S0-CJQ-060

# Educational Media and Technology Yearbook

‹

More information about this series at http://www.springer.com/series/8617

Michael Orey • Robert Maribe Branch

Editors

# Educational Media and Technology Yearbook

Volume 40

 Springer

*Editors*
Michael Orey
Learning, Design, and Technology
The University of Georgia
Athens, GA, USA

Robert Maribe Branch
Learning, Design, and Technology
The University of Georgia
Athens, GA, USA

LB 1028.3 .E37 2017
Eds: Michael Orey &
Robert Maribe Branch
Educational Media &
Technology Yearbook, V. 40

ISSN 8755-2094
Educational Media and Technology Yearbook
ISBN 978-3-319-45000-1        ISBN 978-3-319-45001-8   (eBook)
DOI 10.1007/978-3-319-45001-8

Printed on acid-free paper

This Springer imprint is published by Springer Nature
The registered company is Springer International Publishing AG
The registered company address is: Gewerbestrasse 11, 6330 Cham, Switzerland

# Preface

The audience for the *Yearbook* consists of media and technology professionals in schools, higher education, and business contexts. Topics of interest to professionals practicing in these areas are broad, as the Table of Contents demonstrates. The theme unifying each of the following chapters is the use of technology to enable or enhance education. Forms of technology represented in this volume vary from traditional tools such as the book to the latest advancements in digital technology, while areas of education encompass widely ranging situations involving learning and teaching which are idea technologies.

As in prior volumes, the assumptions underlying the chapters presented here are as follows:

1. Technology represents tools that act as extensions of the educator.
2. Media serve as delivery systems for educational communications.
3. Technology is *not* restricted to machines and hardware but includes techniques and procedures derived from scientific research about ways to promote change in human performance.
4. The fundamental tenet is that educational media and technology should be used to:

    (a) achieve authentic learning objectives,
    (b) situate learning tasks,
    (c) negotiate the complexities of guided learning,
    (d) facilitate the construction of knowledge,
    (e) aid in the assessment/documenting of learning,
    (f) support skill acquisition, and
    (g) manage diversity.

The *Educational Media and Technology Yearbook* has become a standard reference in many libraries and professional collections. Examined in relation to its companion volumes of the past, it provides a valuable historical record of current ideas and developments in the field. Part I, "Trends and Issues in Learning, Design, and Technology," presents an array of chapters that develop some of the current themes listed above, in addition to others. In Part II, "Leadership Profiles," authors provide biographical sketches of the careers of instructional technology leaders. Part III, "Organizations and Associations in North America," and Part IV, "Worldwide List of Graduate Programs in Learning, Design, Technology, Information, or Libraries," are, respectively, directories of instructional technology-related organizations and institutions of higher learning offering degrees in related fields. Finally, Part V, the "Mediagraphy," presents an annotated listing of selected current publications related to the field.

The Editors of the *Yearbook* invite media and technology professionals to submit manuscripts for consideration for publication. Contact Michael Orey (mikeorey@uga.edu) for submission guidelines.

For a number of years, we have worked together as editors and the tenth with Dr. Michael Orey as the senior editor. Within each volume of the Educational Media and Technology Yearbook (EMTY), we try to list all the graduate programs, journals, and organizations that are related to both Learning, Design, and Technology (LDT) and Library and Information Science (LIS). We also include a section on trends in LDT, trends in LIS, and we have a section profiling some of the leaders in the field. Beginning with the 2007 volume, we have attempted to generate a list of leading programs in the combined areas of LDT and LIS. One year, we were able to compose an alphabetical list of 30 of the programs that people told us were among the best. However, each year we have worked on being more systematic. Instead of following the *US News and World Report* model and have one top program list, we decided to use some of the same numbers that they use and generate a collection of top 20 lists, rather than attempt to generate a statistical model to generate the rankings list. One thought was to rank programs according to the number of publications that were produced; however, deciding which journals to include was an issue. We have decided to use a 4-year span, in this case 2011 through 2014, as the years to count (since at the time of writing, it is still 2015 and so we do not have a complete year). Furthermore, we decided to only count actual research reports that appeared in one of two journals, *Educational Technology Research and Development* and the *Journal of the Learning Sciences*. These two journals were primarily selected based on the general sense that they are the leading journals in the area of LDT. Noticeably absent is the area of information and library science. So, while these numbers are pretty absolute, choosing to only count these journals is somewhat arbitrary.

The other top 20 lists are based on self-report data collected as part of the program information in the Educational Media and Technology Yearbook. Every year, we collect general information about programs in LDT and LIS and publish this information in the Yearbook. Each year we also collect some additional data. We asked the representatives of each of the institutions to enter the US dollar amount of grants and contracts, the number of PhD graduates, the number of master's graduates, and the number of other graduates from their programs. We also asked them for the number of full-time and part-time faculty. We then generated a top 20 list for some of these categories. The limitation in this case is that it is self-report data and there is no real way of verifying that the data is accurate. So, while the list of the 30 top programs from the first year lacked hard data, and the lists this year are based on numbers, those numbers may be just as unreliable. In the end, we have a collection of lists that we hope will be of use to our readers. Many of the universities that

**Table 1** Top 20 Graduate Programs in the area of Learning, Design, and Technology as measured by the number of publications in *Educational Technology Research and Development* and the *Journal of the Learning Sciences* during the years 2011 through 2014, inclusive

| Rank | Institutions | Points |
|------|-------------|--------|
| 1 | The University of Georgia | 6.6 |
| 2 | Stanford University | 5.3 |
| 3 | Brigham Young University | 4.9 |
| 4 | Utah State University | 4.4 |
| 5 | University of Twente | 4.1 |
| 6 | Purdue University | 4.0 |
| 7 | University of Wisconsin-Madison | 3.7 |
| 8 | San Diego State University | 3.4 |
| 9 | McGill University | 3.2 |
| 10 | Aristotle University of Thessaloniki | 3.0 |
| 11 | University of Missouri | 2.8 |
| 12 | Columbia University | 2.7 |
| 13 | University of Pittsburgh | 2.7 |
| 14 | University of California Berkeley | 2.5 |
| 15 | National Central University | 2.3 |
| 15 | Virginia Tech | 2.3 |
| 17 | The Pennsylvania State University | 2.2 |
| 18 | The University of Texas at Austin | 2.1 |
| 19 | Florida State University | 2.0 |
| 19 | Nanyang Technological University | 2.0 |
| 19 | National Institute of Education, Singapore | 2.0 |
| 19 | University of Southern California | 2.0 |

appeared in the list last year are here again, in addition to many others. More information about many of these universities can be found in Part V of this edition.

There are five top 20 lists in this preface. The first of these top 20 lists is based on a count of publications. We used every issue from the 2011 through 2014 volume years of the *Educational Technology Research and Development* journal and the *Journal of the Learning Sciences*. We eliminated all book reviews and letters-to-the-editor and such. We only used the primary academic articles of these journals. Each publication counted 1 point. If the article had two authors, then each author's institution received 0.5 points. If there were three authors, then 0.33 was spread across the institutions. Also, as an additional example, if there were three authors and two of them were from the same institution, then that institution received 0.66 points and the institution of the remaining author received 0.33. Finally, the unit receiving the points was the university. So, in some cases, you might have publications from two completely different departments in the same journal. Table 1 shows our results. The University of Georgia and Stanford University remained as the top 2 LDT programs in the world. Utah State University (3 to 4), University of Wisconsin (4 to 7), Brigham Young University (9 to 3), University of Twente (7 to 5), and San Diego State (4 to 8) all remained in the top 10 this year. Arizona State dropped from 3 to 12 and Nanyang Technological University dropped from 5 to 20. Indiana University dropped out of the top 20 completely from the number 2 position last year. The University of Texas (6 to 18), Penn State University (10 to 17), and University of

Missouri (7 to 11) all dropped out of the top 10. Purdue University (12 to 6), McGill University (20 to 9), and Aristotle University of Thessaloniki (12 to 10) all cracked the top 10 this year. Those are some of the biggest moves this year.

The two primary measures of research achievement are publications and grants. While choosing ETRD and IJLS was somewhat arbitrary, the numbers are verifiable. For Grants and Contracts, I ask a representative of each institution whose program is described in the section of this book about LDT institutions to report the amount of grants and contracts for their program or department. In Table 2, we present the top 20 programs according to the self-report dollar amount of grants and contracts for that program during the calendar year of 2014. The only institutions that are both on the list for publications and grants are the Utah State University (4 for publications and 7 for grants), University of Missouri (11 for publications and 7 for grants), and Virginia Tech (15 for publications and 6 for grants). So, using publications and grants, Utah State may be the top program in the world for research productivity.

Tables 1 and 2 are measures of research productivity. The remaining three tables are more related to teaching than research. The first, Table 3, shows the top 20 programs in terms of the number of full-time faculty. We also show the total number of faculty which is the sum of full-time and part-time faculty. Southern Illinois University Edwardsville is the number one LDT program in the country with 43 full-time faculty members. Rutgers drops from first to fifth on the list. The University of Balearic Islands has very large number of part-time faculty. It will be interesting to look at those on this list and relate them to the number of graduates (Tables 4, 5 and 6).

The next top 20 list is the number of PhD graduates. This list might be a good measure of research productivity as well as teaching productivity. The number of graduates and grants is self-reported. The number of publications is verifiable, so it is interesting to compare who is on these lists. The only school that is on all three lists is Virginia Tech (15 for publications, 6 for grants, and tied for 4 for PhD graduates). Comparing publications and PhD graduates, those that are on just these two top 20 lists are Brigham Young University (3 for publications and 4 for PhD graduates), University of Georgia (1 for publications and 18 for PhD graduates), and Florida State University (19 for publications and 18 for PhD graduates).

Our last top 20 list is based on the number of master's graduates. In our mind, we might consider this an indication of whether the program is more practitioner oriented than say the number of PhD graduates. There were six universities that were on both the number of faculty and the number of master's degrees—University of North Carolina (3 faculty and 2 master's), Rutgers University (5 faculty and 3 master's), Boise State University's Educational Technology program (9 faculty and 1 master's), University of Hong Kong (7 faculty and 16 master's), Towson University (12 faculty and 7 master's), and University of British Columbia (19 faculty and 9 master's).

For this year, we thought we would also include a table that is the top 20 programs in terms of total graduates. While this list is similar to the total master's degree, there is a bit of shifting around of programs due to the large number of other

**Table 2** Top 20 LDT programs by the amount of grant and contract monies

| Rank | University | Department | Monies |
|---|---|---|---|
| 1 | Old Dominion University | Instructional Design and Technology | 25000000 |
| 2 | Arizona State University; Educational Technology programs | Division of Educational Leadership and Innovation; Mary Lou Fulton Teachers College | 18000000 |
| 3 | Boise State University | Educational Technology | 12000000 |
| 4 | Georgia State University | Learning Technologies Division | 7850000 |
| 5 | University of Massachusetts, Amherst | Learning, Media and Technology Masters Program/Math Science and Learning Technology Doctoral Program | 5300000 |
| 6 | Virginia Tech | Instructional Design and Technology | 4100000 |
| 7 | Utah State University | Department of Instructional Technology and Learning Sciences, Emma Eccles Jones College of Education and Human Services | 3600000 |
| 8 | University of Missouri-Columbia | School of Information Science and Learning Technologies | 2728506 |
| 9 | University of North Texas | Learning Technologies (College of Information) | 2000000 |
| 9 | The Ohio State University | Learning Technologies | 2000000 |
| 11 | Wayne State University | Instructional Technology | 1600000 |
| 12 | University of Virginia | Instructional Technology Program, Department of Curriculum, Instruction, and Special Education, Curry School of Education | 1500000 |
| 13 | Université de Poitiers | Ingénierie des médias pour léducation | 1000000 |
| 13 | University of North Carolina | School of Information and Library Science | 1000000 |
| 15 | Ohio University | Instructional Technology | 500000 |
| 15 | University of Geneva | TECFA—Master of Science in Learning and Teaching Technologies | 500000 |
| 15 | Lehigh University | Teaching, Learning, and Technology | 500000 |
| 18 | University of Florida | School of Teaching and Learning | 459871 |
| 19 | University of Central Florida | College of Education and Human Performance, Educational and Human Sciences, Instructional Design and Technology | 360000 |
| 20 | North Carolina State University | Digital Teaching and Learning Program | 325000 |

**Table 3** Top 20 LDT and LIS programs by the number of full-time faculty during the calendar year of 2014 (also shown is the total faculty which includes both full- and part-time faculty)

| Rank | Name of university | Department | FT faculty | Total faculty |
|---|---|---|---|---|
| 1 | Southern Illinois University Edwardsville | Instructional Technology Program | 43 | 46 |
| 2 | University of Balearic Islands | Sciences of Education | 37 | 100 |
| 3 | University of North Carolina | School of Information and Library Science | 29 | 74 |
| 4 | Université de Poitiers | Ingénierie des médias pour l'éducation | 25 | 50 |
| 5 | Rutgers–The State University of New Jersey | School of Communication and Information | 21 | 67 |
| 6 | Valley City State University | School of Education and Graduate Studies | 20 | 31 |
| 7 | The University of Hong Kong | Master of Science in Information Technology in Education | 19 | 28 |
| 8 | University of Missouri-Columbia | School of Information Science and Learning Technologies | 18 | 20 |
| 9 | Boise State University | Educational Technology | 14 | 26 |
| 10 | University of North Texas | Learning Technologies (College of Information) | 14 | 20 |
| 11 | Anadolu University | Computer Education and Instructional Technology | 13 | 38 |
| 12 | Towson University | College of Education | 13 | 22 |
| 13 | The University of Oklahoma | Instructional Psychology and Technology, Department of Educational Psychology | 11 | 11 |
| 14 | Anton Chekhov Taganrog Institute | Media Education (Social Pedagogic Faculty) | 10 | 30 |
| 15 | Hacettepe University | Computer Education and Instructional Technology | 10 | 26 |
| 16 | Utah State University | Department of Instructional Technology and Learning Sciences, Emma Eccles Jones College of Education and Human Services | 10 | 11 |
| 17 | Brigham Young University | Department of Instructional Psychology and Technology | 10 | 10 |

| 17 | University of Georgia | Department of Career and Information Studies; Learning, Design, and Technology Program | 10 | 10 |
|---|---|---|---|---|
| 19 | University of British Columbia | Master of Educational Technology degree program | 9 | 17 |
| 20 | Valdosta State University | Curriculum, Leadership, and Technology | 8 | 15 |
| 21 | Ball State University | Masters of Arts in Curriculum and Educational Technology | 8 | 12 |
| 22 | Keimyung University | Department of Education | 8 | 11 |
| 22 | Arizona State University; Educational Technology programs | Division of Educational Leadership and Innovation; Mary Lou Fulton Teachers College | 8 | 11 |

I included the list all the way to 22nd place because there was a tie for full-time faculty, but I used total faculty as the tie breaker. I thought I should include all the institutions that had eight full-time faculty

**Table 4** Top 20 LDT and LIS programs by the number of PhD graduates

| Rank | University | Department | PhDs granted |
|---|---|---|---|
| 1 | University of Central Florida | College of Education and Human Performance, Educational and Human Sciences, Instructional Design and Technology | 11 |
| 1 | Wayne State University | Instructional Technology | 11 |
| 1 | University of Balearic Islands | Sciences of Education | 11 |
| 4 | Virginia Tech | Instructional Design and Technology | 10 |
| 4 | Brigham Young University | Department of Instructional Psychology and Technology | 10 |
| 4 | Arizona State University; Educational Technology programs | Division of Educational Leadership and Innovation; Mary Lou Fulton Teachers College | 10 |
| 4 | Northern Illinois University | Educational Technology, Research and Assessment | 10 |
| 4 | Ohio University | Instructional Technology | 10 |
| 4 | Rutgers–The State University of New Jersey | School of Communication and Information | 10 |
| 10 | University of Houston | Learning, Design, and Technology Graduate Program | 9 |
| 11 | Georgia State University | Learning Technologies Division | 8 |
| 11 | George Mason University | Learning Technologies | 8 |
| 13 | Old Dominion University | Instructional Design and Technology | 7 |
| 13 | University of North Texas | Learning Technologies (College of Information) | 7 |
| 13 | University of North Carolina | School of Information and Library Science | 5 |
| 13 | University of Toledo | Curriculum and Instruction | 5 |
| 13 | University of Virginia | Instructional Technology Program, Department of Curriculum, Instruction, and Special Education, Curry School of Education | 5 |
| 18 | University of Memphis | Instructional Design and Technology | 4 |
| 18 | Florida State University | Educational Psychology and Learning Systems | 4 |
| 18 | University of Georgia | Department of Career and Information Studies; Learning, Design, and Technology Program | 4 |

Please note that the list only goes to 18, but since there was a three-way tie for 18th, the next university would be 21st place

**Table 5** Top 20 LDT and LIS programs by the number of master's graduates

| Rank | Name of organization or association | Department | Masters # |
|---|---|---|---|
| 1 | Boise State University | Educational Technology | 186 |
| 2 | University of North Carolina | School of Information and Library Science | 130 |
| 3 | Rutgers-The State University of New Jersey | School of Communication and Information | 114 |
| 4 | Nova Southeastern University—Fischler Graduate School of Education and Human Services | Programs in Instructional Technology and Distance Education (ITDE) | 100 |
| 5 | Azusa Pacific University | School of Education—Teacher Education | 90 |
| 6 | Michigan State University | College of Education | 85 |
| 7 | Towson University | College of Education | 79 |
| 8 | Georgia Southern University | College of Education | 75 |
| 8 | University of British Columbia | Master of Educational Technology degree program | 75 |
| 10 | California State University Fullerton | Program: Educational Technology | 68 |
| 11 | George Mason University | Learning Technologies | 60 |
| 12 | Kennesaw State University | Instructional Technology | 59 |
| 13 | University of Colorado Denver | School of Education and Human Development | 58 |
| 14 | Northern Illinois University | Educational Technology, Research and Assessment | 56 |
| 15 | Virginia Tech | Instructional Design and Technology | 55 |
| 16 | The University of Hong Kong | Master of Science in Information Technology in Education | 52 |
| 17 | Bloomsburg University | Instructional Technology and Institute for Interactive Technologies | 50 |
| 18 | Wayne State University | Instructional Technology | 48 |
| 19 | Boise State University | Organizational Performance and Workplace Learning | 45 |
| 20 | University of Nebraska-Omaha | College of Education; Department of Teacher Education | 44 |

**Table 6** Total degrees granted in 2014

| Rank | Name of organization or association | Department | Total degrees |
|---|---|---|---|
| 1 | Rutgers–The State University of New Jersey | School of Communication and Information | 364 |
| 2 | University of North Texas | Learning Technologies (College of Information) | 194 |
| 3 | Boise State University | Educational Technology | 186 |
| 4 | University of North Carolina | School of Information and Library Science | 185 |
| 5 | Kennesaw State University | Instructional Technology | 122 |
| 6 | Nova Southeastern University–Fischler Graduate School of Education and Human Services | Programs in Instructional Technology and Distance Education (ITDE) | 100 |
| 7 | George Mason University | Learning Technologies | 93 |
| 8 | Azusa Pacific University | School of Education—Teacher Education | 90 |
| 9 | Michigan State University | College of Education | 85 |
| 10 | Towson University | College of Education | 81 |
| 11 | Georgia Southern University | College of Education | 75 |
| 12 | University of British Columbia | Master of Educational Technology degree program | 75 |
| 13 | University of Nebraska-Omaha | College of Education; Department of Teacher Education | 73 |
| 14 | University of Central Florida | College of Education and Human Performance, Educational and Human Sciences, Instructional Design and Technology | 71 |
| 15 | California State University Fullerton | Program: Educational Technology | 68 |
| 16 | Wayne State University | Instructional Technology | 67 |
| 17 | University of Missouri-Columbia | School of Information Science and Learning Technologies | 67 |
| 18 | University of Balearic Islands | Sciences of Education | 67 |
| 19 | Virginia Tech | Instructional Design and Technology | 66 |
| 20 | Northern Illinois University | Educational Technology, Research and Assessment | 66 |

degrees (this could be undergraduate or perhaps other things at the graduate level like certificates and specialist or CAGS degrees that are beyond the master's but not quite a doctorate).

We acknowledge that any kind of rankings of programs is problematic. We hope you find our lists useful. If you have suggestions, please let us know and we will try to accommodate those changes in future publications of the *Yearbook*. If your program is not represented, please contact one of us and we can add you to the database so that you can be included in future issues.

Athens, GA, USA                                                        Michael Orey
                                                              Robert Maribe Branch

# Contents

# Contributors

**Ferry Boschman** Teacher training institute for technical vocational education, Windesheim University of Applied Sciences, Zwolle, The Netherlands

**Robert Maribe Branch** Learning, Design, and Technology, The University of Georgia, Athens, GA, USA

**Abbie Brown** Department of Mathematics, Science, & Instructional Technology Education, East Carolina University, Greenville, NC, USA

**Tonia A. Dousay** Instructional Technology, University of Wyoming, Laramie, WY, USA

**Erkan Er** Learning, Design, and Technology, The University of Georgia, Athens, GA, USA

**Bruce W. Gabbitas** Brigham Young University, Provo, UT, USA

**Benjamin H. George** Department of Landscape Architecture & Environmental Planning, Utah State University, Utah State University, Logan, UT, USA

**Andrew S. Gibbons** Instructional Psychology and Technology, Brigham Young University, Provo, UT, USA

**Tim Green** California State University, Fullerton, CA, USA

**Karah Zane Hagins** The University of Georgia, Athens, GA, USA

**Kadir Kozan** Department of Curriculum and Instruction, Purdue University, West Lafayette, IN, USA

**Michael T. Matthews** Instructional Psychology and Technology, Brigham Young University, Provo, UT, USA

**Susan McKenney** ELAN, Department of Teacher Professional Development, Faculty of Behavioral Sciences, University of Twente, Enschede, The Netherlands

**Michael Orey** Learning, Design, and Technology, The University of Georgia, Athens, GA, USA

**Roy Pea** Graduate School of Education, Stanford University, Stanford, CA, USA

**Jules Pieters** ELAN, Department of Teacher Professional Development, Faculty of Behavioral Sciences, University of Twente, Enschede, The Netherlands

**Jennifer C Richardson** Department of Curriculum and Instruction, Purdue University, West Lafayette, IN, USA

**Steve Schlichtenmyer** Learning Design and Technology, San Diego State University, San Diego, CA, USA

**Bertrand Schneider** Graduate School of Education, Stanford University, Stanford, CA, USA

**Sheng-Shiang Tseng** The University of Georgia, Athens, GA, USA

**Joke Voogt** College of Child Development and Education, University of Amsterdam & Windesheim University of Applied Sciences, Amsterdam, The Netherlands

**Andrew Walker** Department of Landscape Architecture & Environmental Planning, Utah State University, Logan, UT, USA

**Minjuan Wang** Learning Design and Technology, San Diego State University, San Diego, CA, USA

**Stephen C. Yanchar** Instructional Psychology and Technology, Brigham Young University, Provo, UT, USA

# Part I
# Trends and Issues in Learning, Design, and Technology

# Chapter 1
# EMTY Introduction

**Karah Zane Hagins**

Integrating technology and learning has become ubiquitous over the last few years. Access to emerging and innovative technologies has increased in both the private and public sectors. The prevalence of technology has influenced the number of individuals entering the field of instructional technology and instructional design. The increased need for schools, private business, and institutions of higher education to train their employees and faculty in the successful application of technology for education and training will continue to dominate most positions in the field. Therefore, the ability for researchers and practitioners to stay current and competent with these technologies can be a challenge.

Whether these technologies are implemented in educational environments or for business and industry, the correct application to achieve intentional learning goals is imperative. The push for educators to provide integrative and digital learning to their students has increased as funding for technology continues to be popular. Brown and Green (in press) contend that there has been, "continued growth in various instructional approaches (e.g., blended learning, Flipped Classrooms) to online learning, increased use and creation of digital content and curriculum by educators and students, and persistent interest in the use of mobile technologies - especially student owned devices they bring to learning environments" (p. 2). In higher education, the use of learning analytics to identify challenges and improve the student experience has led to questions about physical classroom spaces and how to design them to support mobile learning and technology-enhanced experiences. Guidance and support for organizational use and implementation of innovative technologies will continue to be the role that instructional designers and instructional technologists occupy.

K.Z. Hagins (✉)
The University of Georgia, 116 River's Crossing, Athens, GA 30602-4809, USA
e-mail: khagins@uga.edu

© Springer International Publishing Switzerland 2017
M. Orey, R.M. Branch (eds.), *Educational Media and Technology Yearbook*,
Educational Media and Technology Yearbook 40,
DOI 10.1007/978-3-319-45001-8_1

Understanding the needs of teachers in regards to organizing and utilizing technology appropriately within their classrooms is another area of interest to the field. Curriculum design is important in the classroom to effectively create and achieve learning goals. McKenney, Boschman, Pieters, and Voogt (2016) provide insight into the process by which teachers engage in design talk to determine methods for technology integration and learner success. Exploring the reasoning and internal dynamics of these kinds of decisions are, "especially useful to members of (future) teams or facilitators, to mitigate unrealistic ideals and prepare well for the challenging yet invigorating work of collaborative curriculum design" (McKenney et al., 2016, p. 2). Working together in collaborative teams has proven to be an effective approach to learning and affords access to multiple perspectives as resources when designing learning experiences.

Investigating methods for integrating social learning in online environments is one of the current goals within the field. Faculty and students have displayed concerns with re-purposing collaborative studio design courses into an online environment. However, with the continued growth and demand for online courses perhaps, "social learning theories [can] provide a mechanism to mitigate faculty concerns and facilitate the creation of an online collaborative learning and design space" (George & Walker, in press, p. 1). With the increase of technology tools specifically adapted for communication and interaction, George and Walker's chapter focuses on working with faculty and students to understand these technologies in an online studio context. Learning can be enhanced with peer-to-peer interactions, especially regarding the master to novice relationship. George and Walker (in press) conclude that with proper design, online environments can provide the same authenticity for this relationship as traditional studio courses.

Having a more knowledgeable other (MKO) as a resource has proven invaluable to the novice or intermediate learner. The ability for a student to seek out help when needed allows them to place their learning goals within a context and adjust their cognitive schema appropriately. Er et al.'s chapter expresses the importance of help-seeking behavior in students in a Flipped Classroom. As instructional designers it is important that we understand and meet the needs of the learners regardless of the medium in which the information is delivered. Their chapter emphasizes the benefits of students' ability to receive assistance as well as increase student efficacy within the subject matter. Learning to learn is a valuable skill developed over time within learning environments that are conducive and designed for allowing students to seek-help. Er, Kopcha, Orey, and Dustman (2015) state that, "in help-seeking, students regulate their environments by using use peers, teachers, and parents as sources of support for coping with learning difficulties" (p. 1).

Continuing the discussion of the importance of a collaborative learning environment that provides resources for learners, Richardson and Kozan's (in press) chapter identifies, "the importance of empirically testing theoretical assumptions, which can provide unique insights into how to enhance both theory and practice in online education" (p. 1). Especially important to online learning is providing a community of inquiry, teacher presence, and social presence according to Richardson and Kozan (in press). However, these elements should be thoughtfully considered regardless of the delivery method of the learning materials. Instructional designers need to find innovative ways to integrate all three for each course they design. Collaboration between learners has long been considered a beneficial element for achieving learning goals. New technologies are emerging that allow the field to study this phenomenon using an empirically based scientific method. Using eye-tracking technology, Schneider and Pea (2013) delve deep into the educational psychology behind collaborative problem-solving dyads . Studies like this, "have further implications for teachers' practices; with training, we posit that gaze-awareness tools could teach students the value of achieving joint attention in collaborative groups" (Schneider & Pea, 2013, p. 19). The presence of tools for studying learning such as these, open doors for instructional technology research that has not undergone significant study in the past.

The foundation of instructional technology continues to be the presence of solid design and development practices that provide learning content to achieve intentional goals. Critical thinking can be a difficult element to implement in both online and traditional learning environments. Highlighting activities that allow for critical thinking, Yanchar, Gibbons, Gabbitas, and Matthews (in press) provide an in-depth investigation of the importance of critical thinking activities. This is important to the field, as stakeholders demand more from their learners and the type of content created by instructional technologists. Implementing activities conducive to critical thinking help prepare learners for cross-contextual applications of learning both in educational environments and the real world.

Technology enables people, communities, and companies to be connected more than ever and the globalization of learning is increasing in popularity. Not only is it important for designers to understand the content to design and develop effective learning artifacts, but also the need to explore the end-user or learner within a cultural context is equally important. Wang and Schlichtenmyer (in press) express the importance to the field of integrating cultural research as another step when conducting analysis of learners and determining content design. "In today's increasingly global and digitally connected society, it is essential to assure the alignment between the learning needs of the individuals from different cultures and the way content is designed and delivered, both online and face-to-face" (Wang & Schlichtenmyer, in press, p. 1).

This book provides a series of chapters written by scholars in the field of instructional technology and design. This introduction presents a brief summary of the chapters, which have been categorized into the following topics: (a) Issues and trends in instructional technology, (b) Pedagogical approaches in educational environments, (c) Current researches on teaching and learning with technologies, and (d) Instructional technology challenges and future studies.

## Issues and Trends in Instructional Technology

The field of instructional technology, by definition, is in constant flux. With new technologies coming to market and creative ways to integrate them for learning, staying current with such trends is of utmost importance. Brown and Green's chapter provides an overview of their research results on the most popular topics and concerns in instructional technology for 2015. Compiling their information from major annual reports, Brown and Green (in press) categorized this data into four main focus areas: overall developments, corporate training and development, higher education, and K-12 settings. In regards to overall developments, the authors found that the use of instructional technology is a priority due to the slight increase in spending on hardware, software, and training. Unique instructional delivery methods such as blended-learning and the flipped classroom remained steady as all sectors utilized instructional technology's ability to fulfill the learning needs of both private and public institutions. In corporate training and development the authors reported: (a) a slight increase in the average learning expenditure per employee with smaller organizations spending more than larger organizations; (b) one third of corporate instructional content entails management and supervision, mandatory and compliance training, and professional or industry specific training. The remaining two thirds of corporate training content focused on procedures, customer service, sales, and executive training, and (c) 70 % of all corporate training hours were instructor-led with a slight increase in the use of online delivery from the previous year with 25 % of training hours completed online (Brown & Green, in press).

Results on trends and issues in higher education determined that mobile computing is currently the most important campus technology concern. Students and faculty in higher education are using these applications for both academic and nonacademic purposes. Learning analytics and assessment are another emerging technology being considered in higher education as a method to identify challenges and improve student success (Brown & Green, in press). Online learning continues to grow in importance as 74 % of academic leaders that responded to the Babson survey feel learning outcomes are the same or similar to traditional instruction approaches (Brown & Green, in press). Blended learning is an expectation of students and learning management systems continue to facilitate flipped classroom environments on campus. The student demands for technology integrated online and blended courses place greater pressure on faculty to utilize these tools for instruction and communication. Concerns about faculty and student digital literacy have arisen due to the need for intermediate-levels of technology use, beyond simply using social media and/or answering emails (Brown & Green, in press). This trend predicts demands for administrative and instructional support personnel will increase in higher education. Faculty and student training on tool implementation and the use of innovative technology in online, blended, and flipped classrooms will be necessary as technology continues to increase in higher education.

As for K-12 there has been a 6.4 % increase on the total expenditure in instructional technology (Brown & Green, in press). Student access to mobile devices both personal and school owned continues to increase in the K-12 sector. Students continue to utilize mobile devices for emailing their teachers, using online textbook, accessing Web 2.0 resources, and viewing teacher created media (Brown & Green, in press). Initiatives such as BYOT/BOYD, flipped classroom, and virtual K-12 programs continue to influence the procurement and use of mobile devices for education with the biggest challenge being consistent Internet access away from educational locations.

In conclusion, Brown and Green (in press) explain that the growth and acceptance of online learning, mobile devices, and instructional technology in all three sectors will continue to increase. Instructional support personnel and specialists will continue to be in demand as various stakeholders require the implementation of innovative technologies (e.g., mobile learning, information and personalized learning, and gaming) into private and public institutions (Brown & Green, in press).

## Pedagogical Approaches in Educational Environments

Pedagogical approaches regarding technology in learning are increasingly important to the field due to the widespread access to a variety of tools. However, technology should not be implemented as a solution, until a problem is clearly identified. A lack of thorough analysis creates situations where technological tools and/or hardware are found in closets gathering dust. Teachers and support personnel must be trained in the uses of technology beginning with a pedagogical approach. McKenney et al.'s (2016) chapter presents a study of the benefits of collaborative curriculum design talks in teacher teams to integrate ICT (Information and Communication Technology) according to subject matter and pedagogy within a specific context. This chapter reports the results of a study in a kindergarten context with a specific focus on developing functional literacy. The teachers in the study designed learning materials for use with PictoPal. PictoPal is a learning environment that entails computer and non-computer supported activities that result in a written product and using this product in an application activity in the classroom (McKenney et al., 2016).

The study explores how teachers make decisions using collaborative curriculum design discussions while designing learning materials and implementing them into their classrooms. The study took place over the course of a 3-year period and involved 21 kindergarten teachers divided into six teacher design teams (TDTs). Using a micro-perspective to explore what design actually is, how it is being conducted by teachers, and how it occurs in and through conversation, their chapter investigates the collaborative design conversations that occurred as TDTs designed PictoPal material (McKenney et al., 2016). Using a qualitative case study methodology, the study explored design talk as it occurred in a real life kindergarten school context. The study investigates the nature of design talk by way of: deliberative interactions, depth of conversations, and how substantive expertise is provided and utilized (McKenney et al., 2016). McKenney et al. (2016) conducted the analyses using four sub-studies and three consecutive design conversations. The conversations in the TDTs were analyzed systematically on three levels: episodes, topic exchanges, and individual utterances. The key findings provide an in-depth exploration of four identified areas: understanding intuitive decision making in collaborative curriculum designs, how do teachers use and develop TPACK during collaborative design, the role of content knowledge in collaborative design, and individual teachers' design knowledge during collaborative design (McKenney et al., 2016).

In conclusion, McKenney et al. (2016) provides recommendations for practice for facilitators and subject-matter experts that desire to provide procedural and substantive support to teachers. They explain that facilitators should be aware of moments in design talk where teachers struggle or when they witness teachers employing designs that have not been thoroughly considered. Subject-matter support should be aligned with teachers' natural inclinations during design. Teachers utilize their pedagogical knowledge and beliefs to create their course designs, but utilized subject-matter expertise when it was offered via recommendations and explanations (McKenney et al., 2016). Finally, preservice teachers require explicit facilitator support when they are designing integrated technology content that aligns with their pedagogical knowledge (McKenney et al., 2016). The chapter provides several recommendations for further research to investigate collaborative design of technology-rich learning.

George and Walker's (in press) chapter continues the exploration of pedagogical approaches in education with a study of social learning theories and communities of practice through the contextual lens of barriers to implementing online education in a higher education setting. The study investigates social aspects of learning and the formation of learning communities. In the context of a landscape architecture course, George and Walker (in press) provide a hypothesis that the slow growth of online design education or distributed design education (DDE) is not due to pedagogical or technological barriers, but rather from faculty reticence to implement DDE. The use of studio courses in design fields provides a learning relationship between master and student in addition to providing the benefit of an open learning community (George & Walker, in press). In the studio space, the master–student relationship is enhanced by interactions with other students as they view and learn from each other. The studio is meant to be a social-based learning environment in which students engage with the complexities of real world design experiences in order to advance their understanding and skills (George & Walker, in press).

This chapter provides an historical overview of DDE, beginning in 1995 with the development of the virtual design studio (VDS). The early VDS were considered innovative explorations of the use of technology for both design and collaboration (George & Walker, in press). However, despite the benefits of DDE, its use remains rare in landscape architecture programs. George and Walker (in press) employed a 1-year Delphi study to develop consensus on the critical barriers to the adoption of DDE using a panel of experts in the field of landscape architecture. Using a 7-point Likert scale to evaluate the importance of each of 24 identified barriers; panelists were then asked to justify their selections in the form of written feedback. After three rounds of reviewing other panelists' feedback and being asked to reconsider the information, 23 of the 24 barriers achieved stability (George & Walker, in press). The results of the Delphi study revealed that the critical barriers to faculty adoption of DDE were related to social interactions, financial compensation, and a lack of confidence in the online medium (George & Walker, in press). Upon identifying the critical barriers to DDE adoption, George and Walker (in press) provide an in-depth analysis of seven critical barriers in order to determine how best to mitigate these barriers. They contend that such mitigation will require a nuanced effort from educators and researchers to create a pedagogy that emulates the social learning environment of the studio (George & Walker, in press). In conclusion, George and Walker suggest that DDE has not been adopted due to faculty concern over the ability of an online learning environment to provide rich and complex social interactions that occur within physical design studios. They propose that a VDS be constructed specifically utilizing social relationships, potentially using social media networks as inspiration for the platform. By applying social learning theories to DDE pedagogy, George and Walker (in press) believe that it is possible to create a robust learning environment that supports the social framework of the traditional design studio.

Despite the prevalence of innovative technology and the increase in access to mobile devices at school and at home, students still struggle with new information acquisition. It is a concern in the field of instructional technology to understand the needs of the end-users and meet the learners where they are academically or in training environments. Understanding methodologies for providing student support in learning environments such as the flipped classroom is important for student success. Er et al's (2015) chapter provides an approach to college student support by investigating help-seeking behaviors of students in a flipped science classroom. Students display help-seeking behaviors by relying on peers, teachers, and parents for support when they experience learning challenges (Er et al., 2015). Despite the positive effects of help-seeking behavior, not every student utilizes this resource. The chapter provides an overview of the literature describing the factors that influence a student's inclination towards help-seeking behaviors and identifies factors that create impediments.

Er et al. (2015) provide a conceptual mediation model that explores the direct and indirect effects of help-seeking behavior concerning instructor support, relatedness, and goal orientation using students' perceptions of costs and benefits as the mediator. Focusing on students' intentions to seek help and individual students' styles, Er et al. (2015) determined that there are two types of help: executive and instrumental help. The research findings further support the understanding of students' help-seeking behavior in a flipped classroom. Students' intention to seek help and the styles utilized were influenced by instructor support, relatedness, and goal orientations (Er et al. 2015). Student perceptions regarding the benefits and costs of exhibiting help-seeking behavior played the role of both determinants and mediators. The implications of instructors cultivating an environment in which help-seeking behavior is encouraged are discussed and contextual applications of instructor support designs are provided. In conclusion, Er et al. (2015) provide a better understanding of college students' help-seeking behavior in flipped classrooms, which informs the design of such classrooms, and therefore student learning.

## Current Researches on Teaching and Learning with Technologies

In the field of instructional technology the importance of integrating theory with practice is a foundational principle for technology and design integration. Facilitating online learning by encouraging online learning communities is one of many tactics employed to bridge the gap between theory and application. Richardson and Kozan's (in press) chapter researches the theoretical and practical implications of research within online learning communities at Purdue University . The authors conducted this research using the Community of Inquiry (CoI) lens (2015). Their research is comprised of eight studies conducted from 2013–2015 in the context of Purdue's online Learning, Design, and Technology Master's (MS) program (Richardson & Kozan, in press). The study highlights the importance of empirically testing theoretical assumptions, which can provide insight into the enhancement of both theory and practice in online education (Richardson & Kozan, in press). Richardson and Kozan's (in press) study empirically tests the theoretical foundations of the CoI in order to ensure efforts spent on the quality of online learning are effective.

Richardson and Kozan (in press) explain that the CoI framework assumes a learning community or a community of inquiry depends on three interdependent constructs of teaching presence, cognitive presence, and social presence. The chapter continues with historical research and outcomes of several studies conducted related to the CoI framework at Purdue University. Using a Likert scale, the data analysis was utilized for two purposes: (1) to provide summative evaluations for instructors/courses; and (2) to gather information that could be used to improve the online MS program (Richardson & Kozan, in press). The chapter continues as the following three insights from previous research are discussed in more detail: (a) interrelationships between and among teaching, cognitive, and social presence; (b) validity of the CoI Framework; and (c) extending the CoI framework to include instructor presence (Richardson & Kozan, in press). Research continues at Purdue University using the CoI framework, including a study focusing on an instructor's use of social presence, teaching presence, and dissonance for attitudinal change in a massive open online course (MOOC) (Richardson & Kozan, in press). Although there is limited research regarding the potential of the CoI in an MOOC setting, the concept of collaborative learning and instructor as co-participant are at the center of a social constructivist environment (Richardson & Kozan, in press). The authors seek to continue their line of inquiry in online learning environments via CoI based upon the results of this study in addition to continuing to investigate similar studies (2015).

Investigative methodologies to support collaboration among students in learning environments continue to be a topic of interest in the field of instructional technology. Students often respond positively to working in teams and can learn more from each other as they work to solve complex problems. Schneider and Pea (2013) research this concept from an educational psychology perspective by way of an eye-tracking study on collaborative problem-solving dyads. Using an experimental design combined with qualitative and quantitative data analysis, Schneider and Pea (2013) studied two groups of students. In one condition, dyads were able to view the gazes of their partner on the screen; in the control group, the dyads did not have access to this information (Schneider & Pea, 2013). Schneider and Pea (2013) concluded that the real-time mutual gaze intervention allowed students to engage in a higher level of collaboration and thus, a higher learning gain overall. The chapter continues as the authors present implications for supporting group collaboration.

Schneider and Pea (2013) investigate the benefits of joint attention as a fundamental mechanism for establishing connection between individuals. The goal of their study is to design technological interventions to facilitate this process. The authors assume that higher levels of visual synchronization are positively associated with students' quality of collaboration and learning experiences (2013). They provide an in-depth analysis of previous work on joint attention and awareness tools finding that eye-trackers are a possible way to understand and influence factors responsible for high-quality collaboration (Schneider & Pea, 2013). Basing their study on the "Preparing for Future Learning" (PFL) framework, Schneider and Pea (2013) designed tasks to prepare students for traditional instructional activities (e.g., attending a lecture or reading a textbook chapter). By employing PFL tenets, Schneider and Pea (2013) hope that their study will be more likely to have an impact on existing classroom practices when eye-trackers are commonly utilized in society. The authors validated their hypothesis in that they found that participants in the "visible-gaze" group outperformed the dyads in the "no-gaze" group with a total learning gain of: $F(1,40)=7.81$, $p<0.01$ (2013). These findings demonstrate the importance of mediating technologies in order to support joint attention in collaborative learning activities (Schneider & Pea, 2013). The results of their study have provided further implications for teachers' practices; with training, the authors posit that gaze-awareness tools could teach students the value of achieving joint attention in collaborative groups (Schneider & Pea, 2013).

## Instructional Technology Challenges and Future Studies

The field of instructional technology, while constantly evolving and providing new opportunities for growth and innovation also presents challenges. By incorporating concepts like critical thinking, instructional designers can implement approaches to projects that directly address challenges from the preliminary stages of design. In the chapter by Yanchar et al. (in press), the need for critical thinking as an integral piece of the foundations of educational technology is discussed. Critical thinking, although widespread in its importance to a variety of fields, is especially relevant as a target skill for learners in a new and changing world (Yanchar et al., in press). The chapter provides an exploration into the nature, theory, methods, practices, and importance of implementing activities that encourage critical thinking in education. The authors explain that in educational technology critical thinking is primarily a skill to be cultivated in learners through a variety of techniques such as technology-mediated activities, facilitated peer interactions in a learning environment, and methods for scaffolding the development of critical thinking (Yanchar et al., in press). Yanchar et al. (in press) continues by discussing critical thinking in education using a twofold approach: (1) they describe two critical thinking activities determined to be needed in the field; and (2) they identify areas of educational technology that seem to require critical thinking at its most advanced levels.

The chapter continues with an examination of assumptions and implications of critical thinking in the context of scholarly literature and explores the use of Finn's criteria for professionalism (Yanchar et al., in press). Specifically, in the audio-visual field, Finn argued for increased professionalism. This emerging field eventually evolved into the professional community referred to today as Educational Technology (Yanchar et al., in press). Yanchar et al. (in press) continue their chapter with an investigation and explanation of three criteria developed by Finn as well as provide the corresponding Vincenti knowledge categories for each criterion. Finn's primary concerns were of the use and implementation of theory into practice. Yanchar et al. (in press) explains that research indicates that the average instructional designer is confused when it comes to theory and thus, ignores it completely and looks to models of other existing products to find learning solutions. This ignorance or uncertainty about theory may still be a concern today as rapid-prototyping methods of development continue to be intrinsic to the empirical methods for instructional development and in the systematic textbooks of today (Yanchar et al., in press).

Yanchar et al. (in press) provides some activities conducive to generating critical thinking within areas of instructional design that they believe would have the most impact. These areas of the field include: the nature of human action, inquiry methods, and professionalism (Yanchar et al., in press). Yanchar et al. (in press) concludes that one way to combat the challenge of a lack of critical thinking in the field of instructional design could be in the training of future designers. Instructional design programs could include a course on critical thinking in curricula, and thus facilitate the importance of this particular type of inspection (Yanchar et al., in press). Successful implementation of critical-focused programs could bring many positive benefits to the field and could be a major step in the field's progress into a future that demands creative, forward-thinking educational technologists (Yanchar et al., in press).

In the field of instructional design, understanding the end-user is very important. The needs of the learners and end-users may derive from diverse backgrounds and cultures. Therefore, the designer must conduct thorough learner-analysis and attempt to align the learning materials and content delivery accordingly. Wang and Schlichtenmyer's (in press) chapter focuses on working with learners that have different backgrounds and cultures from the instructional designer developing the materials. The authors present a review of theories and models related to instructional design, learning preference, motivation, and culture (2015). It is the responsibility and the challenge for instructional designers and project managers to conduct the appropriate research in order to develop training that motivates and clearly communicates expectations according to culture and background of the learners (Wang & Schlichtenmyer, in press). The chapter continues with explaining the importance of Cultural Sensitivity Training (CSI) and culture-integrated instructional design models in the context of learning styles and learning preferences (Wang & Schlichtenmyer, in press). A Multicultural Model of Learning Style is presented as a possible solution for the increasing globalization of industry and learning that account for the cultural diversity within and among groups of learners (Wang & Schlichtenmyer, in press). Studies utilizing this model demonstrated that cultural dimensions play a role in shaping the learning preferences of people from different nations (Wang & Schlichtenmyer, in press). Another contextual framework, the Cultural Dimensions of Learning (CDLF) is presented and explained in detail. The CDLF investigates how the cognitive styles of cultural learners are created from three main areas: personality, human nature, and culture (Wang & Schlichtenmyer, in press).

The authors highlight that the learning style models presented in their chapter were developed in the west and that further research and development is necessary for East Asian cultures specifically (2015). Wang and Schlichtenmyer (2015) then investigate the cultural perspectives presented in detail through the lens of motivation and contend that motivation may be the biggest factor in achieving learning goals. The authors express the need for researchers to engage in additional studies that are not derived solely from Western theories, concepts, and learning styles (2015). Referencing such additional studies will provide globalized learning styles that can be successful for a wider range of learners from different nationalities and cultures (Wang & Schlichtenmyer, in press).

## Implications of These Studies to the Field

According to the chapters summarized in this introductory portion of this book, themes have emerged in the field of instructional technology: (a) Exploration of trends and issues in implementing innovative technology tools to improve teaching, learning, and corporate training, agility, and mobile learning; (b) Investigations into collaborative and group learning environments that support novice learners and social learning theories for achieving intentional learning goals; (c) Continuing research on pedagogical approaches to learning using foundational learning theories; and (d) Implementing investigations on how best to create learning content and expectations in a cross-cultural context for learners with varying backgrounds. These trends have been researched and explored for 2015, however, each year it is important to understand that topics and research focus will evolve, change, and improve. The field of instructional technology is organic and mercurial. The continuous improvements to technology, education, and training will provide further research topics and areas for discussion next year. It is essential to stay current with technology tools, pedagogy, and implementation practices for new methods of learning in instructional technology. Nonetheless, it is just as vital to allow room for failure and prototype testing of methodologies, procedures, and processes prior to implementation via formative evaluation. It is the responsibility of the instructional technologist to clearly identify learning goals and/or educational problems prior to assigning any technology tool or method of learning delivery, whether online, blended, flipped classroom, or traditional learning context.

# References

McKenney, S., Boschman, F., Pieters, J., & Voogt, J. (2016). Collaborative design of technology-enhanced learning: What can we learn from teacher talk? *TechTrends, 60*(4), 385–391. doi:10.1007/s11528-016-0078-8

Brown, A., & Green, T. (in press). Issues and trends in instructional technology: Increased use of mobile technologies and digital content to provide un-tethered access to training and learning opportunities. *In Educational Media and Technology Yearbook.*

Er, E., Kopcha, T.J., Orey, M., & Dustman, W. (2015). Exploring college students' online help-seeking behavior in a flipped classroom with a webbased help-seeking tool. *Australasian Journal of Educational Technology, 31*(5), 537–555.

George, B.H., & Walker, A. (in press). Social learning in a distributed environment: Lessons learned from online course design. *In Educational Media and Technology Yearbook.*

Richardson, J., & Kozan, K. (in press). Digging deeper into online learning communities at purdue: Research-informed insights into theory and practice. In *Educational Media and Technology Yearbook.*

Schneider, B., & Pea, R. (2013). Real-time mutual gaze perception enhances collaborative learning and collaboration quality. *International Journal of Computer-supported collaborative learning, 8*(4), 375–397. doi:10.1007/s11412-013-9181-4.

Wang, M., & Schlichtenmyer, S. (in press). Exploring the cultural dimensions of instructional design: Models, instruments, and future studies. *In Educational Media and Technology Yearbook.*

Yanchar, S., Gibbons, A., Gabbitas, B., & Matthews, M. (in press). Critical thinking in the field of educational technology: Approaches, projects, and challenges. *In Educational Media and Technology Yearbook.*

# Chapter 2
# Issues and Trends in Instructional Technology: Increased Use of Mobile Technologies and Digital Content to Provide Untethered Access to Training and Learning Opportunities

**Abbie Brown and Tim Green**

We continue the tradition of reporting the past year's issues and trends that shape attitudes and approaches to instructional technology. This chapter is composed of four sections: Overall Developments; Corporate Training and Development; Higher Education; and K-12 Settings. The trends and issues described are based on major annual reports sponsored and/or conducted by organizations including the Association for Talent Development (ATD), EDUCAUSE, Gartner Incorporated, The New Media Consortium, The Online Learning Consortium (formerly the Sloan Consortium), and Project Tomorrow. These reports require time in terms of data collection, interpretation, and publication, the shortest of which take a year to complete, and therefore reflect the issues and trends of large groups over long periods of time. For a more immediate review of trending topics in instructional technology, please refer to the authors' biweekly podcast, *Trends & Issues in Instructional Design, Educational Technology, & Learning Sciences* (Brown & Green, 2015a).

## Overall Developments

The use of instructional technology in all three sectors was once again a priority as evidenced through the slight growth in funding for purchases in hardware, software, and training related to instructional technology integration. Overall spending on

A. Brown, Ph.D. (✉)
Department of Mathematics, Science, & Instructional Technology Education,
East Carolina University, Flanagan Hall, Greenville, NC 27858, USA
e-mail: brownab@ecu.edu

T. Green
California State University, Fullerton, Fullerton, CA 92831, USA

© Springer International Publishing Switzerland 2017
M. Orey, R.M. Branch (eds.), *Educational Media and Technology Yearbook*,
Educational Media and Technology Yearbook 40,
DOI 10.1007/978-3-319-45001-8_2

instructional technology in all sectors is predicted to continue in the near future. The use of instructional technology remained consistent in providing unique instructional delivery methods and approaches (e.g., blended-learning) that take advantage of the unique affordances technology can provide.

## Corporate Training and Development

Similar to previous issues and trends chapters of this yearbook (e.g., Brown & Green, 2014, 2015b), we continue to track corporate application of instructional technologies primarily by referring to the, *State of the Industry* (Miller, 2014) report published by the Association for Talent Development (ATD). The report is based on data collected from organizations regularly submitting annual data, BEST award winners (organizations recognized by ATD for their exceptional efforts in support of learning within the enterprise); and a consolidated group of organizations that submitted their data via an online survey. This represents data collected from 340 business organizations; the average number of employees is 16,719 with an average payroll of $1,016,000,000.

Secondary sources used this section are the eLearning Guild's report, *Today's Instructional Designer: Competencies and Careers* (Munzenmaier, 2014), and the Gartner Group's, *Top 10 Strategic Predictions for 2015 and Beyond: Digital Business Is Driving 'Big Change'* (Plummer, 2014).

### *Learning Expenditures*

In 2013, the average learning expenditure per employee was $1208; smaller organizations spent a bit more ($1888 per employee on average) while larger organizations spent only $838 per employee (Miller, 2014); this is a small increase from the previous year (Brown & Green, 2015b). Miller points out the discrepancy can be attributed to the larger organizations' costs to develop and maintain materials are spread over a larger employee population (2014). Large organizations provided an average of 36 h of training, with mid-size organizations providing 27 h on average; the cost per learning hour was on average $1798, which is a slight increase from the previous year (Miller, 2014).

Sixty-three percent of learning costs are internal expenditures including staff salaries, travel costs for staff (not learner-travel costs), as well as administrative costs, and classroom and online delivery costs (Miller, 2014). Twenty-seven percent of learning costs are attributable to external providers, and 10 % is attributable to tuition reimbursement; roughly the same as the previous year (Miller, 2014).

## Instructional Content

Roughly one-third of corporate instructional content focuses on management and supervision; mandatory and compliance training; and professional or industry-specific training (Miller, 2014). The remaining two third covers topics including procedures, customer service, sales, and executive training (Miller, 2014).

The Gartner Group predicts the need for fewer business process workers and more "key digital business jobs" (Plummer, 2014) within the next few years. This suggests the need to shift attention toward corporate instruction that supports greater understanding of innovative concepts and procedures such as data science (big data analysis) and the Internet of Things. The Gartner Group report also recommends focusing on skill development for business projects that are collaborative, ambiguous, constantly changing (Plummer, 2014).

## Methods of Instructional Delivery

Over 60 % of formal learning hours involved an instructor, and over half of these learning hours took place in a classroom (Miller, 2014). Seventy percent of all training hours were instructor-led (Miller, 2014). A slight increase in the use of online delivery was noted over the previous year; 25 % of training hours were completed online with 16 % using self-paced online programs (Miller, 2014).

Instructional design staff and the employees they reach continue to embrace innovative technologies such as mobile learning, informal learning, and gaming, but Miller observes that at the present time it is difficult to accurately measure use of these strategies. Moreover, the technologies these strategies use are often difficult to interface with organizations' existing learning management systems (Miller, 2014).

## Instructional Designers' Professional Prospects

Job opportunities for instructional designers are promising. Projected growth rates for the field range from 14 % to 19.5 % (Munzenmaier, 2014). Munzenmeier cites CNN's *Best Jobs in America* ranking Instructional Designer as 76 on the list of top 100 jobs with "big growth, great pay and satisfying work," (Menzenmeier, 2014, p. 4).

The past year was similar to the previous one, with corporate organizations continuing to invest in employee training and development (Miller, 2014). Instructors remain essential in delivery, while innovative technologies continue to increase in use and popularity.

# Higher Education

We review higher education's instructional technology application by referring primarily to the, *ECAR Study of Undergraduate Students and Information Technology* (Dahlstrom & Bichsel, 2014); *The NMC Horizon Report: 2015 Higher Education Edition* (Johnson, Adams Becker, Estrada, & Freeman, 2015a, 2015b). *Higher Education's Top 10 Strategic Technologies for 2015* (Grajek, 2015); *Grade Level: Tracking Online Education in the United States* (Allen & Seaman, 2015); *Preparing for the Digital University: a Review of the History and Current State of Distance, Blended, and Online Learning* (Siemens, Gašević, & Dawson, 2015). The ECAR, EDUCAUSE, Inside Higher Ed, and Babson Survey Research Group reports are based on large-scale national and international surveys. *The Horizon Report* (Johnson et al., 2015a, 2015b), sponsored by the New Media Consortium, is generated by an international panel of experts. *Preparing for the Digital University* (Siemens et al., 2015) is an extensive examination and synthesis of meta-analyses and literature-reviews related to distance education, online learning and blended learning.

## *Campus Technology Support and Use of Technology for Instruction*

According to the report, *Higher Education's Top 10 Strategic Strategies for 2015* (Grajek, 2015), mobile computing is currently the most important campus technology concern. Seven of the top ten strategies identified in the report relate to mobile computing. Also appearing in this top ten list are analytics technologies. *The Horizon Report* (Johnson et al., 2015a, 2015b), echoes the importance of both of these, listing data-driven learning and assessment, as well as BYOD (bring your own device) initiatives and the redesign of campus spaces to accommodate groups using mobile devices and laptops as key trends in higher education.

Mobile computing issues of particular importance to higher education in the past year include the use of apps, wireless networking, and device/network security. Mobile app development and deployment, both for nonacademic purposes (e.g., sports schedules, bus routes) and instruction (e.g., learning management system support, in-class creativity, and in-class polling) is maturing (Grajek, 2015). Mobile data protection through encryption and access control is important to the campus enterprise, as is secure and reliable wireless networking (Grajek, 2015). Increased use of personal mobile technologies make it necessary to reconsider campus classroom and informal gathering spaces; colleges and universities are redesigning spaces to accommodate both the technologies (e.g., providing outlets for charging devices) and the teaching/learning strategies the technologies support (e.g., collaborative learning, problem-based learning, and "flipped" instruction), (Johnson et al., 2015a, 2015b).

Learning analytics, or data-driven learning and assessment are based on the use of computing technologies' ability to record, analyze and report details of student activity at a granular level. Information that includes responses to online test questions; time, date, and duration of online course material access; discussion thread contributions; and assignment completion rates can be use to determine how best to identify challenges and improve student success (Johnson et al., 2015a, 2015b). Data-mining and statistical analysis applied to teaching and learning is in its formative stage, and there are a number of ethics and privacy issues that require attention, but it is of particular interest in higher education (Johnson et al., 2015a, 2015b).

A significant and growing number of higher education institutions have recently introduced makerspaces (also known as hackerspaces or fab labs) to their campuses (Johnson et al., 2015a, 2015b). These tend to be housed in the campus library or similarly "neutral ground." Makerspaces support and encourage the use of tools and machines to produce artifacts and prototypes and include 3D printers, large-format poster printing, robotics, hot-glue and soldering tools, to name but a few. These spaces support interdisciplinary, personal, collaborative, and problem-based learning.

## Learning Online

The Babson Research group's twelfth annual report on the state of online learning in U.S. higher education (Allen & Seaman, 2015) indicates online learning is more important to institutions than ever before. Approximately 74 % of academic leaders responding to the Babson survey feel learning outcomes for online education are the same or similar to traditional, face-to-face instruction (Allen & Seaman, 2015). While the number of students who took at least one distance education course decreased slightly, it is still higher than overall higher education enrollments (Allen & Seaman, 2015). A key issue to employing online instruction continues to be the additional production effort necessary (Allen & Seaman, 2015). While MOOCs (Massive Open Online Courses) continue to be a newsworthy subject, the majority of academic institutions have little interest in experimenting with or producing them (Allen & Seaman, 2015).

Siemens et al. (2015) observe that asynchronous online delivery of instruction is most likely superior to traditional classroom delivery (which is in turn superior to synchronous online delivery). The authors caution the results are not yet conclusive, but the authors of this chapter have observed similar results in their own professional practice.

As mentioned in *The Horizon Report*, competing models of education are an important consideration for higher education institutions (Johnson et al., 2015a, 2015b), the majority of which are offered online. This suggests the increased need for institutions to make well-considered and strategic decisions about their own approaches to online learning.

**Blended Learning**

Learning Management Systems and other novel educational software facilitate blended learning on campus (Siemens et al., 2015). The Horizon Report mentions the flipped classroom specifically, drawing attention to its connection with blended learning (Johnson et al., 2015a, 2015b). *The ECAR Study of Undergraduate Students and Technology* (Dahlstrom & Bichsel, 2014), note students' increasing preference and expectation for blended and hybrid learning experiences. As was noted in last year's chapter (Brown & Green, 2015b), the authors note the importance of instructional technology professionals' consideration of support for online and blended-learning at their institution.

## *Faculty use of Technology for Instruction*

Chief academic officers continue to report that roughly three-quarters of their faculty accept "the value and legitimacy of online education" (Allen & Seaman, 2015, p. 6). This represents a relatively constant rate for the Babson survey results over the past 12 years. Student preference for blended and hybrid learning experiences (Dahlstrom & Bichsel, 2014) and increased interest in flipped classroom practices (Johnson et al., 2015a, 2015b) place greater pressure on faculty to make use of innovative technologies for instruction and communication. A growing concern related to these pressures is faculty digital literacy (Johnson et al., 2015a, 2015b). Johnson et al. point out digital literacy for instruction is different than competence with more commonplace proficiencies such as the use of e-mail or social media for personal communication, echoing comments from previous Horizon Reports regarding faculty "digital fluency" (Brown & Green, 2015b; Johnson, Adams Becker, Estrada, & Freeman, 2014). This trend suggest that instructional design/technology and media production experts must be ready to support faculty in developing the skills necessary to make use of new and innovative tools for teaching purposes.

## *Student Use of Technology for Learning*

*The ECAR Study of Undergraduate Students and Technology* (Dahlstrom & Bichsel, 2014) reports that, in general, technology's influence is moderate in terms of active course participation and communication with other students and faculty. Students do make use of mobile devices for academic purposes, and in-class use increases if instructors encourage this. However, students remain concerned about mobile devices as potential distractions during class (Dahlstrom & Bichsel, 2014).

Undergraduates report a preference for blended and hybrid learning and place high value on learning management systems, though they rarely make full use of these systems (Dahlstrom & Bichsel, 2014). Students continue to view traditional college degrees as the "gold standard for résumés" (Dahlstrom & Bichsel, 2014, p. 5); few undergraduates have participated in a MOOC and few would include digital badges, portfolios or other competency credentials on their résumés (Dahlstrom & Bichsel, 2014).

Similar to its importance for teaching faculty, digital literacy is an issue for students (Johnson et al., 2015a). The ECAR study report includes a reminder that students are generally technologically inclined but may not be expert at using technologies to support or enhance academic endeavors (Dahlstrom & Bichsel, 2014). Furthermore, the ECAR study's authors recommend institutions assess incoming students digital literacy and provide supports for those who may have difficulty using the institution's computer-based services and applications (Dahlstrom & Bichsel, 2014),

## K-12 Education

As with previous issues and trends chapters (Brown & Green, 2013, 2014, 2015a, 2015b), we have predominantly consulted annual reports from three organizations as the basis for reporting the use of technology in K-12. The reports we consulted are *Technology Counts 2015* (Education Week, 2015), *The 2015 Horizon Report: K-12 Edition* (Johnson et al., 2015b), and the Project Tomorrow Speak Up reports, *Digital Learning 24/7: Understanding Technology—Enhanced Learning in the Lives of Today's Students* (Project Tomorrow, 2015) and *Trends in Digital Learning: Empowering Innovative Classroom Models for Learning* (Blackboard & Project Tomorrow, 2015).

*Technology Counts 2015* is the 16th annual report published by *Education Week.* This report focuses on the overall state of educational technology in K-12 schools. *The Horizon Report*, produced by the New Media Consortium and the Consortium for School Networking (CoSN), focuses on emerging technologies or practices that are likely to gain use within K-12 over the next year to 5 years. *Digital Learning 24/7: Understanding Technology* and *Trends in Digital Learning* reports are the most recent in a series of reports published by Project Tomorrow that focus on students, parents, teachers, and administrator perceptions about and use of educational technology and the availability these groups have to technology. The Project Tomorrow (2015) reports consists of data collected from 521,846 participants: 431,231 K-12 students; 44,289 teachers and librarians; 35,337 parents; 4324 School/District Administrators/Tech Leaders; and 6656 community members. Data was gathered from over 8000 schools and 2600 districts in the USA and around the world.

As with the past three reviews (Brown & Green, 2013, 2014, 2015b), specific areas regarding the use of instructional technology remain consistent in K-12. These areas are the increased access to and use of mobile devices, the use of digital content and curriculum in traditional and online environments, and the consistent growth of online learning. While these areas remained fixed, developments within these areas were observed.

## Funding for Technology

Reporting funding in K-12 can be problematic due to the various reporting procedures of States and Federal agencies and due to the timing of when this data is reported (there is often a year or two lag in data reporting). As such, some data we report is 2 or more years old. In our previous review (Brown & Green, 2015b), we shared that according to a report published by the Education Division of the Software and Information Industry Association (SIIA), there was an esti-mated 7.9 billion dollars spent during 2013 on digital content and education software. This was an increase of 6.4 % over the past 3 years from 2012–2014 (Richards & Struminger, 2013, p. 1). We indicated that the 42 % of the money spent in this area was on digital content, 41 % on instructional support, and 17 % on platforms and administration. The total spending on all K-12 classroom tech-nology reached $13 billion in 2013. Despite K-12 budget pressures, it is esti-mated that instructional technology spending will continue to grow through 2018 at a rate of 8 % per year. The total pending is predicted to reach $19 billion by 2018 (Nagal, 2014).

## Mobile Devices: More Access, Home Internet Connectivity a Concern

Student access to mobile devices—personal and school owned—continues to increase. Schools have made significant investments equipping students with tech-nology. According to *Digital Learning 24/7: Understanding Technology—Enhanced learning in the Lives of Today's Students* (Project Tomorrow, 2015), schools have spent more resources on "equipping students with school-provided mobile devices, enhancing Internet connectivity on school campuses, modifying policies to allow students to use their own devices, and adopting mobile-enabled content to support instruction" (Project Tomorrow, 2015). When asked, *What type of mobile devices do you use at schools?* students surveyed by Project Tomorrow indicated:

- My Own Device: 23 % (grades 6–8) and 58 % (high school)
- School Laptop: 34 % (grades 6–8) and 32 % (high school)
- School Tablet: 21 % (grades 6–8) and 14 % (high school)
- School Chromebook: 21 % (grades 6–8) and 16 % (high school).

Overall, 47 % of K-12 teachers surveyed by Project Tomorrow reported that their students have regular classroom access to mobile devices (Project Tomorrow, 2015). Adding to this data, the *NMC Horizon Report: 2015 K-12 Edition* reported that, "Research from the nonprofit Mobile Future in the US highlighted that 43 % of Pre-K through 12th-grade students use a smartphone and 73 % of middle and high school teachers use cell phones for classroom activities" (Johnson et al., 2015b, p. 36).

The grade 6–12 students surveyed by Project Tomorrow indicated that the number one use of mobile devices in schools was to take online tests. Creating presentations, using Internet based services, and using a school portal were the next three most cited uses of mobile devices in schools by these students (Project Tomorrow, 2015, p. 4). Students also indicated using the devices for emailing their teachers with questions, using online textbook, finding online videos for homework help, and watching teacher created videos (Project Tomorrow, 2015, p. 4).

A strong delineation exists between student use of technology for learning at school (teacher-facilitated technology use) and student use of technology for learning at home (student self-directed technology use). At home technology use by students, the top four activities are emailing teacher with questions, using a mobile app, finding online videos for homework help, and posting content online for comment (Project Tomorrow, 2015). There is a strong desire of students to use mobile devices. Of the students surveyed, 75 % indicated that, "ever student should be able to use mobile devices during the school day for learning" (Project Tomorrow, 2015, p. 6).

While there has been an increase in mobile device access in schools, an issue remains with reliable Internet access for students outside of school. "Among students who are using school laptops, tablets, and Chromebooks, 51 % of high school students and 46 % of middle school students note that their out of school Internet connectivity is through a mobile data plan" (Project Tomorrow, 2015, p. 3). Providing reliable Internet connectivity outside of school for students was cited by 47 % of school and district technology leaders as being one their greatest challenges — along with providing opportunities for extending the learning day through mobile learning experiences (Project Tomorrow, 2015, p. 3).

## *Mobile Devices: BYOD/BYOT*

Bring Your Own Device (BYOD) or Bring Your Own Technology (BYOT) is an approach that continues to gain momentum in K-12. According to the *NMC Horizon Report: 2015 K-12 Edition* (Johnson et al., 2015b), the increase in the number of BYOD models in practice is helping move BYOD into mainstream practice in K-12 (p. 36). According to the Third Annual *K-12 IT Leadership Report* from the Consortium of School Networking (CoSN), 14 % of districts have fully operational BYOD/BYOT programs while an additional 58 % are either in discussion piloting, or working on large scale BYOD/BYOT initiative (CoSN, 2015, p. 18). The grown in BYOD/BYOT continues despite the IT security concerns and technology gap issues administrators and educators have regarding BYOD/BYOT models in the classroom (Johnson et al., 2015b). Despite the concerns, only 23 % of administrators (52 % in 2011) surveyed by Project Tomorrow indicated that their students were not allowed to use their own mobile devices at school (Project Tomorrow & Flipped Learning Network, 2015, p. 9).

## *Online Learning: Shift to Different Models*

As reported in the past two reviews (Brown & Green, 2014, 2015b), interest in online learning opportunities in K-12 continues to grow. According to the most recent *Keeping Pace with K-12 Digital Learning: An Annual Review of Policy and Practice* report, fully online schools operating across the entire state were present in 30 states. The report indicated that the number of students attending these schools was over 315,000 in the 2013–2014 school year, which was a 6.2% increase from the previous year (Watson, Pape, Murin, Gemin, & Vashaw, 2014, p. 5). State virtual schools were operating in 26 states to supplemental online courses to students across their states. These schools had approximately 740,000 course enrollments during the 2013–2014 school year, which was close to the same as in the previous school year (Watson et al., 2014, p. 5). Eleven states had course choice policies or programs allowing students to choose online courses from one or more providers (public or private). As the report indicated, "These programs are particularly important, as they are the first significant effort to provide students the option to choose from multiple providers at the course level" (Watson, et al., p. 1).

In addition to the traditional online course offerings, a shift in the type of online learning opportunities available to K-12 students seems to be taken hold—this shift is to blended learning opportunities and teachers flipping their classrooms (Blackboard & Project Tomorrow, 2015; Johnson et al., 2015b). According to Project Tomorrow and the Flipped Learning Network (2015), for the third consecutive year district administrators are reporting a significant increase in teachers moving to a Flipped Classroom approach where teachers are using self-created videos or videos they have found online. The report indicates that, "Over the past three years, school leaders at all grade levels have seen increases from 23 to 32 percent of teachers using videos found online, with a slightly larger overall increase in the number of teachers who are creating their own videos moving from 19 to 29 percent" (Project Tomorrow & Flipped Learning Network, 2015, p. 1).

## Conclusion

Digital content and online learning opportunities remained consistent trends among corporate training, higher education, and K-12 settings. Issues related to resources, while still present, seemed to be less of a concern than in past reviews. Continued spending on instructional technology in all three sectors remained steady. Online learning opportunities continued to be present—a particular focus on blended learning or flipped learning opportunities in higher education and K-12 was evident. Students in higher education and K-12 settings continued to push for using digital resources and social media for educational purposes. Mobile devices continued to be ubiquitous in all three settings. Increased use of mobile devices in all sectors is pushing even greater expectation for their use in teaching and learning in order to provide access to digital content and learning 24/7. Instructional designers and technology specialists continue to be asked to embrace innovative technologies (e.g., mobile learning, informal and personalized learning, and gaming) in order to guide and support organizational use and implementation that is being pushed by various stakeholders.

# References

Allen, I. E., & Seaman, J. (2015). *Grade level: Tracking online education in the United States.* Babson Park, MA: Babson Survey Research Group and Quahog Research Group, LLC.

Blackboard & Project Tomorrow. (2015). *Trends in digital learning: Empowering innovative classroom models for learning.* Retrieved from http://www.tomorrow.org/speakup/2015_ClassroomModels.html.

Brown, A., & Green, T. (2013). Issue and trends in educational technology: Despite lean times, continued interest and opportunity in K-12, business, and higher education. In M. Orey, S. A. Jones, & R. M. Branch (Eds.), *Educational media and technology yearbook* (Vol. 37). New York: Springer.

Brown, A., & Green, T. (2014). Issues and trends in instructional technology: Maximizing budgets and minimizing costs in order to provide personalized learning opportunities. In M. Orey, S. A. Jones, & R. M. Branch (Eds.), *Educational media and technology yearbook* (Vol. 38). New York: Springer.

Brown, A. & Green, T. (Producers). (2015a). *Trends and issues in instructional design, educational technology, and learning sciences* [Audio Podcast Series]. Retrieved from http://trendsandissues.com/.

Brown, A., & Green, T. (2015b). Issues and trends in instructional technology: Leveraging budgets to provide increased access to digital content and learning opportunities. In M. Orey, S. A. Jones, & R. M. Branch (Eds.), *Educational media and technology yearbook* (Vol. 39). New York: Springer.

CoSN. (2015). *2105 K-12 IT leadership report.* Washington, DC: Consortium of School Networks. Retrieved from https://www.documentcloud.org/documents/2094616-cosn-byod.html.

Dahlstrom, E., & Bichsel, J. (2014). *ECAR study of undergraduate students and information technology.* Louisville, CO: ECAR. October. Retrieved from http://www.educause.edu/ecar.

Education Week. (2015). *Technology counts 2015: Learning the digital way.* Retrieved from http://www.edweek.org/ew/toc/2015/06/11/index.html.

Grajek, S. (2015). *Higher education's top 10 strategic technologies for 2015.* Louisville, CO: ECAR. Retrieved from http://www.educause.edu/ecar.

Johnson, L., Adams Becker, S., Estrada, V., & Freeman, A. (2014). *NMC Horizon Report: 2014 higher education edition.* Austin, TX: The New Media Consortium.

Johnson, L., Adams Becker, S., Estrada, V., & Freeman, A. (2015a). *NMC Horizon Report: 2015 higher education edition.* Austin, TX: The New Media Consortium.

Johnson, L., Adams Becker, S., Estrada, V., & Freeman, A. (2015b). *NMC Horizon Report: 2015 K-12 edition.* Austin, TX: The New Media Consortium.

Miller, L. (2014). *2104 state of the industry.* Alexandria, VA: ATD Research.

Munzenmaier, C. (2014). *Today's Instructional Designer: Competencies and Careers.* Santa Rosa, CA: The eLearning Guild.

Nagal, D. (2014, July). Spending on instructional tech to reach $19 billion within 5 years. *T.H.E. Journal.* Retrieved from http://thejournal.com/articles/2014/06/11/spending-on-instructional-tech-to-reach-19-billion-within-5-years.aspx.

Plummer, D. C. (2014). *Top 10 strategic predictions for 2015 and beyond: Digital business is driving 'big change'.* Stamford, CT: Gartner, Inc.. Retrieved from https://www.gartner.com/doc/2864817?refval=&pcp=mpe.

Project Tomorrow. (2015). *Digital learning 24/7: Understanding technology — Enhanced learning in the lives of today's students*. Speak Up 2014 Survey. Retrieved from http://www.tomorrow.org/speakup/SU14DigitalLearning24-7_StudentReport.html.

Project Tomorrow & Flipped Learning Network. (2015). *Speak Up 2014 national research project findings*. Retrieved from http://flippedlearning.org/cms/lib07/VA01923112/Centricity/Domain/4/Speak%20Up%20FLN%202014%20Survey%20Results%20FINAL.pdf.

Richards, J., & Struminger, R. (2013). *2013 U.S. education technology industry market: PreK-12*. Washington, DC: Software & Information Industry Association.

Siemens, G., Gašević, D., & Dawson, S. (2015). *Preparing for the digital university: A review of the history and current state of distance, blended, and online learning*. Arlington, TX: LINK Research Lab at the University of Texas, Arlington. Retrieved from http://linkresearchlab.org/PreparingDigitalUniversity.pdf.

Watson, J., Pape, L., Murin, A., Gemin, B., & Vashaw, L. (2014). *Keeping pace with k-12 digital learning: An annual review of policy and practice*. Evergreen Education Group. Retrieved from http://www.kpk12.com/wp-content/uploads/EEG_KP2014-fnl-lr.pdf.

# Chapter 3
# Design Talk in Teacher Teams: What Happens During the Collaborative Design of ICT-Rich Material for Early Literacy Learning?

**Ferry Boschman, Susan McKenney, Jules Pieters, and Joke Voogt**

## Origins of the Study

For teachers, integrating ICT (Information and Communication Technology) in their teaching and in their teaching materials is conceptually challenging and practically demanding (Labbo et al., 2003; Olson, 2000). While teachers are able to use ICT for every-day personal use (e-mail, word-processing), they often lack competencies to integrate ICT with subject matter and pedagogy in a specific context (Koehler & Mishra, 2008). Scholarship on the subject of ICT integration increasingly promotes teachers' active participation in the design of learning material. Involving teachers as designers has been advocated as a feasible and desirable way of reaching sustained implementation of an innovation in practice (Bakah, Voogt, & Pieters, 2012; Carlgren, 1999; Clandinin & Connelly, 1992; Handelzalts, 2009). Active engagement does not only increase ownership but offer opportunities for learning, and it results in material that is more in line with classroom practice since teachers know their children and the context better than anyone outside of their classrooms (Ben-Peretz, 1990; Borko, 2004; Voogt et al., 2015). A growing number

F. Boschman
Teacher Training Institute for Technical Vocational Education, Windesheim University of Applied Sciences, Campus 2-6, 8017 CA Zwolle, The Netherlands

S. McKenney (✉) • J. Pieters
ELAN, Department of Teacher Professional Development, Faculty of Behavioral Sciences, University of Twente, Postbus 217, 7500 AE Enschede, The Netherlands
e-mail: susan.mckenney@utwente.nl

J. Voogt
College of Child Development and Education, University of Amsterdam & Windesheim University of Applied Sciences, P.O. Box 15776, 10001 NG Amsterdam, The Netherlands

© Springer International Publishing Switzerland 2017
M. Orey, R.M. Branch (eds.), *Educational Media and Technology Yearbook*,
Educational Media and Technology Yearbook 40,
DOI 10.1007/978-3-319-45001-8_3

of studies in which teams of teachers act as designers of ICT integrated curriculum material shows that those teachers actually yield progression in implementing ICT in their classrooms (see for instance Cviko, McKenney, & Voogt, 2013).

The study presented in this chapter is set in the context of kindergarten education, with a specific focus on developing functional literacy. Functional literacy is the understanding that written language has a communicative purpose. Understanding the functions of print develops in many ways, especially when children engage in authentic ways with written products. ICT can enable even non-reading kindergarteners to "write" a variety of products and thereby experience these functions, first hand. In this study, teachers designed learning materials for use with PictoPal. PictoPal is a learning environment consisting of on- and off-computer activities that involve making a written product and using this product in an application activity. An example of a PictoPal on-computer activity is that children compose and print a list of ingredients for making dinner. They do this using a word processor called Clicker®, that features pre-written, spoken, and illustrated words with which children compose their texts. Off-computer, children then engage in an application activity such as "buying" the ingredients on their list (e.g., in the store corner of the classroom) in order to "cook" a dinner (e.g., in the kitchen area of the classroom). PictoPal has shown promising results in children's attainment of functional literacy (Cviko, McKenney, & Voogt, 2012; McKenney & Voogt, 2009).

Teachers' joint participation in designing learning material is a form of collaborative curriculum design. Here, the term *curriculum* is used to refer to a plan for learning (Taba, 1962). This chapter focuses on the technical-professional perspective of curriculum (the making of a plan for learning) as undertaken on the micro-level (learning events and learning materials) (van den Akker, 2003). Consequently, the term, *learning material*, refers to all resources that are used in this plan. In this study, learning material refers to the on-computer learner material as well as the off-computer application activity plans, both of which are designed by teachers. During a 3-year period (2010–2013), a total of 21 kindergarten teachers were involved, divided over six teacher design teams (TDTs). These teams of kindergarten teachers gained experience in designing PictoPal learning materials. All of these teachers participated voluntarily after an open call was issued. Each TDT consisted of at least two teachers.

Little is understood about how teachers make decisions while designing learning material and what they base their decisions on when they collaborate in TDTs. Most studies on TDTs focus on outcomes of the design process in terms of changes in classroom practice, implementation of material, student learning or teachers' knowledge development (Cviko et al., 2013; George & Lubben, 2002; Parke & Coble, 1997). Voogt et al. (2011) conducted a review on literature on TDTs and concluded that there is a lack of studies that take a micro-perspective. Such a micro-perspective means taking a closer look at what design actually is, how it is being conducted by teachers and how it occurs in and through conversation. This study is set out to take such a micro-perspective and investigates in depth, the collaborative design conversations that occur as TDTs design PictoPal material. In accordance with existing work in this area, the collaborative design conversations in this study are referred to as "design talk" (cf. Koehler, Mishra, & Yahya, 2007). The study is guided by the following research question: *What is the nature and content of teachers' design talk during collaborative design of ICT rich learning for early literacy?*

## Theoretical Framework

### *Nature of Design Talk: What Does It Look Like?*

The nature of design talk pertains to the kind of conversation that occurs. The content of design talk reflects key issues raised during these conversations. In this section, the concepts under study regarding the nature of design talk are discussed; thereafter, concepts pertaining to the contents are discussed.

#### Deliberation During Collaborative Design

Walker (1971) provided groundbreaking work in his analysis of deliberation during curriculum design. His Structural Analysis of Curriculum Deliberation (SACD) framework contains a description of the kinds of interactions that may occur during collaborative design. He identified the following types of episodic interactions in his classic study of design team interaction: brainstorms, issues, reports and explication. Underpinning those interactions, typically in the form of utterances by individuals, are ideas, and orientations brought in by design team participants. According to Walker, the kinds of points made within design team interactions are: pointing out problems; proposing solutions; presenting arguments; or offering instances from first or second hand experience. Walker (1971) categories of episodes and single utterances provide a starting point to study the nature of design talk.

#### Depth of Conversations

Collaborative design has the potential to serve as a context for teacher learning (Handelzalts, 2009; Voogt et al., 2011). Addressing design challenges may be considered a form of problem solving. In the case of problems for which teachers do not have ready-made solutions, teachers must use all of their available knowledge. Working in a team to solve a design problem may even be more beneficial to teacher learning. When teachers do not have to work alone but in a team, they may come up with solutions they would not have thought of as individuals. Also, as design problems are complex, solving them together with other teachers might help teachers overcome struggles in solving design problems that they would not have been able to solve individually. Conversations that emerge during problem solving have the potential for teacher learning (Putnam & Borko, 2000). This is particularly the case when teachers participate in sharing information, analyzing a problem, synthesizing information to find a solution, or use their collective thought to envision a solution and reflect on actions taken (Henry, 2012).

To understand the nature of design tasks as a potential context for learning, this study investigates the depth of the inquiry in design talk. Based on Henry (2012), the following depths of inquiry are distinguished and studied in our study: no collaborative inquiry; shallow inquiry by sharing knowledge and information; deep inquiry, building understanding by analyzing and synthesizing information; and deep inquiry by using understanding to achieve learning by planning. The kinds of collaboration that form a context for learning are found in conversations in which teachers not only share information (shallow inquiry) but also construct new knowledge by combining perspectives, applying what they know about the problem, and coming up with novel, effective, and enjoyable solutions (deep inquiry).

### Subject-Matter Expertise

Studies recommend that TDTs benefit from support (Handelzalts, 2009; Huizinga, Handelzalts, Nieveen, & Voogt, 2014). Substantive support to TDTs focuses on subject-matter and how to plan for teaching that subject matter. Substantive support can be provided by an external expert, and by making suggestions and providing information during the design process. Deketelaere and Kelchtermans (1996) found that the goal of such support lies in stating opinions, sharing own knowledge and beliefs, contrasting, fueling discussions, and relinquishing misconceptions.

Substantive support provided by an external expert can influence the nature of design talk. In this study, subject-matter support was provided by an experienced teacher-trainer. The kind of support provided can be seen as "just-in-time": the subject-matter expert aligned her support to the needs the design team displayed through their conversation. At times, design team needs were explicit, such as requests to provide specific information. At other times, the needs were implicit, like when the outside expert felt that information would be helpful to bring the design process one step further. The nature of outside subject matter expertise brought into design conversations can be operationalized as: ask for clarification, make confirming remarks, state critique, provide suggestions, or offer explanations.

## *Content of Design Talk: What Do Teachers Consider?*

In this study, the content of design talk reflects the various considerations underlying collaborative curriculum decision-making. First, teachers bring their own existing orientations to the design table. The term, existing orientations, refers to teachers' own technological pedagogical content knowledge (TPACK) as well as their design knowledge. Second, teachers' practical concerns shape their discussions and decision-making. Third, because teachers' classrooms are part of an educational ecosystem, external priorities (originating from outside the classroom) wield influence on design decision-making. The following sections explain the term TPACK and what is meant by design knowledge. Thereafter, practical concerns and external priorities are briefly explained.

## Existing Orientations

In the context of technology-related design, core knowledge that teachers' need is termed technological pedagogical content knowledge (later abbreviated as TPACK) (Koehler & Mishra, 2005). TPACK can be seen as the whole of knowledge and insights that underlie teachers' actions with ICT in practice (Voogt, Fisser, Pareja Roblin, Tondeur, & van Braak, 2013). The TPACK framework acknowledges that, for effective use of ICT, teachers need integrated knowledge of content and pedagogy and ICT. Several studies employ TPACK as a conceptual framework to understand how teachers explicate their understanding of how knowledge of technology, pedagogy and content interact, for instance during instructional decision-making (Doering, Veletsianos, Scharber, & Miller, 2009; Graham, 2011; Graham, Borup, & Smith, 2012; Manfra & Hammond, 2008).

In this study, teachers' TPACK is investigated with regard to early literacy development in kindergarten. Teaching early literacy entails fostering children's understanding and skills related to reading (readiness), writing (readiness), listening and speaking. Based on international literature (cf. Dickinson & Neuman, 2007; McKenney & Bradley, in press; Verhoeven & Aarnoutse, 1999) three strands of early literacy concepts and skills may be distinguished. The (de)coding strand includes elements such as: linguistic consciousness, phonemic awareness and alphabetic principle. The text comprehension strand includes: book orientation, story understanding and listening comprehension. The functional literacy strand includes: understanding the relationship between spoken and written words and understanding the communicative functions of different genres of text.

This study looks at how knowledge about early literacy, teaching and learning in kindergarten and knowledge about ICT is integrated in curriculum design and expressed in design talk. In this study, the TPACK framework is operationalized as follows:

- Pedagogical knowledge (PK): knowledge about kindergarten teaching and learning as well as socio-emotional development of kindergartners;
- Content knowledge (CK): knowledge about early literacy concepts such as phonological awareness, book-reading, vocabulary development;
- Pedagogical content knowledge (PCK): knowledge about how to apply general instructional strategies in kindergarten to teach and develop early literacy;
- Technological knowledge (TK): general knowledge about technology such as operating computers, web 2.0, email;

- Technological content knowledge (TCK): knowledge about PictoPal that afford the transformation of specific early literacy subject matter;
- Technological pedagogical knowledge (TPK): knowledge about how to use PictoPal in an appropriate kindergarten related fashion such as used to stimulate cooperative learning;
- Technological pedagogical content knowledge (TPCK): how to use the affordances of PictoPal to teach specific early literacy content within a kindergarten appropriate fashion.

As teacher knowledge is intertwined with teacher beliefs (Pajares, 1992), our operationalization of TPACK also includes teacher beliefs. For instance, beliefs about teaching and learning are found to influence, and for a great deal steer, teacher decision making regarding technology use (Ertmer & Ottenbreit-Leftwich, 2010; Prestridge, 2012; Tondeur, Hermans, van Braak, & Valcke, 2008). Tondeur et al. (2008) found that teachers who held constructivist beliefs on teaching and learning, were more inclined to use ICT than teachers who held more traditional beliefs. Similarly, Kim, Kim, Lee, Spector, and DeMeester (2013) conclude that teachers' fundamental beliefs about effective ways of teaching underlie their technology integration practices. In the context of this study (kindergarten), strong pedagogical beliefs have been shown to drive teachers' actions, practices, and decision-making (Buchanan, Burts, Bidner, White, & Charlesworth, 1998; Stipek & Byler, 1997).

Teachers are designers, as Clandinin and Connelly (1992) and Laurillard (2012) have asserted. Teachers design in their everyday lesson preparation and enactment. Whether it is creating tangible material from scratch or adapting existing material to accommodate the instructional needs of their classroom, design is an integral part of the teaching profession. In addition to TPACK, teachers use their design knowledge to adjust plans and resources to meet learning goals and/or make them more useful in their own practice.

Design knowledge entails both the tacit and explicit knowledge that teachers use during design. Following Lundwall and Johnson (1994), McKenney, Kali, Markauskaite, and Voogt (2015) look specifically at the design of technology-enhanced learning. They describe different kinds of knowledge and beliefs that underpin teacher abilities to "engage skilfully in design" (McKenney et al., 2015, p. 3). *Know-what* refers to conceptual knowledge and facts such as subject-matter content, pedagogical theories, and TPACK. *Know-why* pertains to teacher's knowledge and beliefs about principles of learning and teaching. *Know-how* is a teacher's skill to produce what is needed, such as learning materials, instructional events or classroom management.

## Practical Concerns

In addition to existing knowledge and beliefs, practical concerns influence teacher decision-making during design. Practical concerns are what teachers perceive as important factors in classroom practice that influence how designs will (not) function. A classroom is a complex ecology and for designs to function well, this complexity must be taken into consideration. Many teachers intuitively foresee practical concerns during design. As such, they can be quite influential in teachers' decision making (Doyle & Ponder, 1977). In fact, some studies have shown that practical concerns dominate teacher discussions during collaborative curriculum design (Handelzalts, 2009; Kerr, 1981). Types of practical concerns raised during collaborative design include: (a) organizational issues ("how much time is available, how are students seated, what classroom do I have available") (de Kock, Sleegers, & Voeten, 2005); (b) relationship between student and activity (how will students react to this, what will students do with it) (Deketelaere & Kelchtermans, 1996; George & Lubben, 2002; Parke & Coble, 1997); and (c) how subject-matter is presented to students in such a way that it becomes feasible in practice (Handelzalts, 2009).

**External Priorities**

While teachers have a large degree of freedom in deciding what occurs in their classrooms, certain priorities of stakeholders other than the teachers themselves influence both design and implementation. External priorities may be set by stakeholders on different levels varying from macro-level (e.g., national standards), publishers (e.g., textbooks) to the (near) school level, as expressed by school boards (e.g., local policy), principals or colleagues within communities of practice. For instance, subject matter content priorities are often set in curriculum material such as textbooks and software, which are designed by others then teachers themselves. Also, school boards or principals may set a variety of priorities, for instance about the vision on education, teaching or the role of the learner. When designing, teachers often take such external priorities into consideration. In kindergarten, external priorities might for instance be: developmentally appropriate practices in teaching and learning (NAEYC, 2009), appropriate practices in computer use by young children (NAEYC, 1996), early-literacy content knowledge, and policies (Buchanan et al., 1998; Stipek & Byler, 1997; Turbill, 2001). External priorities are often implicitly embedded in the organizational context in which teachers work.

# Methods

## *Research Questions*

The present study focused on the design talk of six teams of kindergarten teachers engaged in the design of PictoPal learning material. Research was conducted to investigate the nature of design talk in terms of: deliberative interactions; depth of conversations; and how substantive expertise is provided and utilized. Simultaneously, the study examined how existing orientations, practical concerns and external priorities featured in the content of design talk. The main research question was: *What is the nature and content of teacher design talk during the collaborative design of ICT rich learning for early literacy?* To answer the main question, four studies were conducted.

## Research Approach

A qualitative case study methodology (Yin, 2003) was applied to understand design talk as it occurred in a real-life context. Qualitative data were gathered through semi-structured interviews and transcripts of three consecutive design conversations. In the first study, three cases of teacher teams' explicated design reasoning were investigated. In each case, existing orientations of the team (before the design) and the explicated design reasoning of the team (during design) were examined. The second study featured one team of teachers. This case study focused on understanding if and how collaborative design conversations could serve as a rich context for teacher learning. In the third study, a subject-matter expert supported two TDTs. Design talk analysis of these two cases focused on how participant content knowledge was intertwined with other domains of knowledge, and how this was reflected in their design talk. Finally, the fourth study took individual teachers as the unit of analysis. Four cases were investigated in this study. The focus was on exploring how the explicated design knowledge of individual teachers contributes to the overall team design.

## Interview Data Analysis

In sub-studies 1 and 4, teachers' existing orientations were investigated using semi-structured interviews. The analysis of the semi-structured interviews occurred on written transcripts. In the first study, teachers' existing orientations were studied with teams as unit of analysis. Individual teachers responses that pertained to either pedagogy or ICT or early literacy or curriculum design were descriptively coded as such (pedagogy, ICT, early literacy, or curriculum design). Codes were refined through constant comparison (Glaser & Strauss, 1999). Then, categories of inductive codes were made through axial coding which resulted in sub-codes within pedagogy, ICT, early literacy, or curriculum design. These category codes were also refined through constant comparison.

The fourth study focused on individual teacher design knowledge. The same semi-structured interview scheme as in the first study was used. In the fourth study, coding however occurred on the categories of design knowledge. Specifically, coding was undertaken to identify: know-why, know-what, and know-how. Through constant comparison (Glaser & Strauss, 1999), these codes were refined.

## Conversation Analysis

The written transcripts of the design talk were analyzed using conversation analysis techniques derived from the work of Sacks, Schegloff, and Jefferson (1974). Throughout the decades in which conversation has matured as an analytical approach (see Schegloff, 2007), conversation analysis has also focused on the contents reflected in conversation. Conversation analysis techniques are being increasingly applied to study teacher learning in collaboration (Adger, Hoyle, & Dickinson, 2004; Ben-Peretz & Kupferberg, 2007; Crespo, 2006; Horn, 2010; Little, 2002). Design talk may seem unstructured; many teachers talk and the conversation is often fast-paced, making it difficult to interpret what teachers say. Still, it is organized following rules of ordinary conversation, derived from Sacks et al. (1974):

- Conversation is interaction, meaning that speakers turn their attention to another speaker.
- Speakers take turns and conversation, while the flow of the conversation may seem unstructured, conversation itself is orderly.
- Finishing each-others' turn and repeating what another speaker said, signals agreement.
- Understanding emerges as speakers talk about the same topics.

The conversations in the teams, capturing design talk, were analyzed systematically. The nature and the content of design talk were studied on three levels: episodes, topical exchanges, and individual utterances. In the first study, the interactions were studied in terms of the kinds of deliberative episodes that occur, and the kinds of individual utterances that emerge when teachers collaboratively design technology-rich learning material for early literacy. In the second study, the focus was on understanding the topical exchanges and how single utterances indicate depth of inquiry (none, shallow, analyze and plan). In the third study, the topical exchanges and single utterances were analyzed in terms of subject-matter expertise utilized and the nature of external support given (clarify, confirm, critique, explain, suggest) under naturalistic circumstances. In the fourth study, the single utterances of individuals were analyzed to portray how individual teachers explicate their design knowledge when working in TDTs.

## Overview of the Sub-Studies

### Study 1

The goal of the first study was to reach a better understanding of the intuitive decisions teachers make when designing a technology-rich learning environment for early literacy. This sub-study answered research questions about existing orientations, design team interactions, and argumentation in design teams. In this first study, three teams of teachers (one with substantial language expertise, one team of four regular teachers and one team of two regular kindergarten teachers) were given an explanation of PictoPal's rationale before designing on- and off-computer materials and activities. Existing orientations (TPACK) were studied through interviews. Analysis of design talk was performed by looking at how existing orientations, practical concerns or external priorities were explicated during the design talk of these three groups of teachers. Furthermore, this study applied Walkers' SACD (see Section "Deliberation during collaborative design") to understand the decision making process itself.

## Study 2

The second study focused on how collaborative design constitutes a context for teacher learning and how TPACK develops across time in design conversations. The research questions that this study answered were oriented to understanding how existing orientations (TPACK) were linked to practical concerns, external priorities and depth of inquiry. One team of teachers was involved. This study analyzed design talk on depth of inquiry (see Section "Depth of conversations"), TPACK and how practical concerns, existing orientations and external priorities influenced decision-making while creating PictoPal learning material.

## Study 3

The third study investigated the role of content knowledge in conversations of kindergarten teachers during collaborative curriculum design of learning material for technology-enhanced learning. The research question of this study pertained to the manifestation of content knowledge in teacher conversations while designing ICT-rich materials for early literacy. In this study, two teams (one team of four and one team of two teachers) each engaged in the design of PictoPal learning material. Each team was supported by an early literacy expert (who was also teacher) with ample experience supporting kindergarten teachers. This study analyzed teachers' existing orientations toward early literacy in their design talk and how early literacy subject matter was integrated with knowledge about teaching (PCK), knowledge about content representations with ICT (TCK) and knowledge about how to teach early literacy with ICT (TPCK). Further, the nature of the contributions by the outside early literacy expert were analyzed.

## Study 4

In the fourth study, individual teacher design knowledge was investigated during the collaborative design of PictoPal learning material. The study focused on how individual differences in design knowledge influenced the design process and the resulting products. The analysis identified individual teacher contributions relating know-what, know-why, and know-how, to understand the kinds of differences individual teachers bring to collaborative design processes.

# Key Findings

## *Understanding Intuitive Decision Making in Collaborative Curriculum Design*

The first study aimed to understand the decision-making that takes place in design teams, when the process is not prestructured. Three teams of teachers were involved in the study: one team of three language expert teachers, and two teams of kindergarten teachers. Semi-structured interviews were held to explore the teams' existing orientations technological pedagogical content knowledge (TPACK) and their curriculum design expertise prior to design. The analysis on decision-making in the teacher design teams focused on: teachers' existing orientations (knowledge and beliefs about technology, pedagogy, content, and curriculum design), practical concerns (concerns related to how to organize the activity and what kind of problems could occur in practice), and external priorities (priorities from outside stakeholders).

The findings of the interviews show that pedagogical beliefs, about teaching and learning in kindergarten, are a dominant lens through which technology is viewed. Furthermore, teachers state that they direct their attention to socio-emotional development of children first, before considering the kind of learning that has to take place. The interviews show that teachers use their own personal experiences most to feed the design of curriculum materials.

The analysis of the design talk suggests that design is mostly a form of brainstorm, occasionally interrupted by short moments in which issues and problems are discussed. These problems are mainly related to practical concerns, and teachers quickly find solutions. Existing orientations and external priorities were scarcely reflected in this data set. Overall, most of what teachers discussed was about practical concerns. However, when comparing the regular kindergarten teacher design talk with that of teachers with extensive early literacy expertise, the latter group explicated more of their knowledge and beliefs throughout the entire conversation. It was concluded in this study that teachers' natural inclination to design is solution-driven and that they frequently make conjectures regarding the functioning of the design in practice. Furthermore, teachers tend to focus their efforts on ensuring that the activities children will do are feasible in practice.

## *How Do Teachers Use and Develop TPACK During Collaborative Design*

The second study focused on how teachers develop TPACK and ways in which design talk provides opportunities for teacher learning. One team of kindergarten teachers was involved in the study. Topical exchanges, units of design talk that focused on one main topic, were analyzed. Analysis focused on: which domains of TPACK were explicated; and how these domains were linked to reasons given during decision-making (existing orientations, practical concerns or external priorities). Furthermore, this study also explored the depth of the conversations in the teams.

Findings revealed that the kinds of knowledge teachers introduced most to the conversations were PCK (pedagogical content knowledge) and TPCK (technological pedagogical content knowledge). General pedagogy did not emerge in isolation, but intertwined with the two other knowledge domains, i.e., as technological pedagogical knowledge (TPK), pedagogical content knowledge (PCK), or technological pedagogical content knowledge (TPCK). PCK and TPCK were closely linked to teachers' practical concerns.

The depth of conversations over time was also examined. The findings of this study showed that, across the three workshop sessions, teachers did reach deeper levels of inquiry (as evidenced by analyzing and planning). However, most of the design talk reflected lower levels of inquiry (sharing information). A pattern emerged in which teachers first share information by proposing what the learning activity could look like. This continues, uncontested, until another teacher casts doubt or makes an evaluative comment about the learning activity. Considerations for decision-making are mainly given by sharing information (what will the learning activity look like). When deeper levels of inquiry are reached, important decisions are made. Along the way, teachers establish a rationale, which then guides further practical design (what kind of learning activity and material, how to organize specific activities). Still, practical concerns dominate discussions of teachers and such discussions on practical concerns are shallow in depth.

This study suggests that deep inquiry emerges less frequently than shallow inquiry. Mostly, design talk reflects shallow inquiry. However, the moments in which teachers' design talk reflects deep inquiry do offer opportunities for learning. It appears that teachers develop their TPACK in such moments.

## *The Role of Content Knowledge in Collaborative Design*

The aim of the third study was to explore the role of content knowledge (CK) of early literacy in teacher design talk. Two teams of teachers designed PictoPal learning material. These two teams were supported by an early literacy expert who elicited and provided subject matter information either upon teachers' request or when deemed useful by the early literacy expert herself. Analysis focused on how CK, TCK, PCK, and TPCK were reflected in the design talk of these teachers.

The findings of this study revealed that CK was utilized when teachers discussed the current goals and objectives of early literacy, set within specific themes in their classrooms. PCK was explicated when relating to current and future classroom learning practices, or activities that would occur with written material. TCK was used when teachers discussed the on-screen layout of written materials that children would conduct. TPCK emerged as teachers discussed how children would produce the written material and how they would use the material in play-related application activities. Findings to the reasoning behind decisions showed that existing orientations (knowledge and beliefs) related mostly to CK and PCK, whereas practical concerns related mostly to TCK and TPCK. The contributions given most by the early literacy were mostly either recommendations or explanations. Recommendations were made pertaining to concrete learning activities, and explanations were provided in relation to CK, explaining concepts pertaining to early literacy. Finally, in this study two different kinds of practical concerns were observed: implementation related (pertaining to how to organize the activity, how much time) and design-related practical concerns (what the material should look like). Content knowledge seems to have served as an internal compass for designing the material and talking about these two kinds of practical concerns.

## *Individual Teachers' Design Knowledge During Collaborative Design*

The fourth study aimed at understanding how individual teachers' design knowledge was utilized during design talk. One team of teachers was investigated (the same team of four teachers as was reported on in the third study). The data of the third study were reanalyzed using a different coding scheme, related to design knowledge (know-what, know-why, and know-how).

Findings of this study suggest that mostly, know-how was expressed during design talk. However, as the interviews also revealed, know-why played an important role because it showed to be underlying the know-how. Know-what was hardly expressed by teachers. This study also found differences between teachers. Of the four teachers, two teachers were inclined mostly to express know-how. These two teachers also made more contributions to the design than the other two teachers did. Of the other teachers, one teacher proportionally expressed more know-what and one teacher more know-why. This study highlights the variety in kinds of contributions made by individuals in teacher design teams.

## Conclusions

This study aimed at understanding the nature and content of design talk in the context of collaborative design of ICT-rich learning material for early literacy. Based on the findings of this study, several conclusions can be drawn.

## *Nature of Design Talk*

### Brainstorms, Directed at Quickly Generating Solutions, Dominate Design Talk

The nature of design talk by teachers largely resembles a brainstorm. The first study showed that these brainstorms were lengthier and more frequent than moments in which problems were discussed. Teachers initiate the design process by brainstorming on a possible learning activity. By sharing ideas, teachers fill in details of these learning activities. Brainstorming is, as the second study showed, a kind of conversation in which teachers share information and opinions about learning activities to be designed, but do not engage in argumentation or reasoning. It can therefore be concluded that the nature of design talk in teachers' collaborative design is that of a brainstorm with a shallow level of inquiry and a strong focus on what learning activity should occur in practice and what the material should look like.

### Conversations on Complex Problems Provide an Opportunity for Learning

While the dominant mode of conversation resembles brainstorm, design talk also includes moments in which teachers reach deeper conversations by discussing problems. These problems are predominantly practical in nature and vary in complexity. Problems that are less complex do not provide opportunities for learning. Teachers gravitate toward quickly finding solutions that are easy to implement. The problems that are more complex provide opportunities for learning. Teachers have to find solutions that work in practice and use their expertise as they reason through justification for the solutions. When justification of the solution is expressed, teachers also discuss the rationale for the decision they make. Eventually, after teachers agree with the solution, they revert back to brainstorming. Though less frequent, bursts of complex problem solving with deep inquiry are present in teacher design conversations.

### Substantive Support Provided by an Outside Expert Matters Most in Recommendations or Explanations

Study three investigated the role of substantive considerations during design, especially through the input of an early literacy expert participating in two TDTs. The findings showed that the expert input frequently, though not always, influenced decision-making. The expert contributions that directly influenced decision-making were recommendations or explanations. Recommendations included advice for addressing specific kinds of problems, or suggestions during brainstorms. Explanations were given at varying moments and provided the other teachers with information on complex or less familiar (language-related) concepts. The expert contributions treated as optional, and only those deemed by the group to be useful and/or feasible were ultimately incorporated into the design.

## Content of Design Talk

### TPCK and TCK Are Mostly Expressed in Relation to Practical Concerns and Dominate the Content of Design Talk

In the first study, practical concerns dominated design talk. In the second and third studies, these practical concerns were linked to TPCK and TCK. Linked to TPCK, these practical concerns related the design of the learning activities; linked to TCK, these practical concerns were related to the elements and layout of those elements on-screen. Teachers focused their design talk largely on fine-tuning these details. Often in design talk, they "picture" what the material and the activities will look like during use. This picture is refined until teachers are satisfied with the completeness and suitability, and judge it to be ready for implementation.

### Teachers Rely Heavily on Their Existing Beliefs About Teaching and Learning to Shape Design

The findings of the first study led to the conclusion that teacher beliefs about teaching and learning in kindergarten influence how they teach early literacy and how they use technology. In other words, both content knowledge and technological knowledge were seen through a pedagogical frame of reference. For example, the first study showed that teacher beliefs about how motivate young children influenced their design of the PictoPal learning material. Specifically, reasons used during decision-making pertained to how they believed the learning activities would engage children when writing their own texts.

### Teachers Rarely Explicate Content Knowledge in Isolation

Content knowledge alone was hardly expressed; most often it was integrated with pedagogy. In the first study, the interviews revealed the importance of creating activities in which children were engaged in authentic writing activities. Analysis of the design talk from the first, second and third studies also showed that teachers did indeed design learning activities to be engaging and authentic. Furthermore, the first study showed that teachers' content knowledge did not appear to be as comprehensive as their knowledge about pedagogy. Teachers mentioned concepts relating to early literacy, yet offered little elaboration of what these concepts meant to them; this was markedly different from the level of detail given when describing their pedagogical perspectives. In the second study, teachers struggled when discussing topics related specifically to content knowledge. The third study showed that (the nonexpert) teachers struggled with subject-matter concepts, yet were able to express the associated learning goals. Yet even these moments were dominated by discussion of how these learning goals could best be attained, thus showing that decisions were more based on teachers' PCK than on their CK.

### Teacher Design Knowledge Is Mostly Expressed as Know-How, Yet Underpinned by Know-Why

The fourth study focused on teachers' individual design knowledge. Know-how was mostly expressed and it related to what the learning activities would look like. Know-what was hardly expressed. The study concluded that what individual teachers know to be true and believe to be important (know-why) steers the contributions that they make to the design (know-how).

### External Priorities Feature Minimally in Teacher Design Talk

Teachers' perceptions of external priorities are occasionally expressed. However, when these reasons conflict with arguments from teachers own existing orientations, their knowledge and beliefs about teaching and learning frequently "outweigh" arguments that are made with relation to external priorities. External priorities were only found most in the form of outside expert viewpoints. In the second and third studies, these viewpoints especially concerned the appropriateness of having children use their own way of spelling words. In the second study, one teacher opposed the idea; in contrast, in the third study both the early literacy expert present and one of the teachers found such practice an important part of early literacy development.

## Reflections

### *Nature of Design Talk*

The studies presented provide insights into teachers' deliberative interactions in design talk, how design talk contains opportunities for learning, and content is manifested and utilized in design talk. This section reflects on the outcomes of this study in light of relevant literature on collaborative design and problem solving. Accordingly, the conclusions given above are taken as starting points in this discussion.

## Brainstorms, Directed at Quickly Generating Solutions, Dominate Design Talk

The use of Walkers' SACD structured approach to curriculum deliberation framework revealed that the design process undertaken by the teachers in this study is mostly a process of brainstorming on possible learning activities. A brainstorm is an approach to solving problems by generating as many solutions as possible and then choosing the optimal solution or combination of solutions. Robust educational design recommends that potential solutions be tested and/or critically judged before selecting one or moving forward with any. In the studies presented here, teachers did not generate multiple solutions, but generated one solution of which the constituent parts were then brainstormed on. However, they did evolve their single idea until it was satisfactory. Design talk in this study closely resembles a solution-driven approach to solving design problems (Hong & Choi, 2011). The solution-driven approach as Hong and Choi (2011) characterize as an "iterative cycle of decision making" (p. 693). As they argue, designers make these decisions on the "constraints, criteria and functions of a design product" (p. 693). In the solution-driven approach, the definition of the problem emerges as the solutions are analyzed, evaluated, and criticized.

The solution-driven approach that was found in this study supports findings on how teachers collaborate in curriculum design. Teachers focus on the to-be-produced learning activities and learning material (Handelzalts, 2009; Kerr, 1981). Furthermore as Huizinga et al. (2014) concluded, teachers skip important and relevant design activities such as defining a problem or conducting an evaluation of initial ideas or draft material. This study portrays how, also from a micro-perspective, the focus remains on creating products.

There are several reasons for this finding. First of all, the design task that was given focused on creating a learning activity. This was done to ensure that teachers worked on a kind of task they already were familiar with. Also it helped teachers to provide them with a picture of the intended curriculum material. Second, teachers are naturally inclined to focus on concrete learning activities rather than on discussing abstract topics from subject matter. In the first study, the interview on the existing orientation regarding curriculum design showed that teachers already focused on designing concrete learning material. During design of PictoPal material, this inclination to designing learning material became even more apparent.

## Conversations on Complex Problems Provide an Opportunity for Learning

Opportunities for learning present themselves during design talk when teachers traverse from sharing proposals on learning activities towards critical inquiry when making decisions or revisiting earlier-made ones. These reflections on action (Hong & Choi, 2011) may be considered contexts in which teachers learn, or at least they provide opportunities in which teachers may learn. Reflection has been considered a context in which teachers may develop knowledge (Bakkenes, Vermunt, & Wubbels, 2010).

The kind of knowledge that teachers learn through design appears to be in line with what Eraut (2007) calls *personal knowledge*. Such personal knowledge develops in interaction, and takes the form of "codified knowledge and/or shared meanings and understandings" (Eraut, 2007, p. 405). Teachers start with an initial idea of what kind of learning material should be designed. Initially, decision-making appears to be more intuitive than rational. Reflection triggers deeper conversations in which knowledge is made explicit. Hearing reasons given by others, and justifying one's own position, contributes to developing teacher personal knowledge.

In the design talk studied, teachers scarcely discussed their understanding of the design problem. It is possible that teachers felt this was clear to everyone and therefore required little clarification. However, this may also have to do with the fact that teachers' natural inclinations toward solving design problems are primarily intuitive in nature (Hoogveld, Paas, & Jochems, 2003). For design conversations to offer opportunities for teacher learning, not just the ideas, but also the reasoned decision-making of teachers must be discussed.

## Substantive Support Provided by an Outside Expert Matters Most in Recommendations or Explanations

Huizinga et al. (2014) argue that TDT support should aim at updating teachers' subject-matter knowledge, their (technological) pedagogical content knowledge, and their design expertise, and their understanding of the reform. In this study, the outside expert was asked to participate naturally, and the contributions that directly influenced TDT decision-making were analyzed. The findings showed that the kind of support wielding influence on teacher decision-making was limited to recommendations and subject matter explanations.

Both the *form* and the *content* of the expert support provided were studied. The form of the support was aligned to the design process and responsive to the needs that teachers have, as recommended in literature (Huizinga et al., 2014). Such just in time support is expected to provide opportunities for learning. The information that the early literacy expert gave was provided was reactive as well as proactive. Reactive support was provided in response to needs expressed by the teachers; proactive support was provided at the early literacy experts' own discretion. In doing so, the information provided to teachers was closely aligned to their needs for subject-matter support.

Content knowledge that teachers need includes knowledge of domain-specific rules and principles, core concepts, and student misconceptions (van Driel, Verloop, & de Vos, 1998). The contents of the support given in this study included early literacy conceptual clarification, as well as ideas about how to foster early literacy in young children through PictoPal. Namely, the early literacy expert explained what specific concepts meant in early literacy and how these concepts related to the design problem that was currently under discussion. Also, the early literacy expert provided information on how kindergartners develop early literacy and how they reach certain goals. This information was aligned with teachers' needs to discuss how vocabulary development was fostered. The early literacy expert provided detailed explanations of her viewpoints and relevant insights from contemporary research on vocabulary development. Finally, the support also contained ideas (provided during brainstorms) in terms of learning activities, which might be feasible and effective.

## *TPACK*

The knowledge that teachers develop and use has been described as personal and situated in the context in which it is developed. As previously stated, the kind of knowledge that teachers may develop during "reflection-on-action" is personal knowledge. In the context of collaborative design, an important subset of personal knowledge that teachers use and develop is their existing orientations. Specifically, these existing orientations consist of teacher technological pedagogical content knowledge (TPACK) and design knowledge.

### TPCK and TCK Are Mostly Expressed in Relation to Practical Concerns and Dominate the Content of Design Talk

TPACK has been conceptualized as the knowledge that teachers need to successfully integrate technology in classroom practice (Koehler & Mishra, 2005). This study has highlighted how teachers use TPACK in design by investigating if and when the three domains of pedagogy, technology and content are integrated during collaborative curriculum design talk. Findings showed that TPACK, the integration of the three knowledge domains, mainly took place in the context of practical concerns.

Teachers' perception and knowledge of the context influence TPACK development (Koehler & Mishra, 2008; Koh, Chai, & Tay, 2014; Voogt et al., 2013). In earlier studies, context knowledge has been conceptualized as knowledge of the classroom practice, the school system and the schools' vision of teaching and learning with or without technology; and the existing beliefs a teacher has gained through experience (Angeli & Valanides, 2009; Koh et al., 2014; Porras-Hernández & Salinas-Amescua, 2013). In this study, especially the contextual knowledge of classroom practice was linked to teacher use of TPCK. Teachers imagined what the learning material would look like and what kind of implementation related issues would be encountered (e.g., time, organization of activity, placement of material). Therefore, this study offers strong support for the notion that knowledge of context (especially foreseeing practical concerns) strongly relates to how teachers weave together their understanding of pedagogy, technology, and early literacy.

This study also found that teachers used their PCK for early literacy as a basis for the decisions they made regarding PictoPal. What this study therefore suggests is that teachers involved in this study integrated their technology knowledge with their existing PCK. That is, despite new affordances of the technology, teachers were more focused on how it enabled them to do more of what they already did (without technology) in teaching early literacy. Koehler and Mishra (2008) suggest that there is reciprocity between the knowledge domains involved. Yet this study finds little support for that claim. One reason for this may be that teachers existing PCK already underlies most of their actions—with or without technology. Furthermore, for most teachers, technology use in kindergarten still somewhat novel and the affordances for this age group seem to be less apparent. The lack of understanding concerning the potential added-value for learning in kindergarten is likely a function of limited technological knowledge (as shown by the lack of T-codes in the conversations) and more widely held beliefs that (much) technology is inappropriate in kindergarten classrooms.

## Teachers Rarely Explicate Content Knowledge in Isolation

Content knowledge was hardly discussed on its own; when it was discussed, it was in relation to setting the learning goals, discuss what current goals could be attained. Analysis of these portions of the conversation showed limited breadth and use of early literacy concepts. Teachers struggled with topics regarding early literacy or even held misconceptions about facts and principles in early literacy development. Teacher knowledge related to early literacy was more evident when connected with pedagogy. One explanation for this is the fact that primary school teachers (and especially kindergarten teachers) have been trained with more emphasis on pedagogy than on content. Building on this, their new knowledge likely enriches pedagogical knowledge and beliefs about learning, which is then applied to reach specific content-related goals. As a result, this study concludes that for these teachers, pedagogical knowledge (rather than teacher knowledge about content or technology), drives decision making in curriculum deign.

Research has shown that teachers' beliefs on teaching and learning influence how they integrate ICT in their classroom (Ertmer, 2005; Prestridge, 2012). In literature, kindergarten teacher beliefs about early literacy promotion have been related to how children were involved in early literacy activities (Burgess, Lundgren, Lloyd, & Pianta, 2001; Sverdlov, Aram, & Levin, 2014). In this study, the teachers' beliefs about teaching and learning clearly steered their decisions on how to promote early literacy. The teachers in this study valued engagement in written activities, making discoveries about literacy, using concrete material in play and collaboration to be the strategies most appropriate. Also, as this study showed, most teachers were inclined to focus these strategies on attaining vocabulary. This is likely because vocabulary development and understanding the link between letters and sounds was a learning goal that could be linked to current classroom practice as well as to future practice with technology.

## *Design Knowledge*

### Teacher Design Knowledge Is Mostly Expressed as Know-How, Yet Underpinned by Know-Why

Teacher design knowledge is the knowledge that teachers use to "engage skillfully in design" (McKenney et al., 2015). This study has provided a realistic account of how design knowledge emerges during design conversations. Teacher knowledge "incorporates aspects of personal expertise, practical wisdom and tacit knowledge" (Eraut, 2007, p. 406). While other studies on teacher knowledge have shown that personal knowledge does indeed underlie the decisions teachers make (Verloop, van Driel, & Meijer, 2001), this one focuses on the specific types of knowledge teachers draw upon when designing.

In the fourth study, the personal knowledge explicated in design talk was categorized as know-how (ways to shape learning materials and activities), know-why (principles, beliefs), and know-what (information, facts). The results showed that, while teachers differ in the kinds of design knowledge they express during design, the conversation was dominated by know-how. This was often related to addressing practical concerns. Indeed, the third study showed that teachers draw upon their integrated their knowledge (TCK and TPCK) to resolve practical concerns. This suggests that integrated technological pedagogical content knowledge might be a specific form of know-how, as both emphasize "knowledge in use" (cf. Koehler & Mishra, 2008).

### External Priorities Feature Minimally in Teacher Design Talk

The finding that external priorities were hardly expressed in this study may be have to do with the context. Specifically, the role of some external priorities in shaping teachers' every day practice may be taken as given, and therefore not discussed. For instance, in the third study, one teacher stated that they worked from a developmental approach to kindergarten education (see Van Oers, 2003). This definitely influenced teacher views on the kinds of learning activities that are conducted in that school, but because this pedagogical vision is already understood and shared, there would have been no need to discuss it.

Another reason why external priorities may not have been addressed much in this study relates to the nature of the design task given. The PictoPal learning environment is clearly related to the national interim targets for early literacy. Additionally, teachers are already aware that the national language tests do not explicitly address the functions of written language. So, because the relationship between the designed PictoPal material and the (measured) attainment targets was clear from the start, there may have been little need to discuss if or how the design should be take such external priorities into consideration.

## *Recommendations*

### Recommendations for Practice

Based on the findings of this study, recommendations for practice are made for facilitators as well as for subject-matter experts that wish to provide procedural and substantive support to teachers. First, taking into account the solution-driven approach teachers employ in design, facilitators should encourage teachers to generate solutions but also guide them in critically evaluating these solutions. Facilitators can help by being aware of moments in design talk in which teachers struggle or when the decisions that teachers do not seemed to have been thought through. At such moments, facilitators could pose questions that require teachers to step back from the ideas/decisions, and elicit teachers reasoning (draw out their know-why).

Second, subject-matter support should be aligned with teachers' natural inclinations during design. This study showed that teachers reason from their pedagogical knowledge and beliefs and that they used extended subject-matter expertise when it was offered in the forms of recommendations and explanations. Teachers appreciated having the outside subject-matter expert serve as co-designer, sharing knowledge not in isolation, but in direct connection to the design problem at hand. To share knowledge in use and serve where needed, technological pedagogical content expertise (as opposed to only content expertise) would likely be most helpful to teachers.

Third, related to developing teachers' integrated technological pedagogical content knowledge, it is recommended that facilitators explicitly support teachers in thinking through the actual use of the design, even in early stages before it is constructed. This is because conversations in which teachers envisioned actual use appeared to draw out their integrated technological pedagogical content knowledge. During such conversations facilitators can expect two kinds of practical concerns: design-related (What should the products look like?) and implementation-related (How should the product be used?). Additionally, facilitators should prepare for and prompt conversations related to both (e.g., what characteristics the product must have to enable a certain kind of use).

### Recommendations for Future Research

Based on the experiences from this study, several recommendations for further research are presented to further investigate collaborative design of technology-rich learning. First, to gain a more complete picture of the knowledge teachers use during design, their products could be investigated. This could be done by means of appraisals from early literacy experts and experts on technology. Additionally, insight into the design could also be gained by studying implementation of the products through observations during or interviews directly after use.

Second, to further explore how collaborative design forms a context for teacher learning, subsequent research should follow teachers through multiple cycles of action and reflection. Such cyclical learning is considered a key aspect of teacher learning (Clarke & Hollingsworth, 2002) in general and in collaborative design teams especially (Voogt et al., 2015). Such a longitudinal study would examine teacher learning as a result of initial design; implementation; reflection on action; reflection on consequences (learner experience and performance) as well as redesign.

Third, this small-scale study involved a limited number of participants. Replicating this study in other kindergarten contexts (e.g., more variety in school types, in other countries) would help ascertain the extent to which the findings from this study could be generalizable. In so doing, attention should be given to not only the teacher designers, but also the kinds of contributions by facilitators and/or subject-matter experts that influence the decisions teachers make and the (quality) of the material designed.

**Closing Comments**

This study has described the nature and content of teacher design talk when centered on technology-rich learning materials for early literacy. It has showed the kinds of knowledge teachers use and has demonstrated that design conversations can provide opportunities for learning. The implications for practice and future research were discussed. According to Fullan (2007), educational innovation rests on what teachers think and do. Through detailed investigation of teacher talk, this study has revealed how teachers reason together and what drives their decision-making during the design of innovative learning material.

# References

Adger, C. T., Hoyle, S. M., & Dickinson, D. K. (2004). Locating learning in in-service education for preschool teachers. *American Educational Research Journal, 41*(4), 867–900. doi:10.3102/00028312041004867.

Angeli, C., & Valanides, N. (2009). Epistemological and methodological issues for the conceptualization, development, and assessment of ICT-TPCK: Advances in technological pedagogical content knowledge (TPCK). *Computers & Education, 52*(1), 154–168.

Bakah, M. A. B., Voogt, J. M., & Pieters, J. M. (2012). Advancing perspectives of sustainability and large-scale implementation of design teams in Ghana's polytechnics: Issues and opportunities. *International Journal of Educational Development, 32*(6), 787–796. doi:10.1016/j.ijedudev.2011.11.002.

Bakkenes, I., Vermunt, J. D., & Wubbels, T. (2010). Teacher learning in the context of educational innovation: Learning activities and learning outcomes of experienced teachers. *Learning and Instruction, 20*(6), 533–548. doi:10.1016/j.learninstruc.2009.09.001.

Ben-Peretz, M. (1990). *The teacher-curriculum encounter: Freeing teachers from the tyranny of texts*. Albany, NY: State University of New York Press.

Ben-Peretz, M., & Kupferberg, I. (2007). Does teachers' negotiation of personal cases in an interactive cyber forum contribute to their professional learning? *Teachers and Teaching: Theory and Practice, 13*(2), 125–143.

Borko, H. (2004). Professional development and teacher learning: Mapping the terrain. *Educational Researcher, 33*(8), 3–15. doi:10.3102/0013189x033008003.

Buchanan, T. K., Burts, D. C., Bidner, J., White, V. F., & Charlesworth, R. (1998). Predictors of the developmental appropriateness of the beliefs and practices of first, second, and third grade teachers. *Early Childhood Research Quarterly, 13*(3), 459–483. doi:10.1016/S0885-2006(99)80052-0.

Burgess, K. A., Lundgren, K. A., Lloyd, J. W., & Pianta, R. C. (2001). *Preschool teachers' self-reported beliefs and practices about literacy instruction.* Washington, DC: Center for the Improvement of Early Reading Achievement.

Carlgren, I. (1999). Professionalism and teachers as designers. *Journal of Curriculum Studies, 31*(1), 43–56.

Clandinin, D. J., & Connelly, F. M. (1992). Teacher as curriculum maker. In P. Jackson (Ed.), *Handbook of research on curriculum* (pp. 363–395). New-York, NY: Macmillan.

Clarke, D., & Hollingsworth, H. (2002). Elaborating a model of teacher professional growth. *Teaching and Teacher Education, 18*(8), 947–967.

Crespo, S. (2006). Elementary teacher talk in mathematics study groups. *Educational Studies in Mathematics, 63*(1), 29–56.

Cviko, A., McKenney, S., & Voogt, J. (2012). Teachers enacting a technology-rich curriculum for emergent literacy. *Educational Technology Research and Development, 60*(1), 31–54.

Cviko, A., McKenney, S., & Voogt, J. (2013). The teacher as re-designer of technology integrated activities for an early literacy curriculum. *Journal of Educational Computing Research, 48*(4), 447–468. doi:10.2190/EC.48.4.c.

de Kock, A., Sleegers, P., & Voeten, M. J. M. (2005). New learning and choices of secondary school teachers when arranging learning environments. *Teaching and Teacher Education, 21*(7), 799–816. doi:10.1016/j.tate.2005.05.012.

Deketelaere, A., & Kelchtermans, G. (1996). Collaborative curriculum development: An encounter of different professional knowledge systems. *Teachers and Teaching: Theory and Practice, 2*(1), 16.

Dickinson, D. K., & Neuman, S. B. (2007). *Handbook of early literacy research.* New York: Guilford Publications.

Doering, A., Veletsianos, G., Scharber, C., & Miller, C. (2009). Using the technological, pedagogical, and content knowledge framework to design online learning environments and professional development. *Journal of Educational Computing Research, 41*(3), 319–346.

Doyle, W., & Ponder, G. A. (1977). The practicality ethic in teacher decision-making. *Interchange, 8*(3), 1–12. doi:10.1007/bf01189290.

Eraut, M. (2007). Learning from other people in the workplace. *Oxford Review of Education, 33*(4), 403–422. doi:10.1080/03054980701425706.

Ertmer, P. (2005). Teacher pedagogical beliefs: The final frontier in our quest for technology integration? *Educational Technology Research and Development, 53*(4), 25–39.

Ertmer, P., & Ottenbreit-Leftwich, A. (2010). Teacher technology change: How knowledge, confidence, beliefs, and culture intersect. *Journal of Research on Technology in Education, 42*(3), 255–284.

Fullan, M. (2007). Change the terms for teacher learning. *National Staff Development Council, 28*(3), 35–36.

George, J. M., & Lubben, F. (2002). Facilitating teachers' professional growth through their involvement in creating context-based materials in science. *International Journal of Educational Development, 22*(6), 659–672.

Glaser, B., & Strauss, A. (1999). *The discovery of grounded theory: Strategies for qualitative research.* Chicago: Aldine Transaction.

Graham, C. R. (2011). Theoretical considerations for understanding technological pedagogical content knowledge (TPACK). *Computers & Education, 57*(3), 1953–1960. doi:10.1016/j.compedu.2011.04.010.

Graham, C. R., Borup, J., & Smith, N. B. (2012). Using TPACK as a framework to understand teacher candidates' technology integration decisions. *Journal of Computer Assisted Learning, 28*(6), 530–546. doi:10.1111/j.1365-2729.2011.00472.x.

Handelzalts, A. (2009). *Collaborative curriculum development in teacher design teams*. PhD Doctoral, Universiteit Twente, Enschede.

Henry, S. (2012). *Instructional conversations: A qualitative exploration of differences in elementary teachers' team discussions*. ED Doctoral Dissertation, Harvard University.

Hong, Y.-C., & Choi, I. (2011). Three dimensions of reflective thinking in solving design problems: A conceptual model. *Educational Technology Research and Development, 59*(5), 687–710. doi:10.1007/s11423-011-9202-9.

Hoogveld, A. W. M., Paas, F., & Jochems, W. M. G. (2003). Application of an instructional systems design approach by teachers in higher education: Individual versus team design. *Teaching and Teacher Education, 19*(6), 581–590.

Horn, I. (2010). Teaching replays, teaching rehearsals, and re-visions of practice: Learning from colleagues in a mathematics teacher community. *Teachers College Record, 112*(1), 225–259.

Huizinga, T., Handelzalts, A., Nieveen, N., & Voogt, J. M. (2014). Teacher involvement in curriculum design: Need for support to enhance teachers' design expertise. *Journal of Curriculum Studies, 46*(1), 33–57. doi:10.1080/00220272.2013.834077.

Kerr, S. T. (1981). How teachers design their materials: Implications for instructional design. *Instructional Science, 10*(4), 363–378.

Kim, C., Kim, M. K., Lee, C., Spector, J. M., & DeMeester, K. (2013). Teacher beliefs and technology integration. *Teaching and Teacher Education, 29*, 76–85. doi:10.1016/j.tate.2012.08.005.

Koehler, M. J., & Mishra, P. (2005). What happens when teachers design educational technology? The development of Technological Pedagogical Content Knowledge. *Journal of Educational Computing Research, 32*(2), 131–152.

Koehler, M. J., & Mishra, P. (2008). Introducing TPCK. In AACTE Committee on Innovation and Technology (Ed.), *The handbook of technological pedagogical content knowledge (TPCK) for educators* (pp. 3–29). New York: Routledge.

Koehler, M. J., Mishra, P., & Yahya, K. (2007). Tracing the development of teacher knowledge in a design seminar: Integrating content, pedagogy and technology. *Computers & Education, 49*(3), 740–762.

Koh, J. H. L., Chai, C. S., & Tay, L. Y. (2014). TPACK-in-action: Unpacking the contextual influences of teachers' construction of technological pedagogical content knowledge (TPACK). *Computers & Education, 78*, 20–29. doi:10.1016/j.compedu.2014.04.022.

Labbo, L. D., Leu Jr, D. J., Kinzer, C., Teale, W. H., Cammack, D., Kara-Soteriou, J., & Sanny, R. (2003). Teacher wisdom stories: Cautions and recommendations for using computer-related technologies for literacy instruction. *Reading Teacher, 57*(3), 300–304.

Laurillard, D. (2012). *Teaching as a design science: Building pedagogical patterns for learning and technology*. London: Taylor & Francis.

Little, J. W. (2002). Locating learning in teachers' communities of practice: Opening up problems of analysis in records of everyday work. *Teaching and Teacher Education, 18*(8), 917–946. doi:10.1016/s0742-051x(02)00052-5.

Lundwall, B., & Johnson, B. (1994). The learning economy. *Journal of Industry Studies, 1*(2), 23–42.

Manfra, M. M., & Hammond, T. C. (2008). Teachers' instructional choices with student-created digital documentaries: Case studies. *Journal of Research on Technology in Education, 41*(2), 223–245.

McKenney, S., & Bradley, B. (2016). Assessing Teacher Beliefs about Early Literacy Curriculum Implementation. *Early Child Development and Care, 186*(9), 1415–1428. http://dx.doi.org/10.1080/03004430.2015.1096784.

McKenney, S., Kali, Y., Markauskaite, L., & Voogt, J. (2015). Teacher design knowledge for technology enhanced learning: An ecological framework for investigating assets and needs. *Instructional Science, 43*(2), 181–202. doi:10.1007/s11251-014-9337-2.

McKenney, S., & Voogt, J. (2009). Designing technology for emergent literacy: The PictoPal initiative. *Computers & Education, 52*, 719–729.

NAEYC. (1996). *Technology and young children—Ages 3 through 8*. A position statement of the National Association for the Education of Young Children.

NAEYC. (2009). *Developmentally appropriate practice in early childhood programs serving children from birth through age 8*. A position statement of the National Association for the Education of Young Children.

Olson, J. (2000). OP-ED Trojan horse or teacher's pet? Computers and the culture of the school. *Journal of Curriculum Studies, 32*(1), 1–8.

Pajares, M. F. (1992). Teachers' beliefs and educational research: Cleaning up a messy construct. *Review of Educational Research, 62*(3), 307–332.

Parke, H. M., & Coble, C. R. (1997). Teachers designing curriculum as professional development: A model for transformational science teaching. *Journal of Research in Science Teaching, 34*(8), 773–789.

Porras-Hernández, L. H., & Salinas-Amescua, B. (2013). Strengthening TPACK: A broader notion of context and the use of teacher's narratives to reveal knowledge construction. *Journal of Educational Computing Research, 48*(2), 223–244.

Prestridge, S. (2012). The beliefs behind the teacher that influences their ICT practices. *Computers & Education, 58*(1), 449–458. doi:10.1016/j.compedu.2011.08.028.

Putnam, R., & Borko, H. (2000). What do new views of knowledge and thinking have to say about research on teacher learning? *Educational Researcher, 29*(1), 4–15. doi:10.3102/0013189x029001004.

Sacks, H., Schegloff, E. A., & Jefferson, G. (1974). A simplest systematics for the organization of turn-taking for conversation. *Language, 50*(4), 696–735. doi:10.2307/412243.

Schegloff, E. A. (2007). *Sequence organization in interaction: Vol. 1: A primer in conversation analysis* (Vol. 1). Cambridge: Cambridge University Press.

Stipek, D. J., & Byler, P. (1997). Early childhood education teachers: Do they practice what they preach? *Early Childhood Research Quarterly, 12*(3), 305–325.

Sverdlov, A., Aram, D., & Levin, I. (2014). Kindergarten teachers' literacy beliefs and self-reported practices: On the heels of a new national literacy curriculum. *Teaching and Teacher Education, 39*, 44–55. doi:10.1016/j.tate.2013.12.004.

Taba, H. (1962). *Curriculum development: Theory and practice*. New York: Harcourt, Brace & World.

Tondeur, J., Hermans, R., van Braak, J., & Valcke, M. (2008). Exploring the link between teachers' educational belief profiles and different types of computer use in the classroom. *Computers in Human Behavior, 24*(6), 2541–2553.

Turbill, J. (2001). A researcher goes to school: Using technology in the kindergarten literacy curriculum. *Journal of Early Childhood Literacy, 1*(3), 255–279. doi:10.1177/14687984010013002.

van den Akker, J. (2003). Curriculum perspectives: An introduction. In J. van den Akker, W. Kuiper, & U. Hameyer (Eds.), *Curriculum landscapes and trends* (pp. 29–44). Dordrecht: Kluwer Academic Publishers.

van Driel, J. H., Verloop, N., & de Vos, W. (1998). Developing science teachers' pedagogical content knowledge. *Journal of Research in Science Teaching, 35*(6), 673–695.

Van Oers, B. (2003). Signatuur van ontwikkelingsgericht onderwijs [The signature of developmental approaches to education]. *Zone, 2*(3), 11–15.

Verhoeven, L., & Aarnoutse, C. (1999). *Tussendoelen beginnende geletterdheid: Een leerlijn voor groep 1 tot en met 3*. Nijmegen: Expertisecentrum Nederlands.

Verloop, N., van Driel, J., & Meijer, P. (2001). Teacher knowledge and the knowledge base of teaching. *International Journal of Educational Research, 35*(5), 441–461. doi:10.1016/s0883-0355(02)00003-4.

Voogt, J., Fisser, P., Pareja Roblin, N., Tondeur, J., & van Braak, J. (2013). Technological pedagogical content knowledge—A review of the literature. *Journal of Computer Assisted Learning, 29*(2), 109–121. doi:10.1111/j.1365-2729.2012.00487.x.

Voogt, J., Laferrière, T., Breuleux, A., Itow, R., Hickey, D., & McKenney, S. (2015). Collaborative design as a form of professional development. *Instructional Science, 43*(2), 259–282.

Voogt, J., Westbroek, H., Handelzalts, A., Walraven, A., McKenney, S., Pieters, J., & de Vries, B. (2011). Teacher learning in collaborative curriculum design. *Teaching and Teacher Education, 27*(8), 1235–1244. doi:10.1016/j.tate.2011.07.003.

Walker, D. F. (1971). A study of deliberation in three curriculum projects. *Curriculum Theory Network, 7*, 118–134.

Yin, R. K. (2003). *Case study research: Design and methods*. Thousand Oaks, CA: SAGE Publications.

# Chapter 4
# Social Learning in a Distributed Environment: Lessons Learned from Online Design Education

**Benjamin H. George and Andrew Walker**

## Introduction

While online education has become prevalent in higher education as universities seek to expand their reach, invest in technological innovation, and restructure budgetary systems, it has remained largely nascent in the design fields of architecture, landscape architecture, and interior design (Bender & Good, 2003; Christensen & Eyring, 2011; Yuan & Powell, 2013). This is despite the widespread adoption of innovations in communication technologies that support social learning environments and the creation of online learning communities (García-Peñalvo, Conde, Alier, & Casany, 2011; Hew & Cheung, 2013). The emergent nature of online education in the design fields is especially perplexing considering the nearly two decades of research on virtual design studios (VDS).

Previous research has identified many of the affordances and constraints of online design education, or distributed design education (DDE), and indicated that DDE can be an effective method for both design instruction and collaboration (Bender & Vredevoogd, 2006; Ham & Schnable, 2011; Kvan, 2001). DDE provides many affordances that are particularly compelling to design education, such as facilitating the sharing of design work, easily preserving and cataloging design iterations, and enabling access to geographically diverse faculty, students, and practitioners (Dave & Danahy, 2000; Ham & Schnable, 2011; Park, 2011). In light of the successful precedents and identified affordances, we hypothesized that the slow growth of DDE stemmed not from pedagogical or technological shortcomings, but from faculty apprehension to adopt DDE.

B.H. George (✉) • A. Walker
Department of Landscape Architecture & Environmental Planning, Utah State University,
4005 Old Main Hill, Logan, UT 84322-4005, USA
e-mail: benjamin.george@usu.edu

© Springer International Publishing Switzerland 2017     53
M. Orey, R.M. Branch (eds.), *Educational Media and Technology Yearbook*,
Educational Media and Technology Yearbook 40,
DOI 10.1007/978-3-319-45001-8_4

This chapter describes the results of a national Delphi study on the barriers to the adoption of DDE by landscape architecture faculty. The results of the study reveal that managing the social aspects of the learning environment and the creation of a community of practice are the most prominent barriers to the adoption of DDE. The application of social learning theories, combined with a knowledge of the function of communities of practice, provides an opportunity to develop pedagogical strategies to mitigate for many faculty concerns.

# Background

## *The Culture of Design Education and the Studio*

While the studio has served as the foundation of design education for nearly two centuries, it was not until the 1980s that the learning processes occurring within the studio were theorized by Donald Schön (Webster, 2009). Schön proposed a theory of design learning called reflective practice, the process whereby a designer constantly analyzes the problem, process, and their own actions in order to develop an optimal design solution (Schön, 1983, 1985). Schön described this process as a conversation between the designer and the design, implying an iterative process not entirely controlled by the designer that results in moments of struggle and serendipity (Schön, 1985).

The complexity and ambiguity of the design process is what precipitates the master–learner relationship in studio pedagogy. On its face, good design may seem easy to achieve; yet a student quickly learns that the process is difficult to master. Schön (1983) emphasizes the need for the master to tutor the student by describing the paradox of the design studio: the student cannot know what needs to be done to design successfully, yet the student can only learn what needs to be done by designing. This can create a frustratingly circular learning situation in which the student must muddle through the process, learning in fits and starts by trial, error, and exploration; and a setting in which the careful guidance of a master to provide instruction and modeling is highly valued.

The master–student relationship is supplemented by interactions with other students in the studio. As an open learning community, students are able to view and learn from each other, especially their more advanced peers. In some extreme cases studios even merge learners studying similar topics irrespective of their level of development or skill—committing to vertical mentoring through peers (Barnes, 1993). Through the combination of mentoring provided by the studio master and other students, individual students become enculturated into the design process, and in so doing they enter the community of designers.

## Theorization of the Design Studio Environment

While curriculum and focus have undergone significant changes over the last two centuries, the physical design studio (PDS) remains the fundamental instructional environment in design education and its basic pedagogical tenants have remained relatively constant (Bender, 2005; Broadfoot & Bennett, 2003). These tenants include a space where with ample opportunities for instruction and modeling from a master and more advanced peers, and where students can freely observe and collaborate with their peers. The studio is meant to be a rich, social-based learning environment in which students must confront the complexities of realistic design situations and, by so doing, advance their understanding and skills.

While Schön (1985) described and theorized the process of design, a deeper understanding of design studio pedagogy and the interactions that occur within the studio can be developed through the application of the social learning theories of legitimate peripheral participation, distributed cognition, and affinity spaces. The purpose of the studio and the nature of the master–learner relationship of the physical design studio (PDS) can best be theorized by legitimate peripheral participation theory (LPP). The social characteristics of the studio environment by the theories of distributed cognition (DC) and affinity spaces (AfS), in which students are exposed to authentic design activities in a cognitive apprenticeship under the guidance of a studio master in an open environment in which students are free to observe, learn, and collaborate with each other (Black, 2008; Gee, 2004; Hutchins, 1995; Lave & Wenger, 1991; Schön, 1985).

The master–learner relationship of the studio is meant to provide students with the opportunity to shadow the actions of a mentor within the design community of practice. However, Lave and Wenger (1991) noted that successful cognitive apprenticeships involved more than the structural establishment of a master–learner duality. The master must provide the learner with contextual and social opportunities for legitimate peripheral participation in the community of practice. In theory, the master–student relationship in design education is meant to function in this manner, with the instructor playing the role of a wise master who provides the student with careful instruction and projects intended to replicate practice (Hokanson, 2012; Schön, 1985)

Much of the design process can be segmented into a series of rational design decisions and, as a result, the social structure of the studio increasingly resembles the collaborative learning environment Hutchins (1995) describes in distributed cognition theory, that is, a rational, replicable approach to design, where the process is separated into discrete tasks. This means that more advanced students are better able to act as tutors to less advanced students as they master each task. As in Hutchins (1995) description of naval crewmen learning from those above them and tutoring those below them, in the design studio there is an expectation that upperclassmen learn from the studio master while simultaneously providing instruction and modeling to lower classmen. It has been recognized that successful tutoring in the studio space is incumbent upon an open layout, a spatial arrangement supported

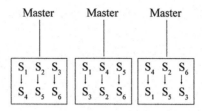

**Fig. 4.1** Studio social hierarchy. This graphic demonstrates the shifting social hierarchy in the studio in which different students may act as mentors within different realms of knowledge

by Hutchins (1995) horizon of observation, which can be distilled to the basic concept that a person is able to learn from what they can physically observe in the environment around them (George & Bussiere, 2015).

As a student masters each task they assume a new role as a teacher and are then able to act in the role of a teacher to help tutor other students. This shifting of social learning roles within the studio, based on knowledge and competencies, is described in AfS theory, wherein a fluid social structure enables members of the learning community to simultaneously maintain an identity as a master and learner, dependent upon the discrete activity being performed. Thus, the social hierarchy of the studio may be envisioned as static only at the top (between the studio master and the students) and then the students engage in a fluid social hierarchy based on their individual competencies in design or other technical tasks (see Fig. 4.1) (Black, 2008; Gee, 2004).

## Research in Distributed Design Education

Beginning in 1995, there was considerable interest generated by the exploration and development of early DDE techniques in the form of the virtual design studio (VDS) (Broadfoot & Bennett, 2003; Dale, 2006; Maher, Bilda, & Gül, 2006; Sagun, Demirkan, & Goktepe, 2001). These early experiments were typically built around a short design project—few appeared to have much longevity beyond their initial use—and they are best viewed as forward-thinking explorations of the use of technology for both design and collaboration.

These early descriptions focus most of their commentary on the technological tools being utilized, a trend that has since continued in most of the disseminated work on DDE, and the majority of articles detailing the use of a VDS do not consider or emphasize the social and pedagogical implications of a VDS (Bender & Good, 2003; Budd, Vanka, & Runton, 1999; Maher & Simoff, 1999; Maher, Simoff, & Cicognani, 1996; Simoff & Maher, 1997). There are notable exceptions to this focus on the novel use of technology for collaboration. For example, Cheng (1998) explored the potential of DDE to mimic and improve upon the social relationships that exist in a PDS, and explicitly discussed the unique challenges of establishing authentic social identities and relationships in a VDS. Kvan (2001) is an early example, and one of only a handful, who addresses the fact that the use of a VDS precipitates a reevaluation of the accepted design studio pedagogy because it dramatically alters the environment in which learning occurs.

Researchers repeatedly discuss the benefits of the VDS to design education, especially noting the ability of DDE to provide students with access to geographically dispersed individuals, enabling collaboration with other students, educators, practitioners, critics, and clients that would not have been possible in a PDS (Dave & Danahy, 2000; Kvan, 2001; Levine & Wake, 2000). DDE offers the ability to expose students to foreign cultures and practices, potentially altering the way they perceive and think about design and social values (Kvan, 2001; Sagun et al., 2001). Utilizing a VDS can increase time flexibility and efficiency in teaching, enabling higher contact rates between the student and instructor and more time spent in deeper discussion about topics (Brown, Hardaker, & Higgett, 2000; Kvan, 2001; Li & Murphy, 2004; Shannon, 2002). Researchers also suggest that DDE could enable a greater emphasis and understanding of the design process through the preservation and efficient organization of data related to the iterative development of a student's design (Brown et al., 2000; Matthews & Weigand, 2001; Sagun et al., 2001; Schnable, Kvan, Kruiff, & Donath, 2001).

Despite the identified benefits of DDE, its use remains rare in landscape architecture programs. A review of studio pedagogy reveals that the social relationships that exist in a studio are critical to facilitating learning and, while most DDE research has focused on the technical aspects of DDE, we speculated that the ill-defined social component of DDE is of most concern to faculty and a great impediment to its adoption. One of the primary purposes of this chapter is to explore the extent to which faculty acknowledge the challenge of including a social component in DDE and the extent to which social learning theory might be a meaningful lens to address that challenge.

## Methodology

A Delphi study was used to develop consensus on the critical barriers to the adoption of DDE from a panel of experts composed of landscape architecture faculty members employed at accredited landscape architecture programs in the USA (Hasson, Keeney, & McKenna, 2000; So & Bonk, 2010). Delphi studies as a consensus building activity are fundamentally aligned with social learning theory. In addition, they are designed to incorporate a heterogeneous pool of participants that represent the full range of opinions in a field. In this particular case we included faculty members who had presented in the Design Teaching and Pedagogy track at the Council of Educators in Landscape Architecture Conference within the previous 3 years, as well as department heads. Forty-three individuals agreed to participate.

The potential barriers were drawn from an extensive literature review that identified the constraints and barriers to the adoption of DDE. A thematic-synthesis was used to produce a list of 22 potential barriers to adoption. Following the development of the barriers, the first round of the Delphi study was carried out. During this first round, panelists had the opportunity to suggest other barriers, and two additional barriers were added to subsequent rounds. Panelists used a 7-point Likert scale to evaluate the importance of each potential barrier. Panelists were also asked to justify their selections by providing written feedback.

At the commencement of the second and third rounds, panelists received the mean and standard deviation of the entire panel's responses on each barrier, as well as their own response from the previous round. They were also provided with the anonymous comments provided by the panel. In light of this additional knowledge, panelists were asked to reconsider each barrier and either change or maintain their response, again being asked to justify their position. The rounds continued until distribution stability (expressed as a percentage change in total scale units) was reached for the individual barriers (Scheibe, Skutsch, & Schofer, 1975). Twenty-three of the 24 barriers achieved stability after the third round and, with diminishing participation rates, the Delphi was ended after the third round.

## Results

The final rank order of the barriers was developed from the mean score of the panel's responses for each barrier. In instances of ties, the rank order was determined first by the mode, and then the IQR (see Table 4.1). Graphing the mean scores revealed a series of natural breaks which were used to divided the barriers into four categories: *critical*, *important*, *less important*, and *not important*. Barriers in the *critical* category had an average mean score of 5.07, those in the *important* category had an average mean of 4.59, those in the *less important* category had an average mean of 4.16, and the average mean of the *not important* category was 3.51. The critical barriers also had the highest level of consensus, with an average SD of 1.26, and only one barrier having an IQR of higher than 1.

The results show that the critical barriers to faculty adoption of DDE are issues related to social interaction (barriers 1, 4–7), issues with financial compensation (barrier 2), and a lack of confidence in the medium (barrier 3). While the first barrier is concerned with the overarching concept of online education, the panelist comments related to this barrier imply that the undergirding concern is social. Combined with the fourth through seventh barriers, it is clear that faculty are preeminently concerned about preserving the social characteristics of traditional studio culture. Mitigating for these barriers will require a nuanced effort from educators and researchers to create a pedagogy that emulates the social learning environment of the studio. Educational theories concerned with the social role of learning and the formation of communities of practice will provide an ideal foundation on which to construct such a pedagogy (Black, 2008; Gee, 2004; Hutchins, 1995).

**Table 4.1** Delphi results for the barriers to adoption

| Barrier | Mean | Mode | SD | IQR | Category |
|---|---|---|---|---|---|
| Instructors believe the studio method cannot be replicated using DDE | 5.61 | 6 | 1.033 | 0 | Critical |
| Faculty not adequately compensated | 5.30 | 6 | 1.105 | 1 | Critical |
| A lack of precedent in DDE | 5.05 | 5 and 6 | 0.999 | 2 | Critical |
| Building rapport with others is difficult | 4.96 | 5 | 1.364 | 1 | Critical |
| Students feel socially isolated from their peers | 4.91 | 6 | 1.443 | 1 | Critical |
| Lack of face-to-face interaction | 4.91 | 5 | 1.379 | 1 | Critical |
| Critiquing student work is difficult | 4.78 | 5 | 1.506 | 1 | Critical |
| Designs produced on a computer are inferior | 4.70 | 6 | 1.941 | 4 | Important |
| Upfront costs may deter development | 4.70 | 5 | 1.329 | 1 | Important |
| DDE constrains a student's creative process | 4.65 | 6 | 1.722 | 3 | Important |
| Only motivated and organized student can succeed | 4.61 | 5 | 1.196 | 1 | Important |
| Faculty have theoretical or pedagogical opposition | 4.57 | 5 | 1.376 | 2 | Important |
| Faculty struggle to adopt necessary technology | 4.52 | 4 and 5 | 1.41 | 1 | Important |
| Students spend less time and energy on DDE projects | 4.52 | 4 | 1.123 | 1 | Important |
| It is difficult for students to collaborate | 4.48 | 5 | 1.675 | 2 | Important |
| Teaching consumes unacceptable amounts of faculty time | 4.32 | 4 and 5 | 1.323 | 2 | Less Imp |
| Faculty concern that DDE will decrease tenured positions | 4.30 | 4 | 1.579 | 2 | Less Imp |
| Internet resources may be unreliable | 4.14 | 4 and 5 | 1.699 | 3 | Less Imp |
| Private concern DDE will threaten personal job security | 4.09 | 4 | 1.505 | 1 | Less Imp |
| Faculty are unwilling to adopt necessary technology | 4.04 | 4 and 5 | 1.397 | 2 | Less Imp |
| Ongoing costs deter continued offering | 4.04 | 4 | 1.147 | 1 | Less Imp |
| Necessary technology is too expensive for students | 3.70 | 4 | 1.329 | 2 | Not Imp |
| Necessary technology is too expensive for programs | 3.61 | 4 | 1.27 | 1 | Not Imp |
| Required technology proficiency is unreasonable for students | 3.22 | 3 | 1.347 | 1 | Not Imp |

## Discussion

With the critical barriers to adoption identified, we turn to an analysis of how we might use the identified social learning theories to mitigate for these barriers while preserving the essence of the studio. Here we discuss the social component of the individual critical barriers, excluding the second and third barriers, which are not tied to pedagogy or the social learning environment of the studio.

## Critical Barrier 1: Instructors Believe the Studio Method Cannot Be Replicated Using DDE

The panel's comments made it clear there is concern about the loss of physical interaction as a means of conveying and converging on information and design ideas. Several comments refer to an intangible quality of the studio, a "something" that is not replicable outside of the physical confines of the studio. These comments are best summarized by a panelist's response: "There is something lost when students can't look across to other's desks and see their works and/or iterations, over-hear conversations, or participate in impromptu pop-up discussions and topics." While it is impossible to define what that something is specifically, from other comments it can be inferred that it refers to the social learning environment that is created within the studio. Comments suggest that students would be unable to interact with each other, and therefore learn from each other through observation and impromptu learning sessions.

There is also a belief that an online education platform that could support all of the communication and design tools necessary simply does not yet exist. Panelists acknowledge that learning goals might be achieved, but believe that design results would be substantially different. There is discussion about the ability of technology to facilitate many of the types of in situ communication that occurs in the studio, but that elements of the learning process are either lost or degraded: "I think that it could be done technically and logistically, but I think that the process and the experience would lose something important."

While the PDS provides students an immediate horizon of observation composed of their proximate peers, research has shown that DDE can provide students with the ability to expand their horizon of observation. However, it appears that the panel is more concerned about the time factor of the horizon. In the studio, students are able to immediately see and interact with their peers, while in many VDSs it is possible to see peer's work, but it is often cumbersome or requires many steps to do so. A possible DDE solution would be to create a social sharing network that is integrated with a file sharing service such, in which digital files that are updated on a student's computer are automatically updated for quick browsing in the VDS. As a social network, this service would accommodate the sharing of more than simply files, enabling students to easily comment on each other's work and provide tutoring on specific tasks.

## Critical Barrier 4: Building Rapport with Others Is Difficult

The most common theme is concern about the ability of existent technological tools to support the rich forms of communication necessary for building rapport. Although panelists discuss many common forms of computer-mediated communication and social media, they express the view that "there is a disconnect between [people]" when using these technologies, and that they are unable to develop the "deeper and more meaningful connections" that can be made face-to-face. There is also concern about if students would learn to communicate with their future clients and the public. One panelist sums up this concern: "What I worry about is if they will continue to be able to design for REAL PEOPLE. Especially if they don't get outside and away from their electronic devices long enough."

Countering this technology gap theme is discussion on the nature of how modern students collaborate. Some panelists feel that students are digital natives, and that they find it as easy (some suggest easier) to communicate and build rapport in an online setting as in a face-to-face setting. One panelist describes building rapport online as being the "preferred method" of modern students and, with the heavy involvement students have in social media, it is possible that "rapport of this kind has come into its own in education."

Between the two sides of this debate, some panelists felt that building rapport is no more or less difficult online as it is face-to-face, and that building good rapport in a face-to-face environment is not a foregone conclusion. These panelists suggest building rapport is dependent upon the characteristics of the individual students and how effectively the scaffolding in the course encourages communication.

Pedagogically, the instructor should introduce course activities that provide scaffolding for rapport building in a DDE course that may not have been necessary in a F2F course. Hutchins (1995) concluded that groups collaborate best when there are social dependencies built into the collaborative tasks. The nature of the task should require rapport building in order to be successful. Returning to the social learning network suggested above, this network could also be made to include practitioners or community members in order to gather feedback and enable students to experience legitimate peripheral participation with the community of practice they are training to enter. In this way, students would be able to build rapport amongst themselves, as well as taking additional steps towards the center of the community of practice.

## Critical Barrier 5: Students Feel Socially Isolated from Their Peers

Within this barrier, the most commonly discussed topic by the panel revolves around modern students and how they socialize. In the first two rounds, comments were dismissive of this barrier, stating that "students don't care" about being isolated and that the large majority of modern students regularly communicate and socialize online via social media. However, by the third round many panelists insisted that students should not be isolated, and that some of the most important learning that happens in the studio happens organically between peers, and that students in a DDE environment are not be able to enjoy a similar type of social experience.

In the third round, another theme emerged focusing on the social interactions of the studio environment, but these comments focused on the development of broader social skills. "Students need to learn to interact with their peers" and "effective social interaction and communication is critical" for designers. These comments took a more global look at the issues of isolation and communication, criticizing computer-mediated discussions as insufficient to teach the social skills required in the landscape architecture profession. However, using the same rationale, a similar argument can be made that students need to be able to master and communicate via new media and technologies, as these become increasingly prominent in practice and broader society (Boyd & Ellison, 2007; Vanderkaay, 2010).

Concerns stemming from this barrier are best understood in the context of the physical environment of the studio, where students are free to observe and interact with their peers. Social isolation is worse than simply reducing the amount of social exchanges between students, it represents the reduction in the quantity of ideas that are shared, and, by extension, the quality of designs that are subsequently produced (Dutton, 1987; Schön, 1983).

As theorized by Hutchins (1995), it is critical that learners are able to observe each other, especially their more advanced peers, in order to facilitate learning and mastery of more advanced skills. Conversely Lave and Wenger (1991) demonstrated that depriving learners of the ability to observe their more advanced peers decreased learning performance. In the studio this observation often takes the form of socialization between students as they move between each other's desks to talk about their designs and other topics.

It is our belief that preventing social isolation in DDE will once again need to rely on social dependencies being built into learning tasks. Requiring basic interaction (á la making discussion posts or participating in chat group) is not sufficient because the social aspect remains either undeveloped or tertiary to the task. Social interactions need to be scaffolded in such a way that they advance the task.

While a concern, DDE can provide an opportunity to reduce the social isolation for some individuals. Because of the power structure of the studio, the studio master holds an inordinate amount of power by virtue of their position. This has led some to note that the student is often kept in a position of subservience in which they do little more than mime and try to please the studio master; a social structure that prevents them from participating in meaningful exploration and keeps them intellectually isolated (Anthony, 1991; Dutton, 1987; Webster, 2009). Online education has been shown to encourage participation from the most socially vulnerable students because it can flatten the power structure of the studio (Matthews & Weigand, 2001). Affinity spaces demonstrate that this is the case, in that otherwise socially isolated students are able to share their specific expertise without having to open themselves for criticism on other aspects of their knowledge (Black, 2008).

## *Critical Barrier 6: Lack of Face-to-Face Interaction*

The panel was most concerned about constraints that technology places on the communication process. While some panelists acknowledge that verbal and nonverbal communication can be facilitated online, they are concerned about the "limitations of technology to replicate all of the factors involved in communication." These limitations impact how students communicate, and therefore what type of culture they form amongst themselves. Panelists also believe that the studio environment is invaluable for providing an embodied experience that "replicates real world situations of design practice."

They recognize that "DDE could facilitate effective communication but may be [sic] not the same type of communication that happens [in the studio]." Out of this there was a discussion of the pros and cons of any potential changes, such as impacts to the time it takes to communicate, the ability to include more stakeholders in the communication process, and the ability to record and revisit conversations later. However, the suggestion is that even though physical face-to-face communication is preferable, not having it is not insurmountable. It is likely this barrier will become less of a concern as technology improves and students have the ability to communicate in a manner ever-closer to F2F interactions.

## *Critical Barrier 7: Critiquing Student Work Is Difficult*

In the initial round, the major concern was related to the technical constraints of technology in facilitating critiques. Panelists worried that what is already "a difficult process in a face-to-face environment" would become more difficult in a distributed one, and that oftentimes "technology complicates simple communication." The concern appears to be not that technology is unable to facilitate a critique, but rather that it would become more difficult to do so.

The panel also expressed concern about the ability to effectively convey emotion during a critique in DDE. Critiquing students "is always a dicey proposition fraught with risks when students have fragile egos, insecurities, and lack emotional resilience." They wonder if the process will become more difficult if there is no adequate way to express "voice inflection, facial expressions, and other non-verbal techniques to communicate feedback" in a considerate manner.

The comments of the panel, especially those that focus on the emotional state and reaction of the students, suggest to us that faculty are focusing too much on the social relationship itself during a critique, and not attributing a large enough role to the actual design product. During the critique, the student's work acts as an open tool. An open tool is a device that is available to multiple individuals to utilize, and can be used to encourage or constrain interaction and learning between individuals (Hutchins, 1995). The student's design provides a shared context and mechanism by which the master can teach, and the student can learn (Anthony, 1991; Hokanson, 2012).

In regards to critiques, DDE pedagogy should emphasize the design itself and, in this particular instance, de-emphasize the social relationship. We propose that more emphasis should be placed on group critiques where one-on-one social interactions are less prominent and the power structure is more balanced, theoretically helping to emphasize the design itself. Additionally, emphasis should be placed on facilitating interaction between students, and the critiques that occur between students as they review each other's work. Emphasizing inter-student critiques is supported by all of the social learning theories we have cited in this chapter, and is supported by design experience (Dutton, 1987).

## Conclusion

In this chapter we describe how design studio pedagogy is based on social relationships, and how it can be theorized using the social learning theories of legitimate peripheral participation, distributed cognition, and affinity spaces. We suggest that distributed design education has not seen widespread adoption largely because of faculty concern over the medium's ability to facilitate rich social interactions of the type that occur within the PDS. The results of the Delphi study support this position, as five of the seven critical barriers referenced social issues.

In analyzing the barriers, we propose that a VDS needed to be built around social relationships, potentially using a platform akin to modern social media networks. Such a platform can enable students to have an expansive horizon of observation and near-immediate access to the work of their peers, receive tutoring from their peers, and potentially enable peripheral participation in the design community of practice through engaging practitioners. Pedagogically, tasks assigned to students need to have social dependencies built in which require students to build social connections in order to be successful. Critiques should focus on utilizing the design as an open tool, preferably through the use of group critiques that reduce the social difficulties that can occur between student and master in a critique. We believe that through the application of these social learning theories to DDE pedagogy, it is possible to create a robust social learning environment that supports most of the social framework of the design studio.

## References

Anthony, K. H. (1991). *Design juries on trial: The renaissance of the design studio.* New York, NY: Van Nostrand Reinhold.

Barnes, J. (1993). A case for the vertical studio. *Journal of Interior Design, 19*(1), 34–38.

Bender, D. M. (2005). Developing a collaborative multidisciplinary online design course. *The Journal of Educators Online, 2*(2), 1–12.

Bender, D. M., & Good, L. (2003). Interior design faculty intentions to adopt distance education. *Journal of Interior Design, 29*(1 and 2), 66–80.

Bender, D. M., & Vredevoogd, J. D. (2006). Using online education technologies to support studio instruction. *Journal of Educational Technology & Society, 9*(4), 114–122.

Black, R. W. (2008). *Adolescents and online fan fiction.* New York: Peter Lang.

Boyd, D. M., & Ellison, N. B. (2007). Social network sites: Definition, history, and scholarship. *Journal of Computer-Mediated Communication, 13*(1), 210–230.

Broadfoot, O., & Bennett, R. (2003). *Design studios: Online? Comparing traditional face-to-face Design Studio education with modern internet-based design studios* (pp. 1–13). Presented at the Apple University Consortium.

Brown, S., Hardaker, C. H. M., & Higgett, N. P. (2000). Designs on the web: A case study of online learning for design students. *Association for Learning Technology Journal, 8*(1), 30–40.

Budd, J., Vanka, S., & Runton, A. (1999). The ID-Online Asynchronous Learning Network: A "Virtual Studio" for interdisciplinary design collaboration. *Digital Creativity, 10*(4), 205–214.

Cheng, N. Y.-W. (1998). Digital identity in the virtual design studio. In *Proceedings of the 86th Associated Collegiate Schools of Architecture's (ACSA)* (pp. 1–13). Cleveland, OH.

Christensen, C., & Eyring, H. J. (2011). *The innovative university: Changing the DNA of higher education.* New York, NY: John Wiley.

Dale, J. S. (2006). A technology-based online design curriculum. In *TCC* (pp. 2–11). Retrieved from http://www.researchgate.net/publication/228611136_A_technology-based_online_design_curriculum.

Dave, B., & Danahy, J. (2000). Virtual study abroad and exchange studio. *Automation in Construction, 9,* 57–71.

Dutton, T. A. (1987). Design and studio pedagogy. *Journal of Architectural Education, 41*(1), 16–25.

García-Peñalvo, F., Conde, M., Alier, M., & Casany, M. (2011). Opening learning management systems to personal learning environments. *Journal of Universal Computer Science, 17*(9), 1222–1240.

Gee, J. (2004). *Situated language and learning: A critique of traditional schooling.* New York, NY: Routledge.

George, B. & Bussiere, S. (2015). Factors impacting students' decisions to stay or leave the design studio: A national study. *Landscape Research Record, 3,* 11–21.

Ham, J. J., & Schnable, M. A. (2011). Web 2.0 virtual design studio: Social networking as facilitator of design education. *Architectural Science Review, 54*(2), 108–116.

Hasson, F., Keeney, S., & McKenna, H. (2000). Research guidelines for the Delphi survey technique. *Journal of Advanced Nursing, 32*(4), 1008–1015.

Hew, K., & Cheung, W. S. (2013). Use of Web 2.0 technologies in K-12 and higher education: The search for evidence-based practice. *Educational Research Review, 9,* 47–64.

Hokanson, B. (2012). The design critique as a model for distributed learning. In L. Moller & J. B. Huett (Eds.), *The next generation of distance education* (pp. 71–83). Boston, MA: Springer US.

Hutchins, E. (1995). *Cognition in the wild.* Cambridge, MA: MIT Press.

Kvan, T. (2001). The pedagogy of virtual design studios. *Automation in Construction, 10,* 345–353.

Lave, J., & Wenger, E. (1991). *Situated learning and legitimate peripheral participation.* Cambridge, UK: Cambridge University Press.

Levine, S. L., & Wake, W. K. (2000). Hybrid teaching: Design studios in virtual space. In *Proceedings of the National Conference on Liberal Arts and the Education of Artists* (Vol. 1). New York City, NY.

Li, M.-H., & Murphy, M. D. (2004). Assessing the effect of supplemental web-based learning in two landscape construction courses. *Landscape Review, 9*(1), 157–161.

Maher, M. L., Bilda, Z., & Gül, L. F. (2006). Impact of collaborative virtual environments on design behavior. In *Proceedings of Design Computing and Cognition '06.* Netherlands: Springer.

Maher, M. L., & Simoff, S. (1999). Variations on the virtual design studio. In *Proceedings of Fourth International Workshop on CSCW in Design.* Compiègne, France.

Maher, M. L., Simoff, S., & Cicognani, A. (1996). *The potential and current limitations in a virtual design studio*. Sydney, Australia: Key Centre of Design Computing, Department of Architecture and Design Science. Retrieved from http://web.arch.usyd.edu.au/~mary/VDSjournal/.

Matthews, D., & Weigand, J. (2001). Collaborative design using the internet: A case study. *Journal of Interior Design, 27*(1), 45–53.

Park, J. Y. (2011). Design education online: Learning delivery and evaluation. *The International Journal of Art & Design Education, 30*(2), 176–187.

Sagun, A., Demirkan, H., & Goktepe, M. (2001). A framework for the design studio in web-based education. *The International Journal of Art & Design Education, 20*(3), 332–342.

Scheibe, M., Skutsch, M., & Schofer, J. (1975). Experiments in Delphi methodology. In H. A. Linstone & M. Turoff (Eds.), *The Delphi method: Techniques and applications* (pp. 257–281). London, England: Addison-Wesley.

Schnable, M. A., Kvan, T., Kruiff, E., & Donath, D. (2001). The first virtual environment design studio. In *Proceedings of the 19th Conference on Education in Computer Aided Architectural Design in Europe*. Helsinki, Finland.

Schön, D. A. (1983). *The reflective practitioner: How professionals think in action*. New York: Basic Books.

Schön, D. A. (1985). *The design studio: An exploration of its traditions and potentials*. London, England: Royal Institute of British Architects.

Shannon, S. J. (2002). Authentic digital design learning. In *Proceedings of the 36th Conference of the Australian and New Zealand Architectural Science Association* (pp. 461–468). Geelong, Australia.

Simoff, S., & Maher, M. L. (1997). Design education via web-based virtual environments. In *Proceedings of the Fourth Congress of Computing in Civil Engineering*. New York, NY: ASCE.

So, H.-J., & Bonk, C. J. (2010). Examining the roles of blended learning approaches in computer-supported collaborative learning (CSCL) environments: A Delphi study. *Educational Technology & Society, 13*(3), 189–200.

Vanderkaay, S. (2010). The social media evolution. *Canadian Architect, 4*(10), 39–40.

Webster, H. (2009). Architectural education after Schön: Cracks, blurs, boundaries and beyond. *Journal for Education in the Built Environment, 3*(2), 63–74.

Yuan, L., & Powell, S. (2013). *MOOCs and open education: Implications for higher education*. Bolton, UK: Center for Educational Technology and Interoperability Standards.

# Chapter 5
# Understanding Help-Seeking Behavior of Students' in a Flipped Classroom: A Structural Equation Modeling Approach

**Erkan Er and Michael Orey**

## Introduction

In any learning context, a learner needs to ask for help from a more advanced person (e.g., peer or teacher) when facing an academic difficulty (Ryan, Gheen, & Midgley, 1998). In the literature, this is referred to as help-seeking behavior (Nelson-Le Gall, 1985). Help-seeking has long been recognized as an important self-regulated learning strategy that is associated with students' academic goals and achievement (Karabenick & Newman, 2006). In help-seeking, students regulate their environments by using peers, teachers, and parents as sources of support for coping with learning difficulties. The need for help emerges in response to the combination of a learning difficulty and insufficient personal resources to overcome the difficulty. For example, a student may have trouble understanding one aspect of a science concept and may not be able to solve the assigned problems in the textbook. The student may try such strategies as rereading the related book section and revisiting the lecture notes. However, when these personal strategies are ineffective, the student may consult teachers, friends, or parents for help.

Even though help-seeking positively influences learning (Aleven, Stahl, & Schworm, 2003; Lee, 2007; Newman, 2000), not every student uses it. The literature has been informative in revealing the determinants of students' help-seeking behavior, which broadly includes motivational factors (e.g., self-efficacy, self-esteem, achievement goal orientation, autonomy orientation), and environmental factors (e.g., classroom goal structure and instructor support). Besides these factors, the literature also notes that students' perceived threats and benefits for help-seeking have a considerable influence on their decision to seek help (Newman, 1990; Ryan

E. Er (✉) • M. Orey
Learning, Design, and Technology, The University of Georgia,
116 River's Crossing, Athens, GA 30602-4809, USA
e-mail: erkaner@uga.edu; mikeorey@uga.edu

© Springer International Publishing Switzerland 2017
M. Orey, R.M. Branch (eds.), *Educational Media and Technology Yearbook*,
Educational Media and Technology Yearbook 40,
DOI 10.1007/978-3-319-45001-8_5

& Pintrich, 1997). These perceptions are particularly critical not only because of their direct influence on help-seeking but also because of their interaction with other factors. For example, students with low self-efficacy are likely to feel threatened by asking for help (Ryan & Shim, 2006), and their perceptions of threat often result in their avoidance of help-seeking (Newman, 1990; Ryan & Pintrich, 1997). On the other hand, students with a mastery goal orientation are likely to perceive help-seeking as a beneficial strategy for their learning, and they tend to seek the necessary help (Karabenick, 2003; Ryan & Pintrich, 1997).

Compared to the vast majority of help-seeking literature that has focused on examining the individual influences of various factors on help-seeking, there is a limited number of studies that examined the interactions among different factors. These interactions, when examined as a whole, can help obtain a more complete picture of why students seek or avoid help. Thus, the present study aims to explore the help-seeking behavior of students in a holistic way; a causal model is proposed and tested to explore the effects of environmental and motivational factors on help-seeking. The mediator role of students' perceptions regarding the costs and benefits of help-seeking is examined as well. It is also noteworthy that this study extends the existing literature beyond the traditional classroom, which has been the dominant context in help-seeking research. The research setting of this study is a flipped classroom, which is an implementation of blended instruction in which students study the lectures themselves, usually at home, and during class time they generally engage in problem-solving activities (Woolf, 2010). Understanding help-seeking behavior in flipped classrooms, which employ a relatively new form of blended instruction, can be valuable for informing the practices for supporting help-seeking in such classrooms.

## The Conceptual Model

This paper conceptualizes a mediation model of help-seeking (see Fig. 5.1) that explores the direct and indirect effects of instructor support, relatedness, and goal orientation on help-seeking, in which students' perceptions of benefits and costs are selected as the mediator. The model is composed of three main groups of constructs: 1) instructor support, relatedness, and students' achievement goal-orientation, 2) students' perceptions of benefits and costs for help-seeking, and 3) students' help-seeking intentions and help-seeking styles.

### *Help-Seeking Intentions and Help-Seeking Styles*

In this study, we focus on students' intentions to seek help, as well as their help-seeking styles. Students often seek two types of help: executive (or expedient) and instrumental (or adaptive) help (Nelson-Le Gall, Gumerman, & Scott-Jones, 1983).

**Fig. 5.1** The conceptual model for studying help-seeking

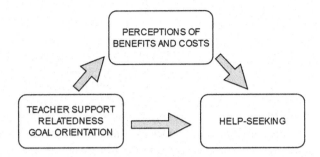

The executive style involves reducing the amount of required effort by utilizing direct help from others. For example, students preferring executive help may solicit a direct answer to a science problem soon after their initial attempts. In contrast, instrumental help-seeking involves receiving minimal assistance from others and solving a problem more independently. Students preferring instrumental help may try to understand the concepts leading to the solution of a problem through hints from others and attempt to solve the problem by their own effort (Karabenick & Knapp, 1991).

## *Instructor Support for Help-Seeking*

Instructor support is included in the model as one of the environmental factors influencing students' help-seeking perceptions and intentions. Instructors' views have an effect on students' attitudes toward help-seeking. Empirical studies reported a correlation between perceived instructor support and the resulting help-seeking activities (Karabenick & Sharma, 1994; Newman & Schwager, 1993). For example, Newman and Schwager (1993) found that students who perceive instructor support for help-seeking are more likely to seek help. Likewise, in a study among college students, Karabenick and Sharma (1994) reported that higher perceptions of instructor support resulted in a higher number of questions asked by students in a classroom environment. Arbreton (1998) added that instructor support for help-seeking results in instrumental help-seeking rather than executive help-seeking, especially in task-focused classrooms. In short, the literature informs us that instructor support helps in decreasing students' feelings of threat and enhancing the belief among students that help-seeking is a useful learning strategy (Arbreton, 1998). Based on this literature, we suggest in the conceptualized model that instructor support directly and indirectly (mediated by perceived costs and benefits) influences students' help-seeking intentions and styles.

## Relatedness

Another factor considered in the conceptual model is relatedness, which is defined as the basic psychological need of an individual to establish bonds with others (Deci, Vallerand, Pelletier, & Ryan, 1991). The need for relatedness can be satisfied by promoting interactions among students and encouraging them to socially support each other. The help-seeking literature highlights the importance of interpersonal relations and social interactions among students in their decisions to seek help (Nelson-Le Gall & Resnick, 1998). Karabenick and Knapp (1988) noted that having higher numbers of friends positively influences help-seeking as students prefer not to seek help from strangers in academic settings. Nelson-Le Gall and Resnick (1998) suggested that being a member of a learning community where help-seeking and help-giving are valued can help students develop a sense of belonging and encourage students to ask for help when needed. Similarly, Hertz-Lazarowitz (1995) found that help-seeking and help-giving behaviors are more likely to occur among students when peer interaction is promoted. Based on the findings from the previous research, it is hypothesized that there exists a positive association between relatedness and students' help-seeking perceptions and intentions.

## Achievement Goal Orientation

The only motivational factor included in the model is students' achievement goal orientations. Students may have different achievement goals influencing their decision to seek help, which can be classified as *mastery* goals and *performance* goals (Nelson-Le Gall, 1985; Wolters, Yu, & Pintrich, 1996). Mastery goals (or task-focused goals, see Ryan & Pintrich, 1997 or learning goals, see Newman, 1998) refer to the desire of a student to learn and improve (Arbreton, 1998; Wolters et al., 1996). Students with mastery goal orientations value learning and spend effort to master a concept. Research shows that students with mastery goal orientations consider help-seeking a beneficial strategy, and they usually prefer the instrumental style (Cheong, Pajares, & Oberman, 2004; Karabenick, 2003; Ryan & Pintrich, 1997).

Students can also adopt performance goals, and these students are likely to have concerns about their abilities and compare themselves to others. Students with a performance goal orientation aim to achieve desirable grades not necessarily by mastery (Wolters et al., 1996). Performance goal oriented students feel threatened by potential negative judgments of others and avoid seeking help (Karabenick, 2004; Tanaka & Murakami, 2001). When they decide to ask for help, these students are likely to seek executive help (Butler, 1998; Cheong et al., 2004; Karabenick, 2003, 2004; Ryan & Pintrich, 1998).

Thus, we include achievement goal orientation in our model and propose that students' achievement goals play a direct and an indirect (mediated by the perceived costs and benefits) role in their help-seeking intentions as well as help-seeking styles.

## *Research Questions*

This study aims to examine the relationships among the constructs in the hypothesized conceptual model by using a Structural Equation Modeling (SEM) approach. As shown in Fig. 5.2, a causal model (or path diagram) is suggested based on the help-seeking literature. This path diagram suggests that (a) instructor support for help-seeking and relatedness have a direct effect on help-seeking and an indirect effect on help-seeking mediated by the perceived costs and benefits, and (b) the perceived costs and benefits of help-seeking have a direct effect on help-seeking.

Based on the causal model, this study attempts to investigate the following research questions:

1. Do instructor support, relatedness, and goal orientation influence students' help-seeking intentions and styles?
2. Do perceptions of benefits and costs for help-seeking influence students' help-seeking intentions and styles?
3. Do perceptions of benefits and costs for help-seeking mediate the indirect effects of instructor support, relatedness, and goal orientation on students' help-seeking intentions and styles?

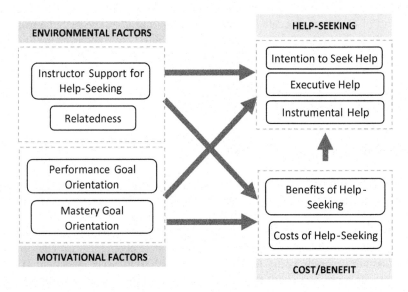

**Fig. 5.2** Hypothesized causal model of help-seeking

# Method

## Context and Participants

The research context was a large-enrollment science course in a southern university in the USA. The course was taught with a flipped classroom approach; students were required to study the video podcasts and supplementary course materials (provided using the university's learning management system) themselves outside the classroom, and in-class time was used to conduct problem solving activities. Additionally, a web-based Q&A tool was integrated to allow students to post any course-related questions. The participants were 356 junior or senior college students (139 males and 217 females) registered in the flipped science course.

## Instruments

A single Likert-type questionnaire was created by combining instruments measuring each individual construct in the causal help-seeking model. The details of these instruments are described as follows.

### Perceived Instructor Support for Help-Seeking (ISFHS) Scale

The ISFHS assesses the degree to which students perceive instructor support for seeking help. This measure consists of items adapted from the Perceived Teacher Support of Questioning Scale (Karabenick & Sharma, 1994) (e.g., "The instructor generally feels good when we ask questions to request help") and from the Students' Perceptions of Teacher Support and Inhibition Scale (Butler & Shibaz, 2008) (e.g., "The instructor encourages us to ask for help any time, even after class"). The reliability of these questionnaires, using the Cronbach's alpha, were 0.82 and 0.79, respectively, indicating a good internal consistency.

### Perceived Relatedness (REL) Scale

This instrument assesses the extent to which students experience satisfaction of relatedness needs in the class. The questionnaire items were adapted from the relatedness section of the Basic Need Satisfaction at Work Scale, which was used by Kasser, Davey, and Ryan (1992) and Baard, Deci, and Ryan (2004). The questionnaire includes such items as "People in the class care about me" or "The people in the class are generally pretty friendly towards me" to measure the extent to which students feels positive about their relationships with others in the class. Previous research reported high internal consistency with a Cronbach's alpha value of 0.89.

**Achievement Goal Orientation Scale**

This instrument assesses the extent to which students are performance or mastery goal-oriented. It is comprised of the items from the Goal Orientation and Learning Strategies Survey (GOALS-S), developed by Dowson and McInerney (2004), to measure students' goal orientations. Four items measure mastery goal-orientation (MGO) (e.g., "I work hard because I am interested in what I am learning"), and six items measure performance goal-orientation (PGO) (e.g., "I want to learn things so that I can get good marks"). Reliability for the mastery-goal orientation subscale was 0.78, and it was 0 .87 for the performance-goal orientation subscale.

**Help-Seeking Scale**

The scale includes 15 items from the help-seeking instrument (Karabenick, 2001); the items are dispersed over five different subscales. The general intention to seek needed help (INTSH) measure asks students to rate three statements about their intentions to seek help (e.g., "If I needed help understanding the lectures in this class I would ask for help") on 5-point Likert scales. The perceived costs (threat) of help seeking (COST) measure asks students to rate four items concerning the costs that they perceive regarding asking for help (e.g., "I would not want anyone to find out that I needed help in this class") on 5-point Likert scales ($\alpha = .84$). The perceived benefits of help seeking (BENF) measure asks students to rate five items regarding the benefits of help-seeking that they perceive in the class (e.g., "Getting help in this class would increase my ability to learn the material") on 5-point Likert scales ($\alpha = .80$). The executive help-seeking (EXECHS) measure asks students to rate three items regarding their tendency to seek executive help (e.g., "Getting help in this class would be a way of avoiding doing some of the work") on 5-point Likert scales ($\alpha = .84$). Finally, the instrumental help-seeking (INSTHS) measure asks students to rate three items regarding their tendency to seek instrumental help on 5-point Likert scales.

## *Procedure and Data Analysis*

The data analysis was carried out in several steps. First, confirmatory factor analysis was conducted to verify the factor structure of the observed variables. After the verification of the factorial structure, a model was created based on the hypothesized path model and estimated. Then, the model was assessed to check whether it fits the data. At the end, the model was re-specified to improve its fit, and then the model was finalized. The data analysis was run with Mplus software. Because of the skewness in the data, MLM (maximum likelihood mean adjusted), an estimator that is robust to non-normality, was used as the estimator (Wang & Wang, 2012).

# Results

## *Correlational Statistics*

Correlational analysis among all measures revealed significant correlations among the constructs in the help-seeking model. First, the perceived instructor support for help-seeking was positively correlated with the perceived benefits ($r = .344, p < .01$) and was negatively correlated with the perceived costs of help-seeking ($r = -.515$, $p < .01$). Similarly, there was a positive correlation between the perceived relatedness and the perceived benefits of help seeking ($r = .194, p < .01$), and a negative correlation between the perceived relatedness and the perceived costs of help-seeking ($r = -.552, p < .01$). Considering the help-seeking behavior, the perceived instructor support for help-seeking was positively correlated with intention to seek help ($r = .461, p < .01$) and instrumental help-seeking ($r = .519, p < .01$), while it was negatively correlated with executive help-seeking ($r = -.329, p < .01$). Similar correlations were found between the perceived relatedness and intention to seek help ($r = .431, p < .01$), perceived relatedness and instrumental help-seeking ($r = .338, p < .01$), and the perceived relatedness and executive help-seeking ($r = -.302$, $p < .01$).

The perceived benefits of help-seeking was positively correlated with students' intentions to seek help ($r = .477, p < .01$) and with their preference for instrumental help-seeking ($r = .571, p < .01$). Conversely, the perceived costs of help-seeking was negatively correlated with intention to seek help ($r = -.404, p < .01$) and with instrumental help-seeking ($r = -.421, p < .01$), while it was positively correlated with their preference for executive help-seeking ($r = .471, p < .01$). The other correlations among the constructs are provided in Table 5.1.

## *Results of the Structural Model Analysis*

Figure 5.3 portrays the hypothesized model that helps examine the relations among instructor support for help-seeking, perceptions of relatedness, achievement goals, and help-seeking behavior (i.e., intention to seek help, instrumental help seeking, and executive help seeking). Relatedness, instructor support for help-seeking, performance goal orientation, and mastery goal orientation are the exogenous variables while intention to seek help, instrumental help-seeking, and executive help-seeking are the endogenous variables of the model. The perceived costs and the perceived benefits serve as both the dependent (endogenous) and independent (exogenous) variables. The standardized regression coefficient (Beta) and coefficient of determination ($r^2$) for equations of endogenous variables are given in Fig. 5.3.

The results of the overall model fit evaluation are presented in Table 5.2. These results indicate that the model fits the data well. In other words, the model supports the plausibility of the hypothesized causal relations among the latent variables.

**Table 5.1** Correlations among the latent variables in the help-seeking path diagram

| [a]Variables | S.E. | INTSH | BENF | MGO | COST | REL | ISFHS | INSTHS | EXECHS |
|---|---|---|---|---|---|---|---|---|---|
| INTSH | 0.053 | 1.000 | – | – | – | – | – | – | – |
| BENF | 0.050 | **0.477 | 1.000 | – | – | – | – | – | – |
| MGO | 0.043 | **0.614 | **0.440 | 1.000 | – | – | – | – | – |
| COST | 0.058 | **−0.404 | **−0.173 | **−0.241 | 1.000 | – | – | – | – |
| REL | 0.047 | **0.431 | **0.194 | **0.295 | **−0.552 | 1.000 | – | – | – |
| ISFHS | 0.033 | **0.461 | **0.344 | **0.490 | **−0.515 | **0.524 | 1.000 | – | – |
| INSTHS | 0.026 | **0.476 | **0.571 | **0.373 | **−0.421 | **0.338 | **0.519 | 1.000 | – |
| EXECHS | 0.028 | −0.073 | 0.101 | −0.055 | **0.471 | **−0.302 | **−0.329 | −0.101 | 1.000 |
| PGO | 0.018 | −0.027 | −0.025 | 0.101 | **0.272 | **−0.178 | −0.062 | 0.062 | **0.424 |

[a]The abbreviated variable names were selected based on the instrument names measuring the latent variable (see Instruments section)

**$p < .01$

**Fig. 5.3** Results of SEM analysis explaining help-seeking behavior. Significant paths of the fully estimated model and standardized regression coefficients are presented. $*p < .01$, $**p < .001$

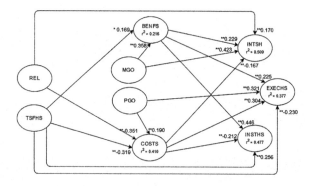

**Table 5.2** Model fit indices indicating the goodness of the model fit to the data

| Chi-Square | DF | p-Value | RMSEA | CFI | TLI | SRMR |
|---|---|---|---|---|---|---|
| 789.454 | 470 | 0.000 | 0.044[a] | 0.955[b] | 0.950[b] | 0.071[c] |

[a]0.00–0.05 good model fit
[b]0.95–1.00 good model fit
[c]0.05–1.00 acceptable model fit

**Table 5.3** Indirect and direct effects between independent and dependent variables in the model

| Independent variables | | Endogenous (dependent) variables | | | | |
|---|---|---|---|---|---|---|
| | | BENF | COST | INTSH | INSTHS | EXECHS |
| TSFHS | Indirect | – | – | **0.092 | **0.143 | −0.059 |
| | Direct | *0.169 | **−0.319 | – | **0.256 | **−0.230 |
| | Total | *0.169 | **−0.319 | **0.092 | **0.399 | **−0.289 |
| REL | Indirect | – | – | **0.059 | **0.074 | – |
| | Direct | – | **−0.351 | **0.170 | – | **−0.107 |
| | Total | – | **−0.351 | **0.228 | **0.074 | **−0.107 |
| MGO | Indirect | – | – | **0.082 | **0.159 | **0.080 |
| | Direct | **0.358 | – | **0.423 | – | – |
| | Total | – | – | **0.505 | **0.159 | **0.080 |
| PMG | Indirect | – | – | *−0.032 | **−0.040 | **0.058 |
| | Direct | – | **0.190 | – | – | **0.321 |
| | Total | – | **0.190 | *−0.032 | **−0.040 | **0.379 |
| BENF | Indirect | – | – | – | – | – |
| | Direct | – | – | **0.229 | **0.446 | **0.225 |
| | Total | – | – | **0.229 | **0.446 | **0.225 |
| COST | Indirect | – | – | – | – | – |
| | Direct | – | – | **−0.167 | **−0.212 | **0.304 |
| | Total | – | – | **−0.167 | **−0.212 | **0.304 |
| $r^2$ | | **0.216 | **0.410 | **0.509 | **0.477 | **0.377 |

$*p < .01$
$**p < .001$

As presented in Table 5.3, the full model explained 21.6 % of the total variance in the perceived benefits of help-seeking and 41% of the total variance in the perceived costs of help-seeking. The perceived benefits were explained by two variables. Instructor support for help-seeking (Beta = .169) and mastery goal orientation (Beta = .358) have positive influences on the perceived benefits for help-seeking. The perceived costs were explained by three variables, which are instructor support for help-seeking (Beta = −.319), relatedness (Beta = −.351), and performance goal orientation (Beta = .190).

These results suggest that when students perceive instructor support for help-seeking, they are more likely to consider help-seeking beneficial and less likely to feel threatened when seeking help. Similarly, when students' relatedness needs are addressed, they are likely to feel less threatened by seeking help. Students' goal orientations also play a significant role in their perceptions regarding the benefits and costs of help-seeking. In particular, mastery goal oriented students are more likely to perceive help-seeking as beneficial, while performance goal orientated students are more likely to perceive help-seeking as threatening.

The full model explained 50.9 % of the total variance in students' intentions to seek help, 47.7 % of the total variance in students' preference for instrumental help-seeking, and 37.7 % of the total variance in students' preference for executive help-seeking. Mastery goal orientations (Beta = .423) had the strongest effect on intentions to seek help, followed by perceptions of benefits (Beta = .229), relatedness (Beta = .170), and perceptions of costs (Beta = −.167). Executive help-seeking was explained by four variables in the model. While perceptions of costs (Beta = .304), perceptions of benefits (Beta = .225), and performance goal orientations (Beta = .321) had positive influences on executive help-seeking, instructor support for help-seeking had a negative effect (Beta = −.230) on executive help-seeking. Instrumental help-seeking was explained by three variables. Perceptions of benefits had the strongest effect (Beta = .446), followed by instructor support for help-seeking (Beta = .256). Perceptions of costs had a negative influence on instrumental help-seeking (Beta = −.212).

The exogenous variables in the model also had indirect effects on help-seeking mediated by students' perceptions regarding the costs and benefits of help-seeking. Instructor support for help-seeking had a positive indirect effect on intention to seek help (Beta = .092) and on instrumental help-seeking (Beta = .143). Similarly, relatedness had a positive indirect effect on intention to seek help (Beta = .059) and instrumental help-seeking (Beta = .074).

## Discussion and Implications

The results of this study support and extend our understanding of students' help-seeking behavior in a flipped science classroom. The model presented projects a bigger picture than previous research and reveals various causal links influencing help-seeking. According to the results, (1) students' intentions to seek help and their help-seeking styles were influenced by instructor support, relatedness, and goal orientations, and (2) their perceptions of benefits and costs of help-seeking were both determinants and mediators of help-seeking. Based on these findings, the implications for promoting help-seeking, particularly in flipped classrooms, are discussed below.

The current study showed that instructor support can predict not only students' perceptions of costs and benefits but also their help-seeking styles. In particular, instructor support can help promote the perceived benefits of help-seeking and decrease the perceived costs of help-seeking, an observation that has been reported consistently by previous research (Karabenick & Sharma, 1994; Kozanitis, Desbiens, & Chouinard, 2007; Nelson-Le Gall & Resnick, 1998). Instructor support was also influential on students' help-seeking styles: it positively influences instrumental help-seeking and negatively influences executive help-seeking. That is, when students perceive instructor support, they are more likely to utilize instrumental help and less likely to seek executive help. Previous research rarely looked into this relationship (Arbreton, 1998; Kozanitis et al., 2007); instead, a great deal of interest around help-seeking styles has been focused on achievement goal orientations. Indeed, this relationship can be inferred from the existing literature. Students with higher levels of perceived instructor support tend to be mastery goal oriented, and thus, they are more inclined to seek instrumental help rather than executive help (Butler & Shibaz, 2008).

Considering the importance of instructor support in promoting help-seeking, the practitioners should design their blended classes in a way that provides opportunities for students to ask questions and receive help. Enabling students to ask questions is an effective approach to promoting students' awareness of instructor support for help-seeking (Karabenick & Sharma, 1994). For example, in flipped classrooms, a web-based questions and answers (Q&A) tool can be integrated to allow students to ask questions outside the classroom, while they are studying the lecture materials. However, only including a Q&A tool may not necessarily promote help-seeking. Instructors may need to explicate that asking and answering questions is essential to learning; therefore, the active use the Q&A tool is important for academic achievement in the class. For example, besides highlighting this point in the syllabus, instructors can provide instructional prompts throughout the semester to inform and remind students that asking questions and receiving the needed help is an important competence. Such prompts can call students' attention to the relevance and necessity of asking for help and encourage students to ask questions when help is needed (Schworm & Gruber, 2012).

Instructor participation in Q&A activities can affect students' use of help-seeking tools to ask and answer questions. First, instructors' positive attitudes toward students' questions and answers might help decrease students' feelings of threat. Help-seeking can be promoted when instructors react to students' help requests in a positive and encouraging manner, because positive instructor attitudes can help students feel safe when posting a question. Reactions from instructors toward students' questions have been found to have a positive influence on help-seeking (Kozanitis et al., 2007). If instructors provide such encouraging feedback as "Great question!" and "Great answer!" to both help-seekers and help-givers, students who were likely to avoid help-seeking before may perceive the instructor support and tend to ask questions when they need help. When using web-based Q&A environments, the instructor–student interactions can be observed by other students, resulting in a classroom-wide effect on students' perceptions of help-seeking. Therefore, it is important that instructors value students' attempts to ask for help in order to increase students' awareness of instructor support and reinforce the belief that help-seeking is an important learning strategy. Furthermore, instructors' participation in Q&A activities is an important factor that can help increase the perceptions of teaching presence. Teaching presence, composed of instructional design, facilitation, and direct instruction, guides students in online learning environments and enhances the quality of interactions in these environments (Garrison, Cleveland-Innes, & Fung, 2010). Instructors' active participation in Q&A activities in terms of answering questions, confirming students' answers, promoting discussions with additional thoughts, supplying additional resources, can support teaching presence and encourage students to ask and answer questions.

Given that help-seeking involves a social interaction, interpersonal relationships among class members is likely to have an influence on help-seeking (Nelson-Le Gall, 1985; Ryan et al., 1998). According to the findings of the study, relatedness directly and indirectly influences students' intentions to seek help in flipped classrooms. Additionally, it has the largest influence on students' perceived costs of help-seeking. These results suggest that building positive relationships with class members has a diminishing effect on students' perceptions of threat and a positive influence on students' intentions to seek help. Similarly, previous research has also indicated that positive relationships with classmates decrease students' concerns about negative judgments of others and encourage students to seek help when it is necessary (Marchand & Skinner, 2007; Nelson-Le Gall & Gumerman, 1984; Ryan, Patrick, & Shim, 2005). There was no influence of relatedness on either students' perceived benefits about help-seeking or their help-seeking styles.

In flipped classrooms, students, who spend considerable amount of time studying the lectures themselves, should be provided with opportunities that help them build and maintain interpersonal relationships with peers. Today's college students, commonly called net generation or millennials (Gloeckler, 2008), are very comfortable using social networking sites to build and maintain friendships (Salaway, Borreson, & Nelson, 2008). Therefore, online learning environments with specific affordances for social networking can appeal to today's college students and allow them to comfortably socialize with peers and build positive relationships (Hurt et al., 2012; Wang, Woo, Quek, Yang, & Liu, 2012). Thus, we suggest that specific affordances that promote social interactions and friendships among students (such as following, friending, bookmarking, likeing, exchanging gifts) should be implemented in new-generation online help-seeking tools. College students could effectively take advantage of the social networking features in building and maintaining positive relationships with classmates, making them feel less threatened to ask questions. Additionally, considering that peers are a source of help frequently preferred by students (Hsu, 2005), increasing connectedness among class members would make this source of help more accessible and indirectly facilitate help-seeking. In this regard, features that enhance the presence of peers can be beneficial.

For example, online help-seeking tools can indicate the number of online users. Furthermore, social networking features can assist students in actively observing peers' Q&A activities. Reviewing existing questions and responses may particularly help those who avoid asking questions because of concerns about being judged by others (Nadler, 1998). These students can keep track of the peers' activities and may observe positive reactions toward asking questions. This observation might help decrease the perceived threat about asking questions and encourage students to post their questions when needed.

Moreover, the results show that students' perceptions of help-seeking have a direct influence on both their intentions to seek help and help-seeking styles. In line with other studies, the perceived costs positively predict executive help-seeking and negatively predict intention to seek help and instrumental help-seeking; the perceived benefits positively predict students' help-seeking styles and intention to seek help. Interestingly and importantly, the positive influence of students' perceived costs about help-seeking on executive help is a finding that is in contrast to other research. For example, Cheong et al. (2004) and Arbreton (1998) found that students who perceive help-seeking as beneficial tend to prefer instrumental rather than executive help. This discrepancy might be due to the fact that students may not recognize different types of helps and may consider help-seeking beneficial whether it is indeed executive or instrumental. To promote instrumental help-seeking among students, instructors can differentiate between these two help-seeking styles and encourage students to seek instrumental help (Cheong et al., 2004). Students can be exposed to this information via syllabus, as well as verbally during class time.

The results indicated that students' goal orientations also play a role in their help-seeking behavior in flipped classrooms. Mastery goal orientation was found to be positively correlated with perceptions of benefits and students' intention to seek help, and performance goal orientation was positively correlated with perceptions of costs and executive help-seeking. These findings, consistent with previous research (Karabenick, 2003, 2004; Ryan & Pintrich, 1997; Tanaka & Murakami, 2001), suggest that mastery goal orientation should be promoted among students in order to support help-seeking. Classroom goal structure can determine students' goal orientation to a great extent (Arbreton, 1993; Butler & Neuman, 1995). Ames and Archer (1988) reported that when students recognize that the learning tasks are mastery goal-oriented, they use effective learning strategies and prefer challenging tasks because they consider achievement associated with mastery and effort. Instructors can emphasize mastery goals in their classroom activities rather than performance and competition. Instructors can discourage students from executive help-seeking and advise them to ask instrumental questions and solve the academic problems mainly by their own effort.

## Limitations and Future Work

The present study examined the role of instructor support, relatedness, and goal orientation in students' help-seeking behavior and tested the mediation effects of the perceived benefits and costs. The findings contribute to a better understanding of college students' help-seeking behavior in flipped classrooms and inform the design of these classrooms in terms of supporting help-seeking, and therefore, student learning. Although the results demonstrate interesting and pertinent findings, several limitations need to be acknowledged. First, the data analysis was conducted with data that were collected at a particular point in time. However, since students' help-seeking behavior is likely to change over time, a cross sectional analysis may not capture the relations among the variables completely. Future studies should examine students' help-seeking behavior over a period of time and capture its change in relation to the other factors. Second, other factors not included in this study may help better predict help-seeking. For example, classroom goal structure directly influences students' help-seeking intentions and styles (Butler & Neuman, 1995; Newman, 1998; Ryan et al., 1998). Additionally, the specific types of performance goals (e.g., performance-avoidance and performance-approach goals) can have different effects on help-seeking (Karabenick, 2003, 2004; Tanaka & Murakami, 2001). Future research can examine the influence of these factors with different path models.

# References

Aleven, V., Stahl, E., & Schworm, S. (2003). Help seeking and help design in interactive learning environments. *Review of Educational Research, 73*(3), 277–320.

Ames, C., & Archer, J. (1988). Achievement goals in the classroom: Students' learning strategies and motivation processes. *Journal of Educational Psychology, 80*(3), 260–267. doi:10.1037/0022-0663.80.3.260.

Arbreton, A. (1993). *When getting help is helpful: Developmental, cognitive, and motivational influences on students' academic help seeking.* Ann Arbor, MI: University of Michigan.

Arbreton, A. (1998). Student goal orientation and help-seeking strategy use. In S. A. Karabenick (Ed.), *Strategic help seeking: Implications for learning and teaching* (pp. 95–116). Mahwah, NJ: Erlbaum.

Baard, P. P., Deci, E. L., & Ryan, R. M. (2004). Intrinsic need satisfaction: A motivational basis of performance and well-being in two work settings. *Journal of Applied Social Psychology, 34*(10), 2045–2068.

Butler, R. (1998). Determinants of help seeking: Relations between perceived reasons for classroom help-avoidance and help-seeking behaviors in an experimental context. *Journal of Educational Psychology, 90*(4), 630–643. doi:10.1037//0022-0663.90.4.630.

Butler, R., & Neuman, O. (1995). Effects of task and ego achievement goals on help-seeking behaviors and attitudes. *Journal of Educational Psychology, 87*(2), 261–271. doi:10.1037//0022-0663.87.2.261.

Butler, R., & Shibaz, L. (2008). Achievement goals for teaching as predictors of students' perceptions of instructional practices and students' help seeking and cheating. *Learning and Instruction, 18*(5), 453–467. doi:10.1016/j.learninstruc.2008.06.004.

Cheong, Y. F., Pajares, F., & Oberman, P. S. (2004). Motivation and academic help-seeking in high school computer science. *Computer Science Education, 14*(1), 3–19. doi:10.1076/csed.14.1.3.23501.

Deci, E. L., Vallerand, R. J., Pelletier, L. G., & Ryan, R. M. (1991). Motivation and education: The self-determination perspective. *Educational Psychologist, 26*(3–4), 325–346. doi:10.1080/00461520.1991.9653137.

Dowson, M., & McInerney, D. M. (2004). The development and validation of the goal orientation and learning strategies survey (GOALS-S). *Educational and Psychological Measurement, 64*(2), 290–310.

Garrison, D. R., Cleveland-Innes, M., & Fung, T. S. (2010). Exploring causal relationships among teaching, cognitive and social presence: Student perceptions of the community of inquiry framework. *Internet and Higher Education, 13*(1-2), 31–36. doi:10.1016/j. iheduc.2009.10.002.

Gloeckler, G. (2008). Here come the millennials. *Business Week.*

Hertz-Lazarowitz, R. (1995). Understanding interactive behaviors: Looking at six mirrors of the classroom. In R. Hertz-Lazarowitz & N. Miller (Eds.), *Interaction in cooperative groups: The theoretical anatomy of group learning* (pp. 71–101). New York, NY: Cambridge University Press.

Hsu, S. (2005). Help-seeking behaviour of student teachers. *Educational Research, 47*(3), 307–318. doi:10.1080/00131880500287716.

Hurt, N. E., Moss, G. S., Bradley, C. L., Larson, L. R., Lovelace, M. D., & Prevost, L. B. (2012). The "Facebook" effect: College students' perceptions of online discussions in the age of social networking. *International Journal for the Scholarship of Teaching & Learning, 6*(2), 1–24.

Karabenick, S. A. (2001). Help seeking in large college classes: Who, why, and from whom. In *The Annual Meeting of the American Educational Research Association.* Seattle.

Karabenick, S. A. (2003). Seeking help in large college classes: A person-centered approach. *Contemporary Educational Psychology, 28*(1), 37–58. doi:10.1016/S0361-476X(02)00012-7.

Karabenick, S. A. (2004). Perceived achievement goal structure and college student help seeking. *Journal of Educational Psychology, 96*(3), 569–581. doi:10.1037/0022-0663.96.3.569.

Karabenick, S. A., & Knapp, J. R. (1988). Help seeking and the need for academic assistance. *Journal of Educational Psychology, 80*(3), 406–408. doi:10.1037//0022-0663.80.3.406.

Karabenick, S. A., & Knapp, J. R. (1991). Relationship of academic help seeking to the use of learning strategies and other instrumental achievement behavior in college students. *Journal of Educational Psychology, 83*(2), 221–230. doi:10.1037//0022-0663.83.2.221.

Karabenick, S. A., & Newman, R. S. (2006). *Help seeking in academic settings: Goals, groups, and contexts.* London: Lawrence Erlbaum Associates.

Karabenick, S. A., & Sharma, R. (1994). Perceived teacher support of student questioning in the college classroom: Its relation to student characteristics and role in the classroom questioning process. *Journal of Educational Psychology, 86*(1), 90–103. doi:10.1037//0022-0663.86.1.90.

Kasser, T., Davey, J., & Ryan, R. M. (1992). Motivation and employee–supervisor discrepancies in a psychiatric vocational-rehabilitation setting. *Rehabilitation Psychology, 37*(3), 175–188.

Kozanitis, A., Desbiens, J.-F., & Chouinard, R. (2007). Perception of teacher support and reaction towards questioning: Its relation to instrumental help-seeking and motivation to learn. *International Journal of Teaching and Learning in Higher Education, 19*(3), 238–250. Retrieved from http://content.ebscohost.com/ContentServer.asp?T=P&P=AN&K=null&S=R &D=ehh&EbscoContent=dGJyMNHX8kSep6440dvuOLCmr0meqLBSsK64SLCWxWXS& ContentCustomer=dGJyMPGuskmzqLBPuePfgeyx44Dt6fIA.

Lee, C. J. (2007). Academic help seeking: Theory and strategies for nursing faculty. *The Journal of Nursing Education, 46*(10), 468–475.

Marchand, G., & Skinner, E. A. (2007). Motivational dynamics of children's academic help-seeking and concealment. *Journal of Educational Psychology, 99*(1), 65–82. doi:10.1037/0022-0663.99.1.65.

Nadler, A. (1998). Relationship, esteem, and achievement perspectives on autonomous and dependent help seeking. In S. A. Karabenick (Ed.), *Strategic help seeking: Implications for learning and teaching* (pp. 61–93). Mahwah, NJ: Lawrence Erlbaum Associates Publishers.

Nelson-Le Gall, S. (1985). Help-seeking behavior in learning. *Review of Research in Education, 12*(1985), 55–90.

Nelson-Le Gall, S., & Gumerman, R. A. (1984). Children's perceptions of helpers and helper motivation. *Journal of Applied Developmental Psychology, 5*(1), 1–12.

Nelson-Le Gall, S., Gumerman, R. A., & Scott-Jones, D. (1983). Instrumental help-seeking and everyday problem solving: A developmental perspective. In B. DePaulo, A. Nadler, & J. Fisher (Eds.), *New directions in helping: Help seeking* (Vol. 2, pp. 265-284). New York: Academic Press.

Nelson-Le Gall, S., & Resnick, L. (1998). Help seeking, achievement motivation and the social practice of intelligence in school. In S. A. Karabenick (Ed.), *Strategic help seeking: Implications for learning and teaching* (pp. 39–60). Hillsdale, NJ: Erlbaum.

Newman, R. S. (1990). Children's help-seeking in the classroom: The role of motivational factors and attitudes. *Journal of Educational Psychology, 82*(1), 71–80. doi:10.1037//0022-0663.82.1.71.

Newman, R. S. (1998). Students' help seeking during problem solving: Influences of personal and contextual achievement goals. *Journal of Educational Psychology, 90*(4), 644–658. doi:10.1037//0022-0663.90.4.644.

Newman, R. S. (2000). Social influences on the development of children's adaptive help seeking: The role of parents, teachers, and peers. *Developmental Review, 20*(3), 350–404. doi:10.1006/drev.1999.0502.

Newman, R. S., & Schwager, M. T. (1993). Students' perceptions of the teacher and classmates in relation to reported help seeking in math class. *The Elementary School Journal, 94*(1), 3–17.

Ryan, A. M., Gheen, M. H., & Midgley, C. (1998). Why do some students avoid asking for help? An examination of the interplay among students' academic efficacy, teachers' social-emotional role, and the classroom goal structure. *Journal of Educational Psychology, 90*(3), 528–535. doi:10.1037//0022-0663.90.3.528.

Ryan, A. M., Patrick, H., & Shim, S. S. (2005). Differential profiles of students identified by their teacher as having avoidant, appropriate, or dependent help-seeking tendencies in the classroom. *Journal of Educational Psychology, 97*(2), 275–285. doi:10.1037/0022-0663.97.2.275.

Ryan, A. M., & Pintrich, P. R. (1997). "Should I ask for help?" The role of motivation and attitudes in adolescents' help seeking in math class. *Journal of Educational Psychology, 89*(2), 329–341. doi:10.1037//0022-0663.89.2.329.

Ryan, A. M., & Pintrich, P. R. (1998). Achievement and social motivational influences on help seeking in the classroom. In S. A. Karabenick (Ed.), *Strategic help seeking: Implications for learning and teaching* (pp. 117–139). Mahwah, NJ: Erlbaum.

Ryan, A. M., & Shim, S. S. (2006). Social achievement goals: The nature and consequences of different orientations toward social competence. *Personality & Social Psychology Bulletin, 32*(9), 1246–1263. doi:10.1177/0146167206289345.

Salaway, G., Borreson, J., & Nelson, M. R. (2008). *The ECAR study of undergraduate students and information technology*. Boulder, CO: Educause (Educause Center for Applied Research).

Schworm, S., & Gruber, H. (2012). e-Learning in universities: Supporting help-seeking processes by instructional prompts. *British Journal of Educational Technology, 43*(2), 272–281. doi:10.1111/j.1467-8535.2011.01176.x.

Tanaka, A., & Murakami, Y. (2001). Achievement goals, attitudes toward help seeking, and help-seeking behavior in the classroom. *Learning and Individual Differences, 13*(1), 23–35.

Wang, J., & Wang, X. (2012). *Structural equation modeling: Applications using Mplus*. Sussex: Wiley.

Wang, Q., Woo, H. L., Quek, C. L., Yang, Y., & Liu, M. (2012). Using the Facebook group as a learning management system: An exploratory study. *British Journal of Educational Technology, 43*(3), 428–438.

Wolters, C. A., Yu, S. L., & Pintrich, P. R. (1996). The relation between goal orientation and students' motivational beliefs and self-regulated learning. *Learning and Individual Differences, 8*(3), 211–238.

Woolf, B. P. (2010). *A Roadmap for education technology*. Amherst, MA: Global Resources for Online Education.

# Chapter 6
# Digging Deeper into Online Communities of Inquiry at Purdue: Research-Informed Insights into Theory and Practice

**Jennifer C. Richardson and Kadir Kozan**

## Background

Over the past decade, enrollment in online higher education has grown significantly with the growth rate outpacing traditional higher education at a 9% or higher rate (Allen & Seaman, 2013). This has led to concerns regarding the quality of learning outcomes (Kozan & Richardson, 2014a). Research has suggested that the CoI framework (e.g., Akyol & Garrison, 2011a, 2011b; Garrison, 2013; Garrison & Akyol, 2013a, 2013b) provides effective guidelines on how to enhance online learning processes (Akyol et al., 2009; Swan, Garrison, & Richardson, 2009). Given this it is reasonable to assume that higher quality learning processes would lead to higher quality learning outcomes. Research has also shown that there is a relationship between the CoI indicators and student persistence in online courses (Boston et al., 2009; Ice, Gibson, Boston, & Becher, 2011) meaning that when particular aspects of the CoI are present in online courses they can help retain students or determine their intention to re-enroll in online courses. Kozan and Richardson (2014a) claimed that theoretical insights related to online learning are of great importance for addressing the quality issue. Accordingly, the authors suggested the need to empirically test the theoretical underpinnings of the CoI in order to ensure that efforts spent on increasing the quality of online learning (Kozan & Richardson, 2014a) are effective.

J.C. Richardson, Ph.D. (✉) • K. Kozan, Ph.D.
Department of Curriculum and Instruction, Purdue University,
Beering Hall, West Lafayette, IN 47907, USA
e-mail: jennrich@purdue.edu; kadirkozan53@gmail.com

© Springer International Publishing Switzerland 2017
M. Orey, R.M. Branch (eds.), *Educational Media and Technology Yearbook*,
Educational Media and Technology Yearbook 40,
DOI 10.1007/978-3-319-45001-8_6

# The Community of Inquiry (CoI) Framework

The CoI framework is a process model of online learning based in Dewey's work on inquiry that results in a collaborative-constructivist learning environment first defined by Garrison, Anderson, and Archer (2000). The CoI framework assumes that a learning community or a community of inquiry depends largely on the three interdependent constructs of teaching, cognitive, and social presence. Garrison (2013) defined a community of inquiry as "A learning community where participants collaboratively engage in purposeful critical discourse and reflection (cognitive presence) to construct personal meaning and shared understanding through negotiation" (p. 10).

## *Teaching Presence*

Teaching presence refers to "the design, facilitation, and direction of cognitive and social processes for the purpose of realizing personally meaningful and educationally worthwhile learning outcomes" (Anderson, Rourke, Garrison, & Archer, 2001, p. 5). Garrison et al. (2000) argued that even though both social and content-related interactions among participants are necessary in online communities, online interactions are not enough to ensure effective online learning. Teaching presence represents the 'methods' that instructors use in online learning environments and is related to successful online learning, specifically in terms of student satisfaction, perceived learning, and sense of community (Garrison & Arbaugh, 2007).

Teaching presence serves three main functions: design and organization, facilitation of discourse, and direct instruction (Akyol & Garrison, 2008; Garrison & Akyol, 2013a). Design and organization involves "planning and design of the structure, process, interaction and evaluation aspects of the online course" (Garrison & Arbaugh, 2007, p. 163). Facilitating discourse has a focus on participant interaction as a means to build knowledge and "requires the instructor to review and comment upon student responses, raise questions and make observations to move discussions in a desired direction, keep discussion moving efficiently" (Garrison & Arbaugh, 2007, p. 164). Finally, direct instruction is the "instructor's provision of intellectual and scholarly leadership, in part through sharing their subject matter knowledge with the students … Responsibilities of the instructor here are to facilitate reflection and discourse by presenting content, using various means of assessment and feedback" (Garrison & Arbaugh, 2007, p. 164). While teaching presence is traditionally considered the responsibility of the instructor, other members of a learning community are encouraged to be involved as well (Garrison, 2011).

## *Cognitive Presence*

Modeled after John Dewey's reflective thought (Garrison, Anderson, & Archer, 2010) cognitive presence is the ability of learners to construct meaning based on sustained communication and reflection and is operationalized through the Practical

Inquiry Model (Garrison et al., 2000, 2001, Garrison, Anderson, & Archer, 2001; Swan et al., 2009). The Practical Inquiry Model is composed of four phases (Garrison et al., 2001): a triggering event, exploration, integration, and resolution. Specifically, (a) the triggering event includes finding a problem to solve; (b) exploration involves exploring different ideas to solve the problem posed; (c) integration consists of synthesizing the ideas produced in the exploration stage; and (d) the final stage, resolution, includes the evaluation of the solution ideas. Transition through these stages is not linear (Garrison & Arbaugh, 2007; Swan et al., 2009) but rather an iterative process in which learners may need to go back and forth. Vaughan and Garrison (2005) presented cognitive presence as "the element within a community of inquiry which reflects the focus and success of the learning experience" (p. 8).

## *Social Presence*

Social presence comprises the extent to which members of a learning community can "project their personal characteristics into the community, thereby presenting themselves to the other participants as 'real people'" (Garrison et al., 2000, p. 89). Based in part on Dewey's work that learning is socially situated and essential for a community of inquiry (Garrison et al., 2010), social presence goes beyond social interactions thus serving the encouragement of critical thinking and higher-level learning outcomes through collaboration and critical discourse (Garrison & Akyol, 2013a).

Social presence consists of three functions "*affective expression*, where learners share personal expressions of emotion, feelings, beliefs, and values; *open communication*, where learners build and sustain a sense of group commitment; and *group cohesion*, where learners interact around common intellectual activities and tasks" (Swan et al., 2009, p. 48). Research on social presence has demonstrated that it can influence students' participation and motivation to participate (Mazzolini & Maddison, 2007; Swan & Shih, 2005; Tu & McIsaac, 2002), course and instructor satisfaction (Akyol & Garrison, 2008; Cobb, 2009; Gunawardena & Zittle, 1997; Hostetter & Busch, 2006; Swan & Shih, 2005), and both actual and perceived learning (Hostetter & Busch, 2013; Joksimović et al., 2015; Picciano, 2002; Richardson & Swan, 2003; Wise et al., 2004).

## **Research on the CoI Framework at Purdue University**

Earlier work on the CoI highlighted the significance of teaching, cognitive and social presence for creating better online learning environments that can also inform other learning contexts including face-to-face and blended learning. These studies bridge the gap between what we currently know about the presences and what we still need to know in order to foster effective learning outcomes in the online environment. To this end, and to serve the practical purpose of evaluating and improving our Learning Design and Technology (LDT) online master's program at Purdue, the faculty and graduate students of the program have conducted a number of studies related to the CoI framework. The data used for the majority of these studies were gathered from instructors and learners in our online master's program.

The online LDT MS program is a 20-month, fully online program that enrolls approximately 200 students on a continuous basis. We have been using the CoI survey (Arbaugh et al., 2008; Swan et al., 2008) at the end of each 8-week session since the online program began in 2011. The CoI survey is a 34 item instrument that operationalizes the CoI framework while using a 0–4 (strongly disagree to strongly agree) Likert scale; it has been shown to be both a valid and reliable measure (Arbaugh et al., 2008; Swan et al., 2008). The data was used for two purposes: (1) to provide summative evaluations for instructors/courses; and (2) to gather information that could be used to improve the online MS program. Research studies have provided insights regarding: (a) interrelationships among the presences; (b) validity of the presences within the CoI framework; and (c) conceptual insights into extensions of the CoI framework such as instructor presence. We discuss each of these in more detail.

## Interrelationships Between and Among Teaching, Cognitive and Social Presence

There has been limited research conducted on the interconnections between and among the presences (Garrison & Arbaugh, 2007); however, several studies have provided evidence of the relationships. For instance, Akyol and Garrison (2008) found a significant correlation between teaching and cognitive presence. Shea et al. (2010) discovered a significant relationship between learner social presence and instructor teaching presence, as well as a significant relationship between learner social presence and instructor social presence. Moreover, Archibald (2010) found that teaching and social presence accounted for 69 % of the variance in cognitive presence, and where therefor significant contributors to the prediction of cognitive presence. Similarly, Ke (2010) found that teaching presence could significantly predict cognitive and social presence.

As the CoI framework assumes close interrelationships between and among teaching, cognitive and social presence, Kozan and Richardson (2014a) tested the theoretically plausible assumption that social presence may serve as a mediator between teaching and cognitive presence. Because teaching presence, particularly in the form of design and organization, starts prior to facilitating discourse and direct instruction, and efforts involved in cognitive and social presence tend to come after these teaching presence efforts, it is theoretically reasonable to assume that teaching presence precedes cognitive and social presence. The assumption of social presence as a mediator further suggests that teaching presence efforts relate first to increased social presence, which in turn relates to increased cognitive presence thereby enhancing learning.

In order to the test the extent to which this assumption was true, Kozan and Richardson (2014a) employed correlation and partial correlation analyses. COI survey data ($N=211$) were collected from six different online courses taught in our online LDT MS program. Correlation analyses identified the relationships between two presence pairs. Results indicated medium to large significant and positive relationships between and among the presences. Particularly, the largest significant relationship was between teaching and cognitive presence, $r_s = .826, p < .01$. The second largest relationship was between social presence and cognitive presence, $r_s = .663, p < .01$ in addition to the significant relationship between teaching and social presence, $r_s = .553, p < .01$ (p. 71). These significant correlations support the assumption of the CoI framework that the presences are closely interconnected with each other. Because each presence is related significantly to the other presences, there is the possibility that at least one of the presences can impact the relationship between the other two presences (Kozan & Richardson, 2014a).

Moreover, the common intersection among the three presences appears to suggest that the relationship between two presences is independent of the effect of any third presence to a certain extent. Kozan and Richardson (2014a) ran partial correlations to test this theoretical assumption. These partial correlations were aimed at determining whether any of the presences could impact the relationship between the other two presences, either partially or completely. Results indicated that when cognitive presence is controlled for, the relationship between teaching and social presence disappears completely, $pr = -.128, p > .05$ (Kozan & Richardson, 2014a). This finding strongly suggests that cognitive presence can function as a full mediator between teaching and social presence. However, after controlling for teaching and social presence, the relationships between cognitive and social presence, and the relationship between teaching and cognitive presence were reduced but stayed significantly positive keeping its size (i.e., medium and large respectively). The second set of findings indicate that neither teaching presence nor social presence act as full mediators between the other presences thereby refuting the assumption that social presence can be the full mediator between teaching and cognitive presence.

Kozan (in press) conducted multiple structural equation modeling (SEM) analyses to further investigate which presence may undertake the full mediator role regarding the interrelationships among the presences. Data for this research came from eleven online MS courses at Purdue based on the CoI survey completed by students ($N = 338$). Previously, two studies examined the interdependence of the presences on one another by applying SEM analyses. Shea and Bidjerano (2009) used the CoI survey to collect data from 2159 participants enrolled in different online learning programs across 30 institutions. The researcher's SEM analyses revealed significant direct links between (a) teaching and social presence; (b) social and cognitive presence; (c) gender and teaching presence; and (d) age and teaching presence. More specifically, while social presence had a direct effect only, teaching presence had both a total and a direct effect that linked it to cognitive presence. Accordingly, Shea and Bidjerano (2009) claimed that teaching presence could significantly and individually relate to cognitive presence, and social presence could function as a partial mediator between teaching and cognitive presence. Likewise, Garrison, Cleveland-Innes, and Fung (2010) showed that teaching and social presence can significantly and directly relate to cognitive presence in addition to the significant direct relationship between teaching and social presence. The overall conclusion was that social presence plays a partial mediator role between teaching and cognitive presence thus confirming a theoretically plausible assumption. Of note, the direct links found between teaching and cognitive presence suggests that social presence is a partial mediator between them.

Pointing at the discrepancy between the SEM results above and the results of Kozan and Richardson (2014a), Kozan (in press) argued for examining the assumption that cognitive presence can be a full mediator between teaching and social presence though an SEM analysis. From an SEM perspective, Bollen and Pearl (2013) argued that SEM models are highly dependent on researchers' informed "causal assumptions" (p. 309). Moreover, Tomarken and Waller (2005) highlighted that there can be different models that can fit a data set equally well in a SEM study. Consequently, Kozan (in press) tested and compared five different models. Among these, the ones in which cognitive presence served as a partial mediator, and cognitive presence served as a full mediator, in addition to a direct link from social presence to cognitive presence did not hold true as a whole. Specifically, in the model with cognitive presence as a partial mediator the relation between teaching and social presence was not significant. Similarly, in the model with a non-recursive relation between cognitive and social presence, the direct link from social to cognitive presence was not significant. Interestingly, when one removes these nonsignificant links from the two models, what remains is the model with cognitive presence as a full mediator between teaching and social presence.

As a result, Kozan (in press) compared three models to see which one could fit the data better using a chi-square difference test. These were the ones with either cognitive presence or social presence as a full mediator, and the one with social presence as a partial mediator. Results indicated that the model with cognitive presence as a full mediator was not significantly different from the model with social presence as a partial mediator. In other words, both of these models achieved equally good data fit. Further, the model with social presence as a partial mediator turned out to be better than the model with social presence as a full mediator. Overall, Kozan (in press) suggested that at the end of a fully online learning experience, the theoretical assumption that cognitive presence may function as a full mediator may be as strong as the one that social presence may be a partial mediator.

## Validity of the CoI Framework

Garrison and Arbaugh (2007) noted that there is a need for further work with a focus on "validating the CoI framework" (p. 167). Similarly, pointing to the importance of increasing the CoI framework's credibility, Garrison (2013) stated, "Explicating and validating such a comprehensive framework is an ongoing challenge" (p. 2). Several recent studies at Purdue have helped to further validate the CoI framework. For example, Kozan and Richardson (2014b) conducted exploratory and confirmatory factor analyses on data collected using the CoI survey. Data were collected through six different online courses taught by 20 instructors in our online LDT MS program, and consisted of student CoI surveys ($N=397$). Different from most of the earlier factor analyses conducted (e.g., Arbaugh et al., 2008; Diaz et al., 2010; Swan et al., 2008), Kozan and Richardson (2014b) implemented an exploratory factor analysis (EFA) using principal axis factoring and promax rotation rather than using a principal component analysis and oblimin rotation. Another significant difference between Kozan and Richardson (2014b) and earlier research was the use of parallel analysis to determine the number of factors that can be extracted from the research data. Overall, Kozan and Richardson (2014b) first explored the three-factor structure of the CoI survey through an EFA, and then confirmed the three-factor structure running a confirmatory factor analysis (CFA), which suggested a very good fit for the model. Consequently, based on the CoI survey data used, these results provided evidence for the construct validity of the CoI framework that was originally based on the existence of three presences and their interrelationships.

Using data from student-completed CoI surveys ($N = 120$) from five online LDT MS courses, the second study involved the CoI framework in relation to its predictive validity of the presences with regard to cognitive load (Kozan, 2015). Cognitive load was measured using a modified version of Leppink, Paas, van Gog, van der Vleuten, and van Merriënboer's 10-item Likert survey (2014). Kozan (2015) ran correlational analyses to see the extent to which teaching, cognitive and social presence could relate to cognitive load that is imposed by performing specific tasks on working memory resources (Sweller, van Merriënboer, & Paas 1998). The results provided strong preliminary evidence that teaching, cognitive, and social presence may significantly predict cognitive load. Because working memory is limited in terms of both capacity and duration (Cowan, 2001, 2010, 2014), it is important to optimize cognitive load or working memory load for learning to occur (van Gog & Paas, 2008). The three cognitive load types are germane, intrinsic and extraneous. Germane or effective load stems from working memory capacity spent on dealing with intrinsic load (Kalyuga, 2011; Sweller et al., 2011). Intrinsic load is the inner complexity of learning materials (Sweller et al., 2011). Accordingly, germane load is also called effective load since it covers the working memory resources allocated to learning itself. On the other hand, extraneous or ineffective load emanates from ineffective instructional design or presentation of information in a way that causes unnecessary information processing (Sweller, 2010). An example would be placing textual information and its corresponding pictorial counterpart far from each other in time and/or space.

As a result, Kozan (2015) theoretically assumed that the presences could relate to cognitive load types since efforts spent on increasing each presence could either increase or decrease certain cognitive load types. Specifically, it was assumed that cognitive presence can increase cognitive load whereas teaching and social presence may be helpful for optimizing or keeping it at a challenging enough level. In line with these assumptions, results revealed that all the presences significantly and positively relate to germane or effective load suggesting that all the presences could contribute to learning. Only did teaching and cognitive presence have a significant and negative relationship with extraneous or ineffective load showing that at least some of teaching presence efforts were spent on decreasing extraneous load in addition to learners' cognitive efforts. Finally, cognitive presence was related significantly and positively to intrinsic load, which may have stemmed from learners' cognitive presence invested in inherent difficulty or complexity of the learning content.

## Extending the CoI Framework: Instructor Presence

Understanding the theoretical assumptions of the CoI framework and demonstrating the relationships between the three presences quantitatively is one aspect of the research that has occurred at Purdue. However, examining the framework conceptually and determining how the various components fit and/or could be extended is also an area of inquiry being addressed. Previous research has lead the way in this effort as demonstrated by Szeto (2015) and Vaughan and Garrison (2005) who moved from researching fully online contexts to blended learning environments while Shea and Bidjerano (2012), Shea et al. (2012), and Hayes et al. (2015) introduced and examined the construct of learning presence.

Beginning with a doctoral level course in the spring of 2014 several faculty and graduate students questioned how the use of adjuncts or limited term lecturers (LTLs) could alter the CoI model as we moved from our traditional paradigm of online instructor-designers to online non-designer instructors. As our online MS program has grown, we have found it necessary to employ a number of LTLs who are charged with implementing an online course that is designed by a full-time faculty member, and so potentially having limited control over the design of social, teaching or cognitive activities. Data were collected from the student participants (e.g., course evaluations, CoI surveys) and instructors (e.g., interviews and archived course observations).

The initial research study focused on conceptualizing Instructor Presence, the intersection between social and teaching presence that is based on "the specific actions and behaviors taken by the instructor that project him/herself as a real person…instructor presence relates to how an instructor positions him/herself socially and pedagogically in an online community" (Richardson et al., 2015, p. 259). For us as researchers, the significant aspect of this lens was that "instructor presence is more likely to be manifested in the 'live' part of courses—as they are being implemented—as opposed to during the course design process" (Richardson, et al., 2015).

Our research used a descriptive multiple-case study approach (Yin, 2009) with the intent to both build an explanation of instructor presence behaviors and actions and conduct a cross-case synthesis. Additionally, by examining instructor presence across 12 instructors and four courses, we developed profiles of online instructor presence. The main data source was archived course observations (e.g., instructors' communications, interactions, and actions from Blackboard) that were coded and analyzed based on a coding schema stemming from the literature and previous social and teaching presence indicators (Richardson, et al., 2015). The results provided a picture of an online instructor's role during the course implementation process that can be especially useful as an example for instructors new to online environments and understanding the expectations of that environment. Similarly, the profiles provided a gauge for balancing social and teaching behaviors in the online environment as a means of developing a learning community. Additionally, the new set of indicators demonstrates how the instructor's role has evolved in the past decade to be more learner-centered and collaborative.

The second phase of our research used an explanatory multiple-case study approach that considered the perspectives of the online instructors about instructor presence ($N$ =13) (Richardson, Besser, Koehler, Lim, & Strait, in press). Interview data were collected and a coding schema was developed. The coding schema was enhanced through inductive coding and allowed codes to emerge through the analysis process, as well as through the revision of existing codes. The final coding schema included categories for (1) importance of instructor presence; (2) actions and behaviors taken to project yourself as a real person; (3) course design; and (4) other.

Instructor perceptions of instructor presence were fuzzy in the beginning of the interviews but as the instructors reflected on the behaviors and actions related to the construct they were able to better describe their actions and why they did what they did as instructors. All instructors indicated that instructor presence was important to the success of students in an online course but their reasons varied. In practice, this translated to letting students know you are approachable, care about their success, and are an expert in the content area. The use of communication strategies to establish instructor presence varied across the instructors but many discussed the need for setting the tone and modeling expected behaviors. The perceptions related to the sharing of personal information ranged across the continuum but the take away is a balance of sharing personal and professional information to create an instructional presence, perhaps by sharing personal stories related to content; a strategy that may not be something that comes naturally to new instructors. The instructors also shared how they felt their instructor presence impacted connections to students and potentially student success within a course. Finally, when asked about being non-designer instructors ($n=9$) almost all indicated they did not feel that teaching a course designed by someone else impacted their instructor presence. However, some instructors felt restricted or frustrated, in part due to the lack of flexibility or level of customization they could bring to the course. Implications for this finding could include training new or non-designer instructors to integrate their presence through existing course structures as well as additional means (e.g., websites, blogs, individual e-mails) designed by the individuals (as permitted).

## Additional Research on the CoI Framework at Purdue University

Several additional studies using the CoI framework as a lens have recently been conducted and others are planned. For example, a recent study focusing on an MOOC instructor's use of social presence, teaching presence, and dissonance for attitudinal change in an MOOC on Human Trafficking was conducted (Watson, Watson, Richardson, & Loizzo, 2016). Our researchers explored the MOOC instructor's use of social presence and teaching presence behaviors, using the CoI framework as a lens, and examined the instructor's facilitation of attitudinal dissonance within the course (e.g., discussion forum, announcements, blog postings). While the focus of this study was on attitudinal change, the CoI lens proved effective as a way to view, evaluate, and express the findings. While limited research has examined the potential of the CoI in an MOOC setting, the concept of collaborative learning and instructor as a co-participant go to the heart of a social constructivist environment.

Yu and Richardson (2015) developed and tested a Korean version of the CoI survey. Participants were undergraduates ($N=995$) at a Cyber University in Korea. The EFA was conducted on the 34 items survey and resulted in three-factor structure composed of 32 items; two items cross-loaded on multiple factors. An item analysis was conducted for reliability purposes and resulted in Cronbach's $\alpha$ of .954 (teaching presence), .913 (social presence), and .956 (cognitive presence) and a Cronbach's $\alpha$ of .972 for the instrument overall. A CFA was conducted for predictive validity that confirmed that the model fit is excellent between the proposed model and the observed data (Yu & Richardson, 2015). The development of the CoI instrument in Korean and other languages will help to serve as a means to determine the usefulness of the CoI framework and survey measure in varying cultural contexts.

Additionally, several studies related to the CoI framework are in the planning stages, including (1) an examination of course design features as mediators for instructor presence; and (2) a comparison of students' CoI measures to instructor's actions and behaviors within the online courses (e.g., archived course data). Beyond that we will continue our line of inquiry using the lens of the CoI framework based on the results of our studies and those of others in the area.

# References

Akyol, Z., Arbaugh, J. B., Cleveland-Innes, M., Garrison, D. R., Ice, P., Richardson, J. C., ..., & Swan, K. (2009). A response to the review of the community of inquiry framework. *Journal of Distance Education, 23*(2), 123–136.

Akyol, Z., & Garrison, D. R. (2008). The development of a community of inquiry over time in an online course: Understanding the progression and integration of social, cognitive and teaching presence. *Journal of Asynchronous Learning Networks, 12*(3–4), 3–22.

Akyol, Z., & Garrison, D. R. (2011a). Assessing metacognition in an online community of inquiry. *Internet and Higher Education, 14*, 183–190.

Akyol, Z., & Garrison, D. R. (2011b). Understanding cognitive presence in an online and blended community of inquiry: Assessing outcomes and processes for deep approaches to learning. *British Journal of Educational Technology, 42*(2), 233–250.

Allen, I. E., & Seaman, J. (2013). *Changing course: Ten years of tracking online education in the United States.* Babson Park, MA: Babson Park Research Group and Quahog Research Group. Retrieved from http://www.onlinelearningsurvey.com/reports/changingcourse.pdf.

Anderson, T., Rourke, L., Garrison, D. R., & Archer, W. (2001). Assessing teaching presence in a computer conferencing context. *Journal of Asynchronous Learning Networks, 5*(2), 1–17.

Arbaugh, B., Cleveland-Innes, M., Diaz, S., Ice, P., Garrison, D. R., Richardson, J. C., ..., Swan, K. (2008). Developing a Community of Inquiry instrument: Testing a measure of the Community of Inquiry framework using a multi-institutional sample. *The Internet and Higher Education, 11*(3–4), 133–136.

Archibald, D. (2010). Fostering the development of cognitive presence: Initial findings using the community of inquiry survey instrument. *The Internet & Higher Education, 13*(1–2), 73–74.

Bollen, K. A., & Pearl, J. (2013). Eight myths about causality and structural equation models. In S. L. Morgan (Ed.), *Handbook of causal analysis for social research* (pp. 301–328). Dordrecht: Springer.

Boston, W., Diaz, S. R., Gibson, A. M., Ice, P., Richardson, J., & Swan, K. (2009). An exploration of the relationship between indicators of the community of inquiry framework and retention in online programs. *Journal of Asynchronous Learning Networks, 13*(3), 67–83.

Cobb, S. C. (2009). Social presence and online learning: A current view from a research perspective. *Journal of Interactive Online Learning, 8*(3), 241–254.

Cowan, N. (2001). The magical number 4 in short-term memory: A reconsideration of mental storage capacity. *Behavioral and Brain Sciences, 24*, 87–185.

Cowan, N. (2010). The magical mystery four: How is working memory capacity limited, and why? *Current Directions in Psychological Science, 19*(1), 51–57.

Cowan, N. (2014). Working memory underpins cognitive development, learning, and education. *Educational Psychology Review, 26*, 197–223.

Diaz, S. R., Swan, K., Ice, P., & Kupczynski, L. (2010). Student ratings of the importance of survey items, multiplicative factor analysis, and the validity of the community of inquiry survey. *The Internet and Higher Education, 13*, 22–30.

Garrison, D. R. (2011). *E-learning in the 21st century: A framework for research and practice* (2nd ed.) [Kindle Fire version]. Retrieved from http://www.amazon.com.

Garrison, D. R. (2013). Theoretical foundations and epistemological insights of the community of inquiry. In Z. Akyol & D. R. Garrison (Eds.), *Educational communities of inquiry: Theoretical framework, research, and practice* (pp. 1–11). Hershey, PA: IGI Global.

Garrison, D. R., & Akyol, Z. (2013a). The community of inquiry theoretical framework. In M. G. Moore (Ed.), *Handbook of distance education* (pp. 104–119). New York, NY: Routledge.

Garrison, D. R., & Akyol, Z. (2013b). Toward the development of a metacognition construct for communities of inquiry. *The Internet and Higher Education, 17*, 84–89.

Garrison, D. R., Anderson, T., & Archer, W. (2000). Critical inquiry in a text-based environment: Computer conferencing in higher education. *The Internet and Higher Education, 2*(2–3), 87–105.

Garrison, D. R., Anderson, T., & Archer, W. (2001). Critical thinking, cognitive presence, and computer conferencing in distance education. *The American Journal of Distance Education, 15*(1), 7–23.

Garrison, D. R., Anderson, T., & Archer, W. (2010). The first decade of the community of inquiry framework: A retrospective. *The Internet and Higher Education, 13*, 5–9.

Garrison, D. R., & Arbaugh, J. B. (2007). Researching the community of inquiry framework: Review, issues, and future directions. *The Internet and Higher Education, 10*(3), 157–172.

Garrison, D. R., Cleveland-Innes, M., & Fung, T. S. (2010). Exploring causal relationships among teaching, cognitive and social presence: Student perceptions of the community of inquiry framework. *The Internet and Higher Education, 13*, 31–36.

Gunawardena, C. N., & Zittle, F. J. (1997). Social presence as a predictor of satisfaction within a computer-mediated conferencing environment. *The American Journal of Distance Education, 11*(3), 8–26.

Hayes, S., Uzuner-Smith, S., & Shea, P. (2015). Expanding learning presence to account for the direction of regulative intent: Self-, co- and shared regulation in online learning. *Online Learning, 19*(3), 15–33.

Hostetter, C., & Busch, M. (2006). Measuring up online: The relationship between social presence and student learning satisfaction. *Journal of Scholarship of Teaching and Learning, 6*(2), 1–12.

Hostetter, C., & Busch, M. (2013). Community matters: Social presence and learning outcomes. *Journal of the Scholarship of Teaching and Learning, 13*(1), 77–86.

Ice, P., Gibson, A. M., Boston, W., & Becher, D. (2011). An exploration of differences between community of inquiry indicators in low and high disenrollment online courses. *Journal of Asynchronous Learning Networks, 15*(2), 44–69.

Joksimović, S., Gašević, D., Kovanović, V., Riecke, B. E., & Hatala, M. (2015). Social presence in online discussions as a process predictor of academic performance. *Journal of Computer Assisted Learning, 31*, 638–654. doi:10.1111/jcal.12107.

Kalyuga, S. (2011). Cognitive load theory: How many types of load does it really need? *Educational Psychology Review, 23*(1), 1–19.

Ke, F. (2010). Examining online teaching, cognitive, and social presence for adult students. *Computers & Education, 55*, 808–820.

Kozan, K. (2015). How does cognitive load relate to teaching, social and cognitive presences? *The AERA Online Paper Repository* (pp. 1–19).

Kozan, K. (2016). A comparative structural equation modeling investigation of the relationships among teaching, cognitive, and social presence. *Online Learning, 20*(3), 210–227.

Kozan, K., & Richardson, J. C. (2014a). Interrelationships between and among social, teaching, and cognitive presence. *The Internet and Higher Education, 21*, 68–73.

Kozan, K., & Richardson, J. C. (2014b). New exploratory and confirmatory factor analysis insights into the Community of Inquiry survey. *The Internet and Higher Education, 23*, 39–47.

Leppink, J., Paas, F., van Gog, T., van der Vleuten, C. P. M., & van Merriënboer, J. J. G. (2014). Effects of pairs of problems and examples on task performance and different types of cognitive load. *Learning and Instruction, 30*, 32–42.

Mazzolini, M., & Maddison, S. (2007). When to jump in: The role of the instructor in online discussion forums. *Computers & Education, 49*(2), 193–213. doi:10.1016/j.compedu.2005.06.011.

Picciano, A. G. (2002). Beyond student perceptions: Issues of interaction, presence, and performance in an online course. *Journal of Asynchronous Learning Networks, 6*(1), 21–40.

Richardson, J.C., Besser, E., Koehler, A., Lim, J. & Strait, M. (2016). Instructors' perceptions of instructor presence in online courses. *International Review of Research in Open and Distributed Learning, 17*(4), 82–104. Available online at: http://www.irrodl.org/index.php/irrodl/article/view/2330/3800

Richardson, J. C., Koehler, A., Besser, E., Caskurlu, S., Lim, J., & Mueller, C. (2015). Conceptualizing and investigating instructor presence in online learning environments. *International Review of Research in Open and Distributed Learning, 16*(3), 256–297.

Richardson, J. C., & Swan, K. (2003). Examining social presence in online courses in relation to students' perceived learning and satisfaction. *Journal of Asynchronous Learning, 7*(1), 68–88. Retrieved from: http://onlinelearningconsortium.org/read/journal-issues/.

Shea, P., & Bidjerano, T. (2009). Community of inquiry as a theoretical framework to foster "epistemic engagement" and "cognitive presence" in online education. *Computers and Education, 52*(3), 543–553.

Shea, P., & Bidjerano, T. (2012). Learning presence as a moderator in the Community of Inquiry model. *Computers and Education, 59*(2), 316–326.

Shea, P., Hayes, S., Uzner, S., Vickers, J., Wilde, J., Gozza-Cohen, M., & Jian, S. (2012). Learning presence: A new conceptual element within the Community of Inquiry (CoI) framework. *Internet and Higher Education, 15*(2), 89–95. doi:10.1016/j.iheduc.2011.08.002.

Shea, P., Hayes, S., Vickers, J., Gozza-Cohen, M., Uzuner, S., Mehta, R., …, Rangan, P. (2010). A re-examination of the community of inquiry framework: Social network and content analysis. *The Internet and Higher Education, 13*, 10–21.

Swan, K., Garrison, D. R., & Richardson, J. C. (2009). A constructivist approach to online learning: The community of inquiry framework. In C. R. Payne (Ed.), *Information technology and constructivism in higher education: Progressive learning frameworks* (pp. 43–57). Hershey, PA: IGI Global.

Swan, K., Richardson, J. C., Ice, P., Garrison, D. R., Cleveland-Innes, M., & Arbaugh, J. B. (2008). Validating a measurement tool of presence in online communities of inquiry. *E-mentor, 2*(24), 1–12.

Swan, K., & Shih, L. F. (2005). On the nature and development of social presence in online course discussions. *Journal of Asynchronous Learning Networks, 9*(3), 115–136.

Sweller, J. (2010). Element interactivity and intrinsic, extraneous and germane cognitive load. *Educational Psychology Review, 22*, 123–138.

Sweller, J., Ayres, P., & Kalyuga, S. (2011). *Cognitive load theory*. New York: Springer.

Sweller, J., van Merriënboer, J. J. G., & Paas, F. (1998). Cognitive architecture and instructional design. *Educational Psychology Review, 10*(3), 251–296.

Szeto, E. (2015). Community of inquiry as an instructional approach: What effects of teaching, social and cognitive presences are there in blended synchronous learning and teaching? *Computers & Education, 81*, 191–201.

Tomarken, A. J., & Waller, N. G. (2005). Structural equation modeling: Strengths, limitations, and misconceptions. *Annual Review of Clinical Psychology, 1*, 31–65.

Tu, C. H., & McIsaac, M. (2002). The relationship of social presence and interaction in online classes. *The American Journal of Distance Education, 16*(3), 131–150. doi:10.1207/S15389286AJDE1603_2.

van Gog, T., & Paas, F. (2008). Instructional efficiency: Revisiting the original construct in educational research. *Educational Psychologist, 43*(1), 16–26.

Vaughan, N., & Garrison, D. R. (2005). Creating cognitive presence in a blended faculty development community. *The Internet and Higher Education, 8*, 1–12.

Watson, S., Watson, B., Richardson, J. C., & Loizzo, J. (2016). Instructor's use of social presence, teaching presence and attitudinal dissonance: A case study of an attitudinal change MOOC. *International Review of Research in Open and Distance Learning, 17*(3), 54–74.

Wise, A., Chang, J., Duffy, T., & Del Valle, R. (2004). The effects of teacher social presence on student satisfaction, engagement, and learning. *Journal of Educational Computing Research, 31*(3), 247–271.

Yin, R. K. (2009). *Case study research: Design and methods* (4th ed.). Los Angeles, CA: Sage Publications.

Yu, T., & Richardson, J. C. (2015). Examining the reliability and validity of a Korean version of the Community of Inquiry instrument using exploratory and confirmatory factor analysis. *The Internet and Higher Education, 25*, 45–52. doi:10.1016/j.iheduc.2014.12.004.

# Chapter 7
# Real-Time Mutual Gaze Perception Enhances Collaborative Learning and Collaboration Quality

**Bertrand Schneider and Roy Pea**

## Introduction

Foundational work in developmental psychology and in the learning sciences demonstrates that joint attention plays a crucial role in any kind of social interaction: From babies learning from their caregivers to parents educating their children, teenagers learning from school teachers, students collaborating on a project or for any group of adults working toward a common goal, joint attention is a fundamental mechanism for establishing common ground between individuals. Our goal is to design technological interventions to facilitate this process.

Technically, joint attention is defined as "the tendency for social partners to focus on a common reference and to monitor one another's attention to an outside entity, such as an object, person, or event […]. The fact that two individuals are simultaneously focused on the same aspect of the environment at the same time does not constitute joint attention. To qualify as joint attention, the social partners need to demonstrate awareness that they are attending to something in common" (Tomasello, 1995, pp. 86–87). Joint attention is fundamental to social coordination: Young infants communicate emotions in a state of synchrony with their caregivers, in turn helping them achieve visual coordination when learning language (Stem, 1977). Parents use deictic gestures such as pointing at a focus of interest to establish joint visual attention so as to signal important features of the environment to their children (Bates, Thal, Whitesell, Fenson, & Oakes, 1989). Professors and mentors teach by highlighting subtle nuances between the conceptual understanding of their students and experts (Roth, 2001). Groups of students manage coordination between their members to reach the problem solution (Barron, 2003), in turn influencing their level of abstract thinking (Schwartz, 1995).

B. Schneider (✉) • R. Pea
Graduate School of Education, Stanford University, Stanford, CA, USA
e-mail: schneibe@stanford.edu; roypea@stanford.edu

© Springer International Publishing Switzerland 2017
M. Orey, R.M. Branch (eds.), *Educational Media and Technology Yearbook*,
Educational Media and Technology Yearbook 40,
DOI 10.1007/978-3-319-45001-8_7

We argue that the construction of joint attention rests significantly though not entirely[1] on two primary channels of communication: people can either point at things physically (i.e., using deictic gestures) or verbally (i.e., by describing the object of interest). Those two mechanisms are subject to inefficiencies because misunderstanding can happen on a verbal and on a physical level. Verbally, communication is prone to misinterpretation from the receiver. This is likely to happen when experts are teaching novices, because novices are still learning the perceptual skills to isolate subtle patterns that separate them from experts. For instance, Biederman and Shiffrar (1987) showed that experts in performing chick-sexing can categorize 1000 chicks per hour with an accuracy of 98 %, but those experts have a lot of trouble explaining to novices (researchers, in that case) how they reached such an impressive speed and precision. Thus, words are sometimes a clumsy medium for teaching perceptual skills. Physically, there is an extra step of taking the point of view of the other person. From a spatial and social point of view, this is not a trivial mental operation (especially for children as demonstrated by Piaget in his studies of egocentrism and in more recent studies on the role of "theory of mind" in human development (Leudar, Costall, & Francis, 2004).

The goal of our work is to develop new ways of supporting the establishment of perceptual joint attention (as distinguished from cognitive, or social joint attention). Our assumption is that higher levels of visual synchronization are positively associated with students' quality of collaboration and learning experience. In our study, we designed an intervention to increase the quantity of student dyads' number of moments of joint attention and studied the effects of the intervention on several interlaced variables: visual synchronization, quality of collaboration and learning gains computed from pre and post-test. We use eye-tracking technologies to make it possible to share users' real-time gaze behaviors during collaborative learning. More specifically, our first attempt in this study involved dyads in a remote collaboration studying contrasting cases (Schwartz & Bransford, 1998). We introduce a new kind of awareness tool that provides participants with the continuous updating of the position of their partner's gaze on the screen. Thus, we depict our intervention as enabling *real-time mutual gaze perception*.

In the following section, we describe previous research in studying joint attention in collaborative learning situations. We then survey studies using eye-trackers and previous attempts at developing "awareness tools" in CSCL (i.e., tools that provide additional information to students about their peers). We conclude by summarizing the literature on joint attention and by formulating our research questions.

## Previous Work on Joint Attention and Awareness Tools

Developmental psychologists have conducted the vast majority of the work on joint attention by highlighting the crucial role of gaze coordination between infants and adults during language learning. Since this work is a primary inspiration for our

---

[1] Attentional alignment is also established partly by body position and orientation (Kendon, 1990).

research, we start by briefly describing a few foundational studies in this area of inquiry and conclude by sketching the significance of those results for the field of the learning sciences.

## The fundamental role of joint attention in infancy

An important developmental milestone is the ability to coordinate visual attention between a partner and an object of interest. Several studies suggest that humans acquire this skill early in life. Baldwin (1991) showed that 16-month-old babies are able to detect nonverbal cues to a referenced object. Bakeman and Adamson (1984) demonstrated that with age, person engagement (i.e., "the infant is engaged just with the other person. Typically such engagement involves face-to-face or person play; For example, a baby giggles and coos as his mother places her face close to his and tickles him") declined while coordinated joint engagement increased (i.e., "The infant is actively involved with and coordinates his or her attention to both another person and the object that person is involved with. For example, the baby pushes the truck the mother has been pushing and then looks back and forth between the mother's face and the truck"); additionally, an infant's social coordination was more likely to happen when the child played with his or her mother. Charman et al. (2000) followed 13 infants aged 20 months for 2 years and administered a battery of cognitive tests at different intervals; across a variety of different measures, they found that only joint attention behaviors were longitudinally associated with increased theory of mind abilities 2 years later. Those studies showed that attentional deployment is one of the first social and emotional regulatory processes to appear. Indeed, young infants communicate their emotions by being in a state of visual synchronization with their caregivers—which in turn help them achieve visual coordination when learning to speak (Stem, 1977). Without the ability of establishing joint attention, infants would have much more trouble acquiring their native language exemplified by the studies of autistic children who show impoverished joint attention behaviors (Mundy, Sigman, & Kasari, 1990), and by studies indicating how greater gaze following by infants in play sessions with their mothers predicts faster vocabulary development (Brooks & Meltzoff, 2008).

For the scope of this chapter, we do not conduct an exhaustive review of the developmental work in this field. However, we can confidently assume that joint attention is an established and relevant concept in developmental and social psychology: meaningful interactions have been shown to be associated with repeated moments of joint visual attention. Humans need to make sure that they are communicating about the same object of interest to avoid misunderstanding. The previous paragraphs demonstrate that babies learn language, in part, by establishing visual coordination with their parents, and that higher levels of joint attention facilitate language acquisition. The following paragraphs suggest that children and teenagers also learn more efficiently by being visually synchronized with their peers.

## *Joint Attention in the Learning Sciences*

During the past decades, research in education has focused substantial efforts on social learning and small group cognition. The inspiration for this effort mainly comes from Piaget (1998), who postulated that socio-cognitive conflicts cause major cognitive restructuration, and Vygotski (1978) who claimed that learning happens first on a social or cultural level, which is then internalized. Those two theories have been joined together under the umbrella of *socio-constructivist* theories of learning. This approach emphasizes the importance of collaboration and negotiation of meaning for thinking and learning; as a consequence, socio-constructivist researchers have devoted their attention to analyzing group interaction and identifying characteristics of successful patterns of collaboration. Over the past two decades, CSCL researchers have begun to extensively study the influence of technology on collaborative learning. A good summary of the goals of the CSCL field can be found in Dillenbourg, Baker, Blaye, and O'Malley (1996, pp. 189–211). And we may note that joint attention is associated with many overlapping concepts in the learning sciences and CSCL—"shared cognition," "intersubjectivity," "grounding processes in conversation," "joint problem-solving," and "distributed cognition" (please refer to Barron & Roschelle, 2009, for more details about these overlapping concepts).

However, as Salomon and Globerson (1989) point out, teams do not always function the way that they should. There are multiple issues that can arise in collaborative learning situations (e.g., the "Free Rider effect," referring to those who benefit from the collaborative activities of the group without contributing their own efforts, or the "Sucker Effect," a tendency for participants to contribute less to a group if they expect others will think negatively of them if they work too hard or contribute too much). Group work can lead to unproductiveness, wasted time and feelings of discouragement. More specifically, Barron (2003) begins to unpack the complexities of collaborative work with detailed analyses of triads solving mathematics problems. Focusing on explanations for variability in outcomes, she contrasted two groups of students who produced radically different outcomes; in one group, students generated, confirmed, documented, and reflected upon correct proposals. In the other group, students generated correct proposals but their partners ignored or rejected them without rationale and left them undocumented. Casebased portraits depicted the challenges that arose as participants attempted (or did not) to coordinate individual perspectives into a joint problem solving space. In the less successful case, relational issues arose that prevented the group from capitalizing on the insights that fellow members had generated. Such relational issues included competitive interactions, differential efforts to collaborate, and self-focused problem-solving trajectories. Behaviorally, these issues were manifest in violation of turn-taking norms, difficulties in gaining the floor, domination of the group workbook, and competing claims of competence. Those differences were not explained by students' prior achievement; rather, the mutuality of exchanges and the achievement of joint attention were found to be better predictors of the groups' success. It seems that the outcome of collaboration not only depends on individuals' contributions, but also on how well group members manage individual and joint attention during the collaborative activities.

As a consequence, we will adopt the point of view expressed by Dillenbourg et al. (1996), who argued that: "collaboration is in itself neither efficient nor inefficient. Collaboration works under some conditions, and it is the aim of research to determine the conditions under which collaborative learning is efficient." Our goal goes beyond observing collaboration: we are interested in designing technological interventions that will support and increase the quality of collaboration. This goal is shared among many researchers in CSCL. More specifically, we base our intervention on the findings of Barron's (2003) study: If joint attention was among the strongest predictors of a good collaboration, then facilitating this process should lead to more productive social interactions.

## *Awareness Features in CSCL*

As mentioned above, teams are not always more efficient than individuals: group members need to sustain mutual understanding, manage a smooth flow of communication, gather as many solution-relevant pieces of information as possible, reach a consensus, divide tasks equally, make sure to finish the current task within the time limit, treat each other with respect, and actively engage in finding a relevant solution to the problem at hand (Meier, Spada, & Rummel, 2007). With so many constraints, it should not be surprising that a good collaboration is difficult to establish and maintain. One promising approach in supporting group collaboration has emerged in CSCL over the last decade: Researchers have begun to design *awareness tools* to support productive interactions among students. Awareness tools provide additional information to a group of students about their peers (e.g., their level of expertise, extraversion, or progression toward a goal). Multiple studies have found that awareness tools increase the quality of collaboration in small teams.

For instance, Sangin (2009) studied pairs of students remotely working on a concept map and found evidence that a knowledge awareness tool (i.e., displaying the level of expertise of each member of the dyad) was associated with a higher density of gaze-coupling to a joint referent (i.e., joint attention), a higher quality of collaboration and increased learning gains. In another line of work, Bachour, Kaplan, and Dillenbourg (2010) described the design of an interactive table displaying the participants' level of participation (i.e., as indexed by the amount of speech produced by each individual); their empirical evaluation suggests that this simple visualization leads to more balanced patterns of collaboration. More specifically, it prevented those who might be described as extroverted users from dominating the discussion and discouraged underparticipation from those who might be described as introverted individuals.[2] Independently but with convergent results, Kim and Pentland (2009) used sociometric sensors to detect group dynamics and found that when these data were used to provide real-time feedback to participants, speaking time and inter-

---

[2] It should be noted that this study did not employ empirical measures of extroversion or introversion to arrive at these characterizations.

activity level of groups changed significantly. Especially interesting was that in groups with one dominant person, the feedback effectively reduced the dynamical difference between co-located and distributed collaboration as well as the behavioral difference between dominant and nondominant individuals. Finally, a slightly different kind of awareness tool supporting interactions between teachers and students was described by Alavi and Dillenbourg (2012). They built an ambient awareness tool to support collaborative work in recitation sections. Each device looks like a lantern and displays the status of the group (e.g., which exercise students are working on, if they have asked for help, how much time they have been waiting). A user study suggested that this kind of tool leads to improved interactions between teams and tutors; they wasted less time waiting for the teaching assistants and spent more time working on their assignments. This last example is conceptually different from the other projects, because it provides awareness at a higher level of social organization (i.e., between a group of students and a teacher). It is slightly less relevant to us since we are interested in raising students' awareness of each other's learning activities as indicated by gaze patterns to learning resources and simultaneous audio channel interchanges.

These four projects show that simple visualizations can be quite powerful for supporting interactions in small groups. As a consequence, we propose to build on this promising body of work to help students coordinate joint visual attention with eye-tracking technologies. In the following section, we summarize existing work on using eye-trackers in education and describe our approach in designing an awareness tool for supporting visual coordination.

## Eye-Tracking and Joint Attention

Even though the first eye-trackers were built and used in research over a century ago (e.g., Dodge & Cline, 1901: see Jacob & Karn, 2003), their use is not widespread in the scientific community. Costs, technological challenges, accuracy and latency, the need for advanced data analysis skills and other obstacles have prevented their propagation. However, the ability to track subjects' gaze can provide rich and insightful data; some researchers even reflect on how eye-trackers may open a new "window into the mind" of the users (Duchowski, 2007) since visual attention often reflects cognitive processes. On a technical level, eye-tracking devices generate three kinds of data: *saccades* ("jumps," that reposition the fovea on a new location of the visual field), *fixations* (prolonged focus of attention on a specific location) and *smooth pursuits* (following an object on the screen). Combined together, these measures provide unique opportunities to understand people's cognitive processes. Furthermore, several eye-tracking devices used in parallel may afford an indication of the level of synchronization of the different members of a group; for instance, by measuring the number of times users look at the same area on the screen within a specified time window (i.e., number of moments of joint attention).

Previous work in CSCL used eye-trackers to study joint attention in collaborative learning situations. For instance, Richardson and Dale (2005) found that the degree of gaze recurrence between individual speaker—listener dyads (i.e., the proportion of times that their gazes are aligned) is correlated with the listeners' accuracy on comprehension questions. Richardson, Dale, and Kirkham (2007) showed that common knowledge grounding (i.e., hearing the same background information before the task) positively influenced the coordination of visual attention in a spontaneous dialogue. Jermann, Mullins, Nuessli, and Dillenbourg (2001) used synchronized eye-trackers to assess how programmers collaboratively worked on a segment of code; they contrasted a "good" and a "bad" dyad, and their results suggested that a productive collaboration is associated with high joint visual recurrence. In another study, Nüssli, Jermann, Sangin, and Dillenbourg (2009) showed that eye-tracking data can be integrated with other measures to build models of group behavior: by using gaze and raw speech data (pitch and speed of the voice), he was able to predict participants' success with an accuracy rate of up to 91 %. As importantly, he was able to make this prediction before the activity was over. In a similar study, Liu et al. (2009) used machine-learning techniques to examine gaze patterns for collaborating dyads, and was able to predict the level of expertise of each subject as soon as 1 min into the collaboration (with 96 % accuracy). In a similar way, Cherubini, Nüssli, and Dillenbourg (2008) designed an algorithm for detecting misunderstanding in a remote collaboration by using the distance between the gaze of the emitter and the receiver; they found that if there is more dispersion, the likelihood of misunderstandings is increased. Finally, Brennan, Chen, Dickinson, Neider, and Zelinsky (2008) studied the effect of shared gaze and speech during a spatial search task; they found that the shared gaze condition was the best of all. It was twice as fast and efficient as solitary search, and significantly faster than other collaborative conditions.

Taken together, those results support the idea that joint attention and, more generally, synchronization between individuals, is crucial for an effective collaboration. They also suggest that eye-trackers are a promising way to understand and influence the factors responsible for a high-quality collaboration.

## *Summary of Previous Work and Hypotheses*

Based on prior work studying joint attention and the effects of awareness tools on collaborative learning, we conjecture that new technologies can facilitate collaboration by supporting the establishment of joint attention. *In a unique application of eye-tracking technologies, we propose that their use to inform a collaborator about their partner's gaze during a collaborative learning situation by creating a new real-time perceptual data stream overlaid on the static representation of the learning resource that they each are studying.* We go beyond prior research using eye tracking as a researcher methodology and representational medium for making scientific inferences about learners or collaborating learners, to use eye tracking in order to provide a new real-time information resource for learners to exploit for enhancing their own collaborative processes.

More specifically, our first attempt in this vector of innovation involves dyads studying contrasting cases (Schwartz & Bransford, 1998) in the domain of neuroscience. In our study, contrasting cases were designed "to help students notice information they might otherwise overlook. As with tasting wines side by side, contrasts can improve discernment"(Schwartz & Martin, 2004). We followed the examples given in Schwartz and Bransford (1998) to help students notice the deep structure of the concepts taught. More specifically, this learning activity is based on the "Preparing for Future Learning" (PFL) framework. The PFL framework proposes to design perceptual tasks to prepare students for traditional instructional activities (e.g., attending a lecture or reading a textbook chapter). The PFL approach encourages students to explore in order to generate their own theories about a class of phenomena, which sets the stage for future learning. Note that we are not testing the PFL approach per se, but we decided to use it for three reasons: First, we assumed that a gaze awareness tool is more likely to produce positive outcomes for a perceptual task, since we are enhancing the ways in which students may perceive their peers' visual behavior. Second, we are interested in improving proven pedagogical strategies; the PFL framework is recognized as being a fruitful approach for teaching in complex domains. For these reasons, our work is more likely to have an impact on existing classroom practices when eye-trackers become commonly used in everyday life. Finally, we care about supporting students' transfer of knowledge to new situations (Pea, 1987), as opposed to rote memorization. PFL activities are known to promote higher gain on transfer questions (Schwartz & Martin, 2004).

## General Description of the Experiment

Our experiment had three distinct steps: during the first 12 min, dyads worked on five contrasting cases in neuroscience that were represented in a single static diagram. We chose contrasting cases as an instructional approach, because joint attention is more likely to be a significant mediator for students' learning gains in a highly perceptual task. In this experiment, we were specifically targeting deictic behavior: by providing gaze information from the participants' partner, we eliminated the need for them to precisely describe which area of the screen they were referring to. However, as we note in our discussion, it is unclear if the results we obtain will generalize beyond diagram-based contrasting cases. Students had to collaboratively explain how visual information is processed in the human brain by studying the models described in Fig. 7.1. In the second step, they then read a text on the same topic for 12 min. In the final step, they answered a learning test. We used a between-subjects design with two conditions. In one condition ("visible-gaze"), dyads were able to see the gaze of their partner on the screen. In the other condition ("no-gaze"), they could not. In both conditions, an audio channel was open between the collaborating participants.

Our hypotheses for results from the two conditions are as follows: first, we expect the dyads in the treatment group (i.e., students who could see their partner's gaze on the screen) to have a higher quality of collaboration, since this visualization will disambiguate their focus of attention and better enable "common ground" for learning conversations (Clark & Brennan, 1991). Second, we assume that a better

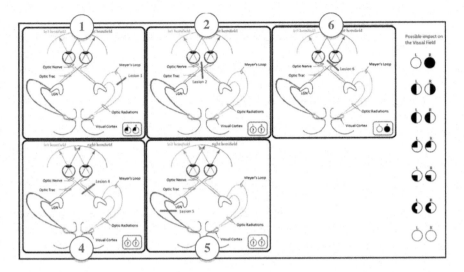

**Fig. 7.1** The dyads worked on the five contrasting cases above. Possible answers are shown on the right side. Answers of two cases (#1, top left and #6, top right) were given to subjects. Participants had to solve the three remaining cases (#2—top middle—and #4 and #5—bottom left and right of the screen, respectively)

collaboration will be positively associated with participants' learning gain (Barron, 2003), since users will more efficiently communicate their understanding of the content taught, and thus better explore the problem space for the information needed for their learning task.

## Methods

*Participants.* Participants were 42 college-level students from a community college (average age 23.0, SD=8.3; 28 females, 14 males). Dyads were randomly assigned to the two experimental conditions: the treatment group was in the "visible-gaze" condition ($N=22$) with 15 females and 7 males; the control group was in the "no-gaze" condition, with 13 females and 7 males ($N=20$). There was no significant difference in terms of GPA (Grade Point Average) between the two conditions: $F(1,36)=0.29$, $p=0.59$ (for "visible-gaze": mean=3.09, SD=0.87; for "no-gaze": mean=3.22, SD=0.59). All participants were taking an introductory class in psychology and were required to participate in an experiment as part of their course. No participant had previous knowledge in neuroscience before completing the task. Participants did not know each other prior to the study.

*Material.* During the first step of the experiment, dyads worked on the contrasting cases shown in Fig. 7.1. Their task was to infer the effect of three particular lesions (labeled 2, 4 and 5 in Fig. 7.1) on the visual field of a patient. Students had two main ideas to discover to be successful in this learning task: first, visual information is crossed after the left geniculate nucleus (LGN): in general, the left hemisphere of one's brain processes the information coming from one's right side of the visual field, and the right hemisphere of one's brain processes the information coming from the left side of one's visual field. Second, participants had to discover that visual information is again divided between the LGN and the visual cortex: the outer optic radiation (called Meyer's Loop) processes information coming from the top half of the visual field, while the inner optic radiation processes information coming from the bottom half of the visual field. Thus, each pathway between the LGN and the visual cortex carries information relative to a quarter of one's visual field. To derive the correct answers, students needed to look both at the color coding of the contrasting cases and the answers for cases 1 and 6.

To compel learner collaboration, the answer for lesion 1 (top left) was visible only to the first member of the dyad while the answer for lesion 6 (top right) was shown only to its second member. This "jigsaw" method is commonly used to make sure that one member of the dyad does not solve the problem alone (Aronson, Blaney, Sikes, Stephan, & Snapp, 1978). The text used in the next step is available online.[3] The document was five pages long, contained 972 words and included six large figures. The content focused on the visual pathways shown on the contrasting cases in Fig. 7.1. It explained why various lesions have different impacts on the visual field. We removed unnecessary paragraphs with heavy medical terminology to keep the task doable in the amount of time provided to the students.

*Experimental design.* Our study used a between-subjects design. Participants were randomly distributed between two conditions: In the treatment group ("visible-gaze"), dyads were able to see the gaze of their partner on the screen. In the control group ("no-gaze"), they could not. The gaze was only visible during the first step of the experiment for the treatment group (i.e., when participants had to collabora-tively solve the contrasting cases shown in Fig. 7.1).

*Procedure.* Upon their arrival, participants were welcomed and thanked for their participation. The experimenter then explained that they would need to collaborate and suggested that they introduce themselves to their partner. They were also told that each member of the dyad would be in a different room, but would be able to communicate via a microphone audio channel. The experimenter explained that participants would learn basic concepts in neuroscience, and he described the struc-ture of the experiment—12 min of analysis of contrasting cases, 12 min of reading a text solitarily and silently, and as much time as needed for the learning test. Each participant then followed the experimenter to different rooms, where he calibrated their personal eye-tracker. At the beginning of the task, the contrasting cases were then presented for approximately one minute to each participant and the experi-menter ensured that they understood the goal of the task. Participants then worked

---

[3] The text used in the second part of the study is accessible here: http://www.scribd.com/doc/98921800 (last access: 03/08/2013). Originally retrieved from Washington University in St-Louis (http://thalamus.wustl.edu/).

on the contrasting cases and tried to determine how different lesions affected the brain's visual field. After 12 min, the screen automatically switched to a text explaining how the human brain processes visual information. The experimenter informed participants that they should read the text individually and afterwards discuss it with their partner. The audio channel remained opened for this step. After 12 min, the screen being observed by the dyads automatically switched to the learning test. The experimenter then told the subjects to individually complete the test and stopped the audio link. Participants took as much time as they needed for completion. They were then debriefed as the experimenter explained the goal of the study.

*Eye-tracking setup.* We used two desktop-based Tobii X1 eye-trackers running at 30 Hz to capture and display participants' gaze. We used an in-house server for synchronizing the two devices. Calibrations were performed using a five-point calibration at the beginning of the experiment. Additionally, since our areas of interest are quite large (for most analyses we used one diagram as an area of interest), we did not correct for gaze deviations. However, we cursorily watched the videos showing the participants' gaze patterns to ensure that no large deviation was present in our dataset.

*Design of the gaze-awareness tool.* The gaze of each participant was displayed to their partner as a light blue dot of 20 pixels of diameter on the screen. The circle was half transparent (40 % opacity) and refreshed approximately four times per second. We determined those values by trial and error to avoid a distracting effect; we found non-transparent circles that were refreshed too often created frustration. During the experiment, students had the opportunity to hide the circle by pressing any key on the keyboard, yet no participant used this function.

*Measures.* Because no participant had previous knowledge in neuroscience, learning gains were computed from the final learning test, which contained 15 questions: five terminology questions (participants were asked to provide the name of a specific brain region or pathway), five conceptual questions (participants had to predict the effect of a specific lesion), and five transfer questions (subjects had to use their new knowledge to solve a vignette; e.g., "patient X is likely to have a lesion in region Y of the brain; should he be allowed to drive?"). The tests were administered electronically and multiple-choice questions were coded automatically (i.e., students were allowed to choose only one option). Transfer questions were open-ended; we gave 1 point for a correct answer, 0.5 points for an ambiguous answer suggesting a correct logic, and 0 points for wrong answers. Two researchers evaluated the answers and agreed on a common definition for "ambiguous," "correct" and "wrong."

The quality of collaboration was rated using dimensions developed in Meier et al. (2007), who assessed collaboration on a five-point scale across nine dimensions (sustaining mutual understanding, dialogue management, information pooling, reaching consensus, task division, task management, technical coordination, reciprocal interaction, and individual task orientation). The evaluation of this rating scheme demonstrated a high inter-rater reliability, consistency and validity, which rendered it as an appropriate tool for assessing collaboration. In addition to those nine dimensions, we also computed a general "collaboration score" by averaging each dyads' scores on those sub-dimensions. This compound variable allowed us to run higher-level correlations between our eye-tracking indicators and students' interactions.

Additionally, we categorized each participant in a binary manner as being either the "leader" or the "follower" in the activity. This distinction is motivated by recent work in HCI (Human-Computer Interaction), where Shaer et al. (2011) noticed that pairs of participants tended to assign "roles" to their members; for instance, in collaborative tasks there tends to be a "driver," who is physically active and controls the interface, and a "passenger," who is physically inactive and merely proposes verbal suggestions. This pattern was also documented in classroom-based uses of microcomputers in Sheingold, Hawkins, and Char (1984), in which the pattern of "I'm the thinkist, you're the typist" was identified. Those profiles of collaboration are interesting, because they inform us about the emergent dynamic of a group. Inspired by this approach, we developed a rough coding scheme to distinguish between "leaders" (the equivalent of Shaer's "drivers") and "followers" (the equivalent of Shaer's "passengers"). We used several indicators to categorize each dyad's members: (1) who started the discussion when the experimenter leaves, (2) who spoke most, (3) who managed turn-taking (e.g., by asking "what do _you_ think?" "how do you understand this part of the diagram?"), and (4) who decides the next focus of attention (e.g., "so to summarize, our answers are [...]. I think we need to spend more time on diagram X"). This measure can be considered as an aggregate estimation over the whole activity of the dyad's dynamic profile, since we acknowledged that subjects are likely to shift roles while solving contrasting cases. We also recognize that this categorization is more likely to be a continuum, and that in a few cases the difference between followers and leaders may be subtle. The decision to only have two categories was made to simplify the coding process and present clearer results (Fig. 7.2), but we acknowledge that this coding presents an oversimplified picture of the dyads' dynamic. Future work will analyze this kind of interaction on a more fine-grained level.

Finally, we collected eye-tracking data during the experiment: approximately 30 datapoints per second were captured for each participant. This gave us ~1,000,000 gaze points in total. Within those measurements, we also collected participants' pupil size as a measure of cognitive load, as we explain subsequently. _Our main motivation for collecting and analyzing eye-tracking data is to compute a quantitative measure of joint attention._ By synchronizing our two eye-trackers, we can see how often dyads looked at the same thing at the same time on the screen. We can then relate this measure to the groups' quality of collaboration and learning gains. Additionally, we can also track students' cognitive load and see: (1) if monitoring an additional channel of information (i.e., the gaze of their partner) increased participants' efforts to complete the task, and (2) if more successful students are characterized by a higher level of cognitive load.

More specifically, from our data we isolated four different measures from the eye-tracking data:

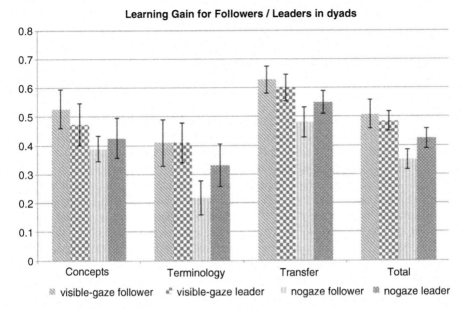

**Fig. 7.2** The total scores of the learning gain and the three sub-dimensions measured: conceptual understanding, participants' recall of the terminology, and transfer questions (crossed with two factors: experimental conditions and individuals' status in the dyad). *Whiskers* represent standard errors

1. First, we counted the number of fixations on the five contrasting cases and on the region showing the potential answers;
2. Second, we aggregated the number of saccades between two regions from the six previously mentioned (i.e., five cases and one area for the answers);
3. Third, we defined a "joint attention" measure, where we counted how many times both participants looked at the same case on the screen. Previous research has shown that subjects need ~2 s to focus their attention on an object after a peer mentions it (Richardson & Dale, 2005). We followed those guidelines to create our measure: for each data point, we checked whether the other member of the dyad was looking at the same area of the screen during the preceding or following two seconds.
4. Fourth, we used the size of the participants' pupil as an indication of his or her cognitive load. When a person is faced with a challenging cognitive task, his or her pupils dilate (the task-evoked pupillary response: Beatty, 1982; Beatty & Lucero-Wagoner, 2000), so pupil dilation may be used for estimating cognitive load. However, it should be noted that there is some debate about using pupil dilation as a measure of cognitive load; consequently, our data for pupil dilation should be provisionally taken as estimations of cognitive load. Additionally, since eye-trackers react differently to the physiology of different eyes, we divided each measure by the total number of data points for each participant. This computation yielded the percentage of fixations, percentage of saccades, and percentage of

joint attention. For the cognitive load, we also subtracted the smallest value from each measure of a particular participant to take into account differences in eyes' morphologies. Participants' pupil size is not always a reliable measure, especially when the lighting conditions vary; however, since the room we used for the experiment did not have a window and thus had a constant lighting, we included those results for our analysis.

*Qualitative analysis.* The previous measures provide quantitative data on the effects of a gaze-awareness tool on students' remote collaboration. However they do not provide us with any explanation for causal mechanisms that may be responsible for such effects. We also tried to qualitatively analyze our data by comparing two dyads in terms of their gaze patterns. We compared two groups: one in the "visible-gaze" condition and one in the "no-gaze" condition. The main goal of this comparison is to illustrate how our intervention changed the behaviors of our participants. More specifically, we focused on four dimensions: (1) students' ability to coordinate themselves, (2) to create convention, (3) to build hypotheses and (4) to share theories. We chose those two groups randomly; it is possible that there are differences between them that go beyond their experimental condition, but our goal here is not to generalize our observations to the entire sample or to a population. Rather, as stated above, our aim was to suggest potential mechanisms for the effect of a gaze-awareness tool on students' collaboration. Thus, we only watched the two videos at 0.5x speed to be able to analyze gaze patterns. We report our observations in the last subsection of the results.

# Results

In this section, we compare main effects for learning gains and collaboration scores across our two experimental groups. We then characterize the dyads of our experiments in terms of their gaze patterns by analyzing our eye-tracking data. We also compare process variables in terms of their predictive effect as mediators. Finally, we conclude by conducting a small qualitative analysis of two dyads (one from each experimental group) to suggest mechanisms for explaining the main effects found.

## *Learning and Collaboration*

For the analyses related to our main hypotheses (learning gains, joint attention and quality of collaboration), we made sure that our Analyses of Variance (ANOVA) met the assumptions of normality and homogeneity of variance by generating and analyzing histograms and boxplots. We also made sure that our distributions did not have outliers beyond two standard deviations.

As predicted, we found that participants in the "visible-gaze" group outperformed the dyads in the "no-gaze" condition for the total learning gain: $F(1,40) = 7.81$,

$p<0.01$. For the sub-dimensions, they also scored higher on the transfer questions $F(1,40)=4.47$, $p<0.05$. The difference is likely to be significant for the terminology questions $F(1,40)=3.59$, $p=0.065$ and for the conceptual questions $F(1,40)=2.11$, $p=0.154$ with a larger sample, since the effect sizes are between medium and large (Cohen's $d$ are 0.62 and 0.5, respectively). Additionally, we took students' GPA (Grade Point Average) into account to perform further analyses (four data points were missing, two in each condition). The difference between our two conditions remained significant when taking the GPA as a covariate: $F(1,36)=6.79$, $p=0.013$ and taking the dyads as the unit of analysis: $F(1,18)=9.19$, $p=0.007$.

The treatment group ("visible gaze") also had a higher quality of collaboration as measured by Meier et al. (2007) rating scheme. The total score is an average across the nine sub-dimensions described in the "measure" section (as a reminder, each group was given a score between $-3$ and $+3$): $F(1,19)=11.73$, $p<0.01$, Cohen's $d=1.24$ (mean for the treatment group$=0.89$, SD$=0.48$; mean for the control group$=-0.08$, SD$=0.79$). More specifically, those visible-gaze condition dyads were better at *sustaining mutual understanding*: $F(1,19)=5.15$, $p<0.05$ (mean for the treatment group$=1.27$, SD$=0.88$; mean for the control group$=0.30$, SD$=1.03$), *pooling information*: $F(1,19)=7.53$, $p<0.05$ (mean for the treatment group$=1.18$, SD$=0.97$; mean for the control group$=-0.20$, SD$=1.28$), *reaching consensus*: $F(1,19)=22.57$, $p<0.001$ (mean for the treatment group$=1.36$, SD$=0.79$; mean for the control group$=-0.1$, SD$=0.55$), and *managing time*: $F(1,19)=4.98$, $p<0.05$ (mean for the treatment group$=1.00$, SD$=0.67$; mean for the control group$=0.00$, SD$=1.29$). A second judge double-coded 20 % of the video data; inter-reliability index using Krippendorff's alpha was 0.81. An alpha higher than 0.8 is considered as a reliable agreement between judges (Hayes & Krippendorff, 2007).

We categorized each member of the dyad as "leader" or "follower" (Fig. 7.2). We found an interaction effect between those two factors (experimental condition and individuals' status) on the total learning score: $F(1,38)=5.29$, $p<0.05$. Followers who could see the gaze of the leader learned significantly more than followers who could not (see the "Total" column in Fig. 7.2). Overall, followers in the "visible-gaze" condition learned more than followers in the "no-gaze" condition: $F(1,19)=10.65$, $p<0.005$ (mean$=0.54$, SD$=0.15$, mean$=0.35$, SD$=0.11$, respectively). There was no significant difference between leaders in the two conditions: $F(1,19)=0.26$, $p=0.61$ (mean$=0.44$, SD$=0.09$, mean$=0.42$, SD$=0.11$, respectively). Additionally, leaders and followers did not differ in terms of their GPA: $F(1,36)<1$ (for followers, mean$=3.19$, SD$=0.75$; for leaders, mean$=3.11$, SD$=0.76$).

*Eye-tracking Data.* We analyzed our eye-tracking data in order to describe the ways in which students' strategies differed when they could see the gaze of their partner on the screen while working on the contrasting cases. We excluded five subjects from those analyses because of missing data (due to the eye-tracker crashing during the activity). Three such participants were in the "no-gaze" condition, and two participants were in the "visible-gaze" condition. We thus have 37 subjects when measuring the number of fixations and saccades, and 16 dyads (32 subjects) when measuring joint attention. We found that participants in the "no-gaze" condition had

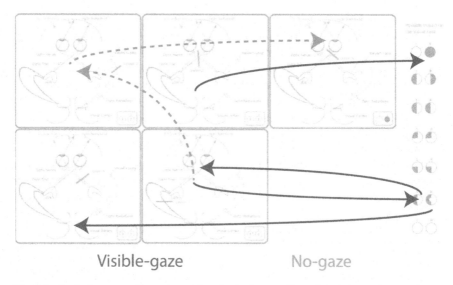

Visible-gaze                          No-gaze

**Fig. 7.3** *Dashed arrows* indicate that subjects in the "no-gaze" condition made more visual comparisons between two regions on the screen compared to subjects in the "visible-gaze" condition; vice versa for the *solid arrows*

significantly more fixations on case one ($F(1,35)=9.69$, $p<0.01$, Cohen's $d=1.28$), and case three ($F(1,35)=4.92$, $p<0.05$, Cohen's $d=0.8$). Participants in the "visible-gaze" condition spent more time looking at the answers ($F(1,35)=10.41$, $p<0.01$ Cohen's $d=1.21$).

In terms of examining the gaze saccades between regions, we divided the screen into six areas: the five contrasting cases and the answers on the right. Figure 7.3 summarizes the results obtained. Subjects in the "visible-gaze" condition made more comparisons between case five and the answers ($F(1, 34)=6.41$, $p<0.05$; Cohen's $d=0.77$; $F(1,34)=7.14$, $p<0.05$; Cohen's $d=0.82$), from the answer to case four ($F(1,34)=7.12$, $p<0.05$; Cohen's $d=0.74$), and from case two to the answers ($F(1,34)=5.12$, $p<0.05$; Cohen's $d=0.73$). Subjects in the "no-gaze" condition made more saccades from case one to case six ($F(1,34)=5,32$, $p<0.05$; Cohen's $d=0.59$) and from case five to case one ($F(1,34)=6.14$, $p<0.05$; Cohen's $d=0.81$). Even though we conducted multiple comparisons, we decided to follow Rothman's advice (1990) to not adjust our results. This researcher suggested that not correcting results led to fewer errors and supported researchers' explorations of alternative hypotheses. Additionally, since those results are descriptive and not central to our claims, we leave it to the reader to hedge their interpretation of those numbers.

We did not find a significant difference for cognitive load between the two gaze conditions: $F(1,35)=1.09$, $p=0.3$ (mean$=1.44$, SD$=0.34$ for "visible-gaze"; mean$=1.31$ SD$=0.41$ for "nogaze"). The interaction effect between experimental condition and leader/follower status within the dyad is also not significant: $F(1,29)=2.51$, $p=0.12$, yet the effect size is between medium and large (partial eta squared$=0.08$; note that we are not using Cohen's $d$, here), which suggests that fol-

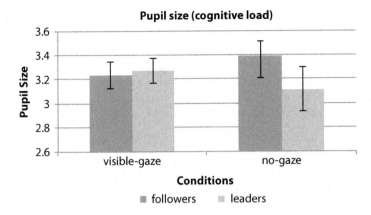

**Fig. 7.4** Participants' pupil size in each condition (distinguishing leaders and followers)

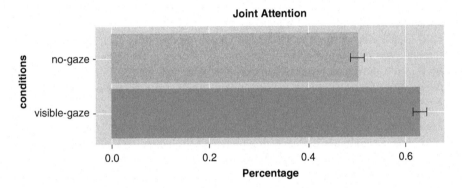

**Fig. 7.5** Percentage of joint attention in each experimental condition

lowers in the "no-gaze" condition made more cognitive effort than followers in the "visible-gaze" condition. It would be interesting to have more subjects to see if this result becomes significant. The pattern is similar in direction to the one described for the learning test (i.e., followers tended to have a higher cognitive load than leaders in the "no-gaze" condition, and followers tended to have a lower cognitive load than leaders in the "visible-gaze" condition; Fig. 7.4).

Participants in the "visible-gaze" condition achieved joint attention more often than the participants in the "no-gaze" condition (see Fig. 7.5; for our analyses, we considered the percentage of moments of joint attention, in order to not give higher scores to subjects whose eyes were more easily detected by our eye-trackers): $F(1,30) = 22.45$, $p < 0.001$, Cohen's $d = 1.73$. This result holds when taking dyads (and not individuals) as the unit of analysis: $F(1, 14) = 16.36$, $p < 0.001$, Cohen's $d = 2.01$. The percentage of joint attention is one of the only measures correlated with a positive learning gain: $r = 0.39$, $p < 0.05$. Recall that our measure for joint attention was determined by whether, for each data point, the other member of the dyad was looking at the same area of the screen during the preceding or following two seconds, regardless of their verbal participation. We did not compute an exact match of $x-y$ coordinates; instead, we considered each diagram and the column of answers to be areas of interest, since they have a conceptual significance for our task. Finally the percentage of moments of joint attention was also correlated with the quality of collaboration of the dyads: $r=0.58, p<0.001$.

*Basic speech processing.* One explanation for students' higher learning gain in the visible-gaze condition is that our intervention provided them with more opportunities for dialogue: By looking at their partners' gaze, they could directly start a discussion on the diagram being looked at. Thus, to examine this conjecture, we analyzed the audio files of the experiment with a custom-made script that estimates the amount of speech produced by each participant. We found that subjects in the "visible-gaze" condition spoke more than the subjects in the "no-gaze" condition: $F(1,38)=6.13, p<0.05$ (mean $=273.72$ s., SD $=125.96$ for "visible-gaze," mean $=189.11$ s., SD $=83.55$ for "no-gaze"). This significant difference remains when taking the dyads as the unit of analysis: $F(1,19)=5.56, p=0.029$. At the individual level (when considering the amount of speech produced by each individual), this measure was not correlated with participants' scores on the learning test: $r=0.24$, $p=0.14$. At the dyadic level (when considering the amount of speech produced by the group), this measure was associated with a higher percentage of joint attention: $r=0.46, p<0.01$.

*Model for potential mediators.* In this section, we tested which process variables were most strongly associated with a positive learning gain. One may hypothesize that the quality of collaboration, the amount of cognitive effort exerted by the participants, or the percentage of joint attention for a dyad during the 12 min session may predict students' learning. We tested for multiple mediation using Preacher and Hayes' (2008) bootstrapping methodology for indirect effects. We used 5000 bootstrap resamples to describe the confidence intervals of indirect effects in a manner making no assumptions about the distribution of the indirect effects. Significance is determined by checking if a confidence interval does *not* contain zero. We tested our model with the following candidates for "mediator": Collaboration, percentage of joint attention, and cognitive load. GPA was used as a covariate, since our goal is to find mediators irrespective of participants' grades. Results for multiple mediation indicated that only joint attention (CI: [0.03; 0.19]) was a mediator for learning (see Fig. 7.6).

*Vignette.* As a reminder, we note that the previous sections provided quantitative data on the effect of a gaze-awareness tool on students' remote collaboration. However, they do not provide us with any explanation for the mechanisms that may be responsible for such effects. Table 7.1 seeks to suggest qualitative explanations for the positive effect of our gaze-awareness tool on students' learning gains and quality of collaboration. We compared two groups: one in the "visible-gaze" condition (Table 7.1 left side) and one in the "no-gaze" condition (Table 7.1 right side).

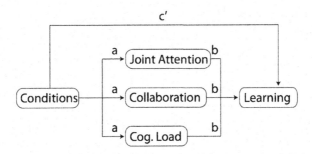

**Fig. 7.6** Mediation model for our experiment. We tested the following potential mediators: cognitive load (measured by the size of participants' pupils), quality of collaboration (measured by Meier, Spada, and Rummel (2007) rating scheme) and percentage of joint attention (estimated with the eye-tracking data)

In terms of coordination, we found substantial differences between our two dyads. More specifically, the four following points summarize our qualitative observations:

1. First, the sequence of actions was reversed: in the "visible-gaze" dyad, the leader would start talking about a lesion, and the follower's gaze would go to the same area on the screen *before* the leader even mentioned the lesion's number (v2). In the "no-gaze" dyad, the follower would have the double burden of finding the lesion of interest, and following the leader's explanation in parallel (n2). We argue that our gaze awareness intervention facilitated coordination and helped the follower anticipate the leader's explanations.

2. Second, we found the emergence of interesting new anaphoric conventions: in the "visible-gaze" dyad (v3), when Lea says "so that would be ... left-left, right-right," neither of them explicitly stated that she was referring to the eyes and hemifields of the diagram. Rather, they implicitly built the convention of moving their gaze as a deictic gesture to complement their explanations—illustrating how conventions of efficient language use such as anaphora when individuals are co-located in a conversation (Clark, 1996) extended to remote collaboration when an alternative referring mechanism (gaze in this case) can be used in the collaborative process of common ground construction during discourse.

3. Third, we hypothesized that our intervention helped students share their cognition, even though they did not master the expert terminology of the domain: sentences as vague as "they are both going to be equal" (v2) suddenly made sense when Lea pointed her gaze at the optic nerves to show that half of the information from each hemifield would be disrupted. This is particularly interesting because novices often lack the vocabulary to effectively communicate their assumptions. In our case, it provided Flo with additional information about the symmetry of the brain and helped her build her own hypotheses.

**Table 7.1** Excerpts of students' dialogue when discussing the contrasting cases

| Visible-gaze (P54-P55) | No-gaze (P07-P08) |
|---|---|
| *Lea (L) is the leader, and Flo the follower (F)*<br>**(v1) building anticipation (1:22)**<br>L: I have an answer for the … *[gaze moving to case 1]*<br>F: *[gaze moving to case 1]*<br>L: … further most left one<br>F: Okay. Where the lesion is the orange colored thing.<br>**(v2) sharing hypotheses (3:45)**<br>L: maybe lesion two is … *[gaze moving back and forth between the two hemifields, eyes and optic nerves]*<br>F: *[her gaze is moving from Lea's gaze to the other lesions]*<br>L: those are both… they would be disrupted … I think that lesion two would be … *[gaze moving to the second answer]*<br>F: *[gaze moving to the second answer]*<br>L: the second one<br>F: why do you say that?<br>L: because they are both going to be equal *[gaze moving to the lesion where two optic nerves (one from the right hemifield, one from the left hemifield) are severed]*<br>F: *[gaze drifting to the same point]* oh right<br>**(v3) creating implicit conventions (6:20)**<br>F: let's look at two again<br>*[both gazes move to lesion 2]*<br>L: everything is sort of cut off …<br>F: well it's just the two in the middle<br>L: yeah so that would be … left-left *[gaze moving from the left hemifield to the left eye, followed by Flo's gaze]* and right-right *[gaze moving from the right hemifield to the right eye followed by Flo's gaze]*<br>F: *[gaze moving to the second answer, followed by Lea's gaze]* … which would be the second one<br>L: yeah, which is the second one<br>**(v4) sharing theories (7:34)**<br>L: so for the fifth we are not sure […]<br>*[both gazes are exploring different cases on their own]*<br>L: so maybe the further away from the eye it is, the less severe *[gaze moving from the eyes to the LGN on lesion 1]*<br>F: *[gaze moving to lesion 1]* Maybe … what was lesion one again?<br>L: that was the top left and top right *[gaze moving to the 4th answer, followed by Flo's gaze]*, the fourth one down<br>F: Oh … Ooooh … Hum *[gaze comparing cases 1 and 5]*<br>L: so the one you had was right by the eye, and it was completely crossed out *[gaze on lesion 6]*<br>F: *[gaze moving to lesion 6, then 5]* so maybe this would be similarly only a quarter of the eye<br>L: *[gaze on answer 5]* yeah, maybe it would be the third one from the bottom *[followed by Flo's gaze on F: maybe … hum … [gaze jumping from lesion 5 to answer 5]* | *Laurie (L) is the leader, and Fiona is the follower (F).* **(n1) establishing common grounds (0–0:30)**<br>L: Hi!<br>F: Hi! *[laughing]* I don't get this stuff.<br>L: I don't either!<br>F: okay, so I have one with the answer *[looking at her case]*<br>L: yeah I have an example too. *[looking at her case]*<br>**(n2) sharing answers (2:37–3:45)**<br>F: so … *[gaze moving to lesion 1]* do you see lesion 1?<br>L: yes *[gaze moving to lesion 1]*<br>F: I think it blocks Meyer's loop somehow<br>L: yes<br>F: so the answer would be the left and the right …<br>L: *[gaze moving between answer 4 and 5]*<br>F: both the visions, they're blocked by one fourth. So it's not like completely blocked. So the answer would be that one *[gaze moving to answer 4]*<br>L: but how is it … hum … *[gaze still moving between answer 4 and 5]*. So you think it's the fourth answer down? Where the quarter is blacked out on the top? On the left?<br>F: yes both right and left vision<br>**(n3) sharing theories (8:19)**<br>F: *[gaze on lesion 5]* you said that lesion 5 would be the third from the bottom, right? *[gaze on answer 5]*<br>L: *[gaze moving from lesion 5 to answer 5]* yeah I think so because it's blocking the left lower part *[gaze moving back and forth between lesion 1 and 5]*<br>F: hu *[gaze moving back and forth between lesion 4 and 6]*<br>L: but then again it kinda doesn't make sense because if the answer for lesion 1 was the top left,<br>F:*[gaze moving to lesion 1, but then going back to lesion 4]* hu hu<br>L: then wouldn't it be blocked on the opposite side of where the lesion is?<br>F: *[gaze moving from lesion 1 to 5]* that's what I thought …<br>**(n4) sharing hypotheses (5:20–6:10)**<br>L: okay lesion 4 …<br>F: lesion 4 would be<br>L: *[gaze moving from the lesion to the third answer]* I think it is the one that's half and half, the third one from the top. Because it blocks … *[gaze moving to the eye]*<br>F: *[gaze moving to the third answer]* the left part of the vision?<br>L: yeah I don't know<br>F: maybe<br>L: *[laughing]*<br>F: Hum … maybe. I don't know *[laughing]*, whatever you say *[both laugh]* |

4. Fourth, we observed a tighter coupling between subjects' attention in the "visible-gaze" condition (v4): gazes would "dance" together during a longer period of time and focus on the same lesions even though they were not explicitly mentioned. In the control group, the follower would briefly attend to the same lesion as the leader talked, and then continue to explore other lesions (n3). This suggests that the theories built during the activity were more the result of the dyad's shared cognition (in the "visible-gaze" condition), and more the results of individuals' cumulative contributions in the "no-gaze" condition.

## Discussion

Our findings demonstrate the importance of mediating technologies for supporting joint attention in collaborative learning activities. We conducted a study where students needed to learn from five contrasting cases in a remote collaboration. In one condition, subjects could see the gaze of their partner on the screen as it was being produced. In the other, they could not. In both conditions, an audio channel was open between the participants in the dyad, as a medium for use in the coordination of their activities. Our results reveal that this simple intervention was associated with subjects in the visible gaze condition producing a higher quality of collaboration and learning more from the contrasting cases. In particular, participants characterized as "followers" saw their learning gain dramatically increase as compared to "leaders." This result was partially confirmed by a similar pattern found for students' cognitive load: followers in the control group expended more effort than leaders while learning less; followers in the treatment group spent less effort than leaders but learned more. We also found that subjects in the "no-gaze" condition spent more time on cases one and six; this suggests that they took more time (and probably had more difficulty) sharing their answers. Participants in the "visible-gaze" condition had a higher percentage of joint attention, which proved to be a significant mediator for learning. Interestingly, our measures of students' quality of collaboration did not significantly correlate with their learning gains. This suggests that perhaps visual coordination is a dimension of collaboration that is not captured by the rating scheme we used. Thus, our results may be an indication of future work for refining Meier, Spada and Rummel's approach for assessing collaboration.

These results provide strong evidence for the important contributions of real-time mutual gaze perception—a special form of technology-mediated shared attention—to the learning gains and collaboration quality of collaborative learning groups. Additional qualitative observations suggest that our intervention helped students on four dimensions: by supporting coordination, creating conventions, sharing cognition and by making knowledge-building a collective process rather than an individual one.

One might argue that a shared pointer could achieve a similar effect. Due to time constraints and limited access to participants, we did not include this condition in our experiment. However, we are interested in studying the effect of shared pointers in future studies compared to gaze-awareness tools. Conceptually, we believe that real-time mutual gaze perception may have several key advantages over a shared pointer: First, there is a cognitive overhead associated with consciously moving a cursor to a region of interest, which may interfere with the learning task. A gaze awareness tool does this work automatically, without requiring additional effort on the part of the user. There is also a certain degree of uncertainty associated with a cursor that stops moving; is your partner thinking, being distracted, or waiting on you? By looking at the videos of our experiment, we saw that members of a dyad would perform some sort of "micro-monitoring" of their partner's behavior, where they would check on their partner's gaze every few seconds. We believe that a continual flux of gaze information reduces uncertainty and helps students regulate the dynamics of their dyad. In summary, we hypothesize that our gaze awareness tool enabled some behaviors that would not be possible with a shared pointer. Future studies are needed to demonstrate the unique affordances of each of those interventions.

There is an alternative interpretation for these results. Most participants were using an eye-tracker for the first time, and it is possible that this novelty effect generated more engagement toward the learning task in the "visible-gaze" condition. If this interpretation is warranted, it would to some extent undermine the usefulness of our results. However, by reviewing the transcripts, we found that only two dyads (17 % of the participants) commented on the gaze-awareness tool or expressed any kind of surprise. We plan on further exploring this question by using natural-language processing algorithms (NLP) on the transcripts and the audio data; more specifically, we will extract the arousal expressed by the participants' voices (Boersma, 2002) to see whether subjects in one condition showed more engagement toward the learning task. One should note, however, that differences in engagement can't explain the differences found in the vignette above. Future work will explore how much variance of the learning effect each of those factors may explain.

## General Discussion

It is well established that joint attention plays a crucial role in any kind of social interaction. Our study provides additional evidence that its role is also preponderant in collaborative learning situations. We predict that in a near future, eye-trackers will become increasingly cheaper and widely available to a broad range of devices (e.g., not only desktops and laptops, but also smartphones and technology-enhanced eye glasses). Our study shows that in some technology-mediated interactions, real-time mutual gaze perception is beneficial for collaboration. Those results have important implications, especially for e-learning environments, since achieving a good remote collaboration is particularly challenging (Kreijns, Kirschner, & Jochems, 2003). Thus, we believe that it will be promising to explore the conditions under which students' visual exploration should be made available to their partners when working remotely. One caveat is that this awareness tool seems to work well for dyads; we are more skeptical of the use of a gaze-awareness tool for triads or large groups where this visualization may become distracting. Future work should investigate whether this effect generalizes to different tasks and group sizes. Our findings also have indirect implications for co-located interactions; as Barron (2003) highlighted in her study, having students collaborate in the same space, either side-by-side or face-to-face, does not make the establishment of joint attention trivial. We hypothesize that our intervention may lead to similar benefits for students working on an interactive surface (as while wearing eye-tracking goggles). Finally, our results have further implications for teachers' practices; with training, we posit that gaze-awareness tools could teach students the value of achieving joint attention in collaborative groups. The ability to effectively collaborate with peers was recently highlighted as a crucial twenty-first century competency (Trilling & Fadel, 2009).

From the standpoint of developing the sciences of collaborative learning, this study has the merit of providing quantitative measures to advance Barron's (2003) data-driven conceptualization of collaboration quality. In her study, she developed qualitative and quantitative indicators for joint attention from discourse and interaction analysis via intensive study of video recordings of collaborative learning dyads (for broader perspective on such analyses, see Barron et al., 2013). In our approach, joint attention is computed in an objective way, without the need for a human coder. We argue that the use of eye-trackers is highly relevant for studying collaborative learning, because it provides the opportunity to speed up the research process by quickly computing metrics of interest and by providing real-time feedback to learners and teachers. With further developments, such measures could be used in real-time in classrooms; Liu et al. (2009) and Nüssli et al. (2009) showed that machine learning techniques can predict students' expertise and task outcomes while the activity is still ongoing. In future classrooms, this approach could prove to be highly powerful in *sensing* and then *re-mediating* students' collaboration difficulties to prevent continued unproductive collaborative activities. Given real-time data processing (gaze and speech) and comprehensible data visualizations, teachers could immediately identify students who are having difficulties, and provide additional assistance to them. This kind of preventive approach is extremely appealing, because it allows teachers to provide help to students before they even realize that they need help. The employment of technological supports for overcoming collaboration challenges could also be triggered when such dyadic difficulties are sensed during eye-tracking, though at this stage of understanding, further studies are needed to guide the development of such real-time collaboration sensing and re-mediation scaffolding tools.

This study has several noteworthy limitations: (1) First, we studied a very specific kind of collaboration: situations where members of a dyad were communicating via a microphone and sharing a computer screen. It is not clear whether this kind of awareness tool would have the same effect in a co-located situation where computer-using collaborators are side by side. One might assume that joint attention is more readily achieved in a face-to-face or side-by-side collaboration, but as we have noted, Barron's (2003) study with co-located middle school collaborators solving math problems indicated real collaboration challenges even when face to face and sharing documents for learning. Future studies using eye-tracking goggles on interactive surfaces could address this question. (2) Second, students had a limited amount of time to work on the contrasting cases. It was unclear how this limitation impacted students' performance. (3) Third, we only cursorily evaluated the transcripts of the dyads. More fine-grained coding schemes may provide additional clues as to how joint attention specifically facilitated collaborative learning; the interaction effect between followers and leaders is especially interesting, and should be analyzed in greater depth. (4) Four, our sample is rather small (especially when considering dyads as the unit of analysis); future studies should seek to replicate this effect with more subjects. (5) Fifth, one may argue about the subcategories describing the learning gains (e.g., it is debatable whether the questions about predicting the effect of a lesion are effectively measuring conceptual understanding). However, because we are not making particular claims about those subcategories, and since the same pattern is repeated across our three learning sub-dimensions (i.e., the interaction effect between followers and leaders), we do not consider this issue to be a serious limitation of our findings. (6) Lastly, most of our statistics are conducted at both the individual and dyadic level. It would be more appropriate to conduct multilevel analyses to account for the learners' non-independence (Cress, 2008). In particular, the fact that we analyzed eye-tracking data (fixations, saccades) at the individual level is a significant limitation of our work. However, since our claims are about joint attention, we made sure that the results related to this measure remained significant when taking dyads as the unit of analysis.

In future work, we plan on evaluating the result of our qualitative observations. More specifically, we want to quantitatively measure the four dimensions we uncovered and examine whether those processes (and others we may uncover) are significantly different across conditions. Second, a next logical step is to investigate this phenomenon in a different setting (e.g., in a co-located situation). Eye-tracking goggles could offer an interesting tool for this purpose. Third, it would be interesting to see if those results generalize beyond contrasting cases; it may be, although we have our doubts, that this intervention is only effective for perceptual tasks. Finally, our results suggested that supporting joint attention between novices and experts could bring interesting results, as real-time mutual gaze perception provides a form of "inter-identity technology" (Lindgren & Pea, 2012). As followers, novices could more easily share their understanding of concepts without having to know the expert terminology; additionally, it would disambiguate experts' explanations by providing perceptual clues to novices (Hanna & Brennan, 2007).

**Acknowledgments** We gratefully acknowledge grant support from the National Science Foundation (NSF) for this work from the LIFE Center (NSF #0835854).

# References

Alavi, H. S., & Dillenbourg, P. (2012). An ambient awareness tool for supporting supervised collaborative problem solving. *IEEE Transactions on Learning Technologies, 5*(3), 264–274.

Aronson, E., Blaney, N., Sikes, J., Stephan, G., & Snapp, M. (1978). *The jigsaw classroom.* Beverly Hills: Sage Publication.

Bachour, K., Kaplan, F., & Dillenbourg, P. (2010). An interactive table for supporting participation balance in face-to-face collaborative learning. *IEEE Transactions on Learning Technologies, 3*(3), 203–213.

Bakeman, R., & Adamson, L. B. (1984). Coordinating attention to people and objects in mother-infant and peer-infant interaction. *Child Development, 55*(4), 1278–1289.

Baldwin, D. A. (1991). Infants' contribution to the achievement of joint reference. *Child Development, 62*(5), 874–890.

Barron, B. (2003). When smart groups fail. *The Journal of the Learning Sciences, 12*(3), 307–359.

Barron, B., Pea, R. D., & Engle, R. (2013). Advancing understanding of collaborative learning with data derived from video records. In C. Hmelo-Silver, A. O'Donnell, C. Chinn, & C. Chan (Eds.), *International handbook of collaborative learning* (pp. 203–219). New York: Taylor & Francis.

Barron, B., & Roschelle, J. (2009). Shared cognition. In E. Anderman (Ed.), *Psychology of classroom learning: An encyclopedia* (pp. 819–823). Detroit: Macmillan Reference USA.

Bates, E., Thal, D., Whitesell, K., Fenson, L., & Oakes, L. (1989). Integrating language and gesture in infancy. *Developmental Psychology, 25*(6), 1004–1019.

Beatty, J. (1982). Task evoked pupillary responses, processing load and structure of processing resources. *Psychological Bulletin, 91*(2), 276–292.

Beatty, J., & Lucero-Wagoner, B. (2000). Pupillary system. In J. T. Cacioppo, L. G. Tassinary, & G. Berntson (Eds.), *Handbook of psychophysiology.* New York: Cambridge University Press.

Biederman, I., & Shiffrar, M. M. (1987). Sexing day-old chicks: A case study and expert systems analysis of a difficult perceptual-learning task. *Journal of Experimental Psychology: Learning, Memory, and Cognition, 13*(4), 640–645.

Boersma, P. (2002). Praat, a system for doing phonetics by computer. *Glot International, 5*(9/10), 341–345.

Brennan, S. E., Chen, X., Dickinson, C. A., Neider, M. B., & Zelinsky, G. J. (2008). Coordinating cognition: The costs and benefits of shared gaze during collaborative search. *Cognition, 106*(3), 1465–1477.

Brooks, R., & Meltzoff, A. N. (2008). Infant gaze following and pointing predict accelerated vocabulary growth through two years of age: A longitudinal, growth curve modeling study. *Journal of Child Language, 35*(1), 207–220.

Charman, T., Baron-Cohen, S., Swettenham, J., Baird, G., Cox, A., & Drew, A. (2000). Testing joint attention, imitation, and play as infancy precursors to language and theory of mind. *Cognitive Development, 15*(4), 481–498.

Cherubini, M., Nüssli, M., & Dillenbourg, P. (2008). Deixis and gaze in collaborative work at a distance (over a shared map): a computational model to detect misunderstandings. In *Proceedings of the 2008 Symposium on Eye Tracking Research & Applications* (Savannah, Georgia, March 26–28, 2008). ETRA '08. (pp. 173–180). New York, NY: ACM.

Clark, H. H. (1996). *Using language.* Cambridge: Cambridge University Press.

Clark, H. H., & Brennan, S. E. (1991). Grounding in communication. In L. B. Resnick, J. Levine, & S. D. Teasley (Eds.), *Perspectives on socially shared cognition* (pp. 127–149). Washington, DC: American Psychological Association.

Cress, U. (2008). The need for considering multilevel analysis in CSCL research—an appeal for the use of more advanced statistical methods. *International Journal of Computer-Supported Collaborative Learning, 3*(1), 69–84.

Dillenbourg, P., Baker, M., Blaye, A., & O'Malley, C. (1996). The evolution of research on collaborative learning. In P. Reimann & H. Spada (Eds.), *Learning in humans and machine: Towards an interdisciplinary learning science* (pp. 189–211). Oxford: Elsevier.

Dodge, R., & Cline, T. S. (1901). The angle velocity of eye movements. *Psychological Review, 8*(2), 145–157.

Duchowski, A. T. (2007). *Eye tracking methodology: Theory and practice*. New York: Springer.

Hanna, J. E., & Brennan, S. E. (2007). Speakers' eye gaze disambiguates referring expressions early during face-to-face conversation. *Journal of Memory and Language, 57*(4), 596–615.

Hayes, A. F., & Krippendorff, K. (2007). Answering the call for a standard reliability measure for coding data. *Communication Methods and Measures, 1*, 77–89.

Jacob, R. J., & Karn, K. S. (2003). Eye tracking in human-computer interaction and usability research: Ready to deliver the promises. *Mind, 2*(3), 4.

Jermann, P., Mullins, D., Nuessli, M. -A., & Dillenbourg, P. (2001). Collaborative gaze footprints: correlates of interaction quality. In Spada, H., Stahl, G., Miyake, N., & Law, N. (Eds.), *Connecting Computer-Supported Collaborative Learning to Policy and Practice: CSCL2011 Conference Proceedings, Hong Kong*, July 4–8, 2011, Volume I—Long Papers, (pp. 184–191).

Kendon, A. (1990). *Conducting interaction: Patterns of behavior in focused encounters*. Cambridge: Cambridge University Press.

Kim, T., & Pentland, A. (2009, March). Understanding effects of feedback on group collaboration. In *Proceedings of the AAAI Spring Symposium on Human Behavior Modeling* (pp. 1–6).

Kreijns, K., Kirschner, P. A., & Jochems, W. (2003). Identifying the pitfalls for social interaction in computer-supported collaborative learning environments: A review of the research. *Computers in Human Behavior, 19*(3), 335–353.

Leudar, I., Costall, A., & Francis, D. (2004). Theory of mind: A critical assessment. *Theory & Psychology, 14*(5), 571–578.

Lindgren, R., & Pea, R. (2012). Inter-identity technologies for learning. *Proceedings of the International Conference of the Learning Sciences* (pp. 427–434). Sydney: Australia.

Liu, Y., Hsueh, P. Y., Lai, J., Sangin, M., Nussli, M. -A., & Dillenbourg, P. (2009, June). Who is the expert? Analyzing gaze data to predict expertise level in collaborative applications. *Proceedings of IEEE International Conference on Multimedia and Expo: ICME 2009* (pp. 898–901).

Meier, A., Spada, H., & Rummel, N. (2007). A rating scheme for assessing the quality of computer-supported collaboration processes. *International Journal of Computer-Supported Collaborative Learning, 2*(1), 63–86.

Mundy, P., Sigman, M., & Kasari, C. (1990). A longitudinal study of joint attention and language development in autistic children. *Journal of Autism and Developmental Disorders, 20*(1), 115–128.

Nüssli, M. A., Jermann, P., Sangin, M., & Dillenbourg, P. (2009). Collaboration and abstract representations: Towards predictive models based on raw speech and eye-tracking data. In *Proceedings of the 9th International Conference on Computer Supported Collaborative Learning* (pp. 78–82).

Pea, R. D. (1987). Socializing the knowledge transfer problem. *International Journal of Educational Research, 11*(6), 639–663.

Piaget, J. (1998). *The language and thought of the child*. Routledge: Psychology Press.

Preacher, K. J., & Hayes, A. F. (2008). Asymptotic and resampling strategies for assessing and comparing indirect effects in multiple mediator models. *Behavior Research Methods, 40*(3), 879.

Richardson, D. C., & Dale, R. (2005). Looking to understand: The coupling between speakers' and listeners' eye movements and its relationship to discourse comprehension. *Cognitive Science, 29*(6), 1045–1060.

Richardson, D. C., Dale, R., & Kirkham, N. Z. (2007). The art of conversation is coordination: Common ground and the coupling of eye movements during dialogue. *Psychological Science, 18*(5), 407–413.

Roth, W. M. (2001). Gestures: Their role in teaching and learning. *Review of Educational Research, 71*(3), 365–392.

Rothman, K. J. (1990). No adjustments are needed for multiple comparisons. *Epidemiology, 1*(1), 43–46.

Salomon, G., & Globerson, T. (1989). When teams do not function the way they ought to. *International Journal of Educational research, 13*(1), 89–100.

Sangin, M. (2009). *Peer knowledge modeling in computer supported collaborative learning.* (Doctoral Dissertation). Retrieved from http://infoscience.epfl.ch/record/133637. Last Access: 03/08/2013.

Schwartz, D. L. (1995). The emergence of abstract representations in dyad problem solving. *Journal of the Learning Sciences, 4*(3), 321–354.

Schwartz, D. L., & Bransford, J. D. (1998). A time for telling. *Cognition & Instruction, 16*(4), 475–522.

Schwartz, D., & Martin, T. (2004). Inventing to prepare for future learning: The hidden efficiency of encouraging original student production in statistics instruction. *Cognition and Instruction, 22*(2), 129–184.

Shaer, O., Strait, M., Valdes, C., Feng, T., Lintz, M., & Wang, H. (2011, May). Enhancing genomic learning through tabletop interaction. In *Proceedings of the SIGCHI Conference on Human Factors in Computing Systems* (pp. 2817–2826). New York: ACM.

Sheingold, K., Hawkins, J., & Char, C. (1984). "I'm the thinkist, you're the typist": The interaction of technology and the social life of classrooms. *Journal of Social Issues, 40*(3), 49–61.

Stem, D. (1977). *The first relationship.* Cambridge: Harvard University Press.

Tomasello, M. (1995). Joint attention as social cognition. In C. Moore & P. J. Dunham (Eds.), *Joint attention: Its origins and role in development* (pp. 103–130). Hillsdale: Erlbaum Associates, Inc.

Trilling, B., & Fadel, C. (2009). *21st century skills: Learning for life in our times.* New York: Wiley.

Vygotski, L. S. (1978). *Mind in society: The development of higher psychological processes.* Cambridge: Harvard University Press.

# Chapter 8
# Critical Thinking in the Field of Educational Technology: Approaches, Projects, and Challenges

Stephen C. Yanchar, Andrew S. Gibbons, Bruce W. Gabbitas, and Michael T. Matthews

Critical thinking is commonly acknowledged as an important endeavor across scholarly fields and professions. It is relevant to a wide expanse of activities and is conceptualized in a number of ways (see, for example, Ennis, 1962; McPeck, 1981). In education it is especially valued as a target skill for learners and often referred to as necessary in a new and changing world (Combs, Cennamo, & Newbill, 2009; Paul & Binker, 1990).

For many scholars and educators, critical thinking refers to thinking directed at purposefully evaluating or making judgments. Some scholars have asserted that this is achieved through the rigorous application of methods (Glaser, 1941), while others have maintained that critical thinking includes a range of analytic thought activity (Ennis, 1987; Paul, 1987). However, traditional definitions of critical thinking can fail to address important aspects of one's practice and beliefs, merely perpetuating current beliefs and ideas (Johnson, 1992; Thayer-Bacon, 2000). Some scholars have argued for critical thinking as a means of developing new perspectives, understandings, and practices. This kind of critical thinking must undertake to uncover assumptions—assumptions held by an individual engaged in practice or by a community of practitioners or assumptions embedded in a body of commonly held theories, methods, and practices. Critical thinking not only entails the explication of assumptions, but also the identification of implications of those assumptions. In this sense, critical thinking becomes a means for improving theory and practice. Additionally, engaging in such critical thinking may include, but extend beyond mere analytic thinking. After all, analytic thinking must rely on the thinking one already possesses, and as

S.C. Yanchar (✉) • A.S. Gibbons • M.T. Matthews
Instructional Psychology and Technology, Brigham Young University, Provo, UT, USA
e-mail: stephen_yanchar@byu.edu; andy_gibbons@byu.edu; mthomasmatthews@gmail.com

B.W. Gabbitas
Brigham Young University, Provo, UT, USA
e-mail: bgabbitas@gmail.com

© Springer International Publishing Switzerland 2017
M. Orey, R.M. Branch (eds.), *Educational Media and Technology Yearbook*,
Educational Media and Technology Yearbook 40,
DOI 10.1007/978-3-319-45001-8_8

such, risks merely reifying existing ideas and beliefs. Other activities can be undertaken to contribute to uncovering assumptions and discovering new perspectives.

In educational technology critical thinking has primarily received attention as a skill to be advanced in learners through a variety of techniques such as technology-mediated activities (Butchart et al., 2009), facilitated peer interactions in a learning environment (Anderson, Howe, Soden, Halliday, & Low, 2001; Chiu, 2009), and methods for scaffolding the development of critical thinking (Belland, Glazewski, & Richardson, 2008; Kim, 2015). This reflects the view that critical thinking is a useful skill that should be developed and supported in others.

However, there has been far less discussion of critical thinking as a form of professional activity within the field of educational technology. To be sure, critical thinking has played an important role in advances and development of the field, including exploring new perspectives and paradigms (Hannafin & Land, 1997; Jonassen, 1991; Spector, 2001), examining practices (McDonald & Gibbons, 2009), exploring methodologies (Amiel & Reeves, 2008), and developing tools aligned with theoretical views (Duffy & Cunningham, 1996). By focusing on critical thinking as professional activity in this chapter, we hope to highlight opportunities for growth for individuals and as a field in general. In what follows, then, we discuss critical thinking in educational technology in two steps: first, we describe two critical thinking activities that we see as particularly needed in the field; second, we identify areas of educational technology that seem to require the most penetrating critical analyses.

## Examining Assumptions and Implications

Of the many forms of critical thinking discussed across scholarly literatures, we wish to focus on two that we consider to be particularly relevant to the field of educational technology. We see these as relevant because of their emphasis on examining the meaning of core disciplinary concepts and practices that have received as yet insufficient critical scrutiny. The first critical thinking activity is concerned primarily with underlying assumptions, particularly those that provide a conceptual foundation for work in the field. The second critical thinking activity, which we will present after our discussion of assumptions, is concerned primarily with reexamining the fundamental and in many cases longstanding questions and practices of the field. More specifically, this critical thinking approach is based on Finn's assessment criteria for professionalism and offers a vehicle for assessing the state of educational technology as a field.

In contrast to critical thinking approaches that emphasize rule following—that is, approaches which emphasize the degree to which various systems of logic, methods, and procedures have been correctly followed (for a review, see Yanchar, Slife, & Warne, 2009)—assumption-based approaches seek to explore what lies beneath such prescriptions, examining the values or precepts they seem to be based on. While rule-following approaches are certainly valuable, in that they place rigorous checks on issues such as invalid logic, erroneous uses of method, and so on, they are not capable of testing their own conceptual undergirdings (Yanchar et al., 2009). For example, thinking critically about traditional experimental research methods usually entails the inspection of issues such as internal validity, sample size, and statistical analysis. Such an approach does not, on the other hand, provide resources for questioning the notion of causation that internal validity is based on (though it has been questioned in other ways) or the notion of generalizability that gives rise to concerns about proper sample size. The examinations we call for are deeper, in a sense, and demand different kinds of critical thinking activities, namely, those that are concerned with basic assumptions that guide work in the field.

This critical thinking activity has been discussed in related fields such as various subareas of psychology, though often by theoretically inclined scholars who seek to foster a critical dialogue regarding the meaning of disciplinary practices (Burgess-Limerick, Abernathy, & Limerick, 1994; Slife, Reber, & Richardson, 2005). It is hoped, from this perspective, that critical thinking and dialogue may expose assumptive frameworks that drive scholarship in a given domain, allowing those frameworks to be scrutinized regarding their implications—that is, regarding where they take practitioners and scholars who explicitly or implicitly accept them. While such analysis is often conducted by scholars associated with critical theory as a unique intellectual movement (Fox, Prilleltensky, & Austin, 2009; Leonardo, 2004; Mezirow, 2009), careful examinations of assumptions and implications are also conducted by adherents of other theoretical positions including various forms of positivism (Smith, 2002), postmodernism (Gergen, 1994), hermeneutics (Yanchar et al., 2009), and feminism (Thayer-Bacon, 2000).

Scholars who engage in this sort of critical analysis pay close attention to several categories assumptions, most commonly, those concerning the nature of human action, motivation, knowledge, development, embodiment, and ethics (e.g., Fox et al., 2009; Slife et al., 2005). Examinations such as these have proven insightful and fostered alternatives in the scholarly literature. As an example, one might consider the rise of situated learning theories (e.g., Lave & Wenger, 1991), which were introduced as significant conceptual alternatives to cognitivist views of learning. As a second example, consider Jonassen's (1991) analysis of objectivist and constructivist views of learning, which offered a useful comparison and contrast of these rival philosophical positions. More general categories of assumptions are often relevant as well, such as those pertaining to the nature of time (Slife, 1993), causation (Rychlak, 1994), technology (Davis, 2006), and sociocultural structure (Giddens, 1979). Again, critical examinations of these and related issues have yielded a number of insights and suggested alternative conceptualizations. Because this activity is designed to explicate what is often taken for granted and lay it bare for examination, has been described as one of the most fundamental or important forms of critical analysis (Brookfield, 1987; Keeley, 1992; Slife & Williams, 1995; Yanchar et al., 2009).

In the field of educational technology, the most traditionally relevant categories of assumptions would seem to have to do with knowledge, mind, human-world interactions, and technology. These are clearly at the base of prominent views of learning such as behaviorism, cognitivism, and constructivism, each of which stakes out a position on the nature of human involvement in the world with a special focus on how humans "know," as well as technologies designed to facilitate the process of knowledge or skill acquisition. Other assumptions are be relevant as well—for example those pertaining to the nature of human identity, communal interaction, and tool use—especially with regard to sociocultural and situated approaches to learning (Daniel, 2008).

One example of such critical analysis in the field was offered by McDonald, Yanchar, and Osguthorpe (2005), who explored parallels between early programmed instruction efforts and contemporary online learning. Through their examination, these authors identified several underlying assumptions of programmed instruction that, according to their analysis, led to the historical demise of this technological movement. In particular, these authors identified assumptions traditionally associated with behaviorism such as social efficiency, ontological determinism, and technological determinism (Delprato & Midgley, 1992; Smith, 1992). Importantly, through this critical examination, these authors identified similar assumptions among many examples of contemporary online instruction, suggesting that they tend to suffer from the same deficiencies as programmed instruction. As a result of this analysis, the authors offered a number of suggestions on how to avoid these assumptions and their negative affects, including a set of critical questions that designers can ask themselves in order to examine their own assumptions and possibly avoid those that appear to be problematic.

It is important to add, however, that this form of critical thinking involves more than the identification of underlying assumptions and an examination of their implications; it is facilitated by comparing the identified assumptions and implications with others in other to provide an illuminating contrast. Often the meaning and consequences of a given assumption's implications becomes clearest when compared against others with different implications. For example, assumptions found in cognitive information-processing models (e.g., acquisition, commoditization, mechanism) are revealed when contrasted with those of constructivist (Jonassen, 1991) or situated learning (Bredo, 1994) approaches. As Sfard (1998) noted, metaphors such as *knowledge acquisition* often do not seem like metaphors at all until compared with others. Indeed, such comparison and contrast is a vital way to clarify ideas and explore where they take those who follow them.

## Finn's Criteria for Professionalism

In the early 1950s, James D. Finn, then Chairman of the Department of Audio-Visual Instruction (DAVI) of the National Educational Association (NEA), noted the increasing specialization of education-related occupations, including "administration, psychologists, curriculum consultants, counselors, and other educational specialists" (Finn, 1953, p. 6). He noted also the emergence of an occupational group "whose main responsibility lies in the preparation, distribution, and use of audio-visual materials" (p. 6). In his article, titled "Professionalizing the Audio-Visual Field," Finn saw this latter group as "unique," in that their concerns cut across all branches of communication and technology, "bringing new disciplines to bear upon the problems of education" (p. 6).

Finn called for increased professionalism in this emerging specialty. His 1953 article was the first of a series of papers written over nearly a decade, as the A-V field transitioned into the professional community today called Educational Technology (Finn, 1953, 1957a, 1957b, 1960a, 1960b, 1962).

At the beginning of this period, the computer was being explored by scientists and psychologists (from outside the A-V field) for its educational potential (Atkinson & Wilson, 1969). By 1962, Finn was describing a new armada of technological innovations that were being ignored by philosophers of education, he felt, because they found them "trivial" and even "dangerous" (p. 30).

From the beginning, Finn urged the A-V field to develop its professionalism by critically examining itself in six areas. Of the six, three are of importance to this discussion of critical thinking: (a) using "an intellectual technique" (p. 2), (b) applying the technique to solve humankind's problems, and (c) possessing "an organized body of intellectual theory constantly expanded by research" (p. 2). These, said Finn, were critical tools of a true profession. For comparison purposes, Finn held up examples of professional fields such as medicine, law, accounting, and engineering.

In his 1953 paper, Finn assessed the state of the art as he saw it, addressing the question: How close is A-V [today educational technology] to being legitimized as a profession? To enable critical thinking regarding the status of educational technology, we suggest questions that members of the educational technology community can use today to assess for themselves the state of the art in educational technology with respect to these three of Finn's criteria, from a 60-year vantage point.

To frame our questions, we will appeal to categories of design knowledge suggested by Vincenti (1990) in his book *What Engineers Know and How They Know It*. Vincenti's categories represent types of knowledge designers in any design field typically use. These categories define focal points for further conversations on Finn's question: "How well does educational technology meet the criteria for being a professional field?" In the quoted text below, in places where Vincenti has used the term "device," we have substituted the term "artifact," which we believe preserves Vincenti's meaning without conveying the notion that educational technologists design only devices. We likewise substitute the term "designer" in place of Vincenti's use of the term "engineer."

## Finn's Intellectual Technique Criterion

The intellectual technique of a field consists its ability to intellectualize its content in ways that lead to the logical, consistent application of principles, as well as connecting key abstractions with elements of practical applications. In this respect,

Finn cited activities such as "think[ing] reflectively," "critical evaluation," and "visualization of abstract concepts" (p. 8). Today, we might refer to this as the ability of a field to engage in critical thinking about itself. Critical thinking is associated with a cloud of intellectual processes by which ideas and processes are formulated, expressed, examined, questioned, tested, proven, discussed, and used within a field.

In our opinion, five of Vincenti's knowledge categories fit under Finn's intellectual technique umbrella. Each category suggests questions about the state of our professional knowledge base.

## Fundamental Design Concepts

Vincenti groups two types of professional knowledge under the heading of fundamental design concepts: Operational Principles, and Normal Configurations. Vincenti describes them in this way: "Designers setting out in any normal design bring with them fundamental concepts about the device [artifact] in question" (p. 208).

## Operational Principles

Operational principle knowledge pertains to "how the [artifact] works" (p. 208). By this, Vincenti means the manner in which an artifact channels energies and information to the point where are applied to accomplish the work.

A visible physical structure, like a building, represents a balance of numerous opposing forces working invisibly to create a stable edifice. Changes in applied forces shift the inner balance of the structure, either strengthening it or weakening it. Likewise, invisible forces that are conveyed through visible means impact the state of mind of a learner. Changes in the balance of forces perceived by a learner shift the learner's state of mind in the direction of either greater understanding or greater processing load and possible confusion. According to Vincenti, "[designers] dealing with any [artifact] must… know its operational principle to carry out normal design" (p. 209). Questions educational technologists should consider include:

- To what extent does educational technology literature deal with the hidden forces at work within the visible means of their technology?
- Do educational technologists have the research tools to ferret out these invisible forces and how visible means apply them?

## Normal Configurations

Vincenti defines normal configurations as "the general shape and arrangement that are commonly agreed to best embody the operational principle" (p. 209). Automotive designers use the concept of "platform" to describe normal configurations. A platform is a standard basic design, which is then featured differently to create visibly distinct models, perhaps by installing a more powerful engine or a different transmission. To the public, platforms fall into categories like "SUV," "van," or "pickup." In this way, the designer's categories of platform result in vehicle categories users want to buy. Questions educational technologists should consider include:

- Are educational technologists aware of the normal configuration concept?
- Do designers have shared normal configurations of educational artifact?
- Do designers use the platform concept to create artifact variations that consumers desire to use?
- Are shared normal configurations useful in an increasingly competitive educational marketplace?

## Criteria and Specifications

Criteria and specifications bridge abstract ideas with real world designs. Criteria "translate the general, qualitative goals for the [artifact] into specific, quantitative goals couched in concrete technical terms" (Vincenti, p. 211). For example, Vincenti explains that the concept of a bridge to carry traffic over a river has to be translated "into specific span and loading requirements" that have "numerical values or limits" (p. 211).

Educational technologists are benefitting from the new concept of learning analytics that suggests that techniques for numerical analysis may, over time, be perfected for the detection and prediction of learner needs, and interaction patterns that match them. This may in turn lead to increased specificity in the description of designs. Questions educational technologists should consider include:

- Do we presently have adequate principles for specifying goals and criteria for outcomes for which designs are being created?
- Do we have methods (and terminology) for detecting (and characterizing) learner needs at any given point in time?
- Do we have languages for describing the characteristics of design elements in terms of the positive learning forces they generate?
- Do we have languages for describing how detected needs can be matched with relevant recommendations for learning experiences?

## Design Instrumentalities

Design instrumentalities include "knowing how," "procedural knowledge," "ways of thinking," and "judgmental skills," according to Vincenti (p. 219). "They give [designers] the power, not only to effect designs where the form of the solution is clear at the outset, but also to seek solutions where some element of novelty is required" (p. 219). Design instrumentalities comprise what a design profession knows about how to design solutions to its problems.

Educational technologists have relied upon systematic design approaches for over 50 years. Recently, new approaches to design have joined them, along with new ways of describing designer thinking and design reasoning (Boling & Gray, 2014; Boling & Smith, 2012; Dorst, 2015; Gibbons, 2014; Gibbons & Yanchar, 2010; Lawson & Dorst, 2009; Rowland, 1993; Smith & Boling, 2009). Likewise, new ways of describing the identity of the designer, design ethics, and the designer's role have emerged (Campbell & Schwier, 2009; Hokanson, Clinton, & Tracey, 2015; Hokanson & Gibbons, 2014; Parrish, 2007, 2008). Since designing implies an understanding of what is being designed, literature trying to describe the nature of learning artifacts is relevant as well (Gibbons, 2003; Krippendorff, 2006).

More mature design professions still have lively internal debates on all of these issues, which often are sources of philosophical and technical innovation within those fields. Educational technologists can profit from looking at design as it is practiced in other fields, while asking:

- Does educational technology have a clear conception of the nature of designing as it applies to educational artifacts and experiences?
- Does educational technology have a clear vocabulary for describing the kinds of artifacts it designs?
- Has educational technology done due diligence to the questions of design competence, design process, design thinking, and design judgment?
- Are there distinguishable levels of design practice that are relevant to the certification of practitioners?
- Are training requirements for different levels of practice well defined?
- What constitute appropriate philosophical and theoretical bases for descriptions of design instrumentalities?

## *Practical Considerations*

Practical considerations, according to Vincenti, represent uncodified, imprecise knowledge, often derived from practical experience rather than research, that is nonetheless a part of expert practice. Practical considerations "do not lend themselves to theorizing, tabulation, or programming into a computer." This kind of knowledge is normally "hard to find written down," and "more or less unconsciously" carried around in designers' minds (p. 217).

A great deal of the knowledge of educational technologists is of this kind. This is typical of a design field in its early development, especially one in which the design problems are what Jonassen called "wicked" (Jonassen, 2004). Wicked problems are not unique to instructional design (see, for example, Rittel & Webber, 1973). It is the non-verbalized, somewhat unconscious nature of the knowledge of a field that makes learning by apprenticeship attractive, and in some cases even necessary (Lave & Wenger, 1991). Fields such as medicine, law, accounting, and engineering today rely on intensive training programs followed by varying degrees of apprenticing. This has not always been the case, and these professions originally all relied on extended apprenticeship experience.

Since they have a particularly invested interest in practical considerations, and since Finn gave as one of his criteria for professional status "a period of long training necessary before entering into the profession" (Finn, 1953, p. 7), educational technologists should be interested in questions like:

- How can a design field aspiring to be professional decrease its reliance on practical considerations and codify its knowledge to a greater extent?
- What kinds of knowledge are required for both theoretical and practical practice in a profession?
- How can programmatic and cooperative research serve to focus and accelerate research aimed at codifying the professional knowledge base in educational technology?

## Finn's Criterion of Applying Intellectual Technique to Solving Problems

The second area of professionalization named by Finn (1953) pertaining to educational technology was an application of intellectual technique to solving humankind's problems. The question of whether educational technology is solving problems can be addressed from different points of view. Indisputably, educational technology is being applied today for educational purposes to an unprecedented degree in virtually every learning venue. The question is whether this is due to the success of "technology" in noticeably improving educational effects, or simply to the everywhere-ness of computer technologies, which are rapidly swallowing all other forms of A-V. Those who grew up in educational technology before the computer remember that the early struggle to achieve adoptions of new technologies was ideological as well as economic. Today, that struggle is much less a matter of convincing stubborn minds and more one of obtaining funds.

Not everyone is convinced that educational technologies like the computer have succeeded in improving learning. Cuban (2001), summarizing a study of the K-12 application of computer technology in the Silicon Valley area, reports: "no advances (measured by higher education achievement of urban, suburban, or rural students) over the last decade can be confidently attributed to broader access to computers" (n.p.). Further, he reports, "the link between test score improvements and computer availability and use is even more contested" (n.p.). He also reports finding no effect on either student or teacher productivity. Similarly, a recent OECD report "Students, Computers, and Learning: Making the Connection" (OECD, 2015) concludes that high expectations of learning improvement through implementation of computers in international classrooms were not supported.

Positive expectations of large-scale computer implementations are sometimes economically motivated. Sometimes the economics can be traced directly to sponsorship by a computer or publishing company. Sometimes political ownership by a government or a school district is a motive. In some cases, subtle connections are traceable, as in a report by the New York Times which showed that the benefit to one school district, which knew that its learning scores had stagnated in comparison with the state, came from "using its computer-centric classes as a way to attract children from around the region, shoring up enrollment [even] as its student population shrinks" (Richtel, 2015, n.p.).

It is largely agreed that media comparison studies have little value, so if technologists wish to demonstrate that their artifacts and interventions have an impact on the problems of humankind, they must make an argument that they employ improved technique rather than technology. This is perhaps a conversation that should be taken up among educational technologists themselves, many of whom are more attracted to the charismatic "gadget" than the actual result demonstrated by research and linked to theory. Reeves (2011) noted that many studies "confound educational delivery modes with pedagogical methods" (n.p.). He notes Bransford's recommendation that:

To heighten the relevance of research that would have demonstrable impact of the kind and level heretofore missing in education, a refocusing of research and educational designs on the fundamental concerns of the practitioner is necessary (Reeves, 2011, n.p.).

As educational technologists discuss among themselves ways they can make their research, theory, and practice more readily applicable to solving humankind's problems, they should also consider other barriers to acceptance. The first is willingness to dialogue with other design fields and adopters of technology in a collegial manner. Selwyn (2014) notes that:

> Unlike most other fields of academic study, educational technology appears particularly resistant to viewpoints that contradict its core beliefs and values—not the least the orthodoxy that technology is a potential force for positive change" (p. 12).

A second issue, also noted by Selwyn, is a kind of arrogance that can be traced to the earliest days of the educational technology field:

> Educational technology has… become a curiously closed field of study—populated by people who consider themselves to be in the somehow more informed position of properly understanding the educational potential of digital technology. This can sometimes lead writers and researchers to adopt an intellectual stance that is evangelical—if not righteousness—in its advocacy of this 'truth' (p. 12).

Educational technologists in one sense *need* to feel defensive about having a profession that dissolves so easily into other professions. Every rocket scientist can jump into instructional design, but educational technologists do not even think about designing rockets. At the same time, if educational technologists had intellectual content that would give a rocket scientist pause, then it might be easier to feel more at ease and less defensive with them. One of the purposes of this writing is to remind educational technologists of the immense task before them in that respect.

## Finn's Criterion of Intellectual Theory Constantly Expanded by Research

Finn found the most important shortfall of educational technology in 1953 to be in the area of theory: its development and application. Specifically, he called for "an organized body of intellectual theory constantly expanding by research" (p. 7). Vincenti's knowledge category of theoretical tools seems most closely related to Finn's concern for a body of formal theory and an accompanying research process to extend it.

## *Theoretical Tools*

Vincenti's category of theoretical tools includes "intellectual concepts for thinking about design as well as mathematical methods and theories for making design calculations" (p. 213). Vincenti points out the scope implied by these tools by explaining that "both the concepts and the methods cover a spectrum running all the way from things generally regarded as part of science to items of particularly engineering character" (p. 213).

## *Intellectual Concepts for Thinking About Design*

Theory is an undeniable feature of the educational technology landscape, but it is a topic with which a surprising number of educational technologists feel uneasy. There are many attempts to define theory in relation to technological applications (Gibbons, 2014; Merrill, 1994; Reigeluth, 1983, 1999; Reigeluth & Carr-Chellman, 2009; Richie, 1986; Richie, Klein, & Tracey, 2011; Snelbecker, 1974; Snow, 1977).

Some link educational design directly to learning theory, while others propose that there is a species of theory especially suited just to designing. Most educational technologists are taught learning theory and told that it should be applied in designs, but there is little guidance in the educational technology literature about how to accomplish that. In the meantime, a body of literature has grown that prefers the term "instructional theory." It is hard to find a clear distinction between instructional theory and learning theory and how they differ in their impact on educational designs.

Strangely little of the publication on theory in educational technology literature has the flavor of a discussion. For example, surprisingly little attention is paid in the educational technology literature to early attempts to promote technological theory from noted authors such as Gage (1964), Bruner (1964, 1966), Glaser (1964), and Lumsdaine (1964). Some of these authors were writing within the paradigm of stimulus–response psychology, and some were not. Nonetheless, many of the observations from both sides sound almost current. For example, Bruner wrote, "a theory of instruction ... is concerned with how one wishes to teach, with improving, rather than describing learning (Bruner, 1964, p. 307). Likewise, Gage stated: "while theories of learning deal with ways in which an organism learns, theories of teaching deal with the ways in which a person influences an organism to learn" (p. 268). Gage went on to propose that, "practical applications have not been gleaned from theories of learning largely because theories of teaching have not been developed" (p. 271). It is important to note that Skinner described his theory of reinforcements as an "instructional theory" rather than a "learning theory." Despite this, Skinner is taught as a learning theory in many graduate programs.

Individual expressions of instructional theory such as those of Merrill (2009), Mayer (2009), van Merrienboer (2007), and others are common. Reigeluth's theory books (Reigeluth, 1983, 1999; Reigeluth & Carr-Chellman, 2009) are an effort to unify theoretical concepts for practitioners. Likewise, Richie et al. (2011) attempt a synthesis. But there is little writing in the literature directed to practitioners about how to unify, connect, and compare theories on their own. Bostwick et al. (2014) attempt to address this issue. Uncertainties about theory seem to have a negative impact on practice. Research indicates that the average instructional designer tends to be confused about theory and tends to ignore the issue of theory, using instead models of other existing products (Cox & Osguthorpe, 2003; Rowland, 2008; Yanchar, South, Williams, Allen, & Wilson, 2010).

Finn was concerned with the state of theory in 1953. He stated that, "on the important test of theory the audio-visual field does not meet professional standards" (p. 15). The extra attention given to theory in this section is meant to illustrate that the degree of uncertainty about theory today may still be a concern. The trial-and-error methods of development predominant in 1953 continued to be embodied in the empirical methods for programmed instruction development of the 1960s, and they are apparent in the systematic design textbooks of today in the form of an emphasis on the tryout and revise cycle at every stage of development. The same design texts have less to say about the application of theory up-front in the design process that might shorten evaluation cycles and reduce the amount of reworking required. Finn criticizes the texts of his day because the theory they appealed to was fragmentary and did not include notions contained in the research literature.

Finn's concerns about research were equally strong. He notes that, "research pertinent to audio-visual education is published throughout the literature of the social sciences and need a staff of detectives to trace it down" (p. 15). His concern was that research results were "inaccessible to the practicing worker" (p. 15). He also noted the lack of evidence that research is influencing the formation of theory. He stated:

> The audio-visual field is in the peculiar position of having much of its research carried on by workers in other disciplines using hypotheses unknown to many audio-visual workers, and reporting results in journals that audio-visual people do not read and at meetings audio-visual people do not attend (p. 16).

In matters of theory and research, Finn contrasts the field of his day with other professional fields like medicine, finding this aspect of the field most lacking. If the state of the art today in research and the development of theory has changed, it is for the educational technology community to determine. As they consider this issue, this question may stimulate a conversation around this question:

- Does educational technology as a field hoping to be considered a profession have a clear concept of what theory is, what kinds there may be, how it is generated, how it relates to research, and how it finds its way into the practices of the average designer?

## *Quantitative Data*

Vincenti points out that even when designers know how to design theoretically they must use materials that have properties that are best described in quantitative form: "such data, essential for design, are usually obtained empirically, though in some cases they may be calculated theoretically" (p. 216). For many educational technologists, their product is in one sense material—consisting of files, programs, and other resources—but in another sense immaterial—consisting of activities, events, and experiences. At the same time, new statistical and computer technologies are able to quantify properties of experience that were not possible 10 years ago. Advances in voice recognition permit the detection of stress; advances in visual analysis permit the recognition of faces and to some extent emotions expressed on faces; advances in statistical analysis permit the recognition of subtle patterns in user responding. These technologies and many others are in their primitive state, but emphasis on their development is high. As educational technologists consider these maturing technologies, they might ask questions like these: What variables of the learner might be useful to monitor and quantify? What kinds of algorithms will make these variables useful during and after instructional experiences?

## Important Topics for Critical Analysis

As a core disciplinary activity, critical thinking can allow for greater understanding of the field's ideas and practices and facilitate progress in a number of areas. In this section, we suggest some of the areas of the field that would benefit from critical inspection of the sorts we have described here.

## The Nature of Human Action

One area of the field that would benefit from critical analysis is assumptions regarding human action, and particularly, human motivation and agency. It seems reasonable to contend that, in order to help humans learn, designers and teachers should know what (or who) they are trying to help—that is, they need a viable concept of humanness and human learning. Some learning theories, for instance, have likened humans to animals (as in behaviorism) or machines (as in cognitivism. In both of these perspectives, human action is explained as being determined by environmental forces acting on individuals (Slife & Williams, 1995). It has been argued that his deterministic assumption, when adopted as the basis for practical design work in the field, often leads to products similar to what was witnessed in the early programmed instruction movement—an educational movement that ultimately failed (McDonald et al., 2005).

Previous writers within educational technology have encouraged both a search for a defensible philosophical foundation for the field (Evans, 2011; Jonassen, 1991; Spector, 2001) and consideration of perspectives that assume human agency instead of determinism (Jonassen et al., 1997). As a step in this direction, we recommend a careful examination of agentic and deterministic ways of conceptualizing humans and human learning, and particularly of how such conceptualizations might influence the design of instruction. For example, how might an instructional design be different if based on the assumptions of self-determination theory (Deci & Ryan, 2002), or some other agency-oriented perspective? Furthermore, if deterministic accounts of learners and learning eliminate the possibility for meaningful human action (Williams, 1992), then accounts of human agency and learning that emphasize that meaningfulness (e.g., Yanchar, Spackman, & Faulconer, 2013) may serve to stimulate further discussion of this issue. Critical examinations and discussions of these issues raise the possibility that agency and deterministic perspective can be better understood, applied, and tested in the context of educational technology. Such examinations offer practitioners and scholars in the field can then base their work on clearer views of human learning and human existence per se.

## Inquiry Methods

Another aspect of the field that would benefit from such critical analyses are various conceptions of research and specific inquiry methods. If the purpose of educational technology is to help learners learn in some sense, then the way learners are conceptualized is key to how they will be studied. As a number of analyses have suggested, any method for studying the world will be based on assumptions and values regarding the target phenomenon and how it exists (Gadamer, 1989; Heideger, 1962; Slife & Williams, 1995; Yanchar & Williams, 2006); thus, an empirical method assumes empirical phenomena, a phenomenological method assumes intentional contents of consciousness, a narrative method assume narratively constructed life experiences, and so on. The logical extension of this basic insight is that a method will only produce findings that are consistent with its assumptions—empirical methods can only produce empirical findings, and so on. While this is obvious in some sense, it also suggests that, in a general way, use of any method ends where it begins—a notion that one observer referred to as the methodological circle (Danziger, 1985). While a study's findings are surely refined, clarified versions of the initial assumptions and hunches of researchers, and include the results of empirical tests, they are not capable of testing empiricism itself, because this assumption is presupposed in the very testing it performs.

Many methods commonly drawn from the social sciences, for instance, are based on the idea that human behavior, including learning behavior, is a lawfully governed phenomenon and should be studied with methods that are designed to provide explanations of the forces that cause human behavior to transpire in a given way under certain circumstances. These methods also commonly assume that what is real is what can be detected via the physical senses—that is, some sort of physical object or process—and thus all relevant phenomena are basically empirical in nature. If not strictly empirical, then a phenomenon of interest must be translated into some measureable operations that are empirical through the use of operational definitions. Thus, such methods—variations on the theme of experimentation—are based on determinism and empiricism, among other assumptions (Slife, 1998).

If scholars within educational technology use these methods, they are implicitly or explicitly engaging in a project that is based on these underlying assumptions; that is, they are using a method that is historically and philosophically designed to fit, and be effective, within a world in which empiricism and determinism are fundamentally real. The method is an appropriate choice for such a world because it was designed to be effective within it.

However, if scholars are not sure that this is the best way to conceive of human action and related phenomena such as learning, then they may wish to explore other inquiry approaches; and a primary way to conduct this exploration is by examining the assumptions of alternative methods, such as various forms of qualitative inquiry, design cases, and so on. While some of these alternative methods may already have been analyzed in this regard and have fairly well-studied assumptive groundings (e.g., phenomenology) that should be considered, others have not (design cases) and thus are in need of just this kind of examination. From our perspective, it is entirely within the purview of educational technology scholarship to perform these kinds of critical analyses. Moreover, resources that can facilitate this kind of examination are available in the social science (e.g., Slife & Williams, 1995; Yanchar & Slife, 2004) and education research (e.g., Paul & Elder, 2002) literatures.

## Professionalism

Finally, in the spirit of Finn's call for professionalism, we briefly identify a number of activities that would allow for educational technology as a profession to be more self-critical and self-aware.

- To be aware of and draw an accurate and detailed history of its own past, its evolution, and its current issues and focusing questions.
- To critically reflect on its history, taking lessons from wrong turns and dead ends openly and honestly.

- To realistically appraise its current state of practice and its areas needing improvement.
- To provide a system for reviewing new ideas, testing them, and assimilating ones that pass the test.
- To revisit and reexamine the fundamental intellectual concepts and assumptions of the field periodically in the light of new knowledge produced in other fields.
- To help set profession-wide goals and voice its aspirations and vision, for the purposes of stimulating productive research and marking progress.
- To welcome and nurture innovative ideas, providing innovation forums where new concepts and processes can be proposed and tested.
- To provide channels to carry proven ideas, methods, theories, and processes from the laboratory into daily practice.
- To establish standards and levels for practice and methods for regulating and certifying members of the profession, including standards for training professionals.
- To provide impartial judging of professional communications, avoiding control of communications from falling into the hands of commercial, political, or social interests.
- To provide methods for detecting and sanctioning malpractice and unethical practices.
- To defend the distinction between professional practice and folk- or popular practice.
- To define acceptable research standards, adopting new methods and technical tools as soon as they are demonstrated effective and reliable.
- To constantly survey neighboring professional fields, investigating innovations, theory, knowledge, and regulatory methods that might be relevant.

## Final Remarks

As we have suggested, the field of educational technology has many dimensions that are worthy of careful critical examination, the results of which would more defensibly ground the field philosophically, and strengthen the legitimacy of the field academically and professionally. However, critical analysis focused on personal as well as disciplinary assumptions can be difficult and demanding. It can be challenging for individuals to question their reasons for doing what they do, and in larger groups with a reasonably long institutional history, that tendency may be multiplied.

However, the process of training future instructional designers holds one potential key in helping the field to critically examine its practices. From our perspective, instructional design programs across the nation could include a course on such critical thinking in their curricula, and thus facilitate this important kind of inspection. However, we also suggest that Instead of teaching critical thinking in a single place in our curricula, opportunities for critical analysis could be embedded throughout the training of instructional design students. According to Wenger (1998), the generational encounter inherent in the training of newcomers to any community of practice can potentially both perpetuate past practices as well as introduce innovative insights. There is thus an opportunity for critical reflection and analysis of the field in every course of every instructional design program, and students in such critically focused programs could bring much to the field, and themselves be benefitted all the more by participating in this way.

Even if critical thinking of this sort cannot be adequately addressed in often-overburdened training programs, the pursuit of clarity, awareness, and self-examination can be a continual ideal toward which professionals in the field strive. The kinds of reflection we suggest, whenever they occur, and however they may be facilitated, are a major step in the field's progress into a future that calls for creative, forward-thinking educational technologists.

# References

Amiel, T., & Reeves, T. C. (2008). Design-based research and educational technology: Rethinking technology and the research agenda. *Educational Technology & Society, 11*(4), 29–40.

Anderson, T., Howe, C., Soden, R., Halliday, J., & Low, J. (2001). Peer interaction and the learning of critical thinking skills in further education students. *Instructional Science, 29*(1), 1–32.

Atkinson, R., & Wilson, H. (1969). *Computer-assisted instruction: A book of readings*. New York: Academic.

Belland, B., Glazewski, K., & Richardson, J. (2008). A scaffolding framework to support the construction of evidence-based arguments among middle school students. *Educational Technology Research & Development, 56*(4), 401–422.

Boling, E., & Gray, C. (2014). Design: The topic that should not be closed. *TechTrends, 58*(6), 17–19.

Boling, E., & Smith, K. M. (2012). The changing nature of design. In R. Reiser & J. V. Dempsey (Eds.), *Trends and issues in instructional design technology* (3rd ed.). New York: Pearson.

Bostwick, J., Calvert, I., Francis, J., Hawkley, M., Henrie, C., Hyatt, F., et al. (2014). A process for critical analysis of instructional theory. *Education Technology Research and Development, 62*, 571–582.

Bredo, E. (1994). Reconstructing educational psychology: Situated cognition and Deweyian pragmatism. *Educational Psychologist, 29*, 23–35.

Brookfield, S. (1987). *Developing critical thinkers: Challenging adults to explore alternative ways of thinking*. San Francisco: Jossey Bass.

Bruner, J. S. (1964). Some theorems on instruction illustrated with reference to mathematics. In E. R. Hilgard (Ed.), *Theories of learning and instruction: The sixty-third yearbook of the national society for the study of education* (pp. 306–335). Chicago, IL: University of Chicago Press.

Bruner, J. S. (1966). *Toward a theory of instruction*. Cambridge, MA: Harvard University Press.

Burgess-Limerick, R., Abernathy, B., & Limerick, B. (1994). Identification of underlying assumptions is an integral part of research: An example from motor control. *Theory and Psychology, 4*, 139–146.

Butchart, S., Forster, D., Gold, I., Bigelow, J., Korb, K., Oppy, G., et al. (2009). Improving critical thinking using web based argument mapping exercises with automated feedback. *Australasian Journal of Educational Technology, 25*(2), 268–291.

Campbell, K., & Schwier, R. (2009). The critical relational practice of instructional design in higher education: An emerging model of change agency. *Educational Technology Research and Development, 57*, 645–663.

Chiu, Y.-C. J. (2009). Facilitating Asian students' critical thinking in online discussions. *British Journal of Educational Technology, 40*(1), 42–57.

Combs, L. B., Cennamo, K. S., & Newbill, P. L. (2009). Developing critical and creative thinkers: Toward a conceptual model of creative and critical thinking processes. *Educational Technology, 49*(5), 3–14.

Cox, S., & Osguthorpe, R. T. (2003). How do instructional design professionals spend their time? *TechTrends, 47*(3), 45–47.

Cuban, L. (2001). *Oversold and underused: Computers in the classroom*. Cambridge, MA: Harvard University Press.

Daniel, H. (2008). *Vygotsky and research*. New York: Routledge.

Danziger, K. (1985). The methodological imperative in psychology. *Philosophy of the Social Sciences, 15*, 1–13.

Davis, G. H. (2006). *Means without ends*. Lanham, MD: University Press of America.

Deci, E. L., & Ryan, R. M. (2002). *Handbook of self-determination research*. Rochester, NY: University of Rochester Press.

Delprato, D. J., & Midgley, B. D. (1992). Some fundamentals of B. F. Skinner's behaviorism. *American Psychologist, 47*(11), 1507–1520.

Dorst, K. (2015). *Frame innovation*. Cambridge, MA: The MIT Press.

Duffy, T. M., & Cunningham, D. J. (1996). Constructivism: Implications for the design and delivery of instruction. In D. H. Jonassen (Ed.), *Handbook of research for educational communications and technology* (pp. 170–198). New York: Simon & Schuster.

Ennis, R. H. (1962). A concept of critical thinking. *Harvard Educational Review, 32*(1), 81–111.

Ennis, R. H. (1987). A taxonomy of critical thinking dispositions and abilities. In J. B. Baron & R. J. Sternberg (Eds.), *Teaching thinking skills: Theory and practice* (pp. 9–26). New York: W.H. Freeman.

Evans, M. A. (2011). A critical-realist response to the postmodern agenda in instructional design and technology: A way forward. *Educational Technology Research and Development, 59*(6), 799–815. doi:10.1007/s11423-011-9194-5.

Finn, J. (1953). Professionalizing the audio-visual field. *Audiovisual Communication Review, 1*(1), 6–17.

Finn, J. (1957a). Automation and education: I. General aspects. *Audiovisual Communication Review, 5*(1), 343–360.

Finn, J. (1957b). Automation and education: II. Automatizing the classroom—background of the effort. *Audiovisual Communication Review, 5*(2), 451–467.

Finn, J. (1960a). Automation and education: III. Technology and the instructional process. *Audiovisual Communication Review, 8*(1), 5–26.

Finn, J. (1960b). A new theory for instructional technology. *Audiovisual Communication Review, 8*(6), 84–94.

Finn, J. (1962). A walk on the altered side. *Phi Delta Kappan, 44*(1), 29–34.

Fox, D., Prilleltensky, I., & Austin, S. (Eds.). (2009). *Critical psychology: An introduction* (2nd ed.). London: Sage Publications.

Gadamer, H. G. (1989). *Truth and method* (2nd ed.). New York: Continuum (original work published 1975).

Gage, N. L. (1964). Theories of teaching. In E. R. Hilgard (Ed.), *Theories of learning and instruction: The sixty-third yearbook of the national society for the study of education* (pp. 268–285). Chicago, IL: University of Chicago Press.

Gergen, K. J. (1994). *Realities and relationships: Soundings in social construction*. Cambridge, MA: Harvard University Press.

Gibbons, A. S. (2003). What and how do designers design? A theory of design structure. *TechTrends, 47*(5), 22–27.

Gibbons, A. S. (2014). *An architectural approach to instructional design*. New York: Routledge.

Gibbons, A. S., & Yanchar, S. (2010). An alternative view of the instructional design process: A response to Smith and Boling. *Educational Technology, 50*(4), 16–26.

Giddens, A. (1979). *Central problems in social theory*. London: Macmillan.

Glaser, E. M. (1941). *An experiment in the development of critical thinking*. New York: Teachers College.

Glaser, R. (1964). Implications of training research for education. In E. R. Hilgard (Ed.), *Theories of learning and instruction: The sixty-third yearbook of the national society for the study of education* (pp. 153–181). Chicago, IL: University of Chicago Press.

Hannafin, M. J., & Land, S. M. (1997). The foundations and assumptions of technology-enhanced student-centered learning environments. *Instructional Science, 25*(3), 167–202. doi:10.102 3/A:1002997414652.

Heideger, M. (1962). *Being and time*. New York: Harper & Row.

Hokanson, B., Clinton, G., & Tracey, M. (2015). *The design of learning experience: Creating the future of educational technology*. New York: Springer.

Hokanson, B., & Gibbons, A. S. (2014). *Design in educational technology: Design thinking, design process, and the design studio*. New York: Springer.

Johnson, R. H. (1992). The problem of defining critical thinking. In S. P. Norris (Ed.), *The generalizability of critical thinking: Multiple perspectives on an educational ideal* (pp. 38–53). New York: Teachers College Press.

Jonassen, D. H. (1991). Objectivism versus constructivism: Do we need a new philosophical paradigm? *Educational Technology Research and Development, 39*(3), 5–14.

Jonassen, D. H. (2004). *Learning to solve problems: An instructional design guide*. New York: Pfeiffer/Wiley.

Jonassen, D. H., Hennon, R. J., Ondrusek, A., Samouilova, M., Spaulding, K. L., Yueh, H. P., et al. (1997). Certainty, determinism, and predictability in theories of instructional design: Lessons from science. *Educational Technology, 37*(1), 27–34.

Keeley, S. M. (1992). Are college students learning the critical thinking skill of finding assumptions? *College Student Journal, 26*, 316–322.

Kim, N. (2015). Critical thinking in wikibook creation with enhanced and minimal scaffolds. *Educational Technology Research & Development, 63*(1), 5–33.

Krippendorff, K. (2006). *The semantic turn: A new foundation for design*. New York: CRC/Taylor & Francis.

Lave, J., & Wenger, E. (1991). *Situated learning: Legitimate peripheral participation*. New York: Cambridge University Press.

Lawson, B., & Dorst, K. (2009). *Design expertise*. Oxford, UK: Elsevier.

Leonardo, Z. (2004). Critical social theory and transformative knowledge: The function of criticism in quality education. *Educational Researcher, 33*(6), 11–18.

Lumsdaine, A. A. (1964). Educational technology, programmed learning, and instructional science. In E. R. Hilgard (Ed.), *Theories of learning and instruction: The sixty-third yearbook of the national society for the study of education* (pp. 371–401). Chicago, IL: University of Chicago Press.

Mayer, R. E. (2009). *Multimedia learning* (2nd ed.). New York: Cambridge University Press.

McDonald, J., & Gibbons, A. (2009). Technology I, II, and III: Criteria for understanding and improving the practice of instructional technology. *Educational Technology Research & Development, 57*(3), 377–392.

McDonald, J. K., Yanchar, S. C., & Osguthorpe, R. T. (2005). Learning from programmed instruction: Examining implications for modern instructional technology. *Educational Technology Research and Development, 53*(2), 84–98.

McPeck, J. (1981). *Critical thinking and education*. Oxford: Oxford University Press.

Merrill, M. D. (1994). *Instructional design theory*. Englewood Cliffs, NJ: Educational Technology.

Merrill, M. D. (2009). First principles of instruction. In C. M. Reigeluth & A. Carr-Chellman (Eds.), *Instructional design theories and models: Building a common knowledge base* (Vol. III). New York: Routledge.

Mezirow, J. (2009). *Transformative learning in practice: Insights from community, workplace, and higher education*. San Francisco: Jossey-Bass.

OECD (2015). *Students, computers, and learning: Making the connection.* Organization for Economic Cooperation and Development. Retrieved September 15, 2015, from http://www.oecd.org/edu/students-computers-and-learning-9789264239555-en.htm.

Parrish, P. E. (2007). Aesthetic principles for instructional design. *Educational Technology Research and Development, 57*(4), 511–528.

Parrish, P. E. (2008). *Designing compelling learning experiences.* Unpublished doctoral dissertation, University of Colorado, Denver.

Paul, R. W. (1987). Dialogical thinking: Critical thought essential to the acquisition of rational knowledge and patterns. In *Teaching thinking skills: Theory and practice* (pp. 127–148). New York: W.H. Freeman.

Paul, R. W., & Binker, A. J. A. (Eds.). (1990). *Critical thinking: What every person needs to survive in a rapidly changing world.* Rohnert Park: Center for Critical Thinking and Moral Critique.

Paul, R. W., & Elder, L. (2002). *Critical thinking: Tools for taking charge of your professional and personal life.* Upper Saddle River, NJ: Prentice Hall.

Reeves, T. (2011). Can educational research be both rigorous and relevant? *Educational Designer: The Journal of the International Society for Design and Development in Education, 1*(4), 1–24.

Reigeluth, C. M. (Ed.). (1983). *Instructional-design theories and models: An overview of their current status.* Hillsdale, NJ: Lawrence Erlbaum.

Reigeluth, C. M. (Ed.). (1999). *Instructional-design theories and models: A new paradigm of instructional theory.* Hillsdale, NJ: Lawrence Erlbaum.

Reigeluth, C. M., & Carr-Chellman, A. (Eds.). (2009). *Instructional-design theories and models: Building a common knowledge base.* New York: Routledge.

Richie, R. (1986). *The theoretical and conceptual bases of instructional design.* New York: Kogan Page.

Richie, R. C., Klein, J. D., & Tracey, M. W. (2011). *Instructional design knowledge base: Theory, research, and practice.* New York: Routledge.

Richtel, M. (2015). In classroom of future, stagnant scores. *New York Times.* Retrieved September 3, 2011, from http://www.nytimes.com/2011/09/04/technology/technology-in-schools-faces-questions-on-value.html?_r=0.

Rittel, H. W. J., & Webber, M. M. (1973). Planning problems are wicked problems. In N. Cross (Ed.), *Development in design methodology* (pp. 135–144). New York: John Wiley and Sons.

Rowland, G. (1993). Designing and instructional development. *Educational Technology Research and Development, 41*(1), 79–91.

Rowland, G. (2008). Design and research: Partners for educational innovation. *Educational Technology, 48*(6), 3–9.

Rychlak, J. F. (1994). *Logical learning theory: A human teleology and its empirical support.* Lincoln, NE: University of Nebraska Press.

Selwyn, N. (2014). *Distrusting educational technology: Critical questions for changing times.* New York: Routledge.

Sfard, A. (1998). On two metaphors for learning and the dangers of choosing just one. *Educational Researcher, 27*(2), 4–13.

Slife, B. D. (1993). *Time and psychological explanation.* Albany: SUNY Press.

Slife, B. D. (1998). Raising the consciousness of researchers: Hidden assumptions in the behavioral sciences. *Adapted Physical Activity Quarterly, 15*, 208–221.

Slife, B. D., Reber, J. S., & Richardson, F. C. (Eds.). (2005). *Critical thinking about psychology: Hidden assumptions and plausible alternatives.* Washington, DC: APA Books.

Slife, B. D., & Williams, R. N. (1995). *What's behind the research? Discovering hidden assumptions in the behavioral sciences.* Thousand Oaks, CA: Sage Publications.

Smith, L. D. (1992). On prediction and control: B. F. Skinner and the technological ideal of science. *American Psychologist, 47*(2), 216–223.

Smith, R. A. (2002). *Challenging your preconceptions: Thinking critically about psychology* (2nd ed.). Belmont, CA: Wadsworth Thomson Learning.

Smith, K. M., & Boling, E. (2009). What do we make of design? Design as a concept in educational technology. *Educational Technology, 49*(4), 3–17.

Snelbecker, G. E. (1974). *Learning theory, instructional theory, and psychoeducational design.* New York: McGraw-Hill.

Snow, R. E. (1977). Individual differences and instructional theory. *Educational Researcher, 6*(10), 11–15.

Spector, J. M. (2001). Philosophical implications for the design of instruction. *Instructional Science, 29*, 381–402.

Thayer-Bacon, B. J. (2000). *Transforming critical thinking: Thinking constructively.* New York: Teacher's College Press.

van Merrienboer, J. J. G. (2007). *Ten steps to complex learning.* Yahweh, NJ: Lawrence Erlbaum Associates.

Vincenti, W. (1990). *What engineers know and how they know it.* Baltimore, MD: Johns Hopkins University Press.

Wenger, E. (1998). *Communities of practice: Learning, meaning, and identity.* New York, NY: Cambridge University Press.

Williams, R. N. (1992). The human context of agency. *American Psychologist, 47*(6),752–760.

Yanchar, S. C., & Slife, B. D. (2004). Teaching critical thinking by examining assumptions. *Teaching of Psychology, 31*, 85–90.

Yanchar, S. C., Slife, B. D., & Warne, R. T. (2009). Advancing disciplinary practice through critical thinking: A rejoinder to Bensley. *Review of General Psychology, 13*, 278–280.

Yanchar, S. C., South, J. B., Williams, D. D., Allen, S., & Wilson, B. G. (2010). Struggling with theory? A qualitative investigation of conceptual tool use in instructional design. *Educational Technology Research and Development, 58*, 39–60.

Yanchar, S. C., Spackman, J. S., & Faulconer, J. E. (2014). Learning as embodied familiarization. *Journal of Theoretical and Philosophical Psychology, 33*(4), 216–232.

Yanchar, S. C., & Williams, D. D. (2006). Reconsidering the compatibility thesis and eclecticism: Five proposed guidelines for method use. *Educational Researcher, 35*(9), 3–12.

# Chapter 9
# Exploring the Cultural Dimensions of Instructional Design: Models, Instruments, and Future Studies

**Minjuan Wang and Steve Schlichtenmyer**

## Introduction

Global companies often face cultural issues when they conduct training of employees in other countries. In today's increasingly global and digitally connected society, it is essential to assure the alignment between the learning needs of individuals from different cultures and the way content is designed and delivered, both online and face-to-face. Many educators and designers often find themselves in the position of developing instruction for learners with backgrounds and cultures very different from their own. Here we present a comprehensive review of theories and models related to instructional design, learning preference, motivation, and culture. We also present research instruments that can be used to study these variables. In particular, we address the following questions:

1. How do employees from different cultures (countries) learn (e.g., their learning styles and preferences)?
2. What motivates them to learn?
3. What reliable assessment tools are available to help examine these issues?

Culturally Sensitive Teaching, Learner Motivation, New Instructional Design Models Business leaders of today cannot risk a negative business outcome resulting from a cultural misunderstanding. They need to assure that there is no gap between the cultural awareness of their employees and the demands of the regions where they do business. They have responded to this need by increasingly providing effective work-based cultural sensitivity training for their international employees (Reid, Stadler, & Spencer-Oatey, 2009). The challenge for project managers and

M. Wang (✉) • S. Schlichtenmyer
Learning Design and Technology, San Diego State University, 5500 Campanile Dr., PSFA 361, San Diego, 92182-4561 CA, USA
e-mail: mwang@mail.sdsu.edu; art4passion@hotmail.com

© Springer International Publishing Switzerland 2017
M. Orey, R.M. Branch (eds.), *Educational Media and Technology Yearbook*, Educational Media and Technology Yearbook 40, DOI 10.1007/978-3-319-45001-8_9

instructional designers is to develop training that is based on sound research, motivates employees, and reinforces the company's objectives and missions.

In order to accommodate unique employee learning preferences, particularly when the subjects are along the lines of Cultural Sensitivity Intelligence (CSI) training, the instructional designer should begin to view these culturally diverse learners as "cultural resources" who can inform the design throughout the process (Young, 2008). Beyond providing empirical information to researchers in the areas of learning preferences and learner motivation, it may also be possible for learners to play an integral role in the development of their own training.

## Culture-Integrated Instructional Design Models

For decades, the ADDIE Model was the standard used in instructional design and training development. However, some researchers argue that ADDIE does not integrate the knowledge of specific cultures beyond the initial Analysis phase and that this model is systematic but not systemic (Thomas, Mitchell, & Joseph, 2002). They recommend adding a cultural dimension to ADDIE, which requires designers to consider the learners' culture and how the designer's own culture interacts with that of the learners. To expedite the design process, educators and designers may need to consider other instructional design models, such the Cultural Adaptation Process (CAP) Model (Edmundson, 2007), the Successive Approximation Model (SAM) (Allen, 2003), and the Location Technology Culture and Satisfaction (LTCS) Model (Wang, Xiao, & Chen, 2014; Xiao, Wang, & Li, 2011). These approaches hold great promise for extending the fundamental premise of experiential learning into the design process itself, with all stakeholders working together.

Edmundson (2007) proposed the cultural adaptation process (CAP) model as a guideline for evaluating e-learning courses and for aligning them with the cultural profiles of targeted learners. The goal of this model is to facilitate the design and development of culturally adapted courses and activities, so as to help all learners achieve equitable learning outcomes. This model mainly enriches the "A" part of ADDIE, in needs assessment and learner analysis. It encourages several levels of cultural analysis, by identifying variables that can affect the selection of content, how to present the content, and the use of media.

The newest and most successful eLearning instructional design method in use today is likely successive approximation or rapid prototyping (see Fig. 9.1). This design approach is evolutionary, rapid, and allows instructional designers to move quickly through the initial phases of design to a rapid prototype ready for testing (Wang et al., 2012). This model leaves room for taking learners' cultural uniqueness into consideration. For instance, learners from some cultures might prefer completing all learning activities individually, while others would embrace collaboration and teamwork.

The fast growth of mobile learning in recent years demands instructional models and guidelines that are crafted for this unique learning modality. Mobile learning (mLearning) enables learners to access education information, education resources,

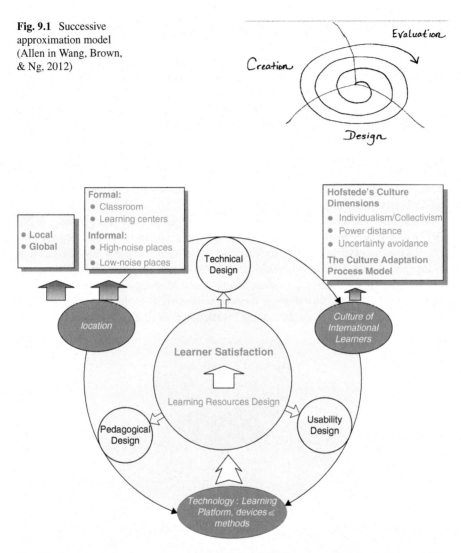

**Fig. 9.1** Successive approximation model (Allen in Wang, Brown, & Ng, 2012)

**Fig. 9.2** Location technology culture and satisfaction (LTCS): a comprehensive design model for mobile learning (Wang et al., 2014; Xiao et al., 2011)

and service with mobile devices. It focuses on anytime-anywhere context-aware learning via portable devices by harnessing the smart contextual capabilities of the devices and mobility of learner. After years of research, Minjuan Wang and her international collaborators proposed the Location, Technology, Culture, and Satisfaction (LTCS) model that can be used to guide the design of mobile learning activities (Wang et al., 2014; Xiao et al., 2011).

Figure 9.2 shows the structure of the LTCS Model. Aligning with the heavy emphasis on learner retention in many online programs, learning resources and learner satisfaction are the foci of this model. To ensure the highest learner satisfaction, learning materials need to be designed with the consideration of Location (local vs global), Technology (learning platform, devices, and methods), and Culture of the learners. Designing instruction for mLearning covers three aspects: pedagogical design, technical design, and usability design. An important aspect of this model is Culture, which refers to the cross-cultural dimensions of globalized eLearning and mLearning. Wang and her collaborators examine culture from two widely used models in teaching and training: Hofstede and Hofstede's (2005) Dimensions of National Culture and Edmundson's (2007) Cultural Adaptation Process (CAP) Model. The authors of LTCS also note that the cultural principles in this model will evolve as cultural theories for design methodologies gradually mature.

Later, through several empirical studies (e.g., Machun, Trau, Zaid, Wang, & Ng, 2012), the LTCS model is further developed and renamed as Mobilegogy (see Fig. 9.3), as an extension of the *Cybergogy for Engaged Learning Model* created by Wang and Kang (2006), viewable at http://edutechwiki.unige.ch/en/Cybergogy. Cybergogy is the pedagogy for online learning, and Mobilegogy is the pedagogy for mobile learning. The Mobilegogy model consists of two tiers: (1) the first one describes the necessary adaptations to instructional design to compensate for the

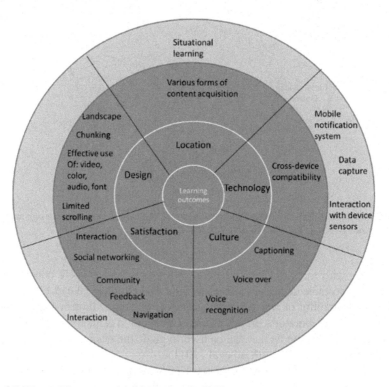

**Fig. 9.3** The mobilegogy model (Machun et al., 2012)

limitations of mobile devices; and (2) the second one encompasses the expansion of the learning experience, things that can only be achieved with mobile devices—making them unique to mLearning. Both Cybergogy and Mobilegogy aim to create a unique experience for the learner, with culture being one of the central elements.

In particular, design guidelines for cultural differences, as presented in the LTCS and Mobilegogy models, both draw on Hofstede and Hofstede's (2005) Dimensions of National Culture. A handful of studies on the influence of cultural attributes on learning or training derived their variables from Hofstede's cultural dimensions, which include six attributes: Power Distance Index (PDI), Individualism (IDV), Masculinity (MAS), Uncertainty Avoidance Index (UAI), Long Term Orientation (LTO), and Indulgence. Three of the six attributes are found to be most influential to learning (Novak & Wang, 2015; Rogers & Wang, 2009; Triandis, 1995; Wang, 2007):

1. PDI refers to the gap between the distribution of power and wealth in a country's society. In learning situations, this may affect students' perception of their instructors and their interactions with them, as peers or as authorities.
2. IDV indicates the degree to which a society values individual over collective achievement.
3. UAI focuses on a society's level of tolerance for new, unknown or surprising situations. A high uncertainty avoidance ranking indicates low acceptance of unforeseen situations and changes, while a low uncertainty avoidance ranking denotes a society's flexibility, adaptability, and acceptance for variations.

We will elaborate on the implications of Hofstede's theory for learner motivation in the latter part of this article.

## Learning Styles and Learning Preferences

When designing instruction and training, we cannot ignore learner preference or learning styles. Learning Style Inventories, such as those developed by Kolb and Kolb (2005), Honey and Mumford (2000), and Gregorc (2004) are tools researchers use to describe an individual's learning preference. Because of subtle differences in the way each person learns, there is no tool that can perfectly describe the unique learning style of every learner. When researchers use the term, they refer to the way individuals tend to use their unique cognitive style (*the way they perceive and think*) in order to process information. If a group of learners exhibits similar tendencies, they are exhibiting a "preference" for a particular learning style. Different researchers have conceived a large number of learning style models to describe the wide variations in tendencies between groups of individuals, different cultures, etc. These learning style inventories provide a way for researchers to gather data that can then be used to help teachers and trainers identify a learner's instructional preferences, or likely comfort with different instructional methods.

Overall, it seems that constructivist learning theories underpin most current educational research. In teaching or training practice, we also believe that educators should carefully design a dynamic curriculum that enables the student to relate their learning to the real world. By so doing, they "construct" meaningful knowledge into the framework of their previous experiences. The most commonly used learning style model is Kolb's (1984) Experiential Learning Theory (ELT) (see Fig. 9.4) which defines learning as: "the process whereby knowledge is created through the transformation of experience" (p. 41). ELT describes a creative cycle that provides two modes of grasping experience and two modes of transforming experience. Learning is a process involving creative tension between the four modes within this learning context. Learning style is based on an individual's preference for different positions within the cycle. As Fig. 9.4 displays, these positions include: Active Experimentation (AE), Concrete Experience (CE), Reflective Observation (RO), and Abstract Conceptualization (AC). In order to acquire knowledge, the learner must possess and use each of these skills. They must be willing and able to be actively involved (AE), to reflect (RO), to analyze (AC), and to apply what they learn (CE) throughout the learning experience.

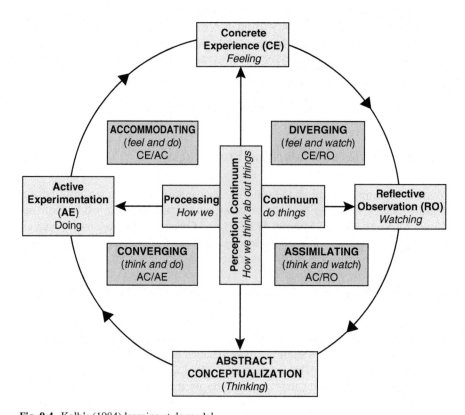

**Fig. 9.4** Kolb's (1984) learning style model

## Toward a Multicultural Model of Learning Style

Because of the increasing globalization of industry and learning, educational researchers have responded to the need to develop learning style models that account for the cultural diversity within and between the groups of learners they study. Joy and Kolb (2009) conducted research to demonstrate that the Experiential Learning Style model is an effective tool for describing differences in Learning Styles between different cultures. In their research, they used the Learning Style Inventory (Kolb & Kolb, 2005) to examine the impact of culture on the ways individuals from different nations learn. Specifically, they sought to determine "… whether culture has an impact on learning styles and which dimensions of culture play a part in shaping them" (Joy & Kolb, 2009, p. 73).

The hypothesis (Joy & Kolb, 2009) that learning style preference is effected by culture challenges the widely held belief among scientists that cognitive learning processes remain consistent across different cultures. From their review of literature, Joy and Kolb (2009) determined that culture might impact learning style, particularly AC (Abstract Conceptualization)-CE (Concrete Experience) and AE-RO (Active Experimentation and Assimilating). They based their research on the framework described in the Global Leadership and Organizational Effectiveness (GLOBE) study (House, 2004). In the GLOBE study, culture is defined as "shared motives, values, beliefs, identities, and interpretations or meanings of significant events that result from common experiences of members of collectives that are transmitted across generations" (House, 2004, p. 15). The GLOBE study further describes cultures as groupings of "countries" which strongly share many of these cultural attributes in common, including Anglo, Latin Europe, Nordic Europe, Germanic Europe, and Eastern Europe. There are also Latin America, Sub-Saharan Africa, Middle East, Southern Asia, and Confucian Asia. Using this framework, Joy and Kolb (2009) collected data from nations that meaningfully represented the heterogeneity of the world.

Their findings clearly demonstrate that cultural dimensions play a role in shaping the learning preferences of people from different nations. This suggests that the Kolb Inventory may be effective in describing differences in learning styles between different cultures. In particular, they found useful correlations as identified in Table 9.1.

Several other studies also suggest that learning styles may differ from one culture to another. Yamazaki (2005) conducted a meta-analysis that summarized the results of these studies (see Fig. 9.5 as in Joy & Kolb, 2009). Yamazaki (2005) notes

**Table 9.1** Learning style preference and cultural dimension

| Learning style preference | Cultural dimension by country |
| --- | --- |
| Abstract | High in in-group collectivism, institutional collectivism, uncertainty avoidance, future orientation and gender egalitarianism |
| Reflective | High in in-group collectivism, uncertainty avoidance and assertiveness |

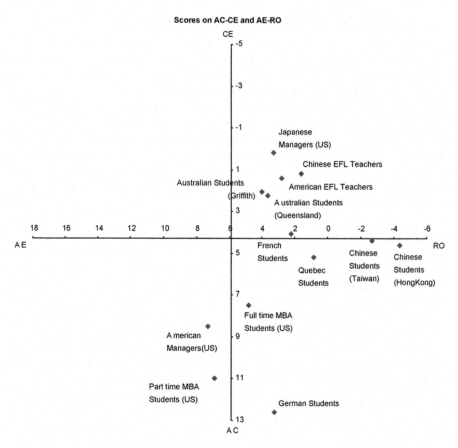

**Fig. 9.5** A meta-analysis of learning style and culture studies (Joy & Kolb, 2009, p. 72)

that few studies have investigated the relationships between particular cultural dimensions and specific learning preferences. In a rigorous study, he examined theoretical relationships between six typologies of culture and specific learning styles or abilities defined in the Kolb model. In the first part of this study, Yamazaki hypothesized that individuals with a particular cultural typology tend to learn through a corresponding Experiential learning style. In Table 9.2, we present a tabulation of the typologies presented in Yamazaki (2005).

Yamazaki (2005) notes the challenge and complexity inherent in gathering truly representative samples within a given population. Nations are culturally and ethnically diverse, and the psychometric characteristics of individuals vary widely. Kolb (1984) also identifies a variety of factors which impact the development of learning styles, including psychology, education, career, and adaptability.

Another factor, which seems to be overlooked, is the possibility that individuals with different or exceptional intelligence may successfully use *multiple* learning preferences identified within the Kolb model. Because of the complexities in

**Table 9.2** Typologies of culture and experiential learning style hypotheses

| Typologies of culture | Experiential learning style hypotheses |
|---|---|
| High context culture | Concrete experience |
| Low context culture | Abstract conceptualization |
| Shame culture | Concrete experience |
| Guilt culture | Reflective observation |
| Strong uncertainty avoidance | Reflective observation |
| Weak uncertainty avoidance | Active experimentation |
| M-type organizations (Western) | Abstract conceptualization |
| O-type organizations (Japanese) | Concrete experience |
| Interdependent self (Collectivism) | Concrete experience and Reflective observation |
| Independent self (Individualism) | Abstract conceptualization and Active experimentation |
| Field-dependent | Concrete experience |
| Field-independent | Abstract conceptualization |

cross-cultural research, studies are unable to adequately explain the *relative* influence of culture on learning style, or the more subtle differences between individual learners in specific educational settings. To better understand this influence, researchers may need to enhance their data gathering methods by using instruments that more accurately describe specific individuals within the group. A well-crafted questionnaire developed by Schlichtenmyer, Rodriquez, and Cerutti (2015), based on the Cultural Dimensions of Learning Framework (CDLF) by Parrish and Linder-VanBerschot (2010), might work in this regard (see Appendix for the Adapted Framework and Survey Questions).

## The Cultural Dimensions of Learning Framework (CDLF)

According to Parrish and Linder-VanBerschot (2010), the cognitive styles of individuals are shaped by three primary forces: personality, human nature, and culture. In order to help educators and designers develop the knowledge to deliver culturally sensitive and adaptive instruction, Parrish and Linder-VanBerschot (2010) created the Cultural Dimensions of Learning Framework (see http://www.irrodl.org/index.php/irrodl/article/view/809/1497, Table 9.1) as a tool that can be used in a variety of contexts including research and educational practice. The CDLF describes a set of eight pairs of deeply rooted cultural values and envisions how they might be exhibited in instructional situations. They proposed that the CDLF might be used "...to determine which preferences appear to cluster together or which appear to be common among a particular group of learners" (p. 9).

The eight cultural parameters within the CDLF Framework are divided into three general categories: Social Relationships, Epistemological Beliefs, and Temporal Perceptions. These categories include questions that reflect the important dimensions identified in earlier research (Hall, 1983; Hofstede & Hofstede, 2005) but also include other dimensions based on more recent research (Levine, 1997; Lewis, 2006; Nisbett, 2003). By understanding the eight dimensions described in this framework, educators may be better able to recognize potential learning differences among students in the instructional setting.

Several preferences appear to exist, suggesting that the Cultural Dimensions of Learning Framework (CDLF) may be useful as a tool to evaluate which preferences appear to be common among a particular group of learners/educators. The CDLF framework can also be used to generate variables and survey questions in cross-cultural research. With the guidance of their professor, teams of students (e.g., Schlichtenmyer et al., 2015) at San Diego State University have used the CDLF framework to conduct employee training and instructional design studies for several global corporations. In their studies, the CDLF served as a guide to construct questions for surveys used in their research (see Appendix). In this adapted CDLF framework, the research team generated survey questions from each dimension. Some of these questions were loosely based on a questionnaire provided by Parrish and Linder-VanBerschot (2009). It is important to note that the original CDLF framework and associated questionnaire do not include the open-ended questions, which were generated from the aforementioned research by Rogers, Graham, and Mayes (2007).

Based on this adapted framework, Schlichtenmyer and his team members modified and tested a survey instrument that integrates sophisticated cultural dimensions into the identification of real-world learning preferences. The survey developed in this study can also provide a rich and valuable reflective tool for instructors and designers to better understand the culturally based learning preferences of their students. As recommended by the authors of the original CDLF framework, a reflective instrument derived from CDLF can be used by learners and instructors, together, as a way to better integrate the learner's culture throughout the entire process of course development. The common intention is for trainers and educators to take the survey, review their preferences, and then think about these preferences (individually or in group discussion) in the context of their open-ended responses, in which they explain their attitudes about how they design and deliver instruction for culturally diverse learners.

## The East Asian Perspective

It is worth noting that all of the Learning Style Models mentioned so far were developed in the West. In *Cultural Foundations of Learning: East and West* (2012), Li describes a distinction between the Western and East Asian models of Learning. Her views are cultivated from 20 years as a teacher in China and the United States. She characterizes the Western learning model as "mind oriented" and the Asian model as "virtue oriented." If true, this distinction could profoundly impact the way Western learning models are used in Japan and East Asia.

Researchers from China (e.g., Cheng et al., 2011) professes a similar sentiment. They describe learning as a path to a meaningful life. For these authors, Confucius is the model teacher. Rather than transmitting knowledge to the student, Confucius is a facilitator, encouraging the active construction of knowledge by the students. They go on to explain that learning relies on prior knowledge and that the fundamental goal is for students to develop the capacity to learn to learn. Ironically, these goals are not dissimilar to those of contemporary Western Constructivist Learning theory.

From the above analysis it would seem that Western learning models could be seamlessly applied in East Asian culture. Pham (2011) presents a different point of view. He discusses the large number of recent failures in learning reforms at Asian Universities. He points out that Western instruction practices may not be appropriate within the cultural context of these universities. He does not condemn Western Learning Models, per se, but recommends that Asian educators need to be active participants in developing student-centered learning.

Another theme which is frequently repeated in the literature is the characterization of people from East Asian nations as "rote learners." These researchers typically point out that, although Confucian culture celebrates the virtues of mindfulness and individual learning, the words of a teacher were considered "absolute truth" and not to be challenged (Richmond, 2007). Although Asian students desire to acquire knowledge for themselves, they tend to enjoy learning in a group setting with their fellow students.

Although most of the studies already discussed describe the learning styles of students in a traditional learning setting, current research indicates that learning theory can be used by employees in the context of reflective process to help them improve their on-the-job learning. As part of a detailed study of nurses in the Netherlands, participants discussed their own learning style dimensions with their colleagues (Berings, Poell, & Simons, 2008). They claimed that this reflection enhanced their self-knowledge, self-confidence and knowledge about differences with others, helping them to become more adaptable in their practice. Although the results were somewhat ambiguous, this study points to the potential usefulness of other studies of this kind.

Reflection was also used in a qualitative study that investigated the real world experiences of 12 instructional design professionals (Rogers et al., 2007). In this study, these professionals reflected on the challenges of developing online instruction for learners from different cultures from their own. They identified areas where they could improve their learning design to become more culturally sensitive. They were asked a series of open-ended survey questions that required them to rethink their assumptions about the practice of instructional design. Through this introspective approach, they learned that culture was not just another isolated factor that they needed to better integrate, but that it defined nearly all of their design decisions. More importantly, they became aware that learners may not be as much like themselves as they once assumed.

## Theories of Motivation

Motivating employees and other learners may be the biggest factor in achieving successful learning outcomes. Moreover, it provides both the primary impetus and the driving force to sustain long-term learning and achieve business objectives. At the most fundamental level, motivation is either Extrinsic or Intrinsic. Deci and Ryan (2008) describe the relationship between Intrinsic and Extrinsic Motivation in their Self Determination Theory (see Table 9.3). They also describe the application of this theory in a work organization (Deci, Connell, & Ryan, 1989). They argue that activities that support a learner's experience of autonomy, competence and relatedness engender motivation and creativity.

Vallerand and his colleagues (1992) describes these three subdivisions of Intrinsic Motivation:

1. To *know*, or the pleasure experienced while learning something new.
2. To *accomplish* things, or the satisfaction derived from achieving or creating something.
3. *Stimulation*, or the stimulation one derives from participating.

In his Flow Theory, Csikszentmihalyi (1990) argues convincingly that people are happiest when they are in a state of *flow*, or complete immersion in the task at hand. Csikszentmihalyi additionally describes these persons who are intrinsically motivated, or purposeful and naturally curious as *autotelic*. They are not motivated by external rewards such as money, power or fame. This has ramifications in the world of business. Employees are likely the most productive, long-term, when they are purposefully engaged in in their work, suggesting that flow theory can play an essential role in the design of on-the-job training.

As with the Theories of Learning Styles, there are a large number of Motivational theories. It is beyond the scope of this review to describe them all. However, the most well-known and referenced Motivation Theory is the ARCS Model of Motivational Design (see Table 9.4), developed by Keller and Kopp (1987). This theory is based on the idea that people will be motivated to learn if they see value in the material or knowledge presented. It is a four part process:

**Table 9.3** Theory of intrinsic and extrinsic motivation

| Intrinsic motivation (internal) | • Enjoyment based "Hedonic"—the individual achieves physical or social well-being and their condition is improved<br>• Obligation or community based "Normative"—the wish to act appropriately is acquired through socialization |
|---|---|
| Extrinsic motivation (external) | • External regulation (rewards)<br>• Introjected regulation-avoiding guilt or obtaining self esteem<br>• Identified regulation-behaviors judged important by individual<br>• Integrated regulation-behaviors that correspond to sense of self |

**Table 9.4** ARCS: motivation components and strategies (Keller & Kopp, 1987)

| Motivation components | Motivation strategies |
|---|---|
| Attention | • Perceptual arousal<br>• Inquiry arousal<br>• Variability |
| Relevance | • Goal orientation<br>• Motive matching<br>• Familiarity |
| Confidence | • Performance requirements<br>• Success opportunities<br>• Personal control |
| Satisfaction | • Intrinsic reinforcement<br>• Extrinsic rewards<br>• Equity |

## Hosftede's Cultural Dimensions for Learner Motivation

In his groundbreaking study, Geert Hofstede (1980) applied his Dimensions of Culture to motivation and leadership theory and discovered that differences in employee motivation can be traced to differences in the "collective mental programming" of people from different cultures. Hofstede's theories have been well tested and validated by at least 140 studies. Moreover, different typologies of culture share similarities with his Dimensions of Culture (Clark, 1990; Hsu, Woodside, & Marshall, 2013). There is no question that Hofstede's approach to understanding similarities and differences between cultures is influential and well-fitted to the world of business and organizations. As such, they are essential to the execution of motivational strategies.

In particular, Hofstede believes that a clear understanding of Power Distance and Uncertainty Avoidance is especially vital in structuring organizations that will work best in different countries. For instance, Hofstede interprets the relationship between subordinates and their superiors from the Power Distance (PD) perspective, in degrees of Small PD, Medium PD, and Large PD. In small power distance, subordinates have weak dependence needs and expect superiors to consult them in decision-making. In Medium PD, subordinates expect superiors to consult them but will accept autocratic behavior. In Large OD, subordinates have strong dependence needs and expect superiors to act autocratically. Power distance, when applied to learning and training setting, affects how learners perceive their instructors and their interaction dynamics. The effects of Power Distance and Uncertainty Avoidance have been confirmed in several studies conducted by faculty and students of Learning Design and Technology, San Diego State University (Novak & Wang, 2015; Wang, 2007; Wang et al., 2012, 2014).

## Conclusions

Several principal themes emerge from this literature review that combine to suggest potential avenues of future study and data collection.

1. There is a strong need to provide Cultural Sensitivity Training to the Global workforce.
2. Individuals within particular cultural groups may be best informed to design their training.
3. Cultural groups exhibit particular Learning Style preferences.
4. A better understanding of Learning Styles within cultural groups may provide insight into effective Instructional Design.
5. Specific motivational techniques seem to relate directly to particular Cultural Dimensions.

## Suggested Studies

- More studies need to be conducted to fine tune the new instructional design models (LTCS and Mobilegogy). Detailed instructional guidelines should be in place to guide learning or training design for global learners.
- Currently, there appear to be few studies of employee Learning Style Preferences. The Adult Version of the Kolb Learning Style Inventory could be successfully used for this purpose.
- Researchers will need to establish a baseline of cultural awareness for individuals who will be participating in training. The Developmental Model of Intercultural Sensitivity (DMIS) or similar assessment could be used for this purpose.
- It would be helpful to better understand the relation between learning style preferences and the Cultural groups that exhibit them. The Cultural Dimensions of Learning (CDLF) might be used in concert with other assessments to better parse the results from the Globe study. This might help to determine the learning preference of groups from particular regions and cultures.

Finally, we need to point out that researchers may be misguided by engaging in studies that are solely based on Western theories, concepts, learning style inventories, and other assessments. Researchers and practitioners should also avoid stereotyping learners from different national cultures. At each step, researchers should consider modifications to their research methods and assessments, which will prevent them from gathering data that can result in false or simplistic conclusions.

## Assessment Tools in Cultural Studies

DMIS—Developmental Model of Intercultural Sensitivity (Bennett, Hammer, & Wiseman, 2003).
CDLF—Cultural Dimensions of Learning (Parrish & Linder-VanBerschot, 2010).

The Learning Style Inventory (Kolb & Kolb, 2005).
The Learning Styles Questionnaire (Honey & Mumford, 2000).
The Personal Adult Style Inventory (Knowles, Holton, & Swanson, 2005).
The Gregorc Style Delineator—Mind Styles Model (Gregorc, 2004).
The NAASP task force model (Keefe, 1985).
Sternberg Triarchic Abilities Test (Sternberg, 2006).

# Appendix

An Adapted Framework and Survey Questions for a Global Learning and Training Study based on the Cultural Dimensions of Learning Framework (Parrish & Linder-VanBerschot, 2009, 2010 [Q1–Q16]) and exploration research (Rogers et al., 2007 [Q18–Q20]).

| Social Relationships (Parrish & Linder-VanBerschot, 2010, p. 7) | |
| --- | --- |
| **More Equality** | **More Authority** |
| How is inequality handled? How is status demonstrated and respect given? What interactions are appropriate for those of unequal status? (Hofstede & Hofstede, 2005; Lewis, 2006) | |
| **Q1a** Instructors can be treated as equals and can be questioned or challenged. **Q2a** Learners should discuss and participate in the selection of learning activities. | **Q1b** It is not appropriate for a learner to question or challenge an instructor. **Q2b** Instructors are solely responsible for what happens during instruction. |
| **More Individualistic** | **More Collectivist** |
| Which prevails, the interests of the individual or the interest of the group? To what degree are interpersonal relationships valued? (Hofstede & Hofstede, 2005; Nisbett, 2003) | |
| **Q3a** Learners should feel comfortable expressing themselves whenever they have something to add. **Q4a** Personal gain is the primary motivation for hard work. | **Q3b** Before expressing themselves, learners should understand what the instructor has to say to the class. **Q4b** Helping the entire group is the motivation for hard work. |
| **More Nurturing** | **More Challenging** |
| Which is the more important set of goals, cooperation and security or recognition and advancement? Which achieves better learning outcomes, supportive acts or challenging acts? (Hofstede & Hofstede, 2005) | |
| **Q5a** Every learner should be praised. **Q6a** Collaboration is the best way for learners to improve. | **Q5b** To set a good example, only the most excellent learners should be praised. **Q6b** Competition is the best way for learners to improve. |
| Epistemological Beliefs (Parrish & Linder-VanBerschot, 2010, p. 8) | |
| **More Stability Seeking** | **More Uncertainty Acceptance** |
| How is uncertainty dealt with? Is it avoided or accepted? Is structure assumed more important than flexibility? What is the status of knowledge—established or in a process of development? (Hofstede & Hofstede, 2005; Nisbett, 2003) | |

| | |
|---|---|
| **Q7a** I am more comfortable with structured learning activities. <br> **Q8a** The learner should rely on course materials to avoid conflicting information. | **Q7b** I am more comfortable with open-ended and self-directed learning activities. <br> **Q8b** The learner should seek information from a variety of other sources. |
| **More Logical** | **More Practical** |
| How are arguments developed? Which is more important, logical consistency or practical outcomes? How is disagreement managed? (Nisbett, 2003) | |
| **Q9a** Contradictions should be debated until the correct answer is found. <br> **Q10a** The best solution is found through logical argumentation. | **Q9b** Contradictions should be tolerated for the sake of good working relationships. <br> **Q10b** The most practical solutions are arrived at through consensus. |
| **More focus on Causality** | **More focus on Systems and Situations** |
| How is causality assigned typically? Is it assigned to a single, most likely source, or is it assigned to the broader context? (Nisbett, 2003) | |
| **Q11a** Preestablished knowledge and principles are the starting point for learning. <br> **Q12a** Learners are primarily responsible for their own success or failure. | **Q11b** Practical situations are the starting point for learning. <br> **Q12b** The design of instruction is the primary reason for the success or failure of learners. |
| **Temporal Perceptions** (Parrish & Linder-VanBerschot, 2010, p. 9) | |
| **More Clock Focus** | **More Event Focus** |
| Do people conform to an external measure of time, or do they allow the event at hand to unfold on its own time? Which are more important, deadlines or relationships? (Levine, 1997) | |
| **Q13a** It is best for learning activities to start and stop promptly. <br> **Q14a** Students learn more by working alone quietly and efficiently to achieve planned outcomes. | **Q13b** Learning activities should be allowed to continue as long as they are useful. <br> **Q14b** Students learn more by socializing and discussing issues with their peers. |
| **More Linear Time** | **More Cyclical Time** |
| Do people see time as a path and goals as necessary destinations, or do they see time as a pattern of interlocking cycles into which they step in and out over the course of a life? (Hall, 1983; Lewis, 2006) | |
| **Q15a** A focus on the future and meeting established goals is best for learning. <br> **Q16a** Schedules need to be carefully managed and followed in order for goals to be met. | **Q15b** Frequent reflection about past experiences allows one to learn best from present experiences. <br> **Q16b** Schedules are expendable and should be adapted to allow the learner to draw as much as possible from each activity. |
| **Open-ended Questions** (derived from Rogers et al., 2007) | |
| **Q17** A specific culture can be identified by describing the patterns of thinking, feeling and acting shared by particular groups of people. Do you work, study or provide instruction or training to persons from cultures other than your own? | Yes; No |

| **Q18** Are you aware of differences between yourself and the people from cultural groups with whom you work, study or provide instruction or training? (p. 199) | Yes; No |
|---|---|
| **Q19** Please describe how you became aware of differences between yourself and the cultural groups with whom you work, study or provide instruction or training. (p. 199) | Open-ended response |
| **Q20** Please describe how your understanding of cultural differences affects your work? (p. 199) | Open-ended response |

# References

Allen, M. (2003). *Michael Allen's guide to eLearning: Building interactive, fun, and effective learning programs for any company*. Hoboken, NJ: Wiley.

Bennett, M., Hammer, M., & Wiseman, R. (2003). Measuring intercultural sensitivity: The intercultural development inventory. *International Journal of Intercultural Relations, 27*, 421–443.

Berings, M. G., Poell, R., & Simons, P. (2008). Dimensions of on-the-job learning styles. *Applied Psychology, 57*(3), 417–440.

Cheng, K., Liy, Y., Cheng, L., Xu, N., Bai, T., & Tan, S. (2011). Responses to Wu's interpretation, autonomy, and transformation: Chinese pedagogic discourse in a cross-cultural perspective. *Journal of Curriculum Studies, 43*(5), 591–630.

Clark, T. (1990). International marketing and national character: A review and proposal for an integrative theory. *Journal of Marketing, 54*(4), 66–79.

Csikszentmihalyi, M. (1990). *Flow: The psychology of optimal experience*. New York: Harper and Row.

Deci, E. L., Connell, J. P., & Ryan, R. M. (1989). Self-determination in a work organization. *Journal of Applied Psychology, 74*(4), 580.

Deci, E. L., & Ryan, R. M. (2008). Self-determination theory: A macrotheory of human motivation, development and health. *Canadian Psychology, 49*, 182–185.

Edmundson, A. (2007). The cultural adaptation process (cap) model: Designing e-learning for another culture. In A. Edmundson (Ed.), *Globalized e-learning cultural challenges* (pp. 267–290). Hershey, PA: Idea Group, Inc.

Gregorc, A. (2004). *The gregorc style delineator*. Columbia, CT: Gregorc Associates, Inc.

Hall, E. T. (1983). *The dance of life*. New York: Doubleday.

Hofstede, G. (1980). Motivation, leadership, and organization: Do American theories apply abroad? *Organizational Dynamics, 9*(1), 42–63.

Hofstede, G., & Hofstede, G. J. (2005). *Cultures and organizations: Software of the mind* (2nd ed.). New York: McGraw-Hill.

Honey, P., & Mumford, A. (2000). *The learning styles questionnaire: 80 Item version*. Maidenhead: Peter Honey Publications.

House, R. (2004). *Culture, leadership and organizations: The GLOBE study of 62 societies* (pp. 1–818). Thousand Oaks, CA: Sage Publications.

Hsu, S. Y., Woodside, A. G., & Marshall, R. (2013). Critical tests of multiple theories of cultures' consequences: Comparing the usefulness of models by Hofstede, Inglehart and Baker, Schwartz, Steenkamp, as well as GDP and distance for explaining overseas tourism behavior. *Journal of Travel Research*, 0047287512475218.

Joy, S., & Kolb, D. A. (2009). Are there cultural differences in learning style? *International Journal of Intercultural Relations, 33*(1), 69–85.

Keefe, J. (1985). Assessment of learning style variables: The NASSP task force model. *Learning and the Brain, 24*(2), 138–144.

Keller, J. M., & Kopp, T. (1987). Application of the ARCS model of motivational design. In C. M. Reigeluth (Ed.), *Instructional theories in action: Lessons illustrating selected theories and models*. Hillsdale, NJ: Lawrence Erlbaum.

Knowles, M. S., Holton, E. F., III, & Swanson, R. A. (2005). Personal adult style inventory: By Dr. Malcolm S. Knowles. In M. S. Knowles, E. F. Holton III, & R. A. Swanson (Eds.), *The adult learner: The definitive classic in adult education and human resource development* (6th ed., pp. 282–295). Amsterdam: Elsevier Butterworth Heineman.

Kolb, D. A. (1984). *Experiential learning: Experience as the source of learning and development*. New Jersey: Prentice-Hall.

Kolb, A. Y., & Kolb, D. A. (2005). *The Kolb learning style inventory–version 3.1: 2005 Technical secifications*. Philadelphia: Haygroup: Experience Based Learning Systems Inc.

Levine, R. (1997). *A geography of time*. New York: Basic Books.

Lewis, R. D. (2006). *When cultures collide: Leading across cultures* (3rd ed.). Boston: Nicholas Brealey International.

Li, J. (2012). *Cultural foundations of learning: East and west*. New York: Cambridge University Press.

Machun, P., Trau, C., Zaid, N., Wang, M. J., & Ng, J. (2012). MOOCs: Is there an App for that? *IEEE/WIC/ACM International Conferences on Web Intelligence and Intelligent Agent Technology* (Vol. 3, pp. 321–325). MaCau, China.

Nisbett, R. (2003). *The geography of thought: How Asians and Westerners think differently…and why*. New York: Free Press.

Novak, D., & Wang, M. J. (2015). Mobile literacies: Learning in the Mob. In Y. Zheng (Ed.), *Encyclopedia of Mobile Phone Behavior* (pp. 383–398). Hershey, PA: IGI Publishing.

Parrish, P., & Linder-VanBerschot, J. A. (2009). The cultural dimensions of learning framework questionnaire. *The International Review of Research in Open and Distributed Learning, 11*(2). Retrieved from http://www.irrodl.org/index.php/irrodl/article/view/809/1497.

Parrish, P., & Linder-VanBerschot, J. (2010). Cultural dimensions of learning: Challenges of multicultural instruction. *International Review of Research in Open and Distributed Learning, 11*(2), 1–12.

Pham, T.-H.-T. (2011). Issues to consider when implementing student-centred learning practices at Asian higher education institutions. *Journal of Higher Education Policy and Management, 33*(5), 519–528.

Reid, S., Stadler, S., Spencer-Oatey, H. (2009). The global people landscaping study: Intercultural effectiveness in global education partnerships. *Warwick occasional papers in applied linguistics #1* (No. 1, pp. 1–48). The Centre for Applied Linguistics.

Richmond, J. (2007). Bringing critical thinking to the education of developing country professionals. *International Education Journal, 8*(1), 1–29.

Rogers, P. C., Graham, C. R., & Mayes, C. T. (2007). Cultural competence and instructional design: Exploration research into the delivery of online instruction cross-culturally. *Educational Technology Research and Development, 55*(2), 197–217.

Rogers, P. C., & Wang, M. J. (2009). Cross-cultural issues in online learning. In P. Rogers & G. Berg (Eds.), *Encyclopedia of Distance Learning* (2nd ed., pp. 527–536). Hershey, PA: IGI Global Publishing.

Schlichtenmyer, S., Rodriquez, C., & Cerutti, J. (2015). *An exploration of the cultural dimensions of learning: A reflective tool for educators and instructional designers*. Unpublished research report, Learning Design and Technology, San Diego State University.

Sternberg, R. J. (2006). *Cognitive psychology fourth edition* (pp. 234–236). Belmont, CA: Thomson Wadsworth.

Thomas, M., Mitchell, M., & Joseph, R. (2002). The third dimension of ADDIE: A cultural embrace. *TechTrends, 46*(2), 40–45.

Triandis, H. C. (1995). *Individualism and collectivism*. Boulder, CO: Westview Press.

Vallerand, R. J., Pelletier, L. G., Blais, M. R., Briere, N. M., Senecal, C., & Vallieres, E. E. (1992). The academic motivation scale: A measure of intrinsic, extrinsic and motivation in education. *Educational and Psychological Measurement, 52*, 1003–1017.

Wang, M. J. (2007). Designing online courses that effectively engage learners from diverse cultural backgrounds. *British Journal of Educational Technology, 38*(2), 294–311.

Wang, M. J., Brown, F., & Ng, W. P. J. (2012). Current instructional design models and principles for effective e- and cloud-learning. *Open Education Research, 18*(2), 25–35.

Wang, M. J., & Kang, J. (2006). Cybergogy for engaged learning through information and communication technology: A framework for creating learner engagement. In D. Hung & M. S. Khine (Eds.), *Engaged learning with emerging technologies* (pp. 225–253). New York: Springer Publishing.

Wang, M. J., Xiao, J., & Chen, Y. (2014). Mobile learning design: The LTCS model. In: *IE'14: Proceedings of the 10th International Conference on Intelligent Environments* (pp. 80–86). Shanghai, China: IEEE.

Xiao, J., Wang, M. J., & Li, X. (2011). A comprehensive model for designing mobile learning activities and resources. *Modern Educational Technology, 21*(123), 15–21.

Yamazaki, Y. (2005). Learning styles and typologies of cultural differences: A theoretical and empirical comparison. *International Journal of Intercultural Relations, 29*, 521–548.

Young, P. (2008). Integrating culture in the design of ICTs. *British Journal of Educational Technology, 39*(1), 6–17.

# Part II
# Leadership Profiles

# Chapter 10
# Introduction

**Tonia A. Dousay**

The purpose of this section is to profile individuals who have made significant contributions to the field of educational media and communication technology. Leaders profiled in the *Educational Media and Technology Yearbook* have typically held prominent offices, composed seminal works, and made significant contributions that influence the contemporary vision of the field. The people profiled in this section have often been directly responsible for mentoring individuals, who have themselves, become recognized for their own contributions to learning, design, and technology.

You are encouraged to nominate individuals to be featured in this section of the Yearbook. The editors of this Yearbook will carefully consider your nomination. Please direct comments, questions, and suggestions about the selection process to Tonia Dousay <tdousay@uwyo.edu> or Rob Branch <rbranch@uga.edu>.

This volume of the *Educational Media and Technology Yearbook* remembers two outstanding members of the community who continue to positively impact leadership and scholarship. The leaders profiled this year are:

Edward
Caffarella

Sharon Smaldino

T.A. Dousay (✉)
Instructional Technology, University of Wyoming, Education Building 325, 1000 E. University Ave., Dept. 3374, Laramie, WY 82071, USA
e-mail: tdousay@uwyo.edu

© Springer International Publishing Switzerland 2017
M. Orey, R.M. Branch (eds.), *Educational Media and Technology Yearbook*,
Educational Media and Technology Yearbook 40,
DOI 10.1007/978-3-319-45001-8_10

The following people [listed alphabetically] are profiled in earlier volumes of the *Educational Media and Technology Yearbook*:

| | |
|---|---|
| John C. Belland | Kent Gustafson |
| Robert K. Branson | John Hedberg |
| James W. Brown | Robert Heinich |
| Bob Casey | Jacquelyn (Jackie) Hill |
| Betty Collis | Stanley A. Huffman |
| Robert E. De Kieffer | Harry Alleyn Johnson |
| Robert M. Diamond | David H. Jonassen |
| Walter Dick | Roger Kaufman |
| Philip L. Doughty | Jerrold E. Kemp |
| Frank Dwyer | Addie Kinsinger |
| Donald P. Ely | David R. Krathwohl |
| James D. Finn | Jean E. Lowrie |
| Robert Mills Gagné | Wesley Joseph McJulien |
| Castelle (Cass) G. Gentry | M. David Merrill |
| Thomas F. Gilbert | Michael Molenda |
| David Michael Moore | Wilbur Schramm |
| Robert M. Morgan | Charles Francis Schuller |
| Robert Morris | Don Carl Smellie |
| James Okey | Glenn Snelbecker |
| Ronald Oliver | Howard Sullivan |
| Tjeerd Plomp | William Travers |
| Tillman (Tim) James Ragan | Constance Dorothea Weinman |
| W. Michael Reed | Paul Welliver |
| Thomas C. Reeves | Paul Robert Wendt |
| Rita C. Richey | Ronald Zemke |
| Paul Saettler | |

# Chapter 11
# Dr. Edward P. Caffarella

**Tonia A. Dousay**

Find any biography or description of Dr. Caffarella, and you will quickly see that most, if not all, begin with the phrase, "Dr. Edward P. Caffarella is a leader in the field of educational technology." Occasionally, this statement might also include teacher education as an additional area of expertise. Ask any long-standing member of the

T.A. Dousay (✉)
Instructional Technology, University of Wyoming,
Education Building 325, 1000 E. University Ave.,
Dept. 3374, Laramie, WY 82071, USA
e-mail: tdousay@uwyo.edu

© Springer International Publishing Switzerland 2017
M. Orey, R.M. Branch (eds.), *Educational Media and Technology Yearbook*,
Educational Media and Technology Yearbook 40,
DOI 10.1007/978-3-319-45001-8_11

educational technology community, and you will likely hear the same sentiment. Even developing members of the field benefit from Caffarella's long-standing advocacy for students and quiet leadership that has shaped an ever-shifting field. Without question, Dr. Caffarella has cultivated a deliberate and constant commitment to our field, reminding us that the ways in which we impact a discipline are through maintaining a deep and relevant expertise of knowledge and experience.

Originally from Saugus, Massachusetts, Caffarella began his career with an emphasis on education and leadership. He graduated from Springfield College in 1968 with a Bachelor of Science in Community Leadership and Development. Not surprisingly, he combined his passion for leadership with a minor in Teacher Education, Mathematics. It was at Springfield that he developed an interest in media and technology, where he worked in what was then known as the audiovisual lab and was responsible for all of the Springfield College football team game films. While serving as the Coordinator of Educational Media for Oxford Public Schools in Massachusetts, Caffarella continued his own education, graduating with a Master of Education in 1970 from the University of Massachusetts. His background in educational media, systems, and technology helped him forge ahead in this quickly growing educational arena at a time when many schools were still grappling with the idea of media centers and libraries. In 1971, Caffarella enrolled in the Instructional Development and Technology doctoral program at Michigan State University (MSU), under the advisement of Dr. Paul W.F. Witt. During his graduate studies, Caffarella served as a graduate assistant and Assistant Director in the Instructional Media Center, pushing the field forward and establishing himself as a leader early in his career. I would add a new paragraph here.

Since graduating from MSU in 1974, Caffarella has held various faculty appointments at institutions including the University of Maine, Virginia Commonwealth University, University of Northern Colorado, and the State University of New York (SUNY) at Cortland. In addition, he also served as Dean of the School of Education at SUNY Cortland. Even after graduating, Caffarella continued to develop his personal proficiencies by enrolling in Computer Science courses and developing a deep expertise in coding languages and spreadsheet applications. His more than 40 years in the field of educational technology are filled with leadership, scholarship, and service supporting Caffarella's dedication to developing new leaders, effectively preparing teachers to use technology, and examining the role of technology in education. Many members of the Association for Educational Communications and Technology (AECT) fondly remember Caffarella's term as President in 2002–2003. He also served on the Board of Examiners for the National Council for the Accreditation of Teacher Education (NCATE), created the Innovation Adoption Readiness Model (IARM), and developed and tested the Institutional Accreditation Readiness Model for the American Association of Colleges for Teacher Education (AACTE). Caffarella concluded his academic career in 2013 as a Fulbright Scholar at the University of Malaysia and currently holds a Professor Emeritus status at both the University of Northern Colorado at Greeley and SUNY Cortland.

## High Standards and Mentorship

Caffarella set high standards for himself and for his students in a way that deliberately assisted others to develop academic knowledge and individual professional development. He made a pointed effort to mentor students into the field, respective careers, and leadership roles through modeling his own actions. Former students tell stories about how Caffarella expected the very best but never belittled them, focusing instead on how to foster motivation and success. As a student or junior faculty member, Caffarella had a way of questioning you with a look rather than a comment. With one expression, he conveyed concern and question, imploring students and others to really consider their thoughts or actions, and followed up with an opportunity to rethink or revise. Any criticism Caffarella wanted to share was saved for private meetings, and he always maintained a high standard of ethics and his integrity is above reproach. These characteristics made Caffarella an outstanding mentor and leader, but he is so much more. Current leaders of the field can all recount stories of when they were a developing scholar and saw firsthand the dry sense of humor that Caffarella had, which differed greatly from his daily demeanor. When faced with a potentially embarrassing situation, one current leader tells the story of how she confessed her mistake to Caffarella and was pleasantly surprised by his understanding and considerate response. Perhaps the most lasting legacy of Caffarella rests in his chronicling the titles, authors, advisors, and topics of dissertations in educational technology. This compilation continues to help existing and emerging scholars evaluate the issues in our research, methodologies that were and were not accepted, research and mentoring relationships, and the influence of the scholars/researchers in our field through the various evolutions of technology.

Although Caffarella is now retired, he shows no signs of slowing down. He has focused his hobbies and interests on international travel, volunteering, and spending time with family. He and his wife, Rosemary Caffarella, a Cornell University Emeritus Professor, travel around the world, visiting countries to which they've never been. Within a single year, they visited nine countries—Malaysia, India, Bhutan, Nepal, Bulgaria, Macedonia, Kosovo, Albania, and the island of Corfu in Greece. Their next adventure will take them to southern Africa. They plan to take two trips a year and add in visiting places around the USA, like Yellowstone and Glacier National Parks. When they aren't traveling, Caffarella actively volunteers for Habitat for Humanity, specializing in electrical work but happily accepting any tasks that need to be completed. Caffarella also enjoys challenging himself with an n-scale model railroad setup and participating in a railroad club, including model train shows. In between these retirement adventures, the Caffarellas enjoy spending as much time as possible with their two grandchildren and include them in their travels and hobbies. Retirement brings a new set of activities and passions for Caffarella to pursue, but he maintains a presence on the edges of the field, engaging in discussions with colleagues and keeping a watchful eye over the area of study he helped develop.

# References

Caffarella, E. P. (2002). Curriculum vita for Edward P. Caffarella, Ph.D. Retrieved from https://web.archive.org/web/20020820005933/http://www.coe.unco.edu/EdCaffarella/VITA01.htm.
Caffarella, E. P. (2005). Doctoral research in educational technology: A directory of dissertations, 1977–2004. Retrieved from http://aectorg.yourwebhosting.com/publications/EdTechDissertations/Dissdir4.htm.
University of Malaya. (2013). Visiting Professors: Prof. Edward Caffarella. Retrieved from http://cmsad.um.edu.my/index1.php?pfct=umllr&modul=Visiting_Professors&pilihan=Prof._Edward_Caffarella.

# Chapter 12
# Dr. Sharon Smaldino

**Tonia A. Dousay**

If you ask Dr. Sharon Smaldino about how she came into the field of educational technology, she will tell you a story about stumbling into [it] as she was having a conversation with her master's advisor. Dr. Smaldino, the youngest of five children and originally from Binghamton, NY, already possessed a Bachelor of Arts in Speech Pathology/Audiology from SUNY-Albany and was working on a Master of Arts in Elementary Education at the University of Connecticut. Recognizing Smaldino's intellect and innovative spirit, her advisor felt that she needed to be in a field that would allow Sharon to try new things. Taking this advice, Smaldino eventually

T.A. Dousay (✉)
Instructional Technology, University of Wyoming, Education Building 325,
1000 E. University Ave., Dept. 3374, Laramie, WY 82071, USA
e-mail: tdousay@uwyo.edu

© Springer International Publishing Switzerland 2017        177
M. Orey, R.M. Branch (eds.), *Educational Media and Technology Yearbook*,
Educational Media and Technology Yearbook 40,
DOI 10.1007/978-3-319-45001-8_12

graduated in 1987 with a Ph.D. in Educational Media/Computer Applications from Southern Illinois University. Dr. Smaldino spent most of her career at the University Northern Iowa (UNI), starting out as a Research Assistant in 1985. Smaldino climbed the academic ranks, eventually holding the title of Professor in the Department of Curriculum & Instruction and Interim Associate Dean of the College of Education-Graduate Studies. In 2003, Dr. Smaldino left to become the L.D. and Ruth Morgridge Endowed Chair for Teacher Education at Northern Illinois University (NIU), and it is from NIU that Sharon recently retired.

To many, Dr. Smaldino's greatest contributions to the field rest in the preparation of preservice teachers and effective integration of technology, but her legacy extends far beyond the teacher educator arena. Truly, Sharon's impact on the training of thousands of teachers and online educators rests in the continued use of her numerous coauthored scholarly articles, books, book chapters, and monographs. Teacher preparation programs and colleges of education around the United States commonly refer to the *Instructional technology and media for learning* and *Planning for interactive distance education: A handbook* texts, and many of Smaldino's colleagues note that these books are both scholarly as well as practical. However, Dr. Smaldino also has a particular gift for working with students and developing leaders. Her mentoring of future teachers and new professionals in the field is legendary in the eyes of her peers. Smaldino directly advised and mentored more than 175 graduate students while in her faculty positions at UNI and NIU. From challenging gender structures in professional organizations to providing model leadership with great compassion and humility, Dr. Smaldino is often known more for how she treats others rather than what she says.

## A Gentlewoman and a Scholar

Dr. Sharon Smaldino came of age at a time in society when gender roles dictated certain expectations. Most women of the time went into nursing or teaching. She, however, aspired to be an architect. Unfortunately, Smaldino was repeatedly told that architecture was not an appropriate career path for women. She then found herself becoming an educator, knowing that she absolutely did not want to be a classroom teacher. The compromise she devised was to work in the area of speech pathology, assisting learners and teachers. Through her work in special education, Smaldino found that she could reinvent what it meant to be an educator and what her future might look like. This early inclination to forge her own path provided a foundation for her later advancements in the field. Dr. Smaldino's determination and fearless approach to risk, failure, and learning helped as she progressed through the academic and professional ranks that, at the time, were largely dominated by male counterparts and colleagues. In 2004, she achieved something that fewer than 20 women have done when she became President of the Association for Educational

Communications and Technology (AECT). Smaldino has been willing to continually take leadership roles in AECT, both before and after her presidency, and her impact within the organization through her leadership and participation is felt within multiple divisions, association leadership, and the ectFoundation. Smaldino makes no excuses nor does she complain as she continues to acquire the skills and knowledge necessary to get the job done and excel as a scholar in educational technology.

Smaldino's service and research intertwine across the decades, telling both the history of the field and creating a picture of how the field has evolved. Her early presentations and publications, like many of the late 1980s/early 1990s, focused on specific emerging technologies and their place in education. Specifically, Dr. Smaldino was interested in how children interact with materials. When she worked with deaf adolescent learners who had difficulty working with traditional classroom materials, Smaldino became curious about how to better redesign resources to meet individual learning needs in special education contexts. The intersection of this deep interest with emerging technologies in creative and innovative ways was a driving motivation for Dr. Smaldino's foray into educational technology research. Throughout her career, she contributed to early conversations on teacher professional standards, the growing landscape of distance education, and grant-funded projects to implement software and hardware for K12 schools. Today's students who investigate the history of technology initiatives in public education and the numerous programs to fund these initiatives often find themselves reading reports coauthored and/or managed by Smaldino. With respect to distance and online learning, Dr. Smaldino taught herself the technologies and tools of this "new" innovation, bringing her own 300 baud rate modem into the office for experimenting and delivering her first distance course entirely via e-mail. This experience taught Dr. Smaldino much about the interactivity, communication, and tools that are required to accommodate students' needs and how to design these opportunities given available tools.

Despite recently retiring from academia, Dr. Smaldino maintains a willingness to support and nurture others into leadership and scholarship. Through her new hobbies of knitting for grandchildren and playing the ukulele with her husband, Dr. Joseph J. Smaldino, Sharon continues a lifelong passion of learning and sharing learning with others. If you ask Dr. Smaldino about her retirement, she will tell you that she may have left the university, but not the profession. She continues to research and publish, which further illustrates Smaldino's dedication and passion for continuing the legacy of educational technology.

# Reference

Association for Educational Communications & Technology (Producer). (2012). Interview with Dr. Sharon Smaldino. *AECT History Makers*. Video retrieved from http://vtechworks.lib.vt.edu/handle/10919/49419.

# Part III
# Organizations and Associations in North America

# Chapter 13
# Introduction

**Michael Orey**

Part IV includes annotated entries for associations and organizations, most of which are headquartered in North America, whose interests are in some manner significant to the fields of learning, design and technology or library and information science. For the most part, these organizations consist of professionals in the field or agencies that offer services to the educational media community. In an effort to only list active organizations, I deleted all organizations that had not updated their information since 2013. Any readers are encouraged to contact the editors with names of unlisted media-related organizations for investigation and possible inclusion in the 2017 edition.

Information for this section was obtained through e-mail directing each organization to an individual web form through which the updated information could be submitted electronically into a database created by Michael Orey. Although the section editor made every effort to contact and follow up with organization representatives, responding to the annual request for an update was the responsibility of the organization representatives. The editing team would like to thank those respondents who helped assure the currency and accuracy of this section by responding to the request for an update. Figures quoted as dues refer to annual amounts unless stated otherwise. Where dues, membership, and meeting information are not applicable such information is omitted.

M. Orey (✉)
Learning, Design, and Technology, The University of Georgia,
116 River's Crossing, Athens, GA 30602-4809, USA
e-mail: mikeorey@uga.edu

© Springer International Publishing Switzerland 2017
M. Orey, R.M. Branch (eds.), *Educational Media and Technology Yearbook*,
Educational Media and Technology Yearbook 40,
DOI 10.1007/978-3-319-45001-8_13

# Chapter 14
# Organizations and Associations in the USA and Canada

Michael Orey

**Name of Organization or Association** — Adaptech Research Network

**Acronym** — N/A

**Address:**
Dawson College, 3040 Sherbrooke St. West
Montreal, QC
H3Z 1A4
Canada

**Phone Number** — 514-931-8731 #1546; **Fax Number** — 514-931-3567 Attn: Catherine Fichten

**Email Contact** — catherine.fichten@mcgill.ca; **URL** — http://www.adaptech.org

**Leaders** — Catherine Fichten, Ph.D., Codirector; Jennison V. Asuncion, M.A., Codirector

**Description** — Based at Dawson College (Montreal), we are a Canada-wide, grant-funded team, conducting bilingual empirical research into the use of computer, learning, and adaptive technologies by postsecondary students with disabilities. One of our primary interests lies in issues around ensuring that newly emerging instructional and mobile technologies are accessible to learners with disabilities.

**Membership** — Our research team is composed of academics, practitioners, students, consumers, and others interested in the issues of access to technology by students with disabilities in higher education.

M. Orey (✉)
Learning, Design, and Technology, The University of Georgia,
116 River's Crossing, Athens, GA 30602-4809, USA
e-mail: mikeorey@uga.edu

© Springer International Publishing Switzerland 2017
M. Orey, R.M. Branch (eds.), *Educational Media and Technology Yearbook*,
Educational Media and Technology Yearbook 40,
DOI 10.1007/978-3-319-45001-8_14

**Dues**—N/A.

**Meetings**—N/A.

**Publications**—*2015 Jorgensen, M., Fichten, C.S., Nguyen, M.N., Budd, J., Barile, M., Asuncion, J., Amsel, R., Tibbs, A., & Jorgensen, S. (2015). Employment realities of recent junior/community college and university graduates and premature leavers with disabilities. International Journal of Disability, Community, and Rehabilitation, 14(1). Online. Retrieved from http://www.ijdcr.ca/VOL14_01/articles/jorgenson.shtml. *2015 Nguyen, M. N., Fichten, C.S., Budd, J., King, L., Barile, M., Havel, A., Mimouni, Z., Chauvin, A., Raymond, O., Juhel, J. C. & Asuncion, J. (2015). Les TIC pour soutenir l'autodétermination des étudiants postsecondaires ayant des troubles d'apprentissage. Développement humain, handicap et changement social (RIPPH), 21(1), 97–110. *2014 Fichten, C. S., Asuncion, J., & Scapin, R. (2014). Digital technology, learning, and postsecondary students with disabilities: Where we've been and where we're going. Journal of Postsecondary Education and Disability, 27(4), 369–379. *2014 Fichten, C. S., Nguyen, M. N., Amsel, R., Jorgensen, S., Budd, J., Jorgensen, M., Asuncion, J., & Barile, M. (2014). How well does the Theory of Planned Behavior predict graduation among college and university students with disabilities? Social Psychology of Education, 17(4), 657–685. DOI 10.1007/s11218-014-9272-8. *2014 Fichten, C. S., Nguyen, M. N., Budd, J., Barile, M., Asuncion, J., Jorgensen, M., Amsel, R., & Tibbs, A. (2014). College and university students with disabilities: "Modifiable" personal and school related factors pertinent to grades and graduation. Journal of Postsecondary Education and Disability, 27(3), 273–290. *2014 Fichten, C. S., Nguyen, M. N., King, L., Havel, A., Mimouni, Z., Barile, M., Budd, J., Jorgensen, S., Chauvin, A., & Gutberg, J. (2014). How well do they read? Brief English and French screening tools for college students. International Journal of Special Education, 29(1), 33–46. *2014 Nguyen, M. N., Budd, J., Fichten, C. S., & Asuncion, J. V. (2014). Les TIC, les médias sociaux et les étudiants et diplômés canadiens en situation de handicap. Revue Terminal: Technologie de l'Information, Culture et Société, 116. ISBN 978-2-296-13108-8. Retrieved from http://terminal.revues.org/691.

**Name of Organization or Association**—Agency for Instructional Technology

**Acronym**—AIT

**Address:**
8111 N Lee Paul Road
Bloomington, IN
47404
USA

**Phone Number**—(812)339-2203; **Fax Number**—(812)333-4218

**Email Contact**—info@ait.net; **URL**—http://www.ait.net

**Leaders**—Charles E. Wilson, Executive Director

**Description**—The Agency for Instructional Technology has been a leader in educational technology since 1962. A nonprofit organization, AIT is one of the largest providers of instructional TV programs in North America. AIT is also a leading developer of other educational media, including online instruction, CDs, videodisks, and instructional software. AIT learning resources are used on six continents and reach nearly 34 million students in North America each year. AIT products have received many national and international honors, including an Emmy and Peabody award. Since 1970, AIT has developed 39 major curriculum packages through the consortium process it pioneered. American state and Canadian provincial agencies have cooperatively funded and widely used these learning resources. Funding for other product development comes from state, provincial, and local departments of education; federal and private institutions; corporations and private sponsors; and AITs own resources.

**Membership**—None.

**Dues**—None.

**Meetings**—No regular public meetings.

**Publications**—None.

**Name of Organization or Association**—American Association of Community Colleges

**Acronym**—AACC

**Address:**
One Dupont Circle, NW, Suite 410
Washington, DC
20036-1176
USA

**Phone Number**—(202)728-0200; **Fax Number**—(202)223-9390

**Email Contact**—twhissemore@aacc.nche.edu; **URL**—http://www.aacc.nche.edu

**Leaders**—Walter G. Bumphus, President and CEO

**Description**—AACC is a national organization representing the nations more than 1195 community, junior, and technical colleges. Headquartered in Washington, DC, AACC serves as a national voice for the colleges and provides key services in the areas of advocacy, research, information, and leadership development. The nations community colleges serve more than 13 million students annually, almost half (46%) of all US undergraduates.

**Membership**—1100+ institutions.

**Dues**—Vary by category.

**Meetings**—Annual Convention, April of each year; 2016: April 9–12, Chicago, IL.

**Publications**—Community College Journal (bimonthly); Community College Daily (daily online); Annual Fact Sheet; various reports and white papers.

**Name of Organization or Association**—American Library Association

**Acronym**—ALA

**Address:**
50 E. Huron St.
Chicago, IL
60611
USA

**Phone Number**—(800) 545-2433; **Fax Number**—(312) 440-9374

**Email Contact**—library@ala.org; **URL**—http://www.ala.org

**Leaders**—Keith Michael Fiels, Exec. Dir.

**Description**—The ALA is the oldest and largest national library association. Its 56,000 members represent all types of libraries: state, public, school, and academic, as well as special libraries serving persons in government, commerce, the armed services, hospitals, prisons, and other institutions. The ALA is the chief advocate of achievement and maintenance of high-quality library information services through protection of the right to read, educating librarians, improving services, and making information widely accessible. See separate entries for the following affiliated and subordinate organizations: American Association of School Librarians, Association of Library Trustees, Advocates, Friends and Foundations, Association for Library Collections and Technical Services, Association for Library Service to Children, Association of College and Research Libraries, Association of Specialized and Cooperative Library Agencies, Library Leadership and Management Association, Library and Information Technology Association, Public Library Association, Reference and User Services Association, Young Adult Library Services Association, and the Learning Round Table of ALA (formerly the Continuing Library Education Network and Exchange Round Table).

**Membership**—56,000 members at present; everyone who cares about libraries is allowed to join the American Library Association.

**Dues**—Professional rate: $68, first year; $104, second year; third year and renewing: $137 Library Support Staff: $49 Student members: $36 Retirees: $49 International librarians: $82 Trustees: $62 Associate members (those not in the library field): $62.

**Meetings**—Annual Conference: June 23–28, 2016—Orlando, FL; June 22–27, 2017—New Orleans, LA//Midwinter Meetings: January 8–12, 2016—Boston, MA; January 20–24, 2017—Atlanta, GA.

**Publications**—American Libraries; Booklist; BooklistOnline.com; Choice; Choice Reviews Online; Guide to Reference; Library Technology Reports; Newsletter on Intellectual Freedom; RDA Toolkit.

**Name of Organization or Association**—Association for Computers and the Humanities

**Acronym**—ACH

**Address:**
c/o Vika Zafrin, Boston University Libraries, 771 Commonwealth Avenue
Boston, MA
02215
USA

**Phone Number**—+1 617 358 6370

**Email Contact**—secretary@ach.org; **URL**—http://www.ach.org/

**Leaders**—President, ACH

**Description**—The Association for Computers and the Humanities (ACH) is a major professional society for the digital humanities. We support and disseminate research and cultivate a vibrant professional community through conferences, publications, and outreach activities. ACH is based in the USA, but boasts an international membership (as of May 2012, representing 21 countries worldwide).

**Membership**—~450 from over 20 countries. More information available at http://ach.org/membership/.

**Dues**—Membership+print subscription to Digital Scholarship in the Humanities: $153 ACH only, or $181 joint ADHO (the best way to contribute to ACH financially) Student/Senior Citizen membership+print: $76/$91 Joint membership without a subscription to DSH: $40 Joint student/unwaged membership without DSH: $26 Joint membership (without DSH) from developing countries: $26 or free Membership form available at http://dsh.oxfordjournals.org/subscribe.

**Meetings**—General meetings are held at the annual Digital Humanities conference.

**Publications**—ACH Publications:—Digital Humanities Quarterly http://www.digitalhumanities.org/dhq/—DSH: Digital Scholarship in the Humanities http://dsh.oxfordjournals.org/—Humanist http://dhhumanist.org/ More ADHO publications are listed at http://digitalhumanities.org/Publications.

**Name of Organization or Association**—Association for Continuing Higher Education

**Acronym**—ACHE

**Address:**
1700 Asp Ave Rm 129C, OCCE Admin Bldg
Norman, OK
73072
USA

**Phone Number**—800-807-2243; **Fax Number**—405-325-4888

**Email Contact**—admin@acheinc.org; **URL**—http://www.acheinc.org/

**Leaders**—James P. Pappas, Ph.D., Executive Vice President

**Description**—ACHE is an institution-based organization of colleges, universities, and individuals dedicated to the promotion of lifelong learning and excellence in continuing higher education. ACHE encourages professional networks, research, and exchange of information for its members and advocates continuing higher education as a means of enhancing and improving society.

**Membership**—Approximately 1500 individuals in approximately 650 institutions. Membership is open to institutions of higher learning, professionals and organizations whose major commitment is in the area of continuing education.

**Dues**—Institutional dues begin at $550 and are based on student FTE Organizational dues: $550 Professional dues: $90 Student dues: $25 Retiree dues: $25.

**Meetings**—For a list of Annual and Regional Meetings, see http://www.acheinc.org.

**Publications**—Journal of Continuing Higher Education (3/yr.); Five Minutes with ACHE (blog and eNews digest); Proceedings (annual).

**Name of Organization or Association**—Association for Educational Communications and Technology

**Acronym**—AECT

**Address:**
320 West 8th Street Suite 101, Showers Business Plaza
Bloomington, IN
47404
USA

**Phone Number**—(812) 335-7675; **Fax Number**—(812) 335-7678

**Email Contact**—pharris@aect.org; **URL**—http://www.aect.org

**Leaders**—Phillip Harris, Executive Director; Robert Branch Board President

**Description**—AECT is an international professional association concerned with the improvement of learning and instruction through media and technology. It serves as a central clearinghouse and communications center for its members, who include instructional technologists, library media specialists, religious educators, government media personnel, school administrators and specialists, and training media producers. AECT members also work in the armed forces, public libraries, museums, and other information agencies of many different kinds, including those related to the emerging fields of computer technology. Affiliated organizations include the International Visual Literacy Association (IVLA), Minorities in Media (MIM), New

England Educational Media Association (NEEMA), SICET (the Society of International Chinese in Educational Technology), and KSET (the Korean Society for Educational Technology). The ECT Foundation is also related to AECT. Each of these affiliated organizations has its own listing in the Yearbook. AECT Divisions include: Instructional Design & Development, Training & Performance, Research & Theory, Systemic Change, Distance Learning, Media & Technology, Teacher Education, International, and Multimedia Productions.

**Membership**—2500 members in good standing from K-12, college and university and private sector/government training. Anyone interested can join. There are different memberships available for students, retirees, corporations, and international parties. We also have a new option for electronic membership for international affiliates.

**Dues**—$125.00 standard membership discounts are availble for students and retirees. Additional fees apply to corporate memberships.

**Meetings**—Annual Convention held each year at the end of October. Summer meeting held each year the third week in July.

**Publications**—TechTrends (6/yr., free with AECT membership; available by subscription through Springer at www.springeronline.com); Educational Technology Research and Development (6/yr. $46 members; available by subscription through Springer at www.springeronline.com); Quarterly Review of Distance Education (q., $55 to AECT members); many books available on the AECT website for members.

**Name of Organization or Association**—Association for Library and Information Science Education

**Acronym**—ALISE

**Address:**
2150 N 107th St, Suite 205
Seattle, WA
98133
USA

**Phone Number**—206-209-5267; **Fax Number**—206-367-8777

**Email Contact**—office@alise.org; **URL**—http://www.alise.org

**Leaders**—Andrew Estep, Executive Director

**Description**—Seeks to advance education for library and information science and produces annual Library and Information Science Education Statistical Report. Open to professional schools offering graduate programs in library and information science; personal memberships open to educators employed in such institutions; other memberships available to interested individuals.

**Membership**—763 individuals, 69 institutions.

**Dues**—Institutional, sliding scale, $350–2500 International $145.00 Full-Time Personal, $140.00 Part-Time/Retired $75.00 Student $60.00.

**Meetings**—.

**Publications**—Journal of Education for Library and Information Science; ALISE Directory; Library and Information Science Education Statistical Report.

**Name of Organization or Association**—Association for Library Collections & Technical Services

**Acronym**—ALCTS

**Address:**
50 E. Huron St.
Chicago, IL
60611
USA

**Phone Number**—(312)280-5037; **Fax Number**—(312)280-5033

**Email Contact**—alcts@ala.org; **URL**—www.ala.org/alcts

**Leaders**—Keri Cascio, Executive Director

**Description**—A division of the American Library Association, ALCTS is dedicated to acquisition, identification, cataloging, classification, and preservation of library materials; the development and coordination of the country library resources; and aspects of selection and evaluation involved in acquiring and developing library materials and resources. Sections include Acquisitions, Cataloging and Classification, Collection Management and Development, Preservation and Reformatting, and Serials.

**Membership**—3700 Membership is open to anyone who has an interest in areas covered by ALCTS.

**Dues**—$65 plus membership in ALA.

**Meetings**—Annual Conference; Orlando June 23–28, 2016, Chicago June 22–27, 2017, New Orleans June 21–26, 2018.

**Publications**—Library Resources & Technical Services (q.); ALCTS News (q.).

**Name of Organization or Association**—Association for Talent Development (formerly ASTD)

**Acronym**—ATD

**Address:**
1640 King St.
Alexandria, VA
22314
USA

**Phone Number**—(703)683-8100; **Fax Number**—(703)683-8103

**Email Contact**—customercare@td.org; **URL**—http://www.td.org

**Leaders**—Tony Bingham, President and CEO

**Description**—The Association for Talent Development (ATD), formerly ASTD, is the world's largest association dedicated to those who develop talent in organizations. These professionals help others achieve their full potential by improving their knowledge, skills, and abilities. ATD's members come from more than 120 countries and work in public and private organizations in every industry sector. To better meet the needs and represent the work of this dynamic profession, on May 6, 2014 the organization announced its new brand: the Association for Talent Development.

**Membership**—41,000 members in 126 countries.

**Dues**—The Professional Membership ($229.00) is the foundation of ATD member benefits. Publications, newsletters, research reports, discounts, services, and much more, are all designed to help you do your job better. There are also student memberships, joint chapter memberships, and a special rate for international members. Heres what you have to look forward to when you join: TD magazine—Monthly publication of ATD. Stay informed on trends, successful practices, case studies, and more. ATD LINKS—bimonthly newsletter for members. The Buzz—a weekly compilation of news about the talent development profession. Special Reports and Research—Research reports are published on topics that reflect important issues and trends in the industry. The State of the Industry report is published annually and analyzes spending, practices, and other important data related to talent development. Career Navigator Tool—find out where you are in your career and what you need to do to develop professionally. Membership Directory—Online directory and searchable by a variety of criteria. Access to the Membership Directory is for members only. Buyers Guide—A one stop resource for information on hundreds of training suppliers and consultants.

**Meetings**—TechKnowledge Conference & Exposition: January 14–16, 2015, Las Vegas, NV; International Conference & Exposition, May 17–20, 2015, Orlando, FL.

**Publications**—TD (Talent Development) Magazine; TD at Work; State of the Industry Report; ATD Press books; research reports.

**Name of Organization or Association**—Association of Specialized and Cooperative Library Agencies

**Acronym**—ASCLA

**Address:**
50 E. Huron St.
Chicago, IL
60611
USA

**Phone Number**—312-280-4395; **Fax Number**—(312)944-8085

**Email Contact**—ascla@ala.org; **URL**—http://www.ala.org/ascla

**Leaders**—Susan Hornung, Executive Director

**Description**—A division of the American Library Association, the Association of Specialized and Cooperative Library Agencies (ASCLA) enhances the effectiveness of library service by advocating for and providing high quality networking, enrichment and educational opportunities for its diverse members, who represent state library agencies, libraries serving special populations, library cooperatives, and library consultants.

**Membership**—700.

**Dues**—You must be a member of ALA to join ASCLA. See www.ala.org/membership for most current ALA dues rates. ASCLA individual membership: $52; organization membership: $60; State Library Agency dues: $500.

**Meetings**—ASCLA meets in conjunction with the American Library Association.

**Publications**—Interface, quarterly online newsletter; ASCLA Direct, news directly from the ASCLA office; see website http://www.ala.org/ascla for list of other publications.


**Name of Organization or Association**—Canadian Museums Association/ Association des musées canadiens

**Acronym**—CMA/AMC

**Address:**
280 Metcalfe St., Suite 400
Ottawa, ON
K2P 1R7
Canada

**Phone Number**—(613)567-0099; **Fax Number**—(613)233-5438

**Email Contact**—info@museums.ca; **URL**—http://www.museums.ca

**Leaders**—John G. McAvity, Exec. Dir.

**Description**—The Canadian Museums Association is a nonprofit corporation and registered charity dedicated to advancing public museums and museum works in Canada, promoting the welfare and better administration of museums, and fostering a continuing improvement in the qualifications and practices of museum professionals.

**Membership**—2000 museums and individuals, including art galleries, zoos, aquariums, historic parks, etc.

**Dues**—Voting Categories Individual: For those who are, or have been, associated with a recognized museum in Canada. A $10 discount applies if you are associated with a CMA institutional member or if you are a member of a provincial museum association. $85 a year. Senior: For those who are retired and have been associated with a recognized museum in Canada. $50 a year. Institutional Association: For all recognized Canadian museums that are nonprofit, have a collection, and are open to the public. The fee is 0.001 (one tenth of one percent) of your operating budget (i.e., if your budget is $150,000, you would pay $150). The minimum fee payable is $100, and the maximum, $2750. Non-voting Categories Affiliate: For those outside of the museum community who wish to support the aims and programs of the CMA. $100 a year. International: For individuals and institutions outside of Canada. $100 a year. Corporate: For corporations wishing to support the aims and programs of the CMA while developing opportunities within the museum community. $250 a year. Student: For students in Canada. Please enclose a photocopy of your student ID. $50 a year. *Membership fees may be tax deductible. Check with your financial advisor for details.

**Meetings**—CMA Annual Conference, spring.

**Publications**—Muse (bimonthly magazine, color, Canada's only national, bilingual magazine devoted to museums, it contains museum-based photography, feature articles, commentary, and practical information); The Official Directory of Canadian Museums and Related Institutions (online directory) lists all museums in Canada plus information on government departments, agencies, and provincial and regional museum associations.

**Name of Organization or Association**—Computer Assisted Language Instruction Consortium

**Acronym**—CALICO

**Address:**
214 Centennial Hall, Texas State University, 601 University Dr.
San Marcos, TX
78666
USA

**Phone Number**—(512)245-1417; **Fax Number**—(512)245-9089

**Email Contact**—info@calico.org; **URL**—http://calico.org

**Leaders**—Esther Horn, Manager

**Description**—CALICO is devoted to the dissemination of information on the application of technology to language teaching and language learning.

**Membership**—1000 members from the USA and 20 foreign countries. Anyone interested in the development and use of technology in the teaching/learning of foreign languages is invited to join. Members usually come from language teaching fields such as higher education, k-12 education, and even government entities such as the armed services where language learning and teaching are of utmost importance.

**Dues**—$65 annual/individual.

**Meetings**—2016, Michigan State University; 2017, Northern Arizona University.

**Publications**—CALICO Journal Online (three issues per year), CALICO Monograph Series (Monograph IX, 2010: Web 2.0 topics; Monograph V, second edition 2011: teaching languages with technology topics; Monograph X, 2012: teaching writing with technology topics).

**Name of Organization or Association**—Consortium of College and University Media Centers

**Acronym**—CCUMC

**Address:**
306 N. Union Street
Bloomington, IN
47405
USA

**Phone Number**—(812)855-6049; **Fax Number**—(812)855-2103

**Email Contact**—ccumc@ccumc.org; **URL**—www.ccumc.org

**Leaders**—Aileen Scales, Executive Director

**Description**—CCUMC is a professional group whose mission is to provide leadership and a forum for information exchange to the providers of media content, academic technology, and support for quality teaching and learning at institutions of higher education. Fosters cooperative media/instructional technology-related support in higher education institutions and companies providing related products. Gathers and disseminates information on improved procedures and new developments in instructional technology and media center management.

**Membership**—825 individuals at 325 institutions/corporations: Institutional Memberships—Individuals within an institution of higher education who are associated with the support to instruction and presentation technologies in a media center and/or technology support service. Corporate Memberships—Individuals within a corporation, firm, foundation, or other commercial or philanthropic enterprise whose business or activity is in support of the purposes and objectives of CCUMC. Associate Memberships—Individuals not eligible for an Institutional or Corporate membership; from a public library, religious, governmental, or other organizations not otherwise eligible for other categories of membership. Student Memberships—Any student in an institution of higher education who is not eligible for an institutional membership.

**Dues**—Institutional or Corporate Membership: $325 for 1–2 persons, $545 for 3–4 persons, $795 for 5–6 persons, $130 each additional person beyond six Associate Membership: $325 per person Student Membership: $55 per person.

**Meetings**—2015 CCUMC Annual Conference Pittsburgh, PA (October 14–18, 2016).

**Publications**—Leader (newsletter—three issues annually).


**Name of Organization or Association**—Culture, Learning and Technology (a Division of the Association for Educational Communications & Technology)

**Acronym**—AECT-CLT

**Address:**
320 W. 8th St. Ste 101
Bloomington, IN
47404
USA

**Phone Number**—706-897-0664; **Fax Number**—N/A

**Email Contact**—palumpkin@yhc.edu; **URL**—http://aect.site-ym.com/

**Leaders**—Peggy Lumpkin, President (2015–2016); Angela Benson, President-Elect (2015–2016)

**Description**—MISSION STATEMENT: Culture, Learning and Technology's purpose is to encourage the effective utilization of educational media in the teaching learning process; provide leadership opportunities in advancing the use of technology as an integral part of the learning process; provide a vehicle through which minorities might influence the utilization of media in institutions; develop an information exchange network common to minorities in media; study, evaluate, and refine the educational technology process as it relates to the education of minorities and to encourage and improve the production of effective materials for the education of minorities.

**Membership**—Dr. Wesley Joseph McJulien founded Minorities In Media (MIM) around the late 1970s. In the April 1987 issue of Tech Trends, the article Black Contributors to Educational Technology chronicles the history of MIM. John W. Green and Wesley J. McJulien write: "In 1975, a group of Black technologists met in Dallas in an effort to band together and provide more opportunities for Blacks in the Association for Educational Communications and Technology. One of the assignments was to find the Black person who was the outstanding author in the field of educational technology and invite him to speak at the 1977 meeting of BUDDIES (an organization now called Minorities In Media). Dr. Greene was selected and his presentation, "The Role of Blacks in Instructional Technology," stressed that Black must participate in all areas of AECT and especially in research (p. 18)" This history is the foundation of who we are today as an organization. We celebrate our past and continue to spearhead our future. As we move forward, we recognize that societal norms have evolved to include other "minorities" and as such we have expanded our vision to include more areas. These areas are categorized under the cultural umbrella which describes the traditional views such as race, gender, ethnicity and religion but also expands towards a more internationalized view of individualized differences. To further elaborate the Culture, Learning and Technology division is composed of AECT members who are concerned with issues relevant to the intersection of culture, learning and technology. We consider: • Culture as it relates to and is defined in multiple disciplines—sociology, anthropology and psychology; • Learning that is situated in varied environments and involves relevant learning theories; and • Technology that includes approaches to the process of design, information delivery and innovations in technology. We explore relationships between culture, learning and technology in education, politics, economics, science, the arts, and business with the roles they play in the differentiation of individuals in society. Membership is open to professionals and academics whose interests align with CLTs mission.

**Dues**—$75, student; $125—$170 professional.

**Meetings**—Annual meetings held during the Association for Educational Communications & Technology conference—www.aect.org.

**Publications**—Minorities in Media Website: http://aectmim.webs.com/ Facebook Group: www.facebook.com/groups/302061629822972/ Clark, K. (2012). E-Learning and underserved students. In J.A. Banks (Ed.), Encyclopedia of Diversity in Education. Newbury Park, CA: Sage Publications. Clark, K., Brandt, J., Hopkins, R., & Wilhelm, J. (2009). Making games after-school: Participatory game design in non-formal learning environments. Educational Technology, Nov–Dec, pp. 40–44. Eugene, W. & Clark, K. (2012). E-Learning, Engineering and Learners of African Descent: A Needs Analysis. Journal of STEM Education: Innovations and Research, 13(2), 45–57. Eugene, W. and Clark, K. (2009). The Role of Identity and Culture on Website Design. Multicultural Education & Technology Journal, 3(4), p. 256–265. Igoche, D. A., & Branch, R. (2009). Incorporating cultural values into the ADDIE approach to instructional design. Educational Technology, 49(6), 4–8. Joseph, R. & Clark, K. (Eds.) (2009). Culturally relevant technology-based learning environments [Special Issue]. Educational Technology, Nov–Dec. Joseph, R. (2009). Closing the Achievement Gap with Culturally Relevant Technology-based Learning Environments. Educational Technology 49(6), pp. 45–47. Joseph, R. & Clark, K. (2009). Introduction to Special Issue on Culturally Relevant Technology-Based Learning Environments. Educational Technology 49(6), pp. 3–4. Thomas, M., Mitchell, M. & Joseph, R. (2002). The third dimension of ADDIE: A cultural embrace. Tech Trends, 46(2), pp. 40–45. Young, P. A. (2011). The significance of the Culture Based Model in designing culturally-aware tutoring systems. AI & Society. 26(1), 35–47. Young, P. A. (2009). Instructional design frameworks and intercultural models. Hershey, PA: IGI Global/Information Science Publishing.

**Name of Organization or Association**—Education Northwest (formerly Northwest Regional Educational Laboratory)

**Acronym**—N/A

**Address:**
101 SW Main St., Suite 500
Portland, OR
97204
USA

**Phone Number**—(503)275-9500; **Fax Number**—503-275-0448

**Email Contact**—info@educationnorthwest.org; **URL**—http://educationnorthwest.org

**Leaders**—Steve Fleischman, CEO

**Description**—Chartered in the Pacific Northwest in 1966 as Northwest Regional Educational Laboratory, Education Northwest now conducts more than 200 projects annually, working with schools, districts, and communities across the country on comprehensive, research-based solutions to the challenges they face. At Education Northwest, we are dedicated to and passionate about learning. Through our work, we strive to create vibrant learning environments where all youth and adults can succeed. Everything we do is evidence-based, giving us a solid foundation upon which we stand with confidence. We work with teachers, administrators, policy-makers, and communities to identify needs, evaluate programs, and develop new solutions. The breadth of our work—ranging from training teachers, to developing curriculum, to restructuring schools, to evaluating programs—allows us to take a comprehensive look at education and to bring wide-ranging expertise and creativity to our clients' challenges. Our approach is highly customized to meet the needs of our clients, and our staff members take great pride in working closely with customers in the field to design the right approach for each situation. We are proud of our 40-year track record, but we don't rest on our laurels—instead, we strive constantly to identify and address emerging needs and trends in teaching and learning.

**Membership**—921 organizations.

**Dues**—None.

**Meetings**—Annual meeting of membership.

**Publications**—Northwest Matters blog.


**Name of Organization or Association**—Educational Communications, Inc., Environmental, Media and Cultural Projects of

**Acronym**— –

**Address:**
P.O. Box 351419
Los Angeles, CA
90035
USA

**Phone Number**—(310)559-9160; **Fax Number**—on request

**Email Contact**—ECNP@aol.com; **URL**—www.ecoprojects.org

**Leaders**—Nancy Pearlman, Executive Director and Executive Producer

**Description**—Educational Communications is dedicated to enhancing the quality of life on this planet and provides radio programs and television documentaries about the environment, ecotourism and cultural events. Serves as a clearinghouse on ecological issues through the Ecology Center of Southern California. Programming is available on 50 stations in 21 states and the internet. These include: ECONEWS television series and ENVIRONMENTAL DIRECTIONS radio series. Provides ethnic folk dance performances through Earth Cultures. Assists groups in third-world countries through Humanity and the Planet, especially "Wells for Burkina Faso" and "Sustainable Orphanages" and "Environmental Education in Kenya." Services provided include ethnic folk dance performances, a speakers bureau, award-winning public service announcements, radio and television documentaries, video promos, volunteer and intern opportunities, and input into the decision-making process. Its mission is to educate the public about both the problems and the solutions of the ecological crisis. Other projects include Project Ecotourism, Environmental Resources Library and more.

**Membership**—$20.00 for yearly subscription to the Compendium Newsletter.

**Dues**—$20 for regular. All donations accepted.

**Meetings**—As needed.

**Publications**—Compendium Newsletter (bimonthly newsletter) "Culturally Speaking" Newsletter on website Environmental Directions radio audio cassettes, (1900 produced to date) ECONEWS and ECO-TRAVEL television series (over 600 shows in the catalog, available on DVD).

**Name of Organization or Association**—Instructional Technology Council

**Acronym**—ITC

**Address:**
426 C Street, NE
Washington, DC
20002-5839
USA

**Phone Number**—(202)293-3110; **Fax Number**—(202)293-3110

**Email Contact**—cmullins@itcnetwork.org; **URL**—http://www.itcnetwork.org

**Leaders**—Christine Mullins, Executive Director

**Description**—An affiliated council of the American Association of Community Colleges established in 1977, the Instructional Technology Council (ITC) is a leader in advancing distance education. ITCs mission is to provide exceptional leadership and professional development in higher education to its network of eLearning practitioners by advocating, collaborating, researching, and sharing exemplary, innovative practices and potential in educational technologies. ITC tracks federal legislation that will affect distance learning, conducts annual professional development meetings, supports research, and provides a forum for members to share expertise and materials. ITC members receive a subscription to the ITC News and ITC list serv with information on what is happening in distance education, participation in ITCs professional development Webinar series, distance learning grants information, updates on distance learning legislation, discounts to attend the annual eLearning Conference which features more than 80 workshops and seminars.

**Membership**—ITC members include single institutions and multi-campus districts; regional and statewide systems of community, technical and two-year colleges; for-profit organizations; four-year institutions; and nonprofit organizations that are interested or involved in instructional telecommunications.

**Dues**—ITC offers institutional, associate, and consortia memberships and corporate sponsorship opportunities. The institutional, associate, and consortia membership rate is $495 per year. Corporate sponsorship packages are available from $2500 to $10,000.

**Meetings**—ITCs Annual Conference eLearning 2016 will be held on February 14–17, 2016 in Scottsdale Arizona. ITCs 2016 Distance Education Leadership Academy on July 21–23, 2016.

**Publications**—ITC Distance Education Daily; ITC Newsletter—Quarterly; Trends in eLearning: Tracking the Impact of eLearning at Community Colleges; Trends in Distance Education: What College Leaders Should Consider; Quality Enhancing Practices in Distance Education: Vol. 2 Student Services; Quality Enhancing Practices in Distance Education: Vol. 1 Teaching and Learning; New Connections: A Guide to Distance Education (2nd ed.); New Connections: A College President's

Guide to Distance Education; Digital Video: A Handbook for Educators; Faculty Compensation and Support Issues in Distance Education.

**Name of Organization or Association**—International Association for Language Learning Technology

**Acronym**—IALLT

**Address:**
Information Technology Services, Concordia College
Moorhead, MN
56562
USA

**Phone Number**—(218) 299-3464; **Fax Number**—(218) 299-3246

**Email Contact**—business@iallt.org; **URL**—http://iallt.org

**Leaders**—Harold Hendricks, President; Kristy Britt, Treasurer

**Description**—IALLT is a professional organization whose members provide leadership in the development, integration, evaluation and management of instructional technology for the teaching and learning of language, literature, and culture.

**Membership**—400 members Membership/Subscription Categories * Educational Member: for people working in an academic setting such as a school, college, or university. These members have voting rights. * Full-time Student Member: for full-time students interested in membership. Requires a signature of a voting member to verify student status. These members have voting rights. * Commercial Member: for those working for corporations interested in language learning and technology. This category includes for example language laboratory vendors, software and textbook companies. * Library Subscriber: receive our journals for placement in libraries.

**Dues**—1 year: $50, voting member; $25, student; $200 commercial. 2 year: $90, voting member; $380 commercial.

**Meetings**—Biennial IALLT conferences treat the entire range of topics related to technology in language learning as well as management and planning. IALLT also sponsors sessions at conferences of organizations with related interests, including CALICO and ACTFL.

**Publications**—IALLT Journal of Language Learning Technologies (two times annually); materials for language lab management and design, language teaching and technology. Visit our website for details. http://iallt.org.

**Name of Organization or Association**—International Association of School Librarianship

**Acronym**—IASL

**Address:**
65 E. Wacker Place
Chicago, IL
60601
USA

**Phone Number**—312-419-9094; **Fax Number**—312-419-8950

**Email Contact**—iasl@mlahq.org; **URL**—http://www.iasl-online.org/

**Leaders**—Dr. Diljit Singh, President

**Description**—Seeks to encourage development of school libraries and library programs throughout the world; promote professional preparation and continuing education of school librarians; achieve collaboration among school libraries of the world; foster relationships between school librarians and other professionals connected with children and youth and to coordinate activities, conferences, and other projects in the field of school librarianship.

**Membership**—500 members worldwide including students, individuals, institutions, and associations.

**Dues**—Yearly membership to IASL is based on a calendar year—January to December Student membership/Retiree membership: Zone A USD $30.00 Zone B USD $15.00 Zone C USD $10.00 Personal membership: Note Zone A USD $100.00 Zone B USD $60.00 Zone C USD $15.00 LIFE USD $2000.00 Association/Institution membership: Zone A USD $200.00 Zone B USD $120.00 Zone C USD $40.00 For geographic zone information see: http://www.iasl-online.org/member_info.html.

**Meetings**—Annual Conference: August 22–26, 2016 Tokyo, Japan; August 2017, Long Beach, CA, USA.

**Publications**—IASL Newsletter (3/year); School Libraries Worldwide (semiannual); Conference Professionals and Research Papers (annual).


**Name of Organization or Association**—Library and Information Technology Association

**Acronym**—LITA

**Address:**
50 E. Huron St.
Chicago, IL
60611
USA

**Phone Number**—(312)280-4270, (800)545-2433, ext. 4270; **Fax Number**—(312)280-3257

**Email Contact**—lita@ala.org; **URL**—http://www.lita.org

**Leaders**—Jenny Levine, Executive Director

**Description**—LITA is concerned with the planning, development, design, application, and integration of technologies within the library and information environment, with the impact of emerging technologies on library service, and with the effect of automated technologies on people. Its major focus is on interdisciplinary issues and emerging technologies. LITA disseminates information, provides educational opportunities for learning about information technologies and forums for the discussion of common concerns, monitors new technologies with potential applications in information science, encourages and fosters research, promotes the development of technical standards, and examines the effects of library systems and networks.

**Membership**—LITA members come from all types of libraries and institutions focusing on information technology in libraries. They include library decision-makers, practitioners, information professionals, and vendors. Approximately 2500 members.

**Dues**—$60 plus membership in ALA; $25 plus membership in ALA for library school students.

**Meetings**—National Forum takes place in the fall.

**Publications**—LITA Blog: http://litablog.org Information Technology and Libraries: ITAL is the refereed, open access journal of the Library and Information Technology Association. It publishes material related to all aspects of information technology in all types of libraries. LITA Publications List: For information about LITA Guides and monographs, visit http://bit.ly/LITAbooks.

**Name of Organization or Association**—Lister Hill National Center for Biomedical Communications

**Acronym**—LHNCBC

**Address:**
US National Library of Medicine, 8600 Rockville Pike
Bethesda, MD
20894
USA

**Phone Number**—(301)496-4441; **Fax Number**—(301)402-0118

**Email Contact**—lhcques@lhc.nlm.nih.gov; **URL**—http://lhncbc.nlm.nih.gov/

**Leaders**—Clement J. McDonald, MD, Director, ClemMcDonald@mail.nih.gov

**Description**—The Lister Hill National Center for Biomedical Communications is an intramural research and development division of the US National Library of Medicine (NLM). The Center conducts and supports research and development in the dissemination of high quality imagery, medical language processing, high-speed access to biomedical information, intelligent database systems development, multimedia visualization, knowledge management, data mining and machine-assisted indexing.

**Membership**—None.

**Dues**—None.

**Meetings**—None.

**Publications**—Fact sheet (and helpful links to other publications) at: http://www. nlm.nih.gov/pubs/factsheets/lister_hill.html Fellowship and PostDoctoral opportunities are ongoing: http://lhncbc/medical_informatics_training_program.


**Name of Organization or Association**—McREL International

**Acronym**—McREL

**Address:**
4601 DTC Blvd., Suite 500
Denver, CO
80237
USA

**Phone Number**—800-858-6830; **Fax Number**—(303)337-3005

**Email Contact**—info@mcrel.org; **URL**—http://www.mcrel.org

**Leaders**—Bryan Goodwin, CEO

**Description**—McREL International is a nonprofit, nonpartisan organization devoted to improving education through applied research, professional development, and consultative service to teachers and leaders across the USA and around the world. McREL promotes the best research-based instructional and leadership practices that have the strongest effect on student achievement. McREL also provides clients with expertise in academic standards, school and system improvement approaches, use of classroom technology, teacher and leader coaching, and STEM education and programming. McREL manages the US Department of Educations North Central Comprehensive Center, serving the states of Nebraska, North Dakota, South Dakota, and Wyoming. The center provides training and technical assistance to state education agencies in implementing and administering federal education programs. McREL also manages the US Department of Educations Pacific Regional Education Lab, connecting educators in Hawaii, American Samoa, Guam, the Commonwealth of the Northern Mariana Islands, the Federated States of Micronesia, the Republic of the Marshall Islands, and the Republic of Palau with research on teacher effectiveness, family and community engagement, college and career readiness, and more. McREL conducts research and serves as an external evaluator for a variety of local, state, and federal programs at both the K-12 and higher education levels, and also supports public education and outreach for several NASA projects.

**Membership**—Not a membership organization.

**Dues**—No dues.

**Meetings**—NA.

**Publications**—Changing Schools (journal, two issues per year), eNews (monthly electronic newsletter), plus numerous technical reports and other publications. Check website, www.mcrel.org, for current listings.

**Name of Organization or Association**—Media Communications Association—International

**Acronym**—MCA-I

**Address:**
P.O. Box 5135
Madison, WI
53705-0135
USA

**Phone Number**—Use Contact Form

**Email Contact**—info@mca-i.org; **URL**—http://www.mca-i.org

**Leaders**—Melissa Thompson and Sharon Pertzborn-Jensen, Co-Executive Directors

**Description**—MCA-Is mission is to provide media communications professionals opportunities for networking, forums for education, and resources for information. MCA-I also offers business services, such as low-cost insurance, buying programs, etc., to reduce operating costs. MCA-I also confers the highly acclaimed MCA-I Media Festival awarding the Golden Reel. Visit www.mca-i.org for more info.

**Membership**—Individual, student, and corporate members. Membership programs are also available to vendors for relationship and business development.

**Dues**—$90, individual. See website for complete dues schedule.

**Meetings**—Various Partnerships with Association Conferences.

**Publications**—MCA-I eNews (monthly), Find a Pro Directory (online), Facebook, LinkedIn, YouTube, Twitter.

**Name of Organization or Association**—Medical Library Association

**Acronym**—MLA

**Address:**
65 E. Wacker Pl., Ste. 1900
Chicago, IL
60601-7246
USA

**Phone Number**—(312)419-9094; **Fax Number**—(312)419-8950

**Email Contact**—gunn@mail.mlahq.org; **URL**—https://www.mlanet.org/

**Leaders**—Kevin Baliozian, Executive Director

**Description**—MLA, a nonprofit, educational organization, comprises health sciences information professionals with 3000 members worldwide. Through its programs and services, MLA provides lifelong educational opportunities, supports a knowledgebase of health information research, and works with a global network of partners to promote the importance of quality information for improved health to the health care community and the public.

**Membership**—Membership categories: Regular Lower Salary/Regular Membership Institutional Membership International Membership Affiliate Membership Student Membership.

**Dues**—$120/$195, regular lower salary/regular; $130, introductory; $295–695, institutional, based on total library expenditures, including salaries, but excluding grants and contracts; $130, international; $120, affiliate; $50, student.

**Meetings**—National annual meeting held every May; most chapter meetings are held in the fall.

**Publications**—MLA News (newsletter, 10/yr.); Journal of the Medical Library Association (quarterly scholarly publication.); Books copublishers: Rowman & Littlefield; ALA Editions.


**Name of Organization or Association**—National Alliance for Media Arts and Culture

**Acronym**—NAMAC

**Address:**
3965 Linwood Avenue
Oakland, CA
94602
USA

**Phone Number**—(510)336-2555; **Fax Number**—(000)000-0000

**Email Contact**—namac@namac.org; **URL**—http://www.namac.org

**Leaders**—Wendy Levy, Executive Director

**Description**—NAMAC is a nonprofit organization dedicated facilitating collaboration, innovation, strategic growth and cultural impact in the media arts field in the USA and around the world. Members include media centers, arts institutions, funders, independent mediamakers, universities, and civil society NGOs as well as other individuals and organizations providing services for production, education, exhibition, distribution, and preservation of public media. NAMACs information services and interactive resources are available to the general public, arts and non-arts organizations, businesses, corporations, foundations, government agencies, schools, and universities.

**Membership**—300 organizations, 75 individuals.

**Dues**—$200–1000, institutional (depending on annual budget); $50–100, indiv.

**Meetings**—Biennial Conference.

**Publications**—Media Arts Information Network; The National Media Education Directory, annual anthology of case-studies "A Closer Look," periodic White Paper reports, Digital Directions: Convergence Planning for the Media Arts.


**Name of Organization or Association**—National Council of Teachers of English

**Acronym**—NCTE

**Address:**
1111 W. Kenyon Rd.
Urbana, IL
61801-1096
USA

**Phone Number**—(217)328-3870; **Fax Number**—(217)328-0977

**Email Contact**—public_info@ncte.org; **URL**—http://www.ncte.org

**Leaders**—NCTE Executive Director

**Description**—The National Council of Teachers of English, with 30,000 individual and institutional members worldwide, is dedicated to improving the teaching and learning of English and the language arts at all levels of education. Among its position statements and publications related to educational media and technology are "Code of Best Practices in Fair Use for Media Literacy Education," "The NCTE Definition of twenty-first Century Literacies," and "Position Statement on Teaching, Learning, and Assessing Writing in Digital Environments."

**Membership**—NCTE members include elementary, middle, and high school teachers; supervisors of English programs; college and university faculty; teacher educators; local and state agency English specialists; and professionals in related fields.

**Dues**—Membership in NCTE is $50 a year; subscriptions to its journals is in addition to the membership fee.

**Meetings**—http://www.ncte.org/annual/ 104th NCTE Annual Convention, November 20–23, Washington, DC; 105th NCTE Annual Convetion, November 19–22, Minneapolis, MN.

**Publications**—NCTE publishes about ten books a year. Visit http://www.ncte.org/books and http://www.ncte.org/store. NCTEs journals include Language Arts Voices from the Middle English Journal College English College Composition and

Communication English Education Research in the Teaching of English Teaching English in the Two-Year College Talking Points English Leadership Quarterly The Council Chronicle (included in NCTE membership) Journal information is available at http://www.ncte.org/journals/.

**Name of Organization or Association**—National Endowment for the Humanities

**Acronym**—NEH

**Address:**
Division of Public Programs, America's Media Makers Program, 400 7th Street, SW
Washington, DC
20506
USA

**Phone Number**—(202)606-8269; **Fax Number**—(202)606-8557

**Email Contact**—publicpgms@neh.gov; **URL**—http://www.neh.gov

**Leaders**—Karen Mittelman, Director, Division of Public Programs

**Description**—The NEH is an independent federal grant-making agency that supports research, educational, and public programs grounded in the disciplines of the humanities. The Division of Public Programs Media Projects supports film and radio programs in the humanities for public audiences, including children and adults. All programs in the Division of Public Program support various technologies, specifically websites both as stand-alone projects and as extensions of larger projects such as museum exhibitions. The Division of Public Programs has a second film grant program. The Bridging Cultures through Film: International Topics program supports documentary films that examine international and transnational themes in the humanities. These projects are meant to spark Americans' engagement with the broader world by exploring one or more countries and cultures outside of the USA. Proposed documentaries must be analytical and deeply grounded in humanities scholarship. Beginning in 2014, the Division of Public Programs created a new grant category. Digital Projects for the Public grants support projects that are largely created for digital platforms. While these projects can take many forms, shapes, and sizes, you should apply to this program primarily to create digital projects or the digital components of a larger project. NEH is a national funding agency, so these projects should demonstrate the potential to attract a broad, general audience. Projects can have specific targeted audiences (including K-12 students), but they should also strive to cultivate a more inclusive audience.

**Membership**—Nonprofit institutions and organizations including public television and radio stations.

**Dues**—Not applicable.

**Meetings**—Not applicable.

**Publications**—Visit the website (http://www.neh.gov) for application forms and guidelines as well as the Media Log, a cumulative listing of projects funded through the Media Program.


**Name of Organization or Association**—National Freedom of Information Coalition

**Acronym**—NFOIC

**Address:**
101 Reynolds Journalism Institute, Missouri School of Journalism
Columbia, MO
65211-0012
USA

**Phone Number**—573.882.4856; **Fax Number**—NA

**Email Contact**—nfoic@nfoic.org; **URL**—http://www.nfoic.org/

**Leaders**—Daniel Bevarly, interim executive director

**Description**—The National Freedom of Information Coalition is a national membership organization devoted to protecting the publics right to oversee its government. NFOICs goals include helping start-up FOI organizations; strengthening existing FOI organizations; and developing FOI programs and publications appropriate to the membership.

**Membership**—The NFOIC offers active memberships to freestanding nonprofit state or regional Freedom of Information Coalitions, academic centers and First Amendment Centers, and associated memberships to individuals and entities supporting NFOICs mission. Membership information is available at http://www.nfoic.org. Achieving and maintaining active membership in all 50 states is the primary goal of NFOIC.

**Dues**—Membership categories and levels of support are described on the NFOIC website.

**Meetings**—The National Freedom of Information Coalition hosts an FOI Summit.

**Publications**—The FOI Advocate, a blog on FOI, FOIA, and open government matters. Various other audits and white papers.


**Name of Organization or Association**—National Gallery of Art

**Acronym**—NGA

**Address:**
Department of Education Resources, 2000B South Club Drive
Landover, MD
20785
USA

**Phone Number**—(202)842-6269; **Fax Number**—(202)842-6935

**Email   Contact**—EdResources@nga.gov;   **URL**—https://learningresources.nga.gov:7008/vwebv/searchBasic

**Leaders**—Leo J. Kasun, Head, Deparment of Education Resources

**Description**—This department of NGA is responsible for the production and distribution of 120+ educational audiovisual programs, including interactive technologies. Materials available (all loaned free to individuals, schools, colleges and universities, community organizations, and noncommercial television stations) range from DVDs, CD-Roms, and teaching packets with either image CD-ROMs. All DVD programs are closed captioned A free catalog describing all programs is available upon request. We can also provide multiple copies for inservices or large meetings or conferences. Many of these programs are available for long-term loan.

**Membership**—Our free-loan lending program resembles that of a library and because we are a federally funded institution we do not have a membership system. Last year we lent programs directly to over one million borrowers. Our programs are available to anyone who requests them which ranges from individuals to institutions.

**Dues**—None.

**Meetings**—None.

**Publications**—Extension Programs Catalog.


**Name of Organization or Association**—National Telemedia Council Inc.

**Acronym**—NTC

**Address:**
1922 University Ave.
Madison, WI
53726
USA

**Phone Number**—(608)218-1182; **Fax Number**—None

**Email   Contact**—NTelemedia@aol.com;   **URL**—http://www.nationaltelemedia-council.org, and www.journalofmedialiteracy.org

**Leaders**—Karen Ambrosh, President; Marieli Rowe, Exec. Dir.; Belinha De Abreu, Vice-President; Rev. Stephen Umhoefer, Treasurer; Kate Vannoy, Secretary, Dr. Martin Rayala, Past President, (plus 9 Board Members)

**Description**—The National Telemedia Council is a national, nonprofit professional organization that has been promoting a media wise society since 1953. Embracing a positive, nonjudgmental philosophy that values education, evaluation, and reflective judgment, NTC has a long history of a broad array of initiatives that have included annual conferences, workshops, major and innovative interactive forums, local, national and international events for diverse participants (including children); and its major ongoing award, the "Jessie McCanse Award for Individual, Long-Term Contribution to the Field of Media Literacy." NTCs ongoing current activities continue to include its major publication, The Journal of Media Literacy, published two times per year (and a part of the organization since its inception in 1953 and earlier); the development of its archival website; and interactive collaborations to advance the field such as the "media literacy cafes" in connection with issues of the Journal of Media Literacy.

**Membership**—Member/subscribers to the Journal of Media Literacy, currently over 500, including individuals, organizations, schools and University libraries across the Globe including Asia, Australia, Europe, North and South America. Our membership is open to all those interested in media literacy.

**Dues**—Individuals: $40, basic $60, contributing $100, patron Organizations/ Library: $60 Corporate sponsorship: $500 (Additional Postage for Overseas: Canada or Mexico, add $20.00. All other outside North America, add $25.00).

**Meetings**—We are working toward a Symposium showcasing the publication of our archives for our 65th Anniversary in Fall, 2018.

**Publications**—The Journal of Media Literacy.


**Name of Organization or Association**—Reference and User Services Association, a division of the American Library Association

**Acronym**—RUSA

**Address:**
50 E. Huron St.
Chicago, IL
60611
USA

**Phone Number**—(800)545-2433, ext. 4398.; **Fax Number**—(312)280-5273

**Email Contact**—rusa@ala.org; **URL**—http://rusa.ala.org

**Leaders**—Susan Hornung, Executive Director

**Description**—A division of the American Library Association, the Reference and User Services Division (RUSA) is responsible for stimulating and supporting in the delivery of general library services and materials, and the provision of reference and information services, collection development, readers advisory, and resource sharing for all ages, in every type of library.

**Membership**—4200.

**Dues**—Join ALA and RUSA $120; RUSA membership $60 (added to ALA membership); student member $55 ($30 for ALA and $25 for RUSA); retired, support staff or nonsalaried $72 ($42 for ALA and $30 for RUSA).

**Meetings**—Meetings are held in conjunction with the American Library Association.

**Publications**—RUSQ (q.), information provided on RUSA website at www.ala.org/rusa; RUSA Direct, news directly from the RUSA office; RUSA Update, online membership newsletter, select publications.

**Name of Organization or Association**—SERVE Center @ UNCG

**Acronym**—We no longer use the acronym

**Address:**
5900 Summit Avenue, Dixon Building
Browns Summit, NC
27214
USA

**Phone Number**—800-755-3277, 336-315-7457; **Fax Number**—336-315-7457

**Email Contact**—info@serve.org; **URL**—http://www.serve.org/

**Leaders**—Dr. Terri Shelton, Vice Chancellor UNCG Office of Research and Economic Development, Executive Director SERVE Center

**Description**—The SERVE Center at the University of North Carolina at Greensboro, is a university-based education organization with the mission to promote and support the continuous improvement of educational opportunities for all learners. The organizations commitment to continuous improvement is manifest in an applied research-to-practice model that drives all of its work. Building on research, professional wisdom, and craft knowledge, SERVE staff members develop tools, processes, and interventions designed to assist practitioners and policymakers with their work. SERVEs ultimate goal is to raise the level of student achievement in the region. Evaluation of the impact of these activities combined with input from stakeholders expands SERVEs knowledge base and informs future research. The SERVE Center is dedicated to building the capacity of educational leaders in using data, research, and evaluation to improve instructional programs and services. Key aspects of our current work focus on improving services for at-risk students (homeless, migrant, high poverty), studying high school reform initiatives, measuring and improving student engagement, and building the evaluation-capacity of educational and community nonprofit leaders.

**Membership**—None.

**Dues**—None.

**Meetings**—None.

**Publications**—Four titles available in the highlighted products area of website: Reducing Stereotype Threat in Classrooms: A Review of Social-Psychological Intervention Studies on Improving the Achievement of Black Students. Abstract: Stereotype threat arises from a fear among members of a group of reinforcing negative stereotypes about the intellectual ability of the group. The report identifies three randomized controlled trial studies that use classroom-based strategies to reduce stereotype threat and improve the academic performance of Black students, narrowing their achievement gap with White students. A Review Of Methods and Instruments Used In State and Local School Readiness Evaluations Abstract: This report provides detailed information about the methods and instruments used to evaluate school readiness initiatives, discusses important considerations in selecting instruments, and provides resources and recommendations that may be helpful to those who are designing and implementing school readiness evaluations. Levers For Change: Southeast Region State Initiatives To Improve High Schools Abstract: This descriptive report aims to stimulate discussion about high school reform among Southeast Region states. The report groups recent state activities in high school reform into six "levers for change." To encourage critical reflection, the report places the reform discussion in the context of an evidence-based decisionmaking process and provides sample research on reform activities. Evidence-Based Decision making: Assessing Reading Across the Curriculum Intervention. Abstract: When selecting reading across the curriculum interventions, educators should consider the extent of the evidence base on intervention effectiveness and the fit with the school or district context, whether they are purchasing a product from vendors or developing it internally. This report provides guidance in the decision making.

**Name of Organization or Association**—Society of Photo Technologists

**Acronym**—SPT

**Address:**
11112 S. Spotted Rd.
Cheney, WA
99004
USA

**Phone Number**—800-624-9621 or (509)624-9621; **Fax Number**—(509)624-5320

**Email Contact**—cc5@earthlink.net; **URL**—http://www.spt.info/

**Leaders**—Chuck Bertone, Executive Director

**Description**—An organization of photographic equipment repair technicians, which improves and maintains communications between manufacturers and repair shops and technicians. We publish Repair Journals, Newsletters, Parts & Service Directory and Industry Newsletters. We also sponsor SPTNET (a technical email group), Remanufactured parts and residence workshops. Currently our biggest thrust is into Service Adjustment Software, currently featuring Canon models.

**Membership**—1000 shops and manufactures world wide, eligible people or businesses are any who are involved full or part time in the camera repair field.

**Dues**—$125.00–370. Membership depends on the size/volumn of the business. Most one man shops are Class A/$195 dues. Those not involved full time in the field is $125.00/Associate Class.

**Meetings**—SPT Journal; SPT Parts and Services Directory; SPT Newsletter; SPT Manuals—Training and Manufacturer's Tours.

**Publications**—Journals & Newsletters.


**Name of Organization or Association**—The NETWORK, Inc.

**Acronym**—NETWORK

**Address:**
23 NE Morgan St.
Portland, OR
97211-2342
USA

**Phone Number**—800-877-5400, 503-265-8293; **Fax Number**—503-336-1014

**Email Contact**—davidc@thenetworkinc.org; **URL**—www.thenetworkinc.org

**Leaders**—David Crandall, President

**Description**—A nonprofit research and service organization providing training, research and evaluation, technical assistance, and materials for a fee to schools, educational organizations, and private sector firms with educational interests. The NETWORK has been helping professionals manage and learn about change since 1969. Our Leadership Skills series of computer-based simulations extends the widely used board game versions of Making Change (tm) and Systems Thinking/ Systems Changing (tm) with the addition of Improving Student Success: Teachers, Schools and Parents to offer educators a range of proven professional development tools. Networking for Learning, originally developed for the British Department for Education and Skills, offers a contemporary leadership development resource for educators exploring the challenges of complex collaborations involving multiple organizations. Development of Web-based versions is currently underway.

**Membership**—None required.

**Dues**—No dues, fee for service.

**Meetings**—Call.

**Publications**—Making Change: A Simulation Game [board and computer versions]; Systems Thinking/Systems Changing: A Simulation Game [board and computer versions]; Improving Student Success: Teachers, Schools and Parents [computer based simulation].

**Name of Organization or Association**—Vision Maker Media

**Acronym**—NAPT

**Address:**
1800 North 33rd Street
Lincoln, NE
68503
USA

**Phone Number**—(402)472-3522; **Fax Number**—(402)472-8675

**Email Contact**—visionmaker@unl.edu; **URL**—www.visionmakermedia.org

**Leaders**—Shirley K. Sneve, Executive Director

**Description**—Vision Maker Media shares Native stories with the world that represent the cultures, experiences, and values of American Indians and Alaska Natives. Vision Maker Media exists to serve Native producers and Indian country in partnership with public television and radio. Vision Maker Media works with Native producers to develop, produce and distribute educational telecommunications programs for all media including public television and public radio. Vision Maker Media supports training to increase the number of American Indians and Alaska Natives producing quality public broadcasting programs, which includes advocacy efforts promoting increased control and use of information technologies and the policies to support this control by American Indians and Alaska Natives. A key strategy for this work is the development of strong partnerships with tribal nations, Indian organizations and Native communities. Reaching the general public and the global market is the ultimate goal for the dissemination of Native produced media that shares Native perspectives with the world.

**Membership**—No Membership.

**Dues**—None.

**Meetings**—None.

**Publications**—VisionMaker E-Newsletter NAPT General E-Newsletter Producer E-Newsletter Educational Catalog Annual Report Viewer Discussion Guides Educational Guides.

**Name of Organization or Association**—Young Adult Library Services Association

**Acronym**—YALSA

**Address:**
50 E. Huron St.
Chicago, IL
60611
USA

**Phone Number**—(312)280-4390; **Fax Number**—(312)280-5276

**Email Contact**—yalsa@ala.org; **URL**—http://www.ala.org/yalsa

**Leaders**—Beth Yoke, Executive Director

**Description**—A division of the American Library Association (ALA), the Young Adult Library Services Association (YALSA). This is a national association of librarians, library workers and advocates whose mission is to expand and strengthen library services for teens, aged 12–18. Through its member-driven advocacy, research, and professional development initiatives, YALSA builds the capacity of libraries and librarians to engage, serve and empower teens. What We Do YALSA brings together key stakeholders from the areas of libraries, education, research, out of school time, youth development and more to develop and deliver resources to libraries that expand their capacity to support teen learning and enrichment and to foster healthy communities. Advocate By participating in events like National Library Legislative Day and implementing District Days initiatives for libraries to participate in, YALSA works at a national level to inform and engage policy makers and elected officials about the important role libraries and librarians play in preparing teens to become engaged, productive citizens. Research Through efforts such as its Research Agenda and Journal for Research on Libraries and Young Adults, YALSA promotes and disseminates relevant research. Train In order to ensure that librarians and library workers have the skills needed to engage, educate and support teens, YALSA offers a wealth of continuing education activities, including e-learning and a biennial symposium. Through grant funding YALSA is developing digital badges that will provide a new way for librarians and library workers to gain skills and demonstrate their expertise to employers. Build Capacity YALSA provides over $150,000 per year to libraries through grants to help libraries do things like offer summer reading programs, hire teen interns and increase their digital media offerings. YALSA scholarships and stipends support librarians and library workers seeking to further their education or gain leadership skills. Read our 2012 report on Helping Libraries Meet the Needs of Diverse Teens.

**Membership**—5500. YALSA members may be young adult librarians, school librarians, library directors, graduate students, educators, publishers, or anyone for whom library service to young adults is important.

**Dues**—$50; $20 students; $20 retirees (in addition to ALA membership).

**Meetings**—Two ALA conferences yearly, Midwinter (January) and Annual (June); one annual Young Adult Literature Symposium (beginning in 2008).

**Publications**—Young Adult Library Services, a quarterly print journal Attitudes, a quarterly electronic newsletter for members only.

# Part IV
# Graduate Programs

# Chapter 15
# Introduction

**Michael Orey**

Part V includes annotated entries for graduate programs that offer degrees in the fields of learning, design and technology or library and information science. In an effort to only list active organizations, I deleted all programs that had not updated their information since 2013. All readers are encouraged to contact the institutions that are not listed for investigation and possible inclusion in the 2017 edition.

Information for this section was obtained through e-mail directing each program to an individual web form through which the updated information could be submitted electronically into a database created by Michael Orey. Although the section editor made every effort to contact and follow up with program representatives, responding to the annual request for an update was the responsibility of the program representatives. The editing team would like to thank those respondents who helped assure the currency and accuracy of this section by responding to the request for an update. In this year's edition, I asked for some data on numbers of graduates, number of faculty, and amount of grants and contracts. These data were used as self-report top 20 lists in the preface to this book. Readers should be aware that these data are only as accurate as the person who filled the form for their program.

M. Orey (✉)
Learning, Design, and Technology, The University of Georgia,
116 River's Crossing, Athens, GA 30602-4809, USA
e-mail: mikeorey@uga.edu

© Springer International Publishing Switzerland 2017                    221
M. Orey, R.M. Branch (eds.), *Educational Media and Technology Yearbook,*
Educational Media and Technology Yearbook 40,
DOI 10.1007/978-3-319-45001-8_15

# Chapter 16
# Graduate Programs in Learning, Design, and Technology

Michael Orey

**Name of Institution**—University of British Columbia

**Name of Department or Program**—Master of Educational Technology degree program

**Address:**
1304-2125 Main Mall
Vancouver, BC
V6T 1Z4
Canada

**Phone Number**—1-888-492-1122; **Fax Number**—1-604-822-2015

**Email Contact**—info.met@ubc.ca; **URL**—http://met.ubc.ca

**Contact Person**—David Roy

**Specializations**—This innovative online program provides an excellent environment in which to learn the techniques of instructional design including the development and management of programs for international and intercultural populations. Attracting students from more than 30 countries, the program provides a unique opportunity to learn and collaborate with professionals and colleagues from around the world. The MET curriculum is designed for K-12 teachers, college and university faculty, course designers, adult and industry educators.

**Features**—MET fully online graduate degree. MET Graduate Certificate in Technology-Based Distributed Learning. MET Graduate Certificate in Technology-Based Learning for Schools.

M. Orey (✉)
Learning, Design, and Technology, The University of Georgia,
116 River's Crossing, Athens, GA 30602-4809, USA
e-mail: mikeorey@uga.edu

© Springer International Publishing Switzerland 2017
M. Orey, R.M. Branch (eds.), *Educational Media and Technology Yearbook*,
Educational Media and Technology Yearbook 40,
DOI 10.1007/978-3-319-45001-8_16

**Admission Requirements**—Please see website.

**Degree Requirements**—Master's Program: ten courses; Graduate Certificates: five courses.

**Number of Full Time Faculty**—9; **Number of Other Faculty**—8

**Degrees awarded in 2012–2013 Academic Year**—Master's—75; PhD—0; Other—0

**Grant Monies awarded in 2012–2013 Academic Year**—0


**Name of Institution**—University of New Brunswick

**Name of Department or Program**—Faculty of Education

**Address:**
P.O. Box 4400
Fredericton, NB
E3B 5A3
Canada

**Phone Number**—506-452-6125; **Fax Number**—506-453-3569

**Email Contact**—erose@unb.ca; **URL**—http://www.unbf.ca/education/

**Contact Person**—Dr. Ellen Rose

**Specializations**—Courses offered include Introduction to Instructional Design, Designing Constructivist Learning Environments, Needs Assessment, Designing Instructional Materials, Instructional Design for Online Learning, and Educational Technology: Key Issues and Trends. In addition, students are allowed to take other courses in the Faculty of Education or other applicable areas.

**Features**—Students can choose the course, project, or thesis stream. UNBs MEd in Instructional Design is very flexible, allowing students to customize their own learning experiences in order to meet their particular learning outcomes. While this is not an online program, most of the Instructional Design courses, and many other relevant courses in the Faculty of Education, are available online.

**Admission Requirements**—Applicants must have an undergraduate degree in Education or a relevant field, a grade point average of at least 3.0 (B, or its equivalent), and at least 1 year of teaching or related professional experience. Applicants whose first language is not English must submit evidence of their proficiency in the use of the English language. The minimum proficiency levels accepted by the Faculty of Education are scores of 650 on the TOEFL (280 computer-based) and 5.5 on the TWE.

**Degree Requirements**—Course route: ten 3-credit hour courses; Project route: eight 3-credit hour courses and one project/report; Thesis route: five 3-credit hour courses and one thesis; Required courses: Introduction to Instructional Design and Introduction to Research in Education.

**Number of Full Time Faculty**—1; **Number of Other Faculty**—2

**Degrees awarded in 2012–2013 Academic Year**—Master's—5; PhD—0; Other—0

**Grant Monies awarded in 2012–2013 Academic Year**—0

**Name of Institution**—University of Saskatchewan

**Name of Department or Program**—Educational Technology and Design

**Address:**
28 Campus Drive, College of Education
Saskatoon, SK
S7N 0X1
Canada

**Phone Number**—306-966-7558; **Fax Number**—306-966-7658

**Email Contact**—jay.wilson@usask.ca; **URL**—http://www.etad.ca

**Contact Person**—Dr. Jay R. Wilson

**Specializations**—We offer a general educational technology degree, but with a particular emphasis on instructional design in all coursework.

**Features**—Almost all of our courses are delivered in flexible formats. Courses can be taken completely online or blended with classroom experiences. A few courses are only offered face-to-face, but an entire program can be taken online. Many of our courses emphasize authentic learning options, where students work on projects with clients.

**Admission Requirements**—A professional Bachelors degree or the equivalent of a 4-year Bachelor of Arts. Normally, we require a minimum of 1 year of practical experience in education or a related field. An average of 70 % in your most recent 60 credit units of university coursework.

**Degree Requirements**—MEd (course-based) students need to complete 30 credit units of graduate level coursework for the degree. MEd (project) students require 24 credit units of graduate level coursework and the project seminar (ETAD 992.6) supervised by a faculty member in the program. MEd (thesis) students need to complete 21 units of graduate level coursework and a thesis supervised by a faculty member in the program and a committee.

**Number of Full Time Faculty**—3; **Number of Other Faculty**—3

**Degrees awarded in 2012–2013 Academic Year**—Master's—17; PhD—0; Other—0

**Grant Monies awarded in 2012–2013 Academic Year**—200,000

**Name of Institution**—Université de Poitiers

**Name of Department or Program**—Ingénierie des médias pour léducation

**Address:**
UFR Lettres et Langues—Bâtiment A3—1 rue Raymond CANTEL
Poitiers, PC
86000
France

**Phone Number**—+33 5 49 36 62 06; **Fax Number**—/

**Email        Contact**—bruno.devauchelle@univ-poitiers.fr;        **URL**—http://
ll.univ-poitiers.fr/dime/

**Contact Person**—Bruno Devauchelle

**Specializations**—EUROMIME: European Master in Media Engineering for Education (Erasmus Mundus master) EUROMIME is a European Master in Media Engineering for Education. It trains project managers in the field of design, development and implementation of educational and training programs resorting to computer mediated environments. It also trains researchers specializing the study of the use of these technologies. The master, which gives right to continuing to doctoral studies, prepares students to work in various settings such as business firms, government agencies as well as universities. Many of the graduate students work in public or private settings involved in projects related to distance education—MIME: national Master in Media Engineering for Education.

**Features**—The Euromime consortium is composed of seven universities, three in south-west Europe (Université de Poitiers—France; Universidad Nacional de Educación a Distancia, Madrid—España; Universidade Técnica de Lisboa—Portugal) and four in Latin America (Universidad de Los Lagos, Osorno—Chile; Pontificia Universidad Católica del Perú, Lima; Universidade de Brasilia—Brasil; Universidad Nacional Autónoma de México—México). More information: http://www.euromime.org/en/home.

**Admission Requirements**—Application and interview.

**Degree Requirements**—Bachelors degree.

**Number of Full Time Faculty**—25; **Number of Other Faculty**—25

**Degrees awarded in 2012–2013 Academic Year**—Master's—30; PhD—0; Other—0

**Grant Monies awarded in 2012–2013 Academic Year**—1,000,000


**Name of Institution**—The University of Hong Kong

**Name of Department or Program**—Master of Science in Information Technology in Education

**Address:**
Pokfulam Road
Hong Kong

**Phone Number**—852 2859-1903; **Fax Number**—852 2517 0075

**Email Contact**—mite@hku.hk; **URL**—http://web.edu.hku.hk/programme/mite/

**Contact Person**—Dr. Timothy Hew

**Specializations**—The Master of Science in Information Technology in Education [MSc(ITE)] program offers the following three specialist strands: E-leadership —E-learning—Learning technology design.

**Features**—The program aims to provide—An investigation into learning technology design, e-leadership, e-learning, and other emerging learning and teaching technology applications—an opportunity to apply technology in learning and teaching—an opportunity to work in technology-rich learning environment—an exploration of the cultural, administrative theoretical and practical implications of technology in education—an introduction to research in technology for education— an opportunity for those wishing to develop leadership capabilities in the use of technology in education.

**Admission Requirements**—Applicants should normally hold a recognized Bachelor's Degree with honors or qualifications of equivalent standard. Applicants may be required to sit for a qualifying examination.

**Degree Requirements**—To complete the following modules in 1 year full-time study or no more than 4 years of part-time studies:—three core modules—three modules from a specialist strand plus either of the following: o Independent project and three elective modules; or o Dissertation and one elective module.

**Number of Full Time Faculty**—19; **Number of Other Faculty**—9

**Degrees awarded in 2012–2013 Academic Year**—Master's—52; **PhD**—0; **Other**—0

**Grant Monies awarded in 2012–2013 Academic Year**—0


**Name of Institution**—Andong National University

**Name of Department or Program**—Department of Educational Technology, College of Education

**Address:**
1375 Kyungdong St. (Songchun-dong)
Andong, Kyungbuk
760-749
Korea

**Phone Number**—+82-54-820-5580, 5585; **Fax Number**—+82-54-820-7653

**Email Contact**—ycyang@andong.ac.kr; **URL**—http://home.andong.ac.kr/edutech/

**Contact Person**—Dr. Yong-Chil Yang

**Specializations**—Instruction Systems Design and e-HRD major for Master Degree Educational Technology major for PhD

**Features**—* Only Department supported by Ministry of Education in Korea; * BA, MA and PhD programs are offered; * Established in 1996; * Inexpensive tuition and living expenses; * Small class size; * Edutech, ANU Edutech, Educational Technology.

**Admission Requirements**—English or Korean language.

**Degree Requirements**—BA degree for Master MA degree in Education for PhD

**Number of Full Time Faculty**—5; **Number of Other Faculty**—10

**Degrees awarded in 2012–2013 Academic Year**—Master's—6; PhD—3; **Other**—12

**Grant Monies awarded in 2012–2013 Academic Year**—35,000

**Name of Institution**—Anton Chekhov Taganrog Institute

**Name of Department or Program**—Media Education (Social Pedagogic Faculty)

**Address:**
Iniciativnaya, 48
Taganrog
347936
Russia

**Phone Number**—(8634)601753; **Fax Number**—(8634)605397

**Email Contact**—1954alex@mail.ru; **URL**—http://www.tgpi.ru

**Contact Person**—Prof. Dr. Alexander Fedorov

**Specializations**—Media Education, Media Literacy, Media Competence.

**Features**—No.

**Admission Requirements**—Various per year, please see http://www.tgpi.ru.

**Degree Requirements**—Admission after high school (for BA) and MA for PhD level.

**Number of Full Time Faculty**—10; **Number of Other Faculty**—20

**Degrees awarded in 2012–2013 Academic Year**—Master's—0; PhD—1; **Other**—15

**Grant Monies awarded in 2012–2013 Academic Year**—60,000

**Name of Institution**—Keimyung University

**Name of Department or Program**—Department of Education

**Address:**
1095 Dalgubeldaro
Dalseogu, Daegu
704-701
South Korea

**Phone Number**—82-53-580-5962

**Email Contact**—weom@kmu.ac.kr

**Contact Person**—Wooyong Eom

**Admission Requirements**—For foreigners, should have above three class of TOPIK (Test of Proficiency in Korean).

**Degree Requirements**—Above Bachelor degree for master, master degree for doctoral.

**Number of Full Time Faculty**—8; **Number of Other Faculty**—3

**Degrees awarded in 2012–2013 Academic Year**—Master's—3; PhD—0; Other—0

**Grant Monies awarded in 2012–2013 Academic Year**—0


**Name of Institution**—University of Balearic Islands

**Name of Department or Program**—Sciences of Education

**Address:**
Ctra. Valldemossa km 7,5
Palma de Mallorca, IB
07010
Spain

**Phone Number**—34 071173000; **Fax Number**—34 971173190

**Email Contact**—jesus.salinas@uib.es; **URL**—http://www.uib.es

**Contact Person**—Dr. Jesus Salinas

**Specializations**—Doctorado Interuniversitario de Tecnología Educativa [Interuniversity Doctorate of Educational Technology]. University of Sevilla, University of Murcia, University of Balearic Islands and Rovira i Virgili Universitity—Master en Tecnología Educativa. E-learning y gestión del conocimiento. [Master in Educational Technology. E-learning and knowledge management]. University of Sevilla, University of Murcia, University of Balearic Islands and Rovira i Virgili Universitity—Especialista Universitario en Tecnología Educativa. Diseño y elaboración de medios didácticos multimedia. [Specialist in Educational Technology. Design and development of didactic multimedia environments].

**Number of Full Time Faculty**—37; **Number of Other Faculty**—63

**Degrees awarded in 2012–2013 Academic Year**—Master's—23; **PhD**—11; **Other**—33

**Grant Monies awarded in 2012–2013 Academic Year**—0

**Name of Institution**—University of Geneva

**Name of Department or Program**—TECFA—Master of Science in Learning and Teaching Technologies

**Address:**
40 bd du Pont dArve
Geneva, GE
1205
Switzerland

**Phone Number**—41 22 379 93 20; **Fax Number**—41 22 379 93 79

**Email Contact**—Mireille.Betrancourt@unige.ch; **URL**—http://tecfa.unige.ch/maltt/

**Contact Person**—Prof. Dr. Mireille Bétrancourt

**Specializations**—Basics in information and communication technologies Design of computer-supported learning technology Mediated Communication and e-learning User-centered design and ergonomics Research methods in educational technologies Blended education (face-to-face sessions alternately with tutored distance periods, with a ratio of 1 week F2F for 5 weeks at a distance) 120 ECTS, 2-year program Learning approach: mostly project-based, with authentic project design and collaborative work French language.

**Features**—Information at: http://tecfa.unige.ch/maltt/ Collaborative encyclopedia (with student participation) about educational technologies and related models, concepts and technology: http://edutechwiki.unige.ch/en/Main_Page.

**Admission Requirements**—Applicants should qualify to be admitted in master program at the university of Geneva and be fluent in French. For more information, see http://tecfa.unige.ch/maltt/futurs-etudiants/admission/.

**Degree Requirements**—Bachelor degree Training or experience in teaching, education or psychology.

**Number of Full Time Faculty**—4; **Number of Other Faculty**—2

**Degrees awarded in 2012–2013 Academic Year**—Master's—8; **PhD**—3; **Other**—5

**Grant Monies awarded in 2012–2013 Academic Year**—500,000

**Name of Institution**—Hacettepe University

**Name of Department or Program**—Computer Education and Instructional Technology

**Address:**
Faculty of Education, Hacettepe University, Beytepe
Ankara, Turkey
06800
Turkey

**Phone Number**—+90-312-2977176; **Fax Number**—0

**Email Contact**—kocak@hacettepe.edu.tr; **URL**—http://www.ebit.hacettepe.edu.tr/

**Contact Person**—Yasemin Koçak Usluel

**Specializations**—The CEIT department has been established in 1998. Innovations and improvements in technology have changed so many things in people's life. There have been huge improvements in terms of diffusion of information. Computers continue to make an ever increasing impact on all aspects of education from primary school to university and in the growing areas of open and distance learning. In addition, the knowledge and skills related to computers have become essential for everybody in the information age. However, at all levels in society there is a huge need for qualified personnel equipped with the skills that help them to be successful in their personal and professional life. The department aims to train students (prospective teachers) who would teach computer courses in K-12 institutions. It also provides individuals with professional skills in the development, organization and application of resources for the solution of instructional problems within schools.

**Features**—The department has MS and PhD programs. The research areas are: Learning objects and ontologies, diffusion of innovation, technology integration into education, computerized testing, e-learning environments, design, development and assessment of online learning environments, mobile learning.

**Admission Requirements**—BS in education or computer related fields.

**Degree Requirements**—BS.

**Number of Full Time Faculty**—10; **Number of Other Faculty**—16

**Degrees awarded in 2012–2013 Academic Year**—Master's—3; PhD—3; Other—0

**Grant Monies awarded in 2012–2013 Academic Year**—132

**Name of Institution**—Anadolu University

**Name of Department or Program**—Computer Education and Instructional Technology

**Address:**
Faculty of Education
Eskisehir
26470
Turkey

**Phone Number** — 00902223350580/3519; **Fax Number** — 00902223350579

**Email Contact** — aakurt@anadolu.edu.tr; **URL** — https://academy.anadolu.edu.tr/display.asp?kod=0andacc=aakurt

**Contact Person** — Assoc. Prof. Dr. Adile Askim Kurt

**Specializations** — The basic aim of the department is to equip students, with up-to-date knowledge about computer and other information technologies, required for K12 computer teachers. Graduated students of the department can be employed in public or private schools of The Ministry of National Education, as teachers, instructional technologists, or academicians in the universities. The department offers Bachelor, Master and Doctorate programs. Both department staff and students collaborate with international schools in terms of teaching and research through exchange programs. Some of the themes, having been studied by academic staff of the department, are: computer assisted instruction, computer assisted language instruction, educational technology, computer use in education and school systems, effects of technology on individuals, computer anxiety, industrial design, using Internet in education, instructional design, instructional software design, statistics, professional development, ICT action competence, technology integration into education, technology integration into special education, safe Internet use, cyberbullying and digital storytelling, mobile learning.

**Features** — Computer Education and Instructional Technologies Department has three computer labs. Technical properties of the computers in both of the labs are up to date. In addition, students can use the main library which is around 100 m to department building. Students may reach many books and journals about computers and instructional technologies, and have access to various data bases and electronic journals. There is a nonsmoking cafeteria for students in the faculty building where they can find snacks, sandwiches, hot and cold drinks. There is also a small room for the smokers. There is a main student cafeteria for students on the campus. There are also fast food restaurants on the campus.

**Admission Requirements** — High School Diploma plus required scores from the Student Selection Examination administered by Student Selection and Placement Centre and successful completion of qualification examinations. For foreign students, High School Diploma plus required scores from the Foreign Student Examination and successful completion of qualification examinations. Associate Degree plus placement by Student Selection and Placement Centre according to the score obtained in the Student Selection Examination and the students preferences. In addition, may apply to master's or doctorate programs in any field or proficiency in fine arts programs. May apply to bachelor's degree completion programs in related fields of study in Distance Education System.

**Degree Requirements**—For bachelor degree, students are selected by Student Selection and Placement Center according to the students? scores in the Student Selection Exam. About 50 students are admitted to the department each year. The duration of the program is 4 years. Students must pass all courses and obtain a minimum GPA (Grade Point Average) of 2.00 before they can graduate. The official language of instruction is Turkish. Students who want to learn English can attend a 1-year English preparatory school before taking the department courses. The students are required to take courses and prepare and defend a thesis based on their research. It takes approximately 2 years to complete the Master degree. The doctorate degree requires course work and research. The students will conduct original research and prepare a dissertation, then make an oral defense of their completed research. Students require about 4 years beyond the Master's degree to complete a doctorate program.

**Number of Full Time Faculty**—13; **Number of Other Faculty**—25

**Degrees awarded in 2012–2013 Academic Year**—Master's—0; PhD—2; Other—0

**Grant Monies awarded in 2012–2013 Academic Year**—131,550


**Name of Institution**—The University of Arizona

**Name of Department or Program**—University of Arizona South, Educational Technology Program

**Address:**
Science and Technology Park 9040 S Rita Road, Suite 2260
Tucson, AZ
85747
USA

**Phone Number**—520-626-9381; **Fax Number**—520-626-1794

**Email Contact**—bcozkan@email.arizona.edu; **URL**—http://edtech.arizona.edu/content/welcome

**Contact Person**—Dr. Betul Özkan-Czerkawski

**Specializations**—PhD Minor in Educational Technology; Master's of Science in Educational Technology; Graduate Certificate in Instructional Design and Technology; Master of Arts in Second Language Learning and Educational Technology; Undergraduate Minor in Educational Technology.

**Features**—Fully online.

**Admission Requirements**—Satisfy the admission standards of the UA Graduate College and the Educational Technology Program, including: A completed bachelor's degree (in the last 60 credit hours) or master's program from an accredited institution with an overall Grade Point Average (GPA) of 3.0 on a 4.0 scale; A completed application form, along with copies of all undergraduate and graduate transcripts and payment of Graduate College application fees; Three letters of recommendation dated within 6 months of the date of application and written by professionals who are in a position to address the applicants ability to succeed at the graduate level; A completed student information form that includes a brief statement of long-range professional goals and a 500-word summary on a topic relating to educational technology. PhD Minor Admission Requirements: PhD Minor: Minimum Credit Hours: 9; Core Courses: Only the PhD students at the University of Arizona can minor in Educational Technology and take any course listed for the MS in Educational Technology Program. However, students should contact the Program Director first to set up their Plan of Study before taking any courses. More information is at: http://edtech.arizona.edu/content/phd-minor; Graduate Certificate in Instructional Design and Technology Admission Requirements: A bachelor's degree. from an accredited institution with an overall Grade Point Average (GPA) of 2.0 on a 4.0 scale; A completed application form, along with copies of undergraduate transcripts and payment of Graduate College application fees; One letter of recommendation dated within 6 months of the date of application and written by professionals who are in a position to address the applicants ability to succeed at the graduate level.

**Degree Requirements**—MS in Educational Technology: The master's degree program of study is developed in consultation with a faculty advisor and requires a minimum of 36 units of graduate courses, with at least 24 of these units taken in Educational Technology. The choices within the program of study are based on professional aspirations, scholastic needs, and personal preferences. For completion, the master's degree program requires development of a best-works portfolio. PhD Minor: This program requires minimum of 9 credit/units. Graduate Certificate in Instructional Design and Technology: This program requires 15 credit/units. Undergraduate Minor in Educational Technology: The minor program of study is developed in consultation with an academic advisor and requires a minimum of 18 units of undergraduate courses.

**Number of Full Time Faculty**—2; **Number of Other Faculty**—7

**Degrees awarded in 2012–2013 Academic Year**—Master's—14; **PhD**—0; Other—4

**Grant Monies awarded in 2012–2013 Academic Year**—0

**Name of Institution**—The Ohio State University

**Name of Department or Program**—Learning Technologies

**Address:**
29 W. Woodruff Dr.
Columbus, OH
43210
USA

**Phone Number**—(614) 292-2461; **Fax Number**—(614) 292-8052

**Email Contact**—voithofer.2@osu.edu; **URL**—http://ehe.osu.edu/educational-studies/educational-technology/

**Contact Person**—Rick Voithofer

**Specializations**—The Educational Technology program offers both MA and PhD degrees, in addition to a Computer/Technology Endorsement. This interdisciplinary educational technology program focuses on intersections of learning and technology in formal and informal educational settings and in society at-large. Some of the settings addressed in the program include K-12 environments, distance education, e-learning, online education, higher education, urban education, corporate and non-profit organizations, nongovernmental organizations (NGOs), and community-based organizations and programs. Students in the program are exposed to a variety of technologies and media including educational multimedia, computer-based instruction, pod/video casts, online learning environments, mobile technologies, blogs and wikis, MOOCs, educational games, video, and electronic portfolios. Areas of focus studied by faculty and students include: • Educational technology, digital divides and diverse populations; • Computer-supported collaborative learning; • Education and globalization; • Online educational research; • Artificial intelligence in education; • Education Policy and Technology; • Visual Culture and Visual Media; • Multiliteracies, learning, and technology; • Games and simulations; • Technology, virtuality, and student identities Students in this area integrate theoretical and practical studies of technologies and media through pedagogical, social, cultural, economic, psychological, historical and political inquiry and critique, in addition to the production of educational technologies.

**Features**—See: http://go.osu.edu/jKv.

**Admission Requirements**—Please see: http://ehe.osu.edu/educational-studies/prospective-students/.

**Degree Requirements**—MA: http://ehe.osu.edu/downloads/academics/program-sheets/educational-technology-specialization-in-educational-studies-ma.pdf; PhD: http://ehe.osu.edu/downloads/academics/program-sheets/educational-technology-specialization-in-educational-studies-phd.pdf.

**Number of Full Time Faculty**—2; **Number of Other Faculty**—8

**Degrees awarded in 2012–2013 Academic Year**—Master's—10; PhD—2; Other—20

**Grant Monies awarded in 2012–2013 Academic Year**—2,000,000

**Name of Institution**—University of Central Arkansas

**Name of Department or Program**—Leadership Studies

**Address:**
201 Donaghey
Conway, AR
72035
USA

**Phone Number**—(501)450-5430; **Fax Number**—(501)852-2826

**Email Contact**—steph@uca.edu; **URL**—http://www.coe.uca.edu/

**Contact Person**—Stephanie Huffman, Program Director of the Library Media and Information Technologies Program

**Specializations**—MS in Library Media and Information Technologies is a School Library Media program.

**Features**—Facebook page.

**Admission Requirements**—Minimum of a 2.7 undergraduate GPA. Candidates should submit official transcripts, GRE scores, and a copy of their teaching certificate.

**Degree Requirements**—36 semester hours, practicum (for School Library Media), and a professional portfolio.

**Number of Full Time Faculty**—4; **Number of Other Faculty**—2

**Degrees awarded in 2012–2013 Academic Year**—Master's—40; PhD—0; **Other**—20

**Grant Monies awarded in 2012–2013 Academic Year**—0


**Name of Institution**—Arizona State University; Educational Technology programs

**Name of Department or Program**—Division of Educational Leadership and Innovation; Mary Lou Fulton Teachers College

**Address:**
Box 871811
Tempe, AZ
85287-1811
USA

**Phone Number**—480-965-3225; (480) 965-4963; **Fax Number**—480-965-9035

**Email Contact**—Robin.Boyle@asu.edu;savenye@asu.edu; **URL**—http://education.asu.edu/programs

**Contact Person**—Ms. Robin Boyle, Academic and Application Advisor; Dr. Wilhelmina (Willi) Savenye, Professor and Program Leader

**Specializations**—The Educational Technology programs at Arizona State University offer Graduate Certificates in Instructional and Performance Improvement and in K-12 Online Teaching, an MEd degree and a PhD degree specialization. Programs focus on the design, development, and evaluation of instructional systems and educational technology applications to support learning. (Educational technology is now a specialization area in a new PhD degree: Learning, Literacies, and Technologies, as of 2013.)

**Features**—The programs offer courses in a variety of areas such as instructional design technology, media development, technology integration, performance improvement, evaluation, and distance education. The doctoral program emphasizes research using educational technology in applied settings.

**Admission Requirements**—Requirements for admission to the MEd program include a 4-year undergraduate GPA of 3.0. A score of 550 or above on the paper-based TOEFL (or 213 on the computer-based test or 80 Internet-based test) is also required for students who do not speak English as their first language. The new PhD degree program in Learning, Literacies and Technologies requires that students first have earned a master's degree in a related field. Please see the College website at https://education.asu.edu/ for more information. The ASU Graduate College website includes more detailed requirements.

**Degree Requirements**—The Graduate Certificate programs require just 15 credit hours, with a mix of required and elective courses. The MEd degree requires completion of a minimum of 30 credit hours including 18 credit hours of required course work and a minimum of 12 credit hours of electives. MEd students complete an Applied Project as their culminating experience. PhD students must fulfill a residence requirement and are required to be continuously enrolled in the program. Students also take a comprehensive examination and are given considerable support in order to help them develop research skills and publications en route to their dissertation.

**Number of Full Time Faculty**—7; **Number of Other Faculty**—7

**Degrees awarded in 2012–2013 Academic Year**—Master's—9; PhD—8; Other—2

**Grant Monies awarded in 2012–2013 Academic Year**—475,000

**Name of Institution**—California State University-San Bernardino

**Name of Department or Program**—Dept. of Educational Leadership and Technology

**Address:**
5500 University Parkway
San Bernardino, CA
92407
USA

**Phone Number**—(909)537-5692; **Fax Number**—(909)537-7040

**Email Contact**—aleh@csusb.edu; **URL**—http://etec.csusb.edu

**Contact Person**—Dr. Amy Leh

**Specializations**—Technology integration, online instruction, instructional design.

**Features**—Preparing educators in K-12, corporate, and higher education.

**Admission Requirements**—Bachelor's degree, 3.0 GPA, completion of university writing requirement.

**Degree Requirements**—48 units passing a comprehensive examination; 3.0 GPA; grades of "B" or better in all courses.

**Number of Full Time Faculty**—3; **Number of Other Faculty**—1

**Degrees awarded in 2012–2013 Academic Year**—Master's—9; **PhD**—0; **Other**—0

**Grant Monies awarded in 2012–2013 Academic Year**—8000


**Name of Institution**—San Diego State University

**Name of Department or Program**—Learning Design and Technology

**Address:**
5500 Campanile Dr.
San Diego, CA
92182-4561
USA

**Phone Number**—(619)594-6718; **Fax Number**—(619)594-6246

**Email Contact**—bober@mail.sdsu.edu; **URL**—http://edweb2.net/ldt

**Contact Person**—Dr. Marcie Bober-Michel, Professor and Graduate Advisor

**Specializations**—Certificate in Instructional Technology. Advanced Certificate in Instructional Design. Master's degree in Education with an emphasis in Learning Design and Technology.

**Features**—Focus on the design, development, and implementation of learning opportunities that positively influence both individual and organizational performance via strategies that combine theory and practice in relevant, real-world experiences. Programs offered both on campus and online.

**Admission Requirements**—Please refer to SDSU Graduate bulletin at http://arweb.sdsu.edu/es/catalog/2014-15/GraduateBulletin/!!Graduate%202014-15.pdf. Requirements include satisfactory scores on the GRE (verbal, quantitative, writing), a personal statement, undergraduate GPA of 2.85 or higher, and recommendations from supervisors, previous instructors, etc. See our website for more detail: http://edweb2.net/ldt/prospective-students/apply/.

**Degree Requirements**—30 semester units for the Master's; 15–18 semester hours for the certificates.

**Number of Full Time Faculty**—4; **Number of Other Faculty**—2

**Degrees awarded in 2012–2013 Academic Year**—**Master's**—40; **PhD**—0; **Other**—0

**Grant Monies awarded in 2012–2013 Academic Year**—250,000


**Name of Institution**—Azusa Pacific University

**Name of Department or Program**—School of Education—Teacher Education

**Address:**
701 E. Alosta
Azusa, CA
91702
USA

**Phone Number**—(626)815-5355; **Fax Number**—(626)815-5416

**Email Contact**—kbacer@apu.edu; **URL**—http://www.apu.edu

**Contact Person**—Kathleen Bacer—Online Master of Arts in Educational Technology

**Specializations**—Educational Technology, online learning, Infusing technology in teaching/learning environments, digital learning for the twenty-first century learner.

**Features**—100% Online Master of Arts in Educational Technology program designed for the K-12 educator.

**Admission Requirements**—Undergraduate degree from accredited institution with at least 12 units in education, 3.0 GPA.

**Degree Requirements**—36 unit program.

**Number of Full Time Faculty**—2; **Number of Other Faculty**—8

**Degrees awarded in 2012–2013 Academic Year**—**Master's**—90; **PhD**—0; **Other**—0

**Grant Monies awarded in 2012–2013 Academic Year**—10,000


**Name of Institution**—University of Colorado Denver

**Name of Department or Program**—School of Education and Human Development

**Address:**
Campus Box 106, P.O. Box 173364
Denver, CO
80217-3364
USA

**Phone Number**—(303)315-4963; **Fax Number**—(303)315-6311

**Email Contact**—joni.dunlap@cudenver.edu; **URL**—http://www.ucdenver.edu/academics/colleges/SchoolOfEducation/Academics/MASTERS/ILT/Pages/default.aspx

**Contact Person**—Joni Dunlap, Program Coordinator, Information and Learning Technologies

**Specializations**—MA in Information and Learning Technologies (ILT)—includes options for eLearning, K12 Teaching, Instructional Design/Adult Learning, and School Librarianship. A Graduate Certificate is available in Online Teaching (9 credits). The EdD in Educational Equity is available with concentration in Professional Learning and Technology.

**Features**—Distinctive features of the MA program: Fully online E-portfolio designed to serve as a continuing professional portal Priority to strengthen online professional presence via portal/portfolio and engagement in professional learning activities and networks Project-based curriculum with authentic collaborative work resulting in professional products Generous access to advisement and faculty mentoring Induction into the profession and an ongoing community of learners The doctoral program is cross-disciplinary, drawing on expertise in technology, adult learning, professional development, social justice, systemic change, research methods, reflective practice, and cultural studies.

**Admission Requirements**—MA and EdD: satisfactory GPA, letters of recommendation, transcripts. See website for more detail.

**Degree Requirements**—MA: 30 semester hours; professional portfolio; field experience. EdD: 39 semester hours of coursework and labs, plus 15 dissertation hours; dissertation.

**Number of Full Time Faculty**—3; **Number of Other Faculty**—8

**Degrees awarded in 2012–2013 Academic Year**—Master's—58; PhD—0; **Other**—0

**Grant Monies awarded in 2012–2013 Academic Year**—8300


**Name of Institution**—Fairfield University

**Name of Department or Program**—Educational Technology

**Address:**
N. Benson Road
Fairfield, CT
06824
USA

**Phone Number**—(203)254-4000; **Fax Number**—(203)254-4047

**Email Contact**—graded@mail.fairfield.edu; **URL**—http://www.fairfield.edu

**Contact Person**—Dr. Belinha De Abreu, Director, Educational Technology Program

**Specializations**—MA in Educational Technology; certification (initial and cross-endorsement) in School Library Media.

**Features**—Emphasis on theory, practice, and new instructional developments in computers in education, multimedia, school/media, and applied technology in education.

**Admission Requirements**—See http://fairfield.edu/gseap/gseap_policies.html.

**Degree Requirements**—33 credits. Additional coursework for certification.

**Number of Full Time Faculty**—2; **Number of Other Faculty**—5

**Degrees awarded in 2012–2013 Academic Year**—Master's—12; **PhD**—0; **Other**—0

**Grant Monies awarded in 2012–2013 Academic Year**—0


**Name of Institution**—University of Connecticut

**Name of Department or Program**—Educational Psychology

**Address:**
249 Glenbrook Rd, Unit-3064
Storrs, CT
06269-3064
USA

**Phone Number**—(860)486-0182; **Fax Number**—(860)486-0180

**Email Contact**—myoung@UConn.edu; **URL**—http://www.epsy.uconn.edu/

**Contact Person**—Michael Young, program coordinator

**Specializations**—MA in Educational Technology (portfolio or thesis options), 1-year partially online Master's (summer, fall, spring, summer), Sixth Year certificate in Educational Technology and PhD in Cognition, Instruction and Learning Technology. This program is titled UConn 2 Summers MA in Learning Technology.

**Features**—MA can be on-campus or 2 Summers (blended) and Fall-Spring (Online) that can be completed in a year. The PhD emphasis in Learning Technology is a unique program at UConn. It strongly emphasizes Cognitive Science and how technology can be used to enhance the way people think and learn. The Program seeks to provide students with knowledge of theory and applications regarding the use of advanced technology to enhance learning and thinking. Campus facilities include $2 billion Twenty-first Century UConn enhancement to campus infrastructure, including a new wing to the Neag School of Education. Faculty research interests include interactive video for anchored instruction and situated learning, telecommunications for cognitive apprenticeship, technology-mediated interactivity for learning by design activities, and in cooperation with the National Research Center for Gifted and Talented, research on the use of technology to enhance cooperative learning and the development of gifted performance in all students.

**Admission Requirements**—Admission to the graduate school at UConn, GRE scores (or other evidence of success at the graduate level). Previous experience in a related area of technology, education, or experience in education or training.

**Degree Requirements**—Completion of plan of study coursework, comprehensive exam (portfolio-based with multiple requirements), and completion of an approved dissertation.

**Number of Full Time Faculty**—2; **Number of Other Faculty**—3

**Degrees awarded in 2012–2013 Academic Year**—Master's—13; PhD—0; Other—0

**Grant Monies awarded in 2012–2013 Academic Year**—0


**Name of Institution**—George Washington University

**Name of Department or Program**—Graduate School of Education and Human Development

**Address:**
2134 G Street NW
Washington, DC
20052
USA

**Phone Number**—(866)-498-3382; Fax Number—(202)994-2145

**Email Contact**—nmilman@gwu.edu; **URL**—http://www.gwu.edu/~etl

**Contact Person**—Dr. Natalie B. Milman, Educational Technology Leadership, Program Director

**Specializations**—The Educational Technology Leadership program began in 1988. It was one of the first online degree programs in the field. The program offers a high quality, flexible program rich in knowledge of the field and distance education delivery. The result is an outstanding experience for our students.

MA in Education and Human Development with a major in Educational Technology Leadership as well as the following Graduate Certificates:

(1) Instructional Design, (2) Multimedia Development, (3) Leadership in Educational Technology, (4) E-Learning, (5) Training and Educational Technology, (6) Integrating Technology into Education.

**Features**—https://www.facebook.com/groups/153686921326555/.

**Admission Requirements**—Application fee, transcripts, GRE or MAT scores (OPTIONAL), two letters of recommendation from academic professionals, computer access, undergraduate degree with 2.75 GPA. No GRE or MAT is required for entry into the Graduate Certificate programs.

**Degree Requirements**—MASTERS PROGRAM: 36 credit hours (including 27 required hours and 9 elective credit hours). Required courses include computer application management, media and technology application, software implementation and design, public education policy, and quantitative research methods.

GRADUATE CERTIFICATE PROGRAMS: 18 credit hours.

**Number of Full Time Faculty**—3; **Number of Other Faculty**—0

**Degrees awarded in 2012–2013 Academic Year**—Master's—24; **PhD**—0; **Other**—15

**Grant Monies awarded in 2012–2013 Academic Year**—0

**Name of Institution**—Nova Southeastern University—Fischler Graduate School of Education and Human Services

**Name of Department or Program**—Programs in Instructional Technology and Distance Education (ITDE)

**Address:**
1750 NE 167th Street
North Miami Beach, FL
33162
USA

**Phone Number**—954-262-8572, (800)986-3223, ext. 8572; **Fax Number**—(954)262-3905

**Email Contact**—itdeinfo@nova.edu; **URL**—itde.nova.edu

**Contact Person**—Marsha L. Burmeister, Recruitment Coordinator and Program Professor ITDE

**Specializations**—MS and EdD in Instructional Technology and Distance Education.

**Features**—MS 21 months (MS ITDE program graduates may continue with the EdD program as second year students) EdD 36 months MS and EdD combined: 4+ years Blended/hybrid delivery model with limited face-to-face and via instruction at-a-distance using Web-based technologies.

**Admission Requirements**—• Active employment in the field of instructional technology/distance education. • Completion of bachelor's degree for MS program (2.5 minimum GPA); master's degree required for admission to EdD program (3.0 minimum GPA). • Miller Analogies Test (MAT) score (test taken within last 5 years). •

Submission of application/supplementary materials. • Approval of Skills Checklist (application). • Three letters of recommendation. • Official copies of transcripts for all graduate work. • Resume. • Oral interview (via telephone). • Demonstrated potential for successful completion of the program via acceptance of application. • Internet Service Provider; Laptop computer.

**Degree Requirements**—21 months and 30 semester credits. EdD 3 years and 65 semester credits. MS Program: three "extended weekends:" One extended weekend in the fall (5 days), one extended weekend in the spring (4 days), one summer instructional session (4–5 days; July), final term online delivery. EdD program: same as above, continues throughout the 3 years (three sessions in first year, two sessions in the second year, and one instructional session in the third year for a total of six (6) face-to-face sessions).

**Number of Full Time Faculty**—0; **Number of Other Faculty**—0

**Degrees awarded in 2012–2013 Academic Year**—Master's—100; **PhD**—0; **Other**—0

**Grant Monies awarded in 2012–2013 Academic Year**—0

**Name of Institution**—Florida State University

**Name of Department or Program**—Educational Psychology and Learning Systems

**Address:**
3210 Stone Building
Tallahassee, FL
32306-4453
USA

**Phone Number**—(850)644-4592; **Fax Number**—(850)644-8776

**Email Contact**—mmckee@fsu.edu; **URL**—http://education.fsu.edu/degrees-and-programs/instructional-systems-and-learning-technologies

**Contact Person**—Mary Kate McKee, Program Coordinator

**Specializations**—MS and PhD in Instructional Systems and Learning Technologies with specializations for persons planning to work in academia, business, industry, government, or military, both in the USA and in International settings.

**Features**—Core courses include systems and materials development, performance improvement, online learning, development of multimedia, project management, psychological foundations, current trends in instructional design, and research and statistics. Internships are recommended. Strong alumni network. MS courses available both on campus and online.

**Admission Requirements**—MS: 3.0 GPA in last 2 years of undergraduate program, GRE Verbal minimum score is 150, Quantitative minimum score of 144 and Analytical Writing minimum score of 3.5. Minimum TOEFL score (for international applicants) is 85. PhD: GRE Verbal is 152, Quantitative is 152 and Analytical Writing is 4.0, 3.5 GPA in last 2 years; international students, 90 TOEFL.

**Degree Requirements**—MS: 36 semester hours, 2–4 h internship, comprehensive exam preparation of professional portfolio.

**Number of Full Time Faculty**—5; **Number of Other Faculty**—1

**Degrees awarded in 2012–2013 Academic Year**—Master's—27; **PhD**—4; **Other**—0

**Grant Monies awarded in 2012–2013 Academic Year**—0


**Name of Institution**—University of Central Florida

**Name of Department or Program**—College of Education and Human Performance, Educational and Human Sciences, Instructional Design and Technology

**Address:**
4000 Central Florida Blvd.
Orlando, FL
32816-1250
USA

**Phone Number**—(407)823-4835; **Fax Number**—(407)823-4880

**Email Contact**—richard.hartshorne@ucf.edu; **URL**—http://www.education.ucf. edu/insttech/

**Contact Person**—Dr. Richard Hartshorne, Dr. Atsusi Hirumi, Dr. Glenda Gunter

**Specializations**—Graduate Certificates in (a) Instructional Design of Simulations, (b) Educational Technology, and (c) e-Learning Professional Development. MA in Instructional Design and Technology with professional tracks in: (a) Instructional Systems, (b) Educational Technology, and (c) e-Learning, PhD in Education with Instructional Design and Technology track. EdD in Education with Instructional Technology concentration. There are approximately 200 students in MA program, five in EdD and 15 in PhD programs.

**Features**—All programs rely heavily on understanding of fundamental competencies as reflected by NCATE, ASTD, AECT, AASL, and ISTE. There is an emphasis on the practical application of theory through intensive hands-on experiences. Orlando and the surrounding area is home to many high-tech companies, military training and simulation organizations, and tourist attractions. UCF, established in 1963, now has in excess of 55,000 students, representing more than 90 countries. It has been ranked as one of the leading "most-wired" universities in North America.

**Admission Requirements**—GRE score of 1000 for consideration for doctoral program. No GRE required for MA or graduate certificate programs. GPA of 3.0 of greater in last 60 h of undergraduate degree for MA program; TOEFL of 550 (270 computer-based version) if English is not first language; three letters of recommendation; resume, statement of goals; residency statement, and health record. Financial statement if coming from overseas.

**Degree Requirements**—MA in Instructional Technology/Instructional Systems, 39 semester hours; MA in Instructional Technology/Educational Technology, 39 semester hours, MA in Instructional Technology/eLearning, 39 semester hours. Practicum required in all three programs; thesis, research project, or substitute additional course work. PhD and EdD require between 58–69 h beyond the master's for completion.

**Number of Full Time Faculty**—3; **Number of Other Faculty**—5

**Degrees awarded in 2012–2013 Academic Year**—Master's—40; **PhD**—11; **Other**—20

**Grant Monies awarded in 2012–2013 Academic Year**—360,000

**Name of Institution**—Georgia Southern University

**Name of Department or Program**—College of Education

**Address:**
Box 8131
Statesboro, GA
30460-8131
USA
**Phone Number**—(912)478-5307; **Fax Number**—(912)478-7104

**Email Contact**—lgreen@georgiasouthern.edu; **URL**—http://coe.georgiasouthern.edu/itec/

**Contact Person**—Dr. Lucy Santos Green, EdD, Associate Professor, Dept. of Leadership, Technology, and Human Development

**Specializations**—Online MEd and GA certification for School Library Media and Instructional Technology Specialists. An online EdS is available in both concentrations as well. The Online Teaching and Learning Endorsement is offered at both levels.

**Features**—Completely online program. Strong emphasis on technology and use of Web 2.0 tools Online portfolios as culminating program requirement for MEd students http://www.facebook.com/itec.georgiasouthern.

**Admission Requirements**—BS (teacher certification NOT required for SLM certification) GRE or MAT not required for applicants who are certified teachers with a 2.5 undergraduate grade point average MEd required for admission to the EdS program.

**Degree Requirements**—36 semester hours for the MEd 42 semester hour MEd with dual certification in School Library Media and Instructional Technology 30 semester hours for the EdS 9 semester hour Online Teaching and Learning Endorsement.

**Number of Full Time Faculty**—7; **Number of Other Faculty**—0

**Degrees awarded in 2012–2013 Academic Year**—Master's—75; **PhD**—0; **Other**—0

**Grant Monies awarded in 2012–2013 Academic Year**—0


**Name of Institution**—Georgia State University

**Name of Department or Program**—Learning Technologies Division

**Address:**
Box 3976
Atlanta, GA
30302-3976
USA

**Phone Number**—(404)413-8064; **Fax Number**—None

**Email Contact**—swharmon@gsu.edu; **URL**—http://edtech.gsu.edu

**Contact Person**—Dr. Stephen W. Harmon, contact person.

**Specializations**—MS and PhD in Instructional Design and Technology.

**Features**—Focus on research and practical application of instructional technology in educational and corporate settings. Online MS in Instructional Design and Technology available.

**Admission Requirements**—MS: Bachelor's degree, 2.5 undergraduate GPA, >40th percentile GRE, 550 TOEFL. PhD: Master's degree, 3.30 graduate GPA, >50th percentile verbal plus >50th percentile quantitative GRE.

**Degree Requirements**—MS: 36 sem. hours, internship, portfolio, comprehensive examination. PhD: 60 sem. hours, internship, comprehensive examination, dissertation.

**Number of Full Time Faculty**—6; **Number of Other Faculty**—2

**Degrees awarded in 2012–2013 Academic Year**—Master's—16; **PhD**—8; **Other**—0

**Grant Monies awarded in 2012–2013 Academic Year**—7,850,000

**Name of Institution**—University of Georgia

**Name of Department or Program**—Department of Career and Information Studies; Learning, Design, and Technology Program

**Address:**
216 Rivers Crossing
Athens, GA
30602-4809
USA

**Phone Number**—(706)542-1682; **Fax Number**—(706)542-4054

**Email Contact**—janette@uga.edu; **URL**—http://ldt.uga.edu/

**Contact Person**—Dr. Janette Hill, LDT Program Chair

**Specializations**—MEd and EdS in Learning, Design and Technology with three emphasis areas: Instructional Design and Development, Instructional Technology, and School Library Media; PhD for leadership positions as specialists in instructional design and development and university faculty. The program offers advanced study for individuals with previous preparation in instructional media and technology, as well as a preparation for personnel in other professional fields requiring a specialty in instructional systems or instructional technology. Representative career fields for graduates include designing new courses, educational multimedia (especially web-based), tutorial programs, and instructional materials in state and local school systems, higher education, business and industry, research and nonprofit settings, and in instructional products development.

**Features**—Minor areas of study available in a variety of other departments. Personalized programs are planned around a common core of courses and include practicums, internships, or clinical experiences. Research activities include grant-related activities and applied projects, as well as dissertation studies.

**Admission Requirements**—All degrees: application to graduate school, satisfactory GRE score, other criteria as outlined in Graduate School Bulletin and on the program website.

**Degree Requirements**—MEd: 36 semester hours with 3.0 GPA, portfolio with oral exam. EdS: 30 semester hours with 3.0 GPA and project exam. PhD: three full years of study beyond the Master's degree, two consecutive semesters full-time residency, comprehensive exam with oral defense, internship, dissertation with oral defense.

**Number of Full Time Faculty**—10; **Number of Other Faculty**—0

**Degrees awarded in 2012–2013 Academic Year**—Master's—15; PhD—4; Other—13

**Grant Monies awarded in 2012–2013 Academic Year**—271,000

**Name of Institution**—Valdosta State University

**Name of Department or Program**—Curriculum, Leadership, and Technology

**Address:**
1500 N. Patterson St.
Valdosta, GA
31698
USA

**Phone Number**—(229)333-5633; **Fax Number**—(229)259-5094

**Email Contact**—ewiley@valdosta.edu; **URL**—http://www.valdosta.edu/colleges/education/curriculum-leadership-and-technology/

**Contact Person**—Ellen W. Wiley

**Specializations**—MEd in Instructional Technology with concentrations in: Corporate Training; Library/Media, P-12 Technology Applications (leads to certification in Instructional Technology for applicants with a clear and renewable Georgia Certificate), and Non P-12 Technology Applications. The Corporate Training concentration facilitates students acquisition of four industry recognized certifications—Adobe Certified Associate in Photoshop, Premiere, and Dreamweaver; and, Certified Associate in Project Management from the Project Management Institute. Online EdS in Instructional Technology with two tracks: P-12 Technology Applications (leads to certification in Instructional Technology for applicants with a clear and renewable Georgia Certificate) Non P-12 Technology Applications EdD in Curriculum and Instruction (Leads to certification in Curriculum and Instruction for applicants with a clear and renewable Georgia Certificate).

**Features**—The program has a strong emphasis on systematic design and technology in MEd, EdS, and EdD Strong emphasis on change leadership, reflective practice, applied research in EdS and EdD

**Admission Requirements**—MEd: 3.0 GPA, GRE or MAT accepted EdS: Master's degree, 3 years of experience, 3.0 GPA, GRE or MAT accepted. EdD degree, 3 years of experience, 3.50 GPA, GRE or MAT accepted. GRE and MAT scores are only one of the factors considered in admissions decisions. These test scores are not the sole criteria for admission.

**Degree Requirements**—MEd: 30–36 semester hours. EdS: 27 semester hours. EdD: 55 semester hours.

**Number of Full Time Faculty**—8; **Number of Other Faculty**—7

**Degrees awarded in 2012–2013 Academic Year**—Master's—10; **PhD**—0; **Other**—43

**Grant Monies awarded in 2012–2013 Academic Year**—0

**Name of Institution**—University of Northern Iowa

**Name of Department or Program**—Instructional Technology Program

**Address:**
618 Schinder Education Center
Cedar Falls, IA
50614-0606
USA
**Phone Number**—(319)273-3249; **Fax Number**—(319)273-5886

**Email Contact**—leigh.zeitz@uni.edu; **URL**—http://www.uni.edu/itech

**Contact Person**—Leigh E. Zeitz, PhD

**Specializations**—MA in Curriculum and Instruction: Instructional Technology

**Features**—The Instructional Technology master's is designed to prepare educators for a variety of professional positions in K-12 and adult learning/corporate educational settings. This is a hands-on program that requires students to apply the theoretical foundations presented in the courses. The UNI Instructional Technology Master's program is available completely on-line. An online 2-year cohort is initiated during the summer in even numbered years and another cohort begins in Fall semester in odd numbered years. The programs practical perspective prepares professionals for fulfilling technology leadership roles. On a PK-12 level, these roles include technology coordinators, master teachers, special education media specialists, and county educational specialists. On an adult and corporate level, the roles include instructors at vocational-technical schools, community colleges, and universities. They can work as trainers in the corporate world as well as higher education. Many of our graduates have also become successful instructional designers throughout the country. The master's degree is aligned with the ISTE standards and is focused on addressing specific career choices.

**Admission Requirements**—Bachelor's degree, 3.0 undergraduate GPA, 500 TOEFL Licensure as a teacher is not required for admission to the master's program. The bachelor's degree may be in any field.

**Degree Requirements**—33 semester credits. Research paper (literature review, action research, project report, journal article or research report on original research) is required. A thesis option is available. An online digital portfolio will be created by each student to share and reflect upon the students learning experiences in the program.

**Number of Full Time Faculty**—2; **Number of Other Faculty**—1

**Degrees awarded in 2012–2013 Academic Year**—Master's—14; **PhD**—1; **Other**—0

**Grant Monies awarded in 2012–2013 Academic Year**—4000

**Name of Institution**—Boise State University

**Name of Department or Program**—Organizational Performance and Workplace Learning

**Address:**
1910 University Drive, ENGR-327
Boise, ID
83725
USA

**Phone Number**—(208)426-2489;   (800)824-7017   ext.   61312;   **Fax Number**—(000)000-0000

**Email Contact**—jfenner@boisestate.edu; **URL**—http://opwl.boisestate.edu/

**Contact Person**—Jo Ann Fenner, Manager, Marketing and Outreach Services

**Specializations**—The Master of Science in Organizational Performance and Workplace Learning (OPWL) degree is intended to prepare students for careers in instructional design, performance technology, training and development, training management, workplace e-learning, human resources, organizational development, and performance consulting. The department also offers three graduate certificate programs in; Workplace Performance Improvement (WPI), Workplace E-Learning and Performance Support (WELPS), and Workplace Instructional Design (WIDe). The graduate certificates can be earned en route to the MS with the credits eligible for application to the degree.

**Features**—The degrees curriculum results in students working on virtual teams to resolve an organizational problem for an actual client. The resulting projects become part of the students portfolio. OPWL students write a monthly column called Tales from the Field in the International Society for Performance Improvements free e-newsletter performancexpress; http://opwl.boisestate.edu/about-opwl/tales-from-the-field/. We have a group on LinkedIn called the Organizational Performance and Workplace Learning-Network (OPWL-N) that individuals are invited to join; http://opwl.boisestate.edu/resources/linkedin/.

**Admission Requirements**—undergraduate degree with 3.0 GPA, one-to-two page statement of purpose describing why you want to pursue this program and how it will contribute to your personal and professional development, and a resume of personal qualifications and work experience. For more information, visit; http://opwl.boisestate.edu/admission/admission-process/.

**Degree Requirements**—36 semester hours in organizational performance and workplace learning and related course work; and two options for a culminating activity; thesis or portfolio defense (included in 36 credit hours).

**Number of Full Time Faculty**—7; **Number of Other Faculty**—8

**Degrees awarded in 2012–2013 Academic Year**—Master's—45; **PhD**—0; **Other**—0

**Grant Monies awarded in 2012–2013 Academic Year**—0

**Name of Institution**—Governors State University

**Name of Department or Program**—College of Arts and Sciences

**Address:**
1 University Parkway
University Park, IL
60484
USA

**Phone Number**—(708)534-4051; **Fax Number**—(708)534-7895

**Email Contact**—mlanigan@govst.edu; **URL**—http://www.govst.edu/hpt

**Contact Person**—Mary Lanigan, Associate Prof., Human Performance and Training

**Specializations**—MA in Communication and Training with HP&T major—Program concentrates on building instructional design skills; however, we do follow a performance improvement perspective with an emphasis on evaluation. Most classes are delivered in a hybrid format of online and face to face.

**Features**—Instructional Design overview; front-end analysis including both needs and task; design and delivery using various platforms; evaluation skills and how to predict behavior transfer; various technologies; consulting; project management; systems thinking; principles of message design; and more.

**Admission Requirements**—Undergraduate degree in any field; 2.75 GPA; and, a statement of purpose.

**Degree Requirements**—36 credit hours. 27–30 h in instructional and performance technology; internship or advanced field project required. Metropolitan Chicago area based.

**Number of Full Time Faculty**—1; **Number of Other Faculty**—5

**Degrees awarded in 2012–2013 Academic Year**—Master's—11; PhD—0; Other—0

**Grant Monies awarded in 2012–2013 Academic Year**—0


**Name of Institution**—Southern Illinois University at Carbondale

**Name of Department or Program**—Department of Curriculum and Instruction

**Address:**
625 Wham Drive, Mailcode 4610
Carbondale, IL
62901
USA

**Phone Number**—(618)453-4019; **Fax Number**—(618)453-4244

**Email Contact**—fadde@siu.edu; **URL**—http://ehs.siu.edu/ci/graduate/lsdt/index. php

**Contact Person**—Peter Fadde, Coord., Learning Systems Design and Technology

**Specializations**—MSEd in Curriculum and Instruction (with concentration in Learning Systems Design and Technology); PhD in Education (with concentration in Learning Systems Design and Technology).

**Features**—All specializations are oriented to multiple education settings. The LSDT concentration is designed to prepare students for careers as learning systems designers and learning technologists in higher education, schools, corporations, military, government and nonprofit organizations. The master's program focuses on the principles and techniques of creating learning products and multimedia-based online resources for learning, instruction, and education. Courses cover topics including learning theories, systems design, and principles that apply to the design, development, evaluation, and management of learning systems, resources, and technologies. The doctoral program covers the same knowledge base but with an emphasis on research and scholarship.

**Admission Requirements**—MSEd: Bachelor's degree, 2.7 undergraduate GPA, transcripts. PhD: Master's degree with 3.25 GPA, GRE scores, three letters of recommendation, transcripts, writing sample. International students without a degree from a US institution must submit TOEFL score.

**Degree Requirements**—MSEd, 32 credit hours with thesis; 36 credit hours without thesis; PhD, 46 credit hours beyond the master's degree in courses, 24 credit hours for the dissertation.

**Number of Full Time Faculty**—2; **Number of Other Faculty**—1

**Degrees awarded in 2012–2013 Academic Year**—Master's—6; **PhD**—2; **Other**—0

**Grant Monies awarded in 2012–2013 Academic Year**—71,000


**Name of Institution**—Northern Illinois University

**Name of Department or Program**—Educational Technology, Research and Assessment

**Address:**
208 Gabel Hall
DeKalb, IL
60115
USA

**Phone Number**—(815)753-9339; **Fax Number**—(815)753-9388

**Email Contact**—edtech@niu.edu; **URL**—http://www.cedu.niu.edu/etra

**Contact Person**—Dr. Wei-Chen Hung, Department Chair

**Specializations**—MSEd in Instructional Technology with concentrations in Instructional Design, Distance Education, Educational Computing, and Media Administration; EdD in Instructional Technology, emphasizing instructional design and development, computer education, media administration, and preparation for careers in k-12, business, industry, and higher education. In addition, online cohort and Illinois state certification in school library media and technology specialist is offered in conjunction with either degree or alone.

**Features**—Program is highly individualized. All facilities are updated on a 3-year cycle featuring five smart classrooms and over 150 student use desktop and laptop computers. Specialized equipment for digital audio and video editing, online course development, website and mobile apps creation, and presentations. All students are encouraged to create portfolios highlighting personal accomplishments and works (required at Master's). Master's program started in 1968, doctorate in 1970.

**Admission Requirements**—MSEd: 2.75 undergraduate GPA, GRE verbal and quantitative scores, two references. EdD: 3.25 MS GPA, writing sample, three references, interview.

**Degree Requirements**—MSEd: 39 h, including 30 in instructional technology; portfolio. EdD: 63 h beyond Master's, including 15 h for dissertation.

**Number of Full Time Faculty**—7; **Number of Other Faculty**—2

**Degrees awarded in 2012–2013 Academic Year**—Master's—56; **PhD**—10; **Other**—0

**Grant Monies awarded in 2012–2013 Academic Year**—139,000


**Name of Institution**—Southern Illinois University Edwardsville

**Name of Department or Program**—Instructional Technology Program

**Address:**
School of Education
Edwardsville, IL
62026-1125
USA

**Phone Number**—(618)650-3277; **Fax Number**—(618)650-3808

**Email       Contact**—dknowlt@siue.edu;          **URL**—http://www.siue.edu/instructionaltechnology

**Contact Person**—Dr. Dave S. Knowlton, Instructional Technology Program Director; Department of Educational Leadership

**Specializations**—The Educational Technologies option enables teachers and other school personnel to learn how to plan, implement, and evaluate technology-based instruction and learning activities in p-12 settings. Students pursuing this option will become knowledgeable users of technology as well as designers of curriculum and instruction that effectively utilize and integrate technology to improve student learning. Students interested in leadership roles in educational technology, such as those wishing to become technology coordinators in schools or school districts, can work toward meeting the standards for the Illinois State Board of Education's (ISBE) Technology Specialist endorsement through this program. The Library Information Specialist option enables teachers and other school personnel to learn how to plan, implement, and evaluate library information-based activities in P-12 settings. Students pursuing this option will become knowledgeable users of library information as well as designers of curriculum and instruction that effectively utilize and integrate library information to improve student learning. Students interested in Library Information Specialist endorsement can work towards meeting the standards for the Illinois State Board of Education's Library Information Specialist endorsement through this program. The Instructional Design and Performance Improvement option focuses on skills necessary for careers in the areas of instructional design, training, and performance consulting. Emphasis is placed on systematic instructional design and on the use of various media and technologies for learning and instruction. Students in this option may also focus on the design and development of online learning and other performance improvement strategies.

**Features**—Several unique features of the program provide students with opportunities for important practical experiences that complement course work. First, the program can be taken as 100 % online program. Second, juried portfolios provide students with an opportunity to share their work with a jury of professors and peers, and defend their work in light of their own goals and the content of their degree program. Third, virtual Design Studios provide students with opportunities to work on real-world projects for a variety of real clients in order to develop skills in collaboration, design, development tools and techniques, and project management.

**Admission Requirements**—The requirements for admission are a bachelor's degree in any discipline and a GPA of 3.0 or above during their last 2 years of undergraduate work.

**Degree Requirements**—36 semester hours; Thesis or Final Project options.

**Number of Full Time Faculty**—43; **Number of Other Faculty**—3

**Degrees awarded in 2012–2013 Academic Year**—Master's—10; PhD—0; Other—5

**Grant Monies awarded in 2012–2013 Academic Year**—0


**Name of Institution**—Western Illinois University

**Name of Department or Program**—Instructional Design and Technology

**Address:**
47 Harrabin Hall
Macomb, IL
61455
USA

**Phone Number**—(309)298-1952; **Fax Number**—(309)298-2978

**Email Contact**—hh-hemphill@wiu.edu; **URL**—http://www.wiu.edu/coehs/idt

**Contact Person**—Hoyet H. Hemphill, PhD, Chair. PhD in Instructional Technology

**Specializations**—Graduate Program MS in Instructional Design and Technology (available online) with optional emphasis on K-12 Technology Specialist. Six Post-Baccalaureate Certificates (PBC)—three completely online, including Educational Technology Specialist option.

**Features**—MS program approved by Illinois Board of Higher Education in January 1996 with emphases in Instructional Design and Technology, Web-Design, Interactive Multimedia, and Distance Education. MS can be completed entirely online. MS and Post-Baccalaureate Certificate in K-12 Technology Specialist both offered online.

**Admission Requirements**—MS: Bachelor's degree with minimum 2.75 GPA overall or 3.0 for last two years. Otherwise, 12 semester hours of graduate work with GPA of 3.2 or higher. English proficiency (TOEFL) for international students.

**Degree Requirements**—MS: 32 semester hours, thesis or applied project, or 35 semester hours with portfolio. Certificate Program in Instructional Technology Specialization. Graphic applications, training development, video production. Each track option is made of five courses or a total of 15 semester hours, except for Technology Specialist, which is 24 semester hours.

**Number of Full Time Faculty**—6; **Number of Other Faculty**—2

**Degrees awarded in 2012–2013 Academic Year**—Master's—23; PhD—0; **Other**—6

**Grant Monies awarded in 2012–2013 Academic Year**—0


**Name of Institution**—Iowa State University

**Name of Department or Program**—School of Education

**Address:**
N031 Lagomarcino Hall
Ames, IA
50011
USA

**Phone Number**—(515)294-9141; **Fax Number**—(515)294-2763

**Email Contact**—dschmidt@iastate.edu; **URL**—http://www.educ.iastate.edu/

**Contact Person**—Denise Crawford, Director, Center for Technology in Learning and Teaching

**Specializations**—MEd, MS, and PhD in Curriculum and Instructional Technology. Features: Prepares candidates as practitioners and researchers in the field of curriculum and instructional technology. All areas of specialization emphasize appropriate and effective applications of technology in teacher education. MEd program also offered at a distance.

**Features**—Twitter: @ctltisu Graduate Programs: http://www.education.iastate. edu/graduate/.

**Admission Requirements**—Admission Requirements: MEd and MS: Bachelor's degree, top half of undergraduate class, official transcripts, three letters of reference, autobiography. PhD: top half of undergraduate class, official transcripts, three letters of reference, autobiography, GRE scores, scholarly writing sample.

**Degree Requirements**—Degree Requirements: MEd 32 credit hours (7 research, 12 foundations, 13 applications and leadership in instructional technology); MS 33 credit hours (13 research, 12 foundations, 8 applications and leadership in instructional technology) and thesis; PhD 78 credit hours (minimum of 12 research, minimum of 15 foundations, additional core credits in conceptual, technical and advanced specialization areas, minimum of 12 dissertation) and dissertation.

**Number of Full Time Faculty**—5; **Number of Other Faculty**—1

**Degrees awarded in 2012–2013 Academic Year**—Master's—10; **PhD**—2; **Other**—0

**Grant Monies awarded in 2012–2013 Academic Year**—0


**Name of Institution**—Kansas State University

**Name of Department or Program**—Curriculum and Instruction

**Address:**
261 Bluemont Hall
Manhattan, KS
66506
USA

**Phone Number**—785-532-5716; **Fax Number**—785-532-7304

**Email Contact**—talab@ksu.edu; **URL**—http://coe.ksu.edu/ecdol

**Contact Person**—Dr. Rosemary Talab

**Specializations**—The Educational Computing, Design, and Online Learning Program has these specializations: (I) MS in Curriculum and Instruction with specialties in (1) Educational Computing, Design, and Online Learning (online); (2) Digital Teaching and Learning (online). (II) PhD in Curriculum and Instruction with specialty in Educational Computing, Design, and Online Learning (courses available online). (III) K-State Graduate School Certificate in Online Course Design Master's program started in 1982; PhD in 1987 and OCD Certificate in 2014.

**Features**—All coursework for the Certificate and MA degree specialties can be taken online. PhD can be taken online. ECDOL is an online program that focuses on research, theory, practice, ethics, and the design of learning environments, with an emphasis on emerging technologies. Coursework includes instructional design, virtual learning environments, game-based learning, the design and evaluation of online courses, etc. Classes are offered regularly on a rotating basis. A cohort group is begun each fall for the Professional Seminar 1 and 2 academic year via videoconferencing, in which major areas of the field (change and ID models, distance education and online learning, etc.) are explored, as well as various delivery methods and technologies. E-portfolios are required at the Certificate and Master's degree levels. The PhD program allows the student to tailor the classes to individual needs. The Master's degree specialty in Digital Teaching and Learning offers classroom teachers leadership opportunities as technology facilitators and lead teachers, with coursework available in integrating emerging technologies into instruction to improve student achievement through a blend of practical technology skills with research and theory. The Master's degree specialty in Educational Computing, Design and Online Learning is offered to teachers and to those who have BAs in other fields who wish to pursue a specialty in instructional design, prepare for the PhD in ECDOL or design instruction in online and blended environments. The KSU Graduate School Certificate in Digital Teaching and Learning is a 15-h completely online program for the classroom teacher with uniform exit outcomes and an e-portfolio requirement. The emphasis is on the application of technological and pedagogical theory, knowledge and practical application skills that can be directly translated into the classroom.

**Admission Requirements**—MS in ECDOL: B average in undergraduate work, mid-range scores on TOEFL. MS/Certificate in DTL: B average in undergraduate work and teaching experience. PhD: B average in undergraduate and graduate work, GRE, three letters of recommendation, experience or basic courses in educational computing.

**Degree Requirements**—OCD Certificate is 14 h and requires a final eportfolio and an online course/workshop MS: 31 semester hours (minimum of 15 in specialty); thesis, internship, or practicum not required, but all three are possible; e-portfolio and project are required. The PhD degree is 30–42 h, with 30 h of research, for a total of 60 h, minimum. Of that, 60 h semester hours are required, of which 30 h are required for dissertation research and 30 h are taken from the students previous Master's degree program.

**Number of Full Time Faculty**—1; **Number of Other Faculty**—6

**Degrees awarded in 2012–2013 Academic Year**—Master's—7; **PhD**—3; **Other**—2

**Grant Monies awarded in 2012–2013 Academic Year**—0

**Name of Institution**—Fitchburg State University

**Name of Department or Program**—Division of Graduate and Continuing Education

**Address:**
160 Pearl Street
Fitchburg, MA
01420
USA

**Phone Number**—(978)665-3544; **Fax Number**—(978)665-3055

**Email Contact**—rhowe@fitchburgstate.edu; **URL**—www.fitchburgstate.edu

**Contact Person**—Dr. Randy Howe, Chair

**Specializations**—MEd in Educational Leadership and Management with specialization in Technology Leadership.

**Features**—Collaborating with professionals working in the field both for organizations and as independent producers, Fitchburg offers a unique MEd program. The objectives are to develop in candidates the knowledge and skills for the effective implementation of technology within business, industry, government, not-for-profit agencies, health services, and education.

**Admission Requirements**—MAT or GRE scores, official transcript(s) of a baccalaureate degree, 2 or more years of experience in communications or media or education, three letters of recommendation.

**Degree Requirements**—39 semester credit hours.

**Number of Full Time Faculty**—5; **Number of Other Faculty**—7

**Degrees awarded in 2012–2013 Academic Year**—Master's—4; **PhD**—0; **Other**—0

**Grant Monies awarded in 2012–2013 Academic Year**—0


**Name of Institution**—McDaniel College (formerly Western Maryland College)

**Name of Department or Program**—Graduate and Professional Studies

**Address:**
2 College Hill
Westminster, MD
21157
USA

**Phone Number**—(410)857-2507; **Fax Number**—(410)857-2515

**Email Contact**—rkerby@mcdaniel.edu; **URL**—http://www.mcdaniel.edu

**Contact Person**—Dr. Ramona N. Kerby, Coord., School Librarianship, Graduate Studies

**Specializations**—MS in Education with an emphasis in School Librarianship.

**Features**—School librarianship.

**Admission Requirements**—3.0 Undergraduate GPA, three reference checklist forms from principal and other school personnel, acceptable application essay, acceptable Praxis test scores.

**Degree Requirements**—37 credit hours, including professional digital portfolio.

**Number of Full Time Faculty**—1; **Number of Other Faculty**—5

**Degrees awarded in 2012–2013 Academic Year**—Master's—15; PhD—0; Other—0

**Grant Monies awarded in 2012–2013 Academic Year**—0


**Name of Institution**—Towson University

**Name of Department or Program**—College of Education

**Address:**
Hawkins Hall
Towson, MD
21252
USA
**Phone Number**—(410)704-4226; **Fax Number**—(410)704-4227

**Email Contact**—jkenton@towson.edu; **URL**—http://www.towson.edu/coe/edtl/insttech/

**Contact Person**—Dr. Jeffrey M. Kenton, Assistant Dean—College of Education

**Specializations**—MS degrees in Instructional Development, and Educational Technology (Contact Liyan Song: lsong@towson.edu) MS degree in School Library Media (Contact, David Robinson: derobins@towson.edu). EdD degree in Instructional Technology (Contact, William Sadera, bsadera@towson.edu) (http://grad.towson.edu/program/doctoral/istc-edd/).

**Features**—Excellent labs. Strong practical hands-on classes. Engaging and useful hybrid courses. Several online courses add to programs accessibility. Focus of MS program—Students produce useful multimedia projects for use in their teaching and training. Many group activities within courses. School library media degree confers with Maryalnd State Department of Education certification as a Prek-12 Library Media Specialist. Innovative EdD program with online hybrid courses and strong mix of theory and practical discussions.

**Admission Requirements**—Bachelor's degree from accredited institution with 3.0 GPA. (Conditional admission granted for many applicants with a GPA over 2.75.) Doctoral requirements are listed: http://grad.towson.edu/program/doctoral/istc-edd/ar-istc-edd.asp.

**Degree Requirements**—MS degree is 36 graduate semester hours without thesis. EdD is 63 h beyond the MS degree.

**Number of Full Time Faculty**—13; **Number of Other Faculty**—9

**Degrees awarded in 2012–2013 Academic Year**—Master's—79; **PhD**—0; **Other**—2

**Grant Monies awarded in 2012–2013 Academic Year**—0


**Name of Institution**—Eastern Michigan University

**Name of Department or Program**—Teacher Education
**Address:**
313 John W. Porter Building
Ypsilanti, MI
48197
USA

**Phone Number**—(734)487-3260; **Fax Number**—(734)487-2101

**Email   Contact**—ncopeland@emich.edu;   **URL**—http://www.emich.edu/coe/departments/teacher-education/educational-media-technology/index.php

**Contact Person**—Nanct L. Copeland—Professor/Graduate Coordinator

**Specializations**—MA and Graduate Certificate in Educational Media and Technology. The mission of this program is to prepare professionals who are capable of facilitating student learning in a variety of settings. The program is designed to provide students with both the knowledge base and the application skills that are required to use technology effectively in education. Focusing on the design, development, utilization, management and evaluation of instructional systems moves us toward achieving this mission. Students who complete the educational technology concentration will be able to: (a) provide a rationale for using technology in the educational process; (b) identify contributions of major leaders in the field of educational media technology and instructional theory, and the impact that each leader has had on the field; (c) assess current trends in the area of educational media technology and relate the trends to past events and future implications; (d) integrate technology into instructional programs; (e) teach the operation and various uses of educational technology in instruction; (f) act as consultants/facilitators in educational media technology; (g) design and develop instructional products to meet specified needs; and (h) evaluate the effectiveness of instructional materials and systems.

**Features**—Courses in our 30 credit hour Educational Media and Technology (EDMT) program include technology and student-centered learning, technology enhanced learning environments, issues and emerging technologies, instructional design, development of online materials, psychology of the adult learner, principles of classroom learning, curriculum foundations, research seminar and seminar in educational technology. All of the EDMT courses have been taught online. The program can be completed entirely online. Students who do not want to receive a master's degree may apply for admission to our 20 credit hour Educational Media and Technology certificate. The EDMT courses for the certificate are also offered online. Visit our blog at: http://blogs.emich.edu/edmt/. Like us on Facebook (Group: EDMT, Ypsilanti).

**Admission Requirements**—Individuals seeking admission to this program must: (1) Comply with the Graduate School admission requirements. (2) Score 550 or better on the TOEFL and 5 or better on TWE, if a nonnative speaker of English. (3) Have a 2.75 undergraduate grade point average, or a 3.30 grade point average in 12 h or more of work in a master's program. (4) Solicit two letters of reference. (5) Submit a statement of professional goals.

**Degree Requirements**—In order to graduate, each student is expected to: (1) Complete all work on an approved program of study (30+ semester hours). (2) Maintain a "B" (3.0 GPA) average or better on course work taken within the program. (3) Get a recommendation from the faculty adviser. (4) Fill out an application for graduation and obtain the advisers recommendation. (5) Meet all other requirements for a master's degree adopted by the Graduate School of Eastern Michigan University. (6) Complete a culminating experience (research, instructional development or evaluation project) as determined by the student and faculty adviser.

**Number of Full Time Faculty**—4; **Number of Other Faculty**—0

**Degrees awarded in 2012–2013 Academic Year**—Master's—15; **PhD**—0; **Other**—1

**Grant Monies awarded in 2012–2013 Academic Year**—0

**Name of Institution**—Michigan State University

**Name of Department or Program**—College of Education

**Address:**
620 Farm Lane, Room 513
East Lansing, MI
48824
USA

**Phone Number**—517-432-9259; **Fax Number**—517-353-6393

**Email Contact**—edutech@msu.edu; **URL**—http://edutech.msu.edu

**Contact Person**—Punya Mishra

**Specializations**—MA in Educational Technology with Learning, Design and Technology specialization. Online, overseas and on-campus hybrid options.

**Features**—@maet on Twitter https://www.facebook.com/MAETMSU on Facebook.

**Admission Requirements**—Please visit: http://edutech.msu.edu/apply.

**Degree Requirements**—30 semester hours, Web-based portfolio.

**Number of Full Time Faculty**—6; **Number of Other Faculty**—6

**Degrees awarded in 2012–2013 Academic Year**—Master's—85; PhD—0; **Other**—0

**Grant Monies awarded in 2012–2013 Academic Year**—0


**Name of Institution**—Wayne State University

**Name of Department or Program**—Instructional Technology

**Address:**
399 Education
Detroit, MI
48202
USA

**Phone Number**—(313)577-1728; **Fax Number**—(313)577-1693

**Email Contact**—iguerra@wayne.edu; **URL**—http://coe.wayne.edu/aos/it/

**Contact Person**—Ingrid Guerra-Lopez, PhD, Program Coord., Instructional Technology Programs, Div. of Administrative and Organizational Studies, College of Education

**Specializations**—MEd degrees with specializations in Design and Performance Systems and K-12 Technology Integration. PhD program to prepare individuals for leadership in academic, business, industry, health care, and the K-12 school setting as professor, researcher, instructional design and development specialists; media or learning resources managers or performance consultants; specialists in instructional video; and Web-based instruction and multimedia specialists. The IT program offers certificates in Online Learning, Educational Technology, and University Teaching.

**Features**—Guided experiences in instructional design and development; performance improvement activities in business and industry are available. Specific classes use a variety of technologies, including blogs, wikis, Twitter, Facebook, Google docs, and many others. MEd programs are available online.

**Admission Requirements**—PhD: Master's degree, 3.0 GPA, GRE, strong academic recommendations, interview.

**Degree Requirements**—PhD 90 cr. Hrs, including IT core and electives, research courses, 30 cr. dissertation. MEd: 33–37 semester hours, including required project; internship recommended.

**Number of Full Time Faculty**—4; **Number of Other Faculty**—10

**Degrees awarded in 2012–2013 Academic Year**—Master's—48; PhD—11; **Other**—8

**Grant Monies awarded in 2012–2013 Academic Year**—1,600,000


**Name of Institution**—St. Cloud State University

**Name of Department or Program**—Information Media, School of Education

**Address:**
720 Fourth Avenue South
St. Cloud, MN
56301-4498
USA
**Phone Number**—(308)255-2062; **Fax Number**—None

**Email Contact**—im@stcloudstate.edu; **URL**—http://www.stcloudstate.edu/im

**Contact Person**—Merton E. Thompson Chair, Information Media Department

**Specializations**—Undergraduate certificate in Instructional Technology. Master of Science degrees in Technology Integration, Library Media, and Instructional Design and Training. Graduate certificates in Instructional Technology, Design for E-learning, Technology Integration and Library Media Specialist.

**Features**—All graduate courses are available synchronously through distance delivery as well as face to face.

**Admission Requirements**—Undergraduate GPA: 2.75 A baccalaureate degree from a regionally accredited institution GRE is required unless GPA is 3.25 or higher or previous completion of a master's degree. Written and oral examination required.

**Degree Requirements**—Master's: 42 semester credits with thesis; 39 semester credits with starred paper or portfolio; 200-h practicum is required for library media licensure. Course work for all graduate certificates may be applied to the Master of Science program.

**Number of Full Time Faculty**—5; **Number of Other Faculty**—1

**Degrees awarded in 2012–2013 Academic Year**—Master's—15; PhD—0; **Other**—0

**Grant Monies awarded in 2012–2013 Academic Year**—0

**Name of Institution** — University of Missouri-Columbia

**Name of Department or Program** — School of Information Science and Learning Technologies

**Address:**
303 Townsend Hall
Columbia, MO
65211
USA

**Phone Number** — (877)747-5868; **Fax Number** — (573)884-0122

**Email Contact** — howlandj@missouri.edu; **URL** — http://sislt.missouri.edu

**Contact Person** — Jane Howland

**Specializations** — SISLT is a member of the iSchools caucus, an international coalition of leading information schools. As a member of the iSchool consortium, we share a fundamental interest in the relationships among information, people and technology. The Educational Technology program takes a theory-based approach to designing, developing, implementing, and researching technology-mediated environments to support human activity. We seek individuals who are committed to life-long learning and who aspire to use advanced technology to improve human learning and performance. Graduates of the program will find opportunities to use their knowledge and competencies as classroom teachers (face-to-face and online), media specialists, district technology specialists and coordinators, designers and developers of technology-based learning and information systems, training specialists for businesses, medical settings, and public institutions, as well as other creative positions. The curriculum at the Master's and Specialist levels has three emphasis areas: Technology in Schools, Online Educator, and Learning Systems Design and Development; with coursework tailored to each emphasis area. In addition, an Online Educator Graduate Certificate is offered. For information regarding our PhD, see https://education.missouri.edu/degree/information-science-learning-technologies-phd/.

**Features** — The three emphasis areas in the Educational Technology program are available 100 % online. The Technology in Schools emphasis area is based on the ISTE competencies and culminates in an online portfolio based on these competencies. The Learning Systems Design and Development (LSDD) emphasis area links to business, military, and government contexts. This emphasis area offers a challenging balance of design and development coursework, in addition to coursework dealing with instructional design, needs assessment, and evaluation. LSDD coursework culminates in a professional portfolio. The Online Educator emphasis area emphasizes the development of the knowledge and skills needed to design and provide effective online learning experiences in a variety of settings. For the Capstone project, students design, develop, and evaluate an online course. For information regarding our PhD, see https://education.missouri.edu/degree/information-science-learning-technologies-phd/.

**Admission Requirements**—Certificate: Bachelor's degree with a minimum GPA of 3.00 or higher ($A = 4.00$) on the last 60 h of undergraduate coursework; resume; transcript; statement of purpose. Master: Bachelor's degree with a minimum GPA of 3.00 or higher ($A = 4.00$) on the last 60 h of undergraduate coursework; resume; transcript; statement of purpose; two letters of recommendation. EdS: Master's degree, resume; transcript; statement of purpose; two letters of recommendation. PhD: 3.5 graduate GPA, GRE taken before Aug. 1, 2011: ($V > 500$; $A > 500$; $W > 3.5$) GRE taken on or after Aug. 1, 2011: ($V > 156$; $A > 146$; $W > 4.0$). See https://education.missouri.edu/degree/information-science-learning-technologies-phd/ for details.

**Degree Requirements**—Certificate: Minimum of 12 graduate credit hours required for the certificate. Master's and EdS: Minimum of 30 graduate credit hours required for the degree; 15 h of upper division coursework. Maximum of 6 h of transfer credit. PhD. See website for details.

**Number of Full Time Faculty**—18; **Number of Other Faculty**—2

**Degrees awarded in 2012–2013 Academic Year**—Master's—37; **PhD**—2; **Other**—28

**Grant Monies awarded in 2012–2013 Academic Year**—2,728,506


**Name of Institution**—The University of Southern Mississippi

**Name of Department or Program**—Instructional Technology and Design

**Address:**
118 College Drive #5057
Hattiesburg, MS
39406-0001
USA

**Phone Number**—601-266-5247; **Fax Number**—601-266-4548

**Email Contact**—Taralynn.Hartsell@usm.edu; **URL**—http://www.usm.edu/cise

**Contact Person**—Dr. Taralynn Hartsell

**Specializations**—The Department of Curriculum, Instruction, and Special Education at The University of Southern Mississippi has two graduate programs relating to Instructional Technology and Design. The Master's of Science in Instructional Technology is a 30 h program, and the PhD of Instructional Technology and Design is a 57–66 h program. Both programs are hybrid meaning that over 80 % of the coursework could be taken online. The master's program however, could be taken all online depending upon the electives chosen by the student.

**Features**—The Master's of Science concentrates more on the technology application and integration aspect that helps students learn both hands-on application of technology, as well as theoretical and historical aspects related to the field of study. Depending upon the electives selected, students could take all of their courses online. The PhD program is an advanced study program for those wishing to pursue their education in the application of technology and design, research, and leadership (established in August, 2009). A majority of the coursework in the program can be completed online (60 % or more depending upon courses completed) or hybrid. Research core requirements tend to be more traditional in nature.

**Admission Requirements**—Please review the Department website for more information on the application procedures for each program: http://www.usm.edu/cise. The GRE is mandatory for graduate programs. Applications for the university is now completed online: http://www.usm.edu/graduateschool/admissions.php.

**Degree Requirements**—Please review the Department website for more information on degree requirements for each program: http://www.usm.edu/cise.

**Number of Full Time Faculty**—4; **Number of Other Faculty**—1

**Degrees awarded in 2012–2013 Academic Year**—Master's—6; PhD—3; Other—0

**Grant Monies awarded in 2012–2013 Academic Year**—1


**Name of Institution**—North Carolina State University

**Name of Department or Program**—Digital Teaching and Learning Program

**Address:**
602 Poe Hall, Campus Box 7801
Raleigh, NC
27695-7801
USA

**Phone Number**—(919)515-6229; **Fax Number**—(919)515-6978

**Email Contact**—kmoliver@ncsu.edu; **URL**—http://ced.ncsu.edu/programs/digital-learning-and-teaching-master/

**Contact Person**—Dr. Kevin Oliver, Associate Professor

**Specializations**—Online MEd and MS in Digital Learning and Teaching (DL&T). On-Campus PhD in Learning, Design, and Technology (LD&T). Master's students choose one of three strands for specialization—digital leadership, digital design, or digital inquiry. Licensed teachers in North Carolina may earn the 079 computer educator endorsement after 12 credits or six courses (degree program not required—can simply take courses as a nondegree studies student), and may earn the 077 technology director endorsement after completing either master's program.

**Features**—Fully online Master's programs with flexibility for residents near the Raleigh–Durham area to take some on-campus courses if they wish. Doctoral program is not online. A limited number of assistantships are available for students who live near Raleigh, go to school full-time (9 h/semester), and can work on campus 20 h per week. Pays approximately $21k per academic year with health benefits, and tuition remission for doctoral assistantships only. Program Facebook group: http://www.facebook.com/groups/329701684366/. Program Twitter feed: http://twitter.com/dltncsu. Program LinkedIn group: http://www.linkedin.com/groups?gid=2811382.

**Admission Requirements**—Master's: undergraduate degree from an accredited institution, 3.0 GPA in major or in latest graduate degree program; transcripts; GRE or MAT scores; three references; goal statement. PhD: undergraduate degree from accredited institution, 3.0 GPA in major or latest graduate program; transcripts; recent GRE scores, writing sample, three references, vita, research and professional goals statement.

**Degree Requirements**—Master's: 30 semester hours (MEd), 36 semester hours (MS), thesis required for MS program. PhD: 60 h. Up to 12 h of graduate-level transfer credits may be applied to any program if the transfer credits are from Instructional Technology/Digital Learning courses similar to those in the program and have not been previously applied to a degree at another university.

**Number of Full Time Faculty**—3; **Number of Other Faculty**—3

**Degrees awarded in 2012–2013 Academic Year**—Master's—16; PhD—2; Other—0

**Grant Monies awarded in 2012–2013 Academic Year**—325,000

**Name of Institution**—University of North Carolina

**Name of Department or Program**—School of Information and Library Science

**Address:**
100 Manning Hall, CB#3360
Chapel Hill, NC
27599-3360
USA

**Phone Number**—(919)843-5276; **Fax Number**—(919)962-8071

**Email Contact**—smhughes@email.unc.edu; **URL**—http://www.ils.unc.edu/

**Contact Person**—Sandra Hughes-Hassell, Associate Professor, Coord., School Media Program

**Specializations**—Master of Science Degree in Library Science (MSLS) with specializations in school library media, archives management, public librarianship, and academic librarianship. Post-Master's certification program.

**Features**—Rigorous academic program plus field experience requirement; excellent placement record. Focus on meeting the needs of diverse populations.

**Admission Requirements**—Competitive admission based on all three GRE components (quantitative, qualitative, analytical), undergraduate GPA (plus graduate work if any), letters of recommendation, and student statement of career interest and school choice.

**Degree Requirements**—48 semester hours, field experience, comprehensive exam, Master's paper.

**Number of Full Time Faculty**—29; **Number of Other Faculty**—45

**Degrees awarded in 2012–2013 Academic Year**—Master's—130; **PhD**—5; **Other**—50

**Grant Monies awarded in 2012–2013 Academic Year**—1,000,000

**Name of Institution**—University of Nebraska Kearney

**Name of Department or Program**—Teacher Education

**Address:**
1625 West 24th Street
Kearney, NE
68849-5540
USA

**Phone Number**—(308)865-8833; **Fax Number**—(308)865-8097

**Email Contact**—fredricksons@unk.edu; **URL**—http://www.unk.edu/academics/ecampus.aspx?id=6217

**Contact Person**—Dr. Scott Fredrickson, Professor and Chair of the Instructional Technology Graduate Program

**Specializations**—MSED in Instructional Technology, Emphasis areas: Instructional Technology, School Library, Information Technology, and Leadership in Instructional Technology.

**Features**—Two main emphasis areas—Instructional Technology, School Library. The Instructional Technology track has an Information Technology endorsement module, a Leadership in Instructional Technology endorsement module, and an Instructional Technology module. The School Library track has a module that leads a School Library endorsement. To obtain any of the endorsements requires a current teaching certificate, however the degree itself and the classwork in the endorsement areas, do not.

**Admission Requirements**—Graduate Record Examination or completion of an electronic portfolio meeting dept. requirements, acceptance into graduate school, and approval of Instructional Technology Advising Committee.

**Degree Requirements**—36 credit hours—18 of which are required and 18 are elective (30 h are required for the endorsement with 6 h of electives), and a capstone Instructional Technology project.

**Number of Full Time Faculty**—5; **Number of Other Faculty**—24

**Degrees awarded in 2012–2013 Academic Year**—Master's—38; PhD—0; Other—0

**Grant Monies awarded in 2012–2013 Academic Year**—0


**Name of Institution**—University of Nebraska-Omaha

**Name of Department or Program**—College of Education; Department of Teacher Education

**Address:**
Roskens Hall 308
Omaha, NE
68182
USA
**Phone Number**—(402)554-2119; **Fax Number**—(402)554-2125

**Email Contact**—rpasco@unomaha.edu; **URL**—http://www.unomaha.edu/libraryed/

**Contact Person**—Dr. Rebecca J. Pasco

**Specializations**—Undergraduate Library Science Program (school, public, academic, and special libraries) School Library Endorsement (Undergraduate and Graduate) Master of Science in Secondary Education with School Library concentration Master of Science in Elementary Education with School Library concentration Master of Science in Reading with School Library concentration Master's in Library Science Program (Cooperative program with University of Missouri).

**Features**—Web-assisted format (combination of online and on-campus) for both undergraduate and graduate programs. School Library programs nationally recognized by American Association of School Librarians (AASL) Programs for Public, Academic and Special Libraries Cooperative UNO/University of Missouri MLS program is ALA accredited.

**Admission Requirements**—As per University of Nebraska at Omaha undergraduate and graduate admissions requirements for College of Education and College of Arts and Sciences.

**Degree Requirements**—School Library Endorsement (Undergraduate and Graduate)—30 h MS in Secondary and Elementary Education with School Library endorsement—36 h MS in Reading with School Library endorsement—36 h Master's in Library Science Program (Cooperative program with University of Missouri at Columbia)—42 h.

**Number of Full Time Faculty**—4; **Number of Other Faculty**—14

**Degrees awarded in 2012–2013 Academic Year**—Master's—44; PhD—0; **Other**—29

**Grant Monies awarded in 2012–2013 Academic Year**—52,000

**Name of Institution**—Rutgers-The State University of New Jersey

**Name of Department or Program**—School of Communication and Information

**Address:**
4 Huntington Street
New Brunswick, NJ
08901-1071
USA

**Phone Number**—(848)932-8936; **Fax Number**—(732)932-6916

**Email Contact**—rtodd@rutgers.edu; **URL**—https://comminfo.rutgers.edu/mi/master-of-information.html

**Contact Person**—Dr. Ross Todd, Chair, Dept. of Library and Information Studies, School of Communication and Information

**Specializations**—The Master of Information (MI) program provides professional education for a wide variety of service and management careers in libraries, information agencies, the information industry, and in business, industry, government, research, and similar environments where information is a vital resource. Concentrations include: Library and Information Science; Data Science; Technology, Information and Management; and Informatics and Design. Students may also choose to plan a customized course of study with an advisor.

**Features**—The ALA-accredited MI program, available both on campus and online, provides professional expertise, leadership and innovation across diverse information and technological landscapes. Students choose two of four Foundation courses related to their concentration as well as one technology requirement. A rich array of internship opportunities is available and encouraged. The specialization in School Librarianship is certified with the NJ Department of Education. All students in the New Brunswick MI program work with an advisor to plan a course of study appropriate for their interests and career objectives.

**Admission Requirements**—A Bachelor's degree or its equivalent from a recognized institution of higher education in any discipline is required as is an overall average (cumulative grade point average) of at least mid-B (3.0/4.0 GPA). The GRE (general test) and GMAT are officially accepted. MCAT or LSAT scores may also be accepted in place of GRE/GMAT scores. The standardized test requirement may be waived if the applicant can show proof of a successfully completed Master's degree. Please also submit Master's transcripts, if applicable. For international applicants, English Proficiency Test Scores are also required, in addition to Standardized Test scores. The TOEFL and IELTS are officially accepted. The

English proficiency test requirement may be waived for students who earned a bachelor's or master's degree from an accredited U.S. college or university. Two letters are required. Letters of recommendation should focus on academic capacity (e.g., problem solving, thinking, analytical, and reflective skills) to undertake a rigorous program of graduate study, rather than on workplace efficiency and character traits. The recommender's relationship must be established in the letter of recommendation. Personal friends, clergy, and family members are not appropriate recommenders. Students are asked to supply the names and e-mail addresses for recommenders as part of the online application process. A Personal Statement is required as part of the admissions process. In approximately 750 words, applicants share interests and career aspirations in pursuing an MI degree.

**Degree Requirements**—A minimum of 36 credits, or 12 courses, is required to earn the MI degree. All students are required to enroll in three non-credit classes, 501—Introduction to Library and Information Professions in their first semester, 502—Colloquium in a later semester and 503—e-Portfolio in the last semester. There are no language requirements for the MI degree, and there is no thesis or comprehensive examination.

**Number of Full Time Faculty**—21; **Number of Other Faculty**—46

**Degrees awarded in 2012–2013 Academic Year**—Master's—114; **PhD**—10; **Other**—240

**Grant Monies awarded in 2012–2013 Academic Year**—319,525

**Name of Institution**—Appalachian State University

**Name of Department or Program**—Department of Curriculum and Instruction

**Address:**
College of Education
Boone, NC
28608
USA

**Phone Number**—828-262-2277; **Fax Number**—828-262-2686

**Email Contact**—muffoletto@appstate.edu; **URL**—http://edtech.ced.appstate.edu

**Contact Person**—Robert Muffoletto

**Specializations**—MA in Educational Media and Technology with three areas of concentration: Computers, Media Literacy, and Media Production. A plan of study in Internet distance teaching is offered online. Two certificate programs: (1) Distance Learning-Internet delivered; (2) Media Literacy.

**Features**—Business, university, community college, and public school partnership offers unusual opportunities for learning. The programs are focused on developing learning environments over instructional environments.

**Admission Requirements**—Undergraduate degree.

**Degree Requirements**—36 graduate semester hours. We also have certificates in (1) Distance Learning and (2) Media Literacy.

**Number of Full Time Faculty**—0; **Number of Other Faculty**—0

**Degrees awarded in 2012–2013 Academic Year**—Master's—5; PhD—0; Other—0

**Grant Monies awarded in 2012–2013 Academic Year**—0

**Name of Institution**—State University College of Arts and Science at Potsdam

**Name of Department or Program**—Organizational Leadership and Educational Technology

**Address:**
392 Dunn Hall
Potsdam, NY
13676
USA

**Phone Number**—(315)267-2670; **Fax Number**—(315)267-3189

**Email Contact**—betrusak@potsdam.edu; **URL**—http://www.potsdam.edu/olt

**Contact Person**—Dr. Anthony Betrus, Program Coordinator

**Specializations**—MS in Education in Instructional Technology with the following program concentrations: Educational Technology Specialist, K-12 Track Educational Technology Specialist, Non-K-12 Track Organizational Performance, Leadership, and Technology Organizational Leadership.

**Features**—Live instruction Evening courses 12-week courses Internships.

**Admission Requirements**—(1) Submission of an official transcript of an earned baccalaureate degree from an accredited institution. (2) A minimum GPA of 2.75 (4.0 scale) in the most recent 60 credit hours of coursework. (3) Submission of the Application for Graduate Study (w/$50 non-refundable fee). (4) For students seeking the Educational Technology Specialist Certification, a valid NYS Teaching Certificate is required.

**Degree Requirements**—36 semester hours, including internship or practicum; culminating project required.

**Number of Full Time Faculty**—2; **Number of Other Faculty**—5

**Degrees awarded in 2012–2013 Academic Year**—Master's—19; PhD—0; Other—0

**Grant Monies awarded in 2012–2013 Academic Year**—0

**Name of Institution**—Kent State University

**Name of Department or Program**—Instructional Technology

**Address:**
405 White Hall
Kent, OH
44242
USA

**Phone Number**—(330)672-2294; **Fax Number**—(330)672-2512

**Email Contact**—dtiene@kent.edu; **URL**—http://www.kent.edu/ehhs/itec/index.cfm

**Contact Person**—Dr. Drew Tiene, Coordinator: Instructional Technology Program

**Specializations**—MEd in Instructional Technology, and licensure program in Computing/Technology. PhD in Educational Psychology with concentration in Instructional Technology. Online Teaching and Learning Certificate.

**Features**—Programs are planned with advisors to prepare students for careers in elementary, secondary, or higher education, business, industry, government agencies, or health facilities. Students may take advantage of independent research, individual study, and internships. Most courses and programs can be taken online.

**Admission Requirements**—Master's: Bachelor's degree with 3.00 undergraduate GPA, two references Doctorate: Master's Degree, acceptable graduate GPA and GRE scores, goal statement, three references.

**Degree Requirements**—Master's: 34–37 semester hours, portfolio, practicum (for licensure); Doctoral: minimum of 45 post-master's semester hours, comprehensive exam, dissertation.

**Number of Full Time Faculty**—5; **Number of Other Faculty**—5

**Degrees awarded in 2012–2013 Academic Year**—Master's—30; PhD—3; Other—0

**Grant Monies awarded in 2012–2013 Academic Year**—0

**Name of Institution**—Ohio University

**Name of Department or Program**—Instructional Technology

**Address:**
McCracken Hall
Athens, OH
45701-2979
USA

**Phone Number**—(740)597-1322; **Fax Number**—(740)593-0477

**Email Contact**—moored3@ohio.edu; **URL**—http://www.cehs.ohio.edu/academics/es/it/index.htm

**Contact Person**—David Richard Moore, Instructional Technology Program Coordinator

**Specializations**—Certificate in Instructional Design http://www.ohio.edu/education/academic-programs/educational-studies/instructional-technology/index.cfm. MEd in Computer Education and Technology. PhD in Curriculum and Instruction with a specialization in Instructional Technology also available; call for details (740-593-4561) or visit the website: http://www.ohio.edu/education/dept/es/it/index.cfm.

**Features**—Master's program is a blended online delivery.

**Admission Requirements**—Bachelor's degree, 3.0 undergraduate GPA, GRE scores, 550 TOEFL, three letters of recommendation, Paper describing future goals and career expectations from completing a degree in our program.

**Degree Requirements**—Master's—36 semester credits, electronic portfolio or optional thesis worth 2–10 credits or alternative seminar research paper. Students may earn two graduate degrees simultaneously in education and in any other field. PhD—78 h with 10 h being dissertation work.

**Number of Full Time Faculty**—4; **Number of Other Faculty**—0

**Degrees awarded in 2012–2013 Academic Year**—Master's—18; **PhD**—10; **Other**—0

**Grant Monies awarded in 2012–2013 Academic Year**—500,000

**Name of Institution**—University of Toledo

**Name of Department or Program**—Curriculum and Instruction

**Address:**
2801 W. Bancroft Street, Mail Stop 924
Toledo, OH
43606
USA

**Phone Number**—(419)530-7979; **Fax Number**—(419)530-2466

**Email Contact**—Berhane.Teclehaimanot@utoledo.edu; **URL**—http://tipt3.utoledo.edu

**Contact Person**—Berhane Teclehaimanot, PhD

**Specializations**—Technology Using Educator/Technology Coordinator and Instructional Designer.

**Features**—Graduate students may concentrate in one of the two primary "roles," or may choose a blended program of study. The program was completely redesigned and revised in 2013.

**Admission Requirements**—Master's: 2.7 undergrad. GPA, GRE (if undergrad. GPA < 2.7), All graduate students interested in the doctoral program in C&I must meet the admission requirements of the College of Graduate Studies, the Judith Herb College of Education, and the PhD Program in which they wish to study. Application is made to the College of Graduate Studies (http://www.utoledo.edu/graduate/) of The University of Toledo. The admission requirements are as follows: (1) A complete Application for College of Graduate Studies Admission. (2) A 3.25 cumulative grade point average in all graduate work. (3) An autobiographical sketch that describes why the applicant wishes to pursue the selected doctoral program. This sketch should also include information on previous study, educational experience, professional accomplishments, immediate and future professional goals, a proposed time schedule for completing the degree, and any other information that the applicant believes is relevant for admission into the desired program. (4) Evidence of research and writing ability. Such evidence may include a master's thesis, proctored writing sample, a written research report, one or more reprints of publications, a paper presented to a professional society, or similar evidence of competence in this respect. (5) Two (2) copies of any and all official graduate transcripts, including credits and degrees earned. (6) Acceptable GRE-Verbal and GRE-Quantitative scores, as determined by the department or concentration. For example, the recommended Graduate Record Examination (GRE) for the Educational Technology program is as follows: GRE is not required for applicants with master's degree GPA of 3.5 or higher. If under 3.5 GPA, acceptable GRE scores are: 144 Verbal 144 Quantitative 3.5 Analytical Writing International Students (English Proficiency) TOEFL Score: 550 (paper) 213 (computer) 80 (Internet). (7) Three (3) letters of reference describing the applicant's potential for successfully completing a doctoral program, and (8) A nonrefundable application fee (check or money order payable to The University of Toledo). Please contact University of Toledo, College of Graduate Studies concerning issues related to the admission criteria and financial support for international students related issues at http://grad-school.utoledo.edu/ or (419)530-4723. You may also visit the College Website for additional information at http://www.utoledo.edu/education/departments/ci/programs.html.

**Degree Requirements**—Master's: 30 semester hours, culminating project; Doctorate: 60 semester hours, major exams, and dissertation.

**Number of Full Time Faculty**—2; **Number of Other Faculty**—7

**Degrees awarded in 2012–2013 Academic Year**—Master's—14; PhD—5; **Other**—0

**Grant Monies awarded in 2012–2013 Academic Year**—0

**Name of Institution**—The University of Oklahoma

**Name of Department or Program**—Instructional Psychology and Technology, Department of Educational Psychology

**Address:**
321 Collings Hall
Norman, OK
73019
USA

**Phone Number**—(405)325-5974; **Fax Number**—(405)325-6655

**Email Contact**—Tacullen@ou.edu; **URL**—http://education.ou.edu/ipt/

**Contact Person**—Dr. Theresa Cullen Program Area Coordinator

**Specializations**—Master's degree with emphases in Instructional Design and Technology and Instructional Psychology and Technology (includes tracks: Instructional Psychology and Technology and Integrating Technology in Teaching). Doctoral degree in Instructional Psychology and Technology.

**Features**—Strong interweaving of principles of instructional psychology with instructional design and development. Application of IP&T in K-12, vocational education, higher education, business and industry, and governmental agencies.

**Admission Requirements**—Master's: acceptance by IPT program and Graduate College based on minimum 3.00 GPA for last 60 h of undergraduate work or last 12 h of graduate work; written statement that indicates goals and interests compatible with program goals. Doctoral: minimum 3.25 GPA, GRE scores, written statement that indicates goals and interests compatible with program goals, writing sample, and letters of recommendation.

**Degree Requirements**—Master's: 36 h course work with 3.0 GPA; successful completion of thesis or comprehensive exam. Doctorate: see program description from institution or http://www.ou.edu/content/education/edpy/instructional-psychology-and-technology-degrees-and-programs.html.

**Number of Full Time Faculty**—11; **Number of Other Faculty**—0

**Degrees awarded in 2012–2013 Academic Year**—Master's—8; **PhD**—2; **Other**—0

**Grant Monies awarded in 2012–2013 Academic Year**—0


**Name of Institution**—Bloomsburg University

**Name of Department or Program**—Instructional Technology and Institute for Interactive Technologies

**Address:**
207 Sutliff Hall
Bloomsburg, PA
17815
USA

**Phone Number**—(717)389-4875; **Fax Number**—(717)389-4943

**Email Contact**—hdoll@bloomu.edu; **URL**—http://iit.bloomu.edu

**Contact Person**—Dr. Helmut Doll, contact person

**Specializations**—MS in Instructional Technology—Corporate Concentration MS in Instructional Technology—Instructional Technology Specialist Concentration (education eLearning Developer Certificate).

**Features**—MS in Instructional Technology with emphasis on preparing for careers as Instructional Technologist in corporate, government, healthcare, higher education and K-12 educational settings . The program is highly applied and provides opportunities for students to work on real world projects as part of their coursework. Our program offers a corporate concentration and an Instructional Technology Specialist Concentration for educators. The program offers a complete master's degree online as well as on campus. Graduate assistantships are available for full time students. The program is closely associated with the nationally known Institute for Interactive Technologies.

**Admission Requirements**—Bachelor's degree.

**Degree Requirements**—33 semester credits (27 credits+six credit thesis, or 30 credits+three credit internship).

**Number of Full Time Faculty**—5; **Number of Other Faculty**—3

**Degrees awarded in 2012–2013 Academic Year**—Master's—50; **PhD**—0; **Other**—3

**Grant Monies awarded in 2012–2013 Academic Year**—100,000


**Name of Institution**—Lehigh University

**Name of Department or Program**—Teaching, Learning, and Technology

**Address:**
111 Research Drive
Bethlehem, PA
18015
USA

**Phone Number**—(610)758-3230; **Fax Number**—(610)758-6223

**Email Contact**—tch27@lehigh.edu; **URL**—http://coe.lehigh.edu/academics/disciplines/itech

**Contact Person**—Tom Hammond, Associate Professor and Teaching, Learning, and Technology Program Director

**Specializations**—MS in Instructional Technology. A 30-credit master's degree offered through the Teaching, Learning, and Technology program aimed at those interested in the use of technology in education, particularly preK-12 and post secondary settings. Graduate certificate in Technology Use in the Schools: This 12-credit grad certificate focuses on integrating technology into daily practice in the schools. PhD in Teaching and Learning: The doctorate in Teaching, Learning, and Technology (TLT) is a 48-credit, post master's PhD program. The TLT PhD program employs a scientist/practitioner model of learning. That is, research is not separate from application or practice. Our doctoral students collaborate closely with faculty to generate new theories and classification systems, innovative curricula, technology-integrated learning environments, authentic approaches to assessing learning, and a wide range of creative methods of teaching and learning in a global world highly interconnected by technology.

**Features**—Our professional development programs in instructional technology focus on curriculum integration in preK-16 settings, instructional planning and use of novel technology learning tools. The program is targeted toward individuals from varied backgrounds who wish to help educators or learn themselves to design, develop, and incorporate technology more effectively in diverse educational settings (including preK-12, higher education, and informal learning environments). Both master's and doctoral students collaborate with faculty on projects and studies (including national presentation and publication).

**Admission Requirements**—MS (competitive): 3.0 undergraduate GPA or 3.0 graduate GPA, GREs recommended, transcripts, at least two letters of recommendation, statement of personal and professional goals, application fee. Application deadlines: Rolling admissions PhD (highly competitive): 3.5 graduate GPA, GREs required. Copy of two extended pieces of writing (or publications); statement of future professional goals; statement of why Lehigh best place to meet those goals; identification of which presentations, publications, or research by Lehigh faculty attracted applicant to Lehigh. Application deadline: A December 1 deadline for summer or fall start (eligibility for college scholarship) pril 1 deadline for summer or fall start (past date for eligibility for college scholarship).

**Degree Requirements**—MS: 30 credits; thesis option. PhD: 48 credits post master's (including dissertation). Qualifying Exam (written and oral)+General Examination Research Project (publication quality)+dissertation.

**Number of Full Time Faculty**—5; **Number of Other Faculty**—1

**Degrees awarded in 2012–2013 Academic Year**—Master's—11; **PhD**—3; **Other**—0

**Grant Monies awarded in 2012–2013 Academic Year**—500,000

**Name of Institution**—University of South Carolina Aiken and University of South Carolina Columbia

**Name of Department or Program**—Aiken: School of Education; Columbia: Department of Educational Psychology

**Address:**
471 University Parkway
Aiken, SC
29801
USA

**Phone Number**—803.641.3489; **Fax Number**—803.641.3720

**Email Contact**—smyth@usca.edu; **URL**—http://edtech.usca.edu

**Contact Person**—Dr. Thomas Smyth, Professor, Program Director

**Specializations**—Master of Education in Educational Technology (A Joint Program of The University of South Carolina Aiken and Columbia).

**Features**—The Master's Degree in Educational Technology is designed to provide advanced professional studies in graduate level coursework to develop capabilities essential to the effective design, evaluation, and delivery of technology-based instruction and training (e.g., software development, multimedia development, assistive technology modifications, Web-based development, and distance learning). The program is intended (1) to prepare educators to assume leadership roles in the integration of educational technology into the school curriculum, and (2) to provide graduate-level instructional opportunities for several populations (e.g., classroom teachers, corporate trainers, educational software developers) that need to acquire both technological competencies and understanding of sound instructional design principles and techniques. The program is offered entirely online as high-quality, interactive, Web-based courses. There are occasional synchronous online meetings, but the vast majority of the program is asynchronous. Candidates present a program portfolio for review by the faculty at the end of the program.

**Admission Requirements**—Application to the Educational Technology Program can be made after completion of at least the bachelor's degree from a college or university accredited by a regional accrediting agency. The standard for admission will be based on a total profile for the applicant. The successful applicant should have an undergraduate grade point average of at least 3.0, a score of 45 on the Miller's Analogies Test or scores of 450 on both the verbal and quantitative portions of the Graduate Record Exam, a well-written letter of intent that matches the objectives of the program and includes a description of previous technology experience, and positive letters of recommendation from individuals who know the professional characteristics of the applicant. Any exceptions for students failing to meet these standards shall be referred to the Admissions Committee for review and final decision.

**Degree Requirements**—36 semester hours, including instructional theory, computer design, and integrated media.

**Number of Full Time Faculty**—4; **Number of Other Faculty**—2

**Degrees awarded in 2012–2013 Academic Year**—Master's—21; **PhD**—0; **Other**—0

**Grant Monies awarded in 2012–2013 Academic Year**—0


**Name of Institution**—Dakota State University

**Name of Department or Program**—Educational Technology

**Address:**
820 North Washington Ave.
Madison, SD
57042
USA

**Phone Number**—1-888-DSU-9988; **Fax Number**—(605)256-5093

**Email Contact**—mark.hawkes@dsu.edu; **URL**—http://dsu.edu/graduate-students/mset

**Contact Person**—Mark Hawkes

**Specializations**—No specializations offered. A student can organize course work options to develop an emphasis in distance education or technology systems. See program coordinator for more information.

**Features**—The Master of Science in Educational Technology (MSET) is an instructional technology program designed to meet the rapidly increasing demand for educators who are trained to integrate computer technologies into the curriculum and instruction. As computers and technology have become a significant part of the teaching and learning process, addressing the information needs of teachers has become the key to integrating technology into the classroom and increasing student learning. The primary emphasis of the master's program is to prepare educators who can create learning environments that integrate computing technology into the teaching and learning process. The MSET degree is an advanced degree designed to equip educators to be: leaders in educational technology current in teaching and learning processes and practices current in research technologies and designs knowledgeable of technologies and programming skills knowledgeable of current, technology-based educational tools and products. Specifically by the end of the program MSET students will understand the capabilities of the computer and its impact upon education. They will be proficient in the use and application of computer software and will be able to demonstrate proficiency in using computers and related technologies to improve their own and their students learning needs. The program integrates a highly technological environment with a project-based curriculum. Its focus is supported by an institutionally systemic belief that there is a substantial role for technology in teaching and learning in all educational environments.

**Admission Requirements**—Baccalaureate degree from an institution of higher education with full regional accreditation for that degree. Satisfactory scores on the GRE. The test must have been taken within the last 5 years. The GRE test can be waived if one of the following conditions is met: A cumulative grade point average of 3.25 or higher on a 4.0 scale for a baccalaureate degree from a regionally accredited college or university in the U.S. Official admission into and demonstrated success in a regionally accredited graduate program in the U.S. Demonstrated success is defined as grades of A or B in at least 12 h of graduate work. OR Graduation from a regionally accredited college/university in the U.S. at least 15 years ago or more. Other factors (such as student maturity, references, or special expertise) also may be used to determine admission to the program. Also see program specific admission requirements for additional requirements. Demonstrated basic knowledge of computers and their applications for educational purposes. Basic knowledge can be demonstrated in one of the following ways: Technology endorsement from an accredited university; or In-service position as full or part-time technology coordinator in a public school. A personal statement of technological competency. The statement should not exceed two pages and should be accompanied by supporting documentation or electronic references, e.g., URL.

**Degree Requirements**—The program requires a total of 36 credits beyond the baccalaureate degree. All students must take the following: 23 h of required courses. 7 h of electives. It is possible to select an emphasis in Distance Education or Technology Systems by selecting the designated electives for that area. You can also get a K-12 Educational Technology Endorsement is you have a teacher education credential. It is also possible to select the thesis option from among the electives. The entire program is available online, at a distance. MSET courses are offered using a variety of distance delivery tools and methodologies.

**Number of Full Time Faculty**—2; **Number of Other Faculty**—5

**Degrees awarded in 2012–2013 Academic Year**—Master's—24; PhD—0; Other—0

**Grant Monies awarded in 2012–2013 Academic Year**—30,000

**Name of Institution**—Texas A&M University

**Name of Department or Program**—Educational Technology Program, Dept. of Educational psychology

**Address:**
College of Education and Human Development
College Station, TX
77843-4225
USA

**Phone Number**—(979)845-7276; **Fax Number**—(979)862-1256

**Email Contact**—spedersen@tamu.edu; **URL**—http://epsy.tamu.edu/degrees-and-programs/graduate-degree-programs/online-master's-educational-technology

**Contact Person**—Susan Pedersen (contact Kristie Stramaski for application materials/questions)

**Specializations**—MEd in Educational Technology; PhD in Learning Sciences. The purpose of the Educational Technology Program is to prepare educators with the competencies required to improve the quality and effectiveness of instructional programs at all levels. A major emphasis is placed on the design of educational materials that harness the potential of emerging technologies. The program goal is to prepare graduates with a wide range of skills to work as professionals and leaders in a variety of settings, including education, business, industry, and the military.

**Features**—Master's program can be completed entirely online. The college and university maintain facilities and technology services to support both distance and resident students.

**Admission Requirements**—MEd: Bachelor's degree, GPA, letters of recommendation, general background, and student goal statement TOEFL; PhD: 3.0 GPA, 150 GRE Verbal; letters of recommendation, general background, and student goal statement.

**Degree Requirements**—MEd: 36 semester credits; PhD: course work varies with student goals—degree is a PhD in Learning Sciences with specialization in educational technology.

**Number of Full Time Faculty**—2; **Number of Other Faculty**—0

**Degrees awarded in 2012–2013 Academic Year**—Master's—3; PhD—0; **Other**—0

**Grant Monies awarded in 2012–2013 Academic Year**—200,000


**Name of Institution**—The University of Texas at Austin

**Name of Department or Program**—Curriculum and Instruction

**Address:**
406 Sanchez Building
Austin, TX
78712-1294
USA

**Phone Number**—(512)471-5942; **Fax Number**—(512)471-8460

**Email Contact**—Mliu@austin.utexas.edu; **URL**—http://www.edb.utexas.edu/education/departments/ci/programs/it/

**Contact Person**—Min Liu, EdD, Professor and IT Program Area Coordinator/ Graduate Advisor

**Specializations**—The University of Texas at Austin's College of Education is ranked number one in the nation among public universities by U.S. News & World Report's 2013 edition of "America's Best Graduate Schools." It's ranked number three among public and private universities nationally. The Learning Technologies (LT) Program is a graduate program and offers degrees at the master and doctoral levels. Master's degrees in LT provide students with knowledge and skills of cutting-edge new media technologies, learning theories, instructional systems design, human-computer interaction, and evaluation. They prepare students to be leaders and practitioners in various educational settings, such as K-12, higher education, and training in business and industry. PhD program provides knowledge and skills in areas such as instructional systems design, learning and instructional theories, instructional materials development and design of learning environments using various emerging technology-based systems and tools. Graduates assume academic, administrative, and other leadership positions such as professors, instructional technologists at school district level, managers and researchers of instructional design and instructional evaluators.

**Features**—The program is interdisciplinary in nature, although certain competencies are required of all students. Programs of study and dissertation research are based on individual needs and career goals. Learning resources include state-of-art labs in the Learning Technology Center in the College of Education, and university-wide computer labs. Students can take courses offered by other departments and colleges as relevant to their interests. Students, applying to the program, have diverse backgrounds and pursue careers of their interests. The program caters students with both K-12 as well as corporate backgrounds.

**Admission Requirements**—Learning Technologies program considers only applications for Fall admission, with the deadline of December 15. November 15— Deadline for consideration of financial award Admission decisions are rendered based on consideration of the entire applicant file, including GPA, test scores, references, experience, and stated goals. No single component carries any more significance than another. However, priority may be given to applicants who meet the following preferred criteria: GPA 3.0 or above GRE 1100 or above (verbal + quantitative, with at least 400 verbal) TOEFL 213 or above (computer)/550 or above (paper-based)/79 or 80 (Internet-based) TOEFL http://www.edb.utexas.edu/education/departments/ci/studentinfo/pstudents/grad/application/.

**Degree Requirements**—see http://www.edb.utexas.edu/education/departments/ci/programs/lt/ for details.

**Number of Full Time Faculty**—3; **Number of Other Faculty**—41

**Degrees awarded in 2012–2013 Academic Year**—**Master's**—15; **PhD**—2; **Other**—0

**Grant Monies awarded in 2012–2013 Academic Year**—41,000

**Name of Institution**—East Tennessee State University

**Name of Department or Program**—College of Education, Dept. of Curriculum and Instruction

**Address:**
Box 70684
Johnson City, TN
37614-0684
USA

**Phone Number**—(423)439-7843; **Fax Number**—(423)439-8362

**Email Contact**—danielsh@etsu.edu; **URL**—http://www.etsu.edu/coe/cuai/graduate/mediatech/default.aspx

**Contact Person**—Harold Lee Daniels

**Specializations**—(1) MEd in School Library Media. (2) MEd in Educational Technology. (3) School Library Media Specialist add on certification for those with current teaching license and a master's degree. (4) MEd in Classroom Technology for those with teaching license.

**Features**—Two (MAC and PC) dedicated computer labs (45+ computers). Online and evening course offerings for part-time, commuter, and employed students. Student pricing/campus licensing on popular software (MS, Adobe, Apple, etc.). Off site cohort programs for classroom teachers. Extensive software library (900+ titles) with review/checkout privileges.

**Admission Requirements**—Bachelor's degree from accredited institution with undergraduate GPA of 3.0 or higher, transcripts, personal application essay, and three letters of recommendation. An interview, and/or GRE may be required in some cases.

**Degree Requirements**—36 semester hours, including 12 h in common core of instructional technology and media, 18 professional content hours and 2–5 credit hour practicum (80–200 field experience hours).

**Number of Full Time Faculty**—4; **Number of Other Faculty**—4

**Degrees awarded in 2012–2013 Academic Year**—Master's—11; PhD—0; Other—2

**Grant Monies awarded in 2012–2013 Academic Year**—32,000

**Name of Institution**—University of Houston

**Name of Department or Program**—Learning, Design, and Technology Graduate Program
**Address:**
236 Farish Hall, Mail Code 5027
Houston, TX

77204-5027
USA

**Phone Number**—713-743-4975; **Fax Number**—713-743-4990

**Email     Contact**—smcneil@uh.edu;     **URL**—http://www.coe.uh.edu/degree-programs/cuin-ldt-med/

**Contact Person**—Sara McNeil

**Specializations**—Instructional design; Urban community partnerships enhanced by technology; Integration of technology in teacher education; Visual representation of information; Linking instructional technology with content area instruction; Educational uses of digital media (including digital photography, digital video and digital storytelling); Collaborative design and development of multimedia; Uses of instructional technology in health sciences education.

**Features**—The Learning, Design and Technology Program at the University of Houston can be distinguished from other instructional technology programs at other institutions through our unique philosophy based on a strong commitment to the broad representations of community, the individual, and the collaboration that strengthens the two. We broadly perceive community to include our college, the university, and the local Houston environment. The community is a rich context and resource from which we can solicit authentic learning tasks and clients, and to which we can contribute new perspectives and meaningful products. Our students graduate with real-world experience that can only be gained by experience with extended and coordinated community-based projects, not by contrived course requirements. Our program actively seeks outside funding to promote and continue such authentic projects because we so strongly believe it is the best context in which our students can develop expertise in the field. We recognize that each student brings to our program a range of formal training, career experience, and future goals. Thus, no longer can we be satisfied with presenting a single, static curriculum and still effectively prepare students for a competitive marketplace. Our beliefs have led us to develop a program that recognizes and celebrates student individuality and diversity. Students work with advisors to develop a degree plan that begins from their existing knowledge and strives toward intended career goals. We aim to teach not specific software or hardware operations, but instead focus on transferable technical skills couched in solid problem-solving experiences, theoretical discussions, and a team-oriented atmosphere. Students work throughout the program to critically evaluate their own work for the purpose of compiling a performance portfolio that will accurately and comprehensively portray their individual abilities to themselves, faculty, and future employers. Completing our philosophical foundation is a continuous goal of collaboration. Our faculty operates from a broad collaborative understanding that recognizes how everyone involved in any process brings unique and valuable experiences and perspectives. Within the Learning, Design and Technology program, faculty, staff, and students rely on each other to contribute relevant expertise. Faculty members regularly seek collaboration with other faculty in the College of Education, especially those involved with teacher education, as well as with faculty in other schools across campus. Collaboration is a focus that has been infused through the design of our courses and our relationships with students. Facebook: http://www.facebook.com/groups/189269174434698/.

**Admission Requirements**—Admission information for graduate programs: http://www.coe.uh.edu/admissions/graduate/. Master's program: 3.0 grade point average (GPA) for unconditional admission or a 2.6 GPA or above for conditional admission over the last 60 h of coursework attempted Graduate Record Exam: The GRE must have been taken within five (5) years of the date of application for admission to any Graduate program in the College of Education. Doctoral program: Each applicant must normally have earned a master's degree or have completed 36 semester hours of appropriate graduate work with a minimum GPA of 3.0 ($A = 4.0$). Graduate Record Exam: The GRE must have been taken within five (5) years of the date of application for admission to any Graduate program in the College of Education.

**Degree Requirements**—Master's: Students with backgrounds in educational technology can complete the Master's program with 30 h of coursework. For the typical student, the MEd in Instructional Technology consists of 9 semester hours of core courses required by the College of Education, and an additional 12 h core in Instructional Technology as well as 9 h that are determined by the students career goals (K-12, higher education, business and industry). Students complete a capstone project that demonstrates the depth and breadth of their educational growth throughout the program and highlights their knowledge and skills gained as well as their development as a reflective practitioner. More details about the courses and requirements can be found online at: http://www.coe.uh.edu/degree-programs/cuin-ldt-med/. Doctoral: The minimum hours required in the doctoral program (PhD) is 66. More details about the courses and requirements can be found online at: http://www.coe.uh.edu/degree-programs/cuin-phd/.

**Number of Full Time Faculty**—5; **Number of Other Faculty**—5

**Degrees awarded in 2012–2013 Academic Year**—Master's—10; PhD—9; **Other**—0

**Grant Monies awarded in 2012–2013 Academic Year**—50,000

**Name of Institution**—University of North Texas

**Name of Department or Program**—Learning Technologies (College of Information)

**Address:**
3940 N. Elm Street, Suite G150
Denton, TX
76207
USA

**Phone Number**—(940)565-2057; **Fax Number**—(940)565-4194

**Email Contact**—cathie.norris@unt.edu; **URL**—http://www.lt.unt.edu

**Contact Person**—Dr. Cathie Norris, Department Chair

**Specializations**—MS in Learning Technologies MS in Advanced Training and Performance Improvement PhD in Learning Technologies PhD in Advanced Training and Performance Improvement.

**Features**—Unique applications of theory through research and practice in curriculum integration of technology, instructional design, digital media production, learning game design, human performance improvement, human resource development, online learning development, and general web development.

**Admission Requirements**—Toulouse Graduate School Requirements, 18 h in education.

**Degree Requirements**—36 semester hours for the Master's 69 h for the Doctorate plus tools courses if required.

**Number of Full Time Faculty**—14; **Number of Other Faculty**—6

**Degrees awarded in 2012–2013 Academic Year**—Master's—36; PhD—7; **Other**—151

**Grant Monies awarded in 2012–2013 Academic Year**—2,000,000


**Name of Institution**—Brigham Young University

**Name of Department or Program**—Department of Instructional Psychology and Technology

**Address:**
150 MCKB, BYU
Provo, UT
84602
USA

**Phone Number**—(801)422-5097; **Fax Number**—(801)422-0314

**Email Contact**—charles_graham@byu.edu; **URL**—http://www.byu.edu/ipt

**Contact Person**—Charles Graham, Prof., Chair

**Specializations**—MS degrees in Instructional Design and Development, and Research and Evaluation. PhD degrees in Instructional Design and Development, Second Language Acquisition, and Research and Evaluation.

**Features**—Course offerings include principles of learning, instructional design, assessing learning outcomes, evaluation in education, empirical inquiry in education, project management, quantitative reasoning, microcomputer materials production, multimedia production, naturalistic inquiry, and more. Students participate in internships and projects related to development, evaluation, measurement, and research.

**Admission Requirements**—Both degrees: transcript, three letters of recommendation, letter of intent, GRE scores. Apply by Jan. 1. Students agree to live by the BYU Honor Code as a condition for admission.

**Degree Requirements**—Master's: 39 semester hours, including prerequisite (3 h), core courses (19 h), specialization (7 h), internship (3 h), thesis or project (6 h) with oral defense. PhD: 87 semester hours beyond the Bachelor's degree, including: prerequisite and skill requirements (18–31 h), core course (16 h), specialization (24 h), internship (6 h), projects (9 h), and dissertation (18 h). The dissertation must be orally defended. Also, at least two consecutive 6-h semesters must be completed in residence.

**Number of Full Time Faculty**—10; **Number of Other Faculty**—0

**Degrees awarded in 2012–2013 Academic Year**—Master's—11; PhD—10; Other—0

**Grant Monies awarded in 2012–2013 Academic Year**—0

**Name of Institution**—Utah State University

**Name of Department or Program**—Department of Instructional Technology and Learning Sciences, Emma Eccles Jones College of Education and Human Services

**Address:**
2830 Old Main Hill
Logan, UT
84322-2830
USA

**Phone Number**—(435)797-2694; **Fax Number**—(435)797-2693

**Email Contact**—mimi.recker@usu.edu; **URL**—http://itls.usu.edu

**Contact Person**—Dr. Mimi Recker, Prof., Head

**Specializations**—MS and MEd with concentrations in the areas of Instructional Technology, Learning Sciences, Multimedia, Educational Technology, and Information Technology/School Library Media Administration. PhD in Instructional Technology and Learning Sciences is offered for individuals seeking to become professionally involved in instructional/learning sciences research and development in higher education, corporate education, public schools, community colleges, and government. MEd and MS programs in Instructional Technology/School Library Media Administration and Educational Technology are also available completely online. The doctoral program is built on a strong Master's and Specialists program in Instructional Technology. All doctoral students complete a core with the remainder of the course selection individualized, based upon career goals.

**Features**—Facebook: http://www.facebook.com/usuitls (online: facebook.com/usuitlsonline) Online Students Facebook Page: http://www.facebook.com/usuitlsonline. Twitter: http://www.twitter.com/utahstateitls. LinkedIn: http://www.linkedin.com/. YouTube: http://www.youtube.com/usuitls.

**Admission Requirements**—MS and EdS: 3.0 GPA, a verbal and quantitative score at the 40th percentile on the GRE or 43 MAT, three written recommendations. PhD: relevant Master's degree, 3.0 GPA, verbal and quantitative score at the 40th percentile on the GRE, three written recommendations, essay on research interests.

**Degree Requirements**—MS: 36 sem. hours; thesis or project option. EdS: 30 sem. hours if MS is in the field, 40 h if not. PhD: 43 total hours, dissertation, 3-sem. residency, and comprehensive examination.

**Number of Full Time Faculty**—10; **Number of Other Faculty**—1

**Degrees awarded in 2012–2013 Academic Year**—Master's—37; **PhD**—3; **Other**—0

**Grant Monies awarded in 2012–2013 Academic Year**—3,600,000


**Name of Institution**—George Mason University

**Name of Department or Program**—Learning Technologies

**Address:**
Mail Stop 5D6, 4400 University Dr.
Fairfax, VA
22030-4444
USA

**Phone Number**—(703)993-3798; **Fax Number**—(703)993-2722

**Email Contact**—ndabbagh@gmu.edu; **URL**—http://learntech.gmu.edu/

**Contact Person**—Dr. Nada Dabbagh, Director, Division of Learning Technologies

**Specializations**—PhD Program Learning Technologies Design Research (LTDR) concentration with specialization in Instructional Systems Design, Designing Digital Learning in Schools, or Assistive Technology Master's Degrees—MEd in Curriculum and Instruction with concentrations in:—Instructional Design and Technology—Designing Digital Learning in Schools—Integration of Online Learning in Schools Graduate Certificates in:—eLearning—Executive Chief Learning Officer (ECLO)—Designing Digital Learning in Schools—Digital Learning and Teacher Leadership—Integration of Online Learning in Schools.

**Features**—The Division of Learning Technologies supports the following academic programs: Instructional Design and Technology (IDT): provides professionals with the knowledge and skills to design effective and innovative learning solutions to instructional and performance problems; graduates of this program are workplace-ready for instructional design responsibilities in public, private, government, and educational settings. The IDT program provides professionals with the knowledge and skills to design effective and innovative learning solutions to instructional and performance problems. Learning Technologies in

Schools (LTS): provides the knowledge and skills needed to design effective teaching and learning opportunities for PreK-12 learners using a range of technologies appropriate for face-to-face, online, or blended approaches. Candidates in LTS programs learn strategies that support teachers' abilities to use technology to facilitate robust student learning—to accomplish digital learning goals, the ways in which technology can enable learning opportunities that promote twenty-first century skills, and how teachers can be technology-using, thinking, creating, leading, and practicing designers of digital learning in schools. PhD Concentration in Learning Technologies Design Research (LTDR): an innovative program that engages doctoral students in real world, workplace-based integrated design and research; LTDR addresses cross disciplinary progressive cycles of design, development, and research focused on promoting strategic thinking, innovation and creativity in the design of learning technologies to achieve organizational goals. http://www.facebook.com/MasonLearnTech; https://twitter.com/MasonCEHD.

**Admission Requirements**—Master's and Certificate Programs—Teaching or training experience, undergrad GPA of 3.0, TOEFL of 575(written)/230(computer), three letters of recommendation, goal statement, resume. PhD Program—http://gse.gmu.edu/programs/phd/.

**Degree Requirements**—MEd in Curriculum Instructional Design and Technology, 30 h; MEd in Curriculum and Instruction Designing Digital Learning in Schools, 30 h; MEd in Curriculum and Instruction, Integration of Online Learning in Schools, 30 h. PhD Concentration in Learning Technologies Design Research (LTDR): 65 h beyond Master's degree. Certificate programs: 12–18 h.

**Number of Full Time Faculty**—7; **Number of Other Faculty**—6

**Degrees awarded in 2012–2013 Academic Year**—Master's—60; **PhD**—8; **Other**—25

**Grant Monies awarded in 2012–2013 Academic Year**—100,000

**Name of Institution**—Virginia Tech

**Name of Department or Program**—Instructional Design and Technology

**Address:**
370 Drillfield Drive (0313)
Blacksburg, VA
24061-0313
USA

**Phone Number**—(540)231-5587; **Fax Number**—(540)231-9075

**Email Contact**—jmbrill@vt.edu; **URL**—http://www.soe.vt.edu/idt/

**Contact Person**—Jennifer M. Brill, Program Leader

**Specializations**—MA, EdS, EdD, and PhD in Instructional Design and Technology. Graduates of our Master's and Educational Specialist programs find themselves applying their expertise in a variety of rewarding, professional venues; for example, as instructional designers, trainers, or performance consultants in industrial settings and as teachers or technology coordinators in preK-12. Graduates of our Doctoral program typically assume exciting roles as faculty in higher education, advancing research in the field and preparing the next generation of instructional designers for the profession.

**Features**—Areas of emphasis are Instructional Design, Learning Sciences, and Distance Education. Facilities include dedicated School of Education Educational Technology lab as well as university-wide technology labs.

**Admission Requirements**—EdD and PhD: 3.3 GPA from Master's degree, GRE scores, writing sample, three letters of recommendation, transcripts, TOEFL (as needed). MA: 3.0 GPA from Undergraduate degree, three references, goal statement, transcripts, TOEFL (as needed).

**Degree Requirements**—PhD: 90 h beyond bachelor degree (to include: 15 h research courses, 30 h. dissertation), 2 year residency. MA: 30 h beyond bachelor degree, comprehensive portfolio exam.

**Number of Full Time Faculty**—5; **Number of Other Faculty**—0

**Degrees awarded in 2012–2013 Academic Year**—Master's—55; **PhD**—10; **Other**—1

**Grant Monies awarded in 2012–2013 Academic Year**—4,100,000

**Name of Institution**—University of Virginia

**Name of Department or Program**—Instructional Technology Program, Department of Curriculum, Instruction, and Special Education, Curry School of Education

**Address:**
Bavaro Hall #312, 405 Emmet Street, P.O. Box 400273
Charlottesville, VA
22904-4273
USA

**Phone Number**—(434)924-0831; **Fax Number**—(434)924-7461

**Email Contact**—kdg9g@virginia.edu; **URL**—http://curry.virginia.edu/academics/offerings/instructional-technology

**Contact Person**—Karen Dwier, Dept. of Curriculum, Instruction, and Special Education, Curry School of Education

**Specializations**—The University of Virginias Curry School of Education offers MEd, EdS, EdD, and PhD degrees in Instructional Technology. Our faculty have a range of experience and backgrounds and through our partnerships throughout Curry and around UVa, we offer a very rich range of focal areas:

- Instructional Design and Interactive Development
- Educational Innovation and Product Development
- Online Instruction and Planning
- Educational Multimedia
- Technology Leadership
- Science, Technology, Engineering, and Mathematics (STEM) Education
- Games/Play/Flow
- Systems and Change
- Ethics of Technology in Education <=""ul="">Our Master's degree offers tracks for fully online students as well as residential studies. Our EdD features a blended curriculum design that allows students to complete part of their degree in Charlottesville while completing other courses and their capstone project in the field. Our PhD is a highly selective program emphasizing a close mentored relationship with a limited number of students working closely with faculty in their research groups.

**Features**—The IT program is situated in a major research university with linkages to multiple disciplines. Faculty in the program hold leadership positions with the Center for Advanced Study of Teaching and Learning (CASTL) and the Center for Technology and Teacher Education, among others.

Our students work closely with faculty in a collegial environment on both time-tested and leading-edge practices. You will find yourself working with the most talented students from virtually every discipline and background, learning team leadership skills and forming lifelong friendships. The University of Virginia is one of the top-ranked public universities in the nation, and the Curry School is nationally recognized for its leadership and innovation, particularly in IT. We are the recipient of the American Association of Colleges for Teacher Education (AACTE) Innovative Use of Technology Award for modeling innovative use of technology for others in the profession as well as a recipient of the first International Society for Technology in Education (ISTE) Distinguished Achievement Award for integration of technology into teacher education, among other awards and recognition.

Faculty and students are active in national organizations such as the Association for Educational Communications and Technology (AECT), Society for Information Technology and Teacher Education (SITE), and the American Educational Research Association (AERA). Graduates in IT from the Curry School are creating positive change through positions in research and development and instructional innovation around the world. We invite you to discover, create, and change with us.

**Admission Requirements**—Admission to any graduate program requires: Undergraduate degree from accredited institution in any field, undergraduate GPA 3.0, and TOEFL (if applicable): 600 paper-based, 250 computer-based.

For admission to the Master of Education (MEd), Educational Specialist (EdS), and Doctor of Education (EdD) degrees, minimum 1000 GRE (V+Q).

For admission to the Doctor of Philosophy (PhD) program, minimum GRE 1100 (V+Q). PhD admissions are highly competitive and fully funded, to provide mentored, 4-year program based on research, development, and scholarship.

**Degree Requirements**—MEd: 36 semester hours. EdS: 60 semester hours beyond undergraduate degree.

EdD: 72 semester hours including 48 h of coursework, 12 h of internship experience, and a 12 h capstone project.

PhD: 76 semester hours of coursework and research internship, plus 24 h of dissertation research. All graduate degrees require a comprehensive examination. The PhD also requires completion of a preliminary examination and a juried pre-dissertation presentation or publication.

**Number of Full Time Faculty**—4; **Number of Other Faculty**—16

**Degrees awarded in 2012–2013 Academic Year**—Master's—4; PhD—5; Other—2

**Grant Monies awarded in 2012–2013 Academic Year**—1,500,000

**Name of Institution**—University of South Alabama

**Name of Department or Program**—Department of Professional Studies, College of Education

**Address:**
University Commons 3700
Mobile, AL
36688
USA

**Phone Number**—(251)380-2861; **Fax Number**—(251)380-2713

**Email Contact**—jdempsey@usouthal.edu; **URL**—http://www.southalabama.edu/coe/profstudies/index.shtml

**Contact Person**—Brenda Litchfield, IDD Program Coor.; Edward C. Lomax, Ed Media Program Coor

**Specializations**—MS and PhD in Instructional Design and Development. MEd in Educational Media (Ed Media). Online master's degrees in ED Media and IDD are available for qualified students. For information about online master's degree programs, http://usaonline.southalabama.edu.

**Features**—The IDD master's and doctoral programs emphasize extensive education and training in the instructional design process, human performance technology and multimedia—and online-based training. The IDD doctoral program has an additional emphasis in research design and statistical analysis. The Ed Media master's program prepares students in planning, designing, and administering library/media centers at most levels of education, including higher education.

**Admission Requirements**—For the ED Media and IDD Master's: undergraduate degree in appropriate academic field from an accredited university or college; admission to Graduate School; satisfactory score on the GRE. ED Media students must have completed requirements for a certificate at the baccalaureate or master's level in a teaching field. For IDD PhD: Master's degree, all undergraduate and graduate transcripts, three letters of recommendations, written statement of purpose for pursuing PhD in IDD, satisfactory score on GRE.

**Degree Requirements**—Ed Media master's: satisfactorily complete program requirements (minimum 33 semester hours), 3.0 or better GPA, satisfactory score on comprehensive exam. IDD master's: satisfactorily complete program requirements (minimum 40 semester hours), 3.0 or better GPA; satisfactory complete comprehensive exam. PhD: satisfactory complete program requirements (minimum 82 semester hours of approved graduate coures), 1-year residency, satisfactory score on examinations (research and statistical exam and comprehensive exam), approved dissertation completed. Any additional requirements will be determined by students doctoral advisory committee.

**Number of Full Time Faculty**—0; **Number of Other Faculty**—0

**Degrees awarded in 2012–2013 Academic Year**—Master's—0; **PhD**—0; **Other**—0

**Grant Monies awarded in 2012–2013 Academic Year**—0


**Name of Institution**—University of Arkansas

**Name of Department or Program**—Educational Technology

**Address:**
101 Peabody Hall
Fayetteville, AR
72701
USA

**Phone Number**—479-575-5111; **Fax Number**—479-575-2493

**Email Contact**—etec@uark.edu; **URL**—http://etec.uark.edu

**Contact Person**—Dr. Cheryl Murphy

**Specializations**—The program prepares students for a variety of work environments by offering core courses that are applicable to a multitude of professional venues. The program also allows for specific emphasis area studies via open-ended assignments and course electives that include courses particularly relevant to higher education, business/industry or K-12 environments. The primary focus of the program is on the processes involved in instructional design, training and development, and utilization of instructional technologies. Because technology is continually changing, the program emphasizes acquisition of a process over the learning of specific technologies. Although skills necessary in making Educational Technology products are taught, technology changes rapidly; therefore, a primary emphasis on making technological products would lead to the acquisition of skills that are quickly outdated. However, learning the principles and mental tools critical to producing successful training and education will endure long after "new" technologies have become obsolete. That is why the University of Arkansas ETEC program focuses on the processes as opposed to specific technologies.

**Features**—The Educational Technology Program is a 34-h non-thesis online master's program that prepares students for professional positions as educational technologists of education, business, government, and the health professions. Because the program is offered online, there are no on-campus requirements for the completion of this degree. Check us out on Facebook at UAetec.

**Admission Requirements**—The Educational Technology online master's program admits students in the fall, spring, and summer. Applications and all accompanying documents must be submitted within 3 months of the desired starting semester to ensure adequate processing time. To qualify for admission applicants must have an earned bachelor's degree and an undergraduate GPA of 3.0 within the last 60 h of coursework. Specific application materials can be found at http://etec.uark.edu/admission/index.php. Applicants for the MEd degree must have met all requirements of Graduate School admission, completed a bachelor's degree, and earned a 3.0 GPA in all undergraduate coursework. A Graduate School application, ETEC Program Application, writing sample, autobiographical sketch, and letters of recommendation are required for admission consideration.

**Degree Requirements**—In addition to general admission requirements students must complete a minimum of 34 h to include 22 semester hours of educational technology core courses; nine semester hours of educational technology electives; and three semester hours of research. Additionally, a Culminating Student Portfolio must be successfully completed during the last semester of coursework. There are no on-campus requirements for the completion of this degree, although approved courses that meet the research requirements may be taken on campus if desired.

**Number of Full Time Faculty**—2; **Number of Other Faculty**—4

**Degrees awarded in 2012–2013 Academic Year**—**Master's**—9; **PhD**—0; **Other**—0

**Grant Monies awarded in 2012–2013 Academic Year**—75,000

**Name of Institution**—California State Polytechnic University

**Name of Department or Program**—Educational Multimedia Design

**Address:**
3801 West Temple Ave.
Pomona, CA
91768
USA

**Phone Number**—909-869-2255; **Fax Number**—909-869-5206

**Email Contact**—slotfipour@csupomona.edu; **URL**—www.csupomona.edu/emm

**Contact Person**—Dr. Shahnaz Lotfipour

**Specializations**—Design and production of eLearning materials and educational multimedia software (including audio, video, animation, web programming (three levels), graphics, eBooks, and mobile apps) for educational and corporate training environments using the sound instructional design principles and strategies.

**Features**—Hands-on training, project-based, combination of online and hybrid courses, internship possibilities in educational and corporate settings.

**Admission Requirements**—Undergraduate GPA of 3.0, three strong letters of recommendations for this program, and satisfying graduate writing test (GWT) within the first couple of quarters.

**Degree Requirements**—BA or BS in any area.

**Number of Full Time Faculty**—3; **Number of Other Faculty**—5

**Degrees awarded in 2012–2013 Academic Year**—Master's—30; **PhD**—0; **Other**—0

**Grant Monies awarded in 2012–2013 Academic Year**—50,000


**Name of Institution**—California State University Fullerton

**Name of Department or Program**—Program: Educational Technology
**Address:**
800 N. State College Blvd
Fullerton, CA
92834
USA

**Phone Number**—6572787614; **Fax Number**—6572785133

**Email Contact**—tgreen@fullerton.edu; **URL**—http://www.fullerton.edu/edtech

**Contact Person**—Tim Green, PhD or Loretta Donovan, PhD

**Specializations**—MS in Educational Technology

**Features**—100% online, 16-month, applicable to K-12 and adult educators, all courses are a balance of theory and practice. ISTE Coach Standard Seal of Alignment.

**Admission Requirements**—Teaching credential, undergraduate degree from an accredited institution.

**Degree Requirements**—30 semester hours—ten courses.

**Number of Full Time Faculty**—3; **Number of Other Faculty**—4

**Degrees awarded in 2012–2013 Academic Year**—Master's—68; PhD—0; Other—0

**Grant Monies awarded in 2012–2013 Academic Year**—0

**Name of Institution**—California State University, East Bay

**Name of Department or Program**—MSEd, option Online Teaching and Learning

**Address:**
25800 Carlos Bee Blvd
Hayward, CA
94542
USA

**Phone Number**—510-885-4384; **Fax Number**—510-885-4498

**Email Contact**—nan.chico@csueastbay.edu; **URL**—http://www.ce.csueastbay.edu/degree/education/index.shtml

**Contact Person**—Nan Chico

**Specializations**—A professional development degree for experienced K-12, college/university faculty and corporate or nonprofit trainers at institutions creating new, or building on old, fully online course and program degrees, workshops, trainings. A major focus is on learning how to design courses so that barriers to learning are minimized for those with disabilities, or who are English language learners, etc.

**Features**—Courses are in Blackboard; students are given a Blackboard shell of their own to design in or may choose among other course management systems. We focus on best practices in online teaching and learning, using a CMS and varieties of other social media. Not cohort-based, admission in quarterly (Fall and Spring); maximum two courses per quarter; may skip 1–2 consecutive quarters.

**Admission Requirements**—BA or BS degree from a regionally accredited US institution, in any major; GPA 3.0 in last 60 semester units or last 90 quarter units. Selection is also based on mandatory Letter of Intent.

**Degree Requirements**—Four 5-week courses taken over two quarters (which earn the Certificate in Online Teaching and Learning); two 10-week electives, four 10-week required courses, the last of which is a Capstone Project. Each course earns

4.5 quarter units; all required courses must earn a "B" or better, overall GPA must be 3.0 or better. Total of ten courses, 45 units.

**Number of Full Time Faculty**—0; **Number of Other Faculty**—9

**Degrees awarded in 2012–2013 Academic Year**—Master's—60; **PhD**—0; **Other**—0

**Grant Monies awarded in 2012–2013 Academic Year**—0


**Name of Institution**—California State University, Fresno

**Name of Department or Program**—MA in Education and Certificate of Advanced Study in Educational Technology

**Address:**
5005 N. Maple Ave., MS2
Fresno, CA
93740
USA

**Phone Number**—559-278-0245; **Fax Number**—559-278-0107

**Email Contact**—royb@csufresno.edu; **URL**—http://www.fresnostate.edu/kremen/ci/graduate/ma-education.html

**Contact Person**—Dr. Roy M. Bohlin

**Specializations**—None.

**Features**—Very flexible.

**Admission Requirements**—2.75 undergraduate GPA, writing requirement, three letters of recommendation, letter of interest.

**Degree Requirements**—Bachelor's degree.

**Number of Full Time Faculty**—6; **Number of Other Faculty**—5

**Degrees awarded in 2012–2013 Academic Year**—Master's—17; **PhD**—0; **Other**—5

**Grant Monies awarded in 2012–2013 Academic Year**—0


**Name of Institution**—Metropolitan State University of Denver

**Name of Department or Program**—Department of Secondary and Educational Technology

**Address:**
Teacher Education, Campus Box 21, P.O. Box 173362
Denver, CO
80217
USA

**Phone Number**—(303)556-3322; **Fax Number**—(303)556-5353

**Email Contact**—mchung3@msudenver.edu; **URL**—http://www.mscd.edu/~education

**Contact Person**—Dr. Miri Chung

**Number of Full Time Faculty**—2; **Number of Other Faculty**—1

**Degrees awarded in 2012–2013 Academic Year**—Master's—0; PhD—0; Other—0

**Grant Monies awarded in 2012–2013 Academic Year**—0


**Name of Institution**—Regis University

**Name of Department or Program**—School of Education and Counseling

**Address:**
3333 Regis Boulevard
Denver, CO
80221
USA

**Phone Number**—800-388-2366; **Fax Number**—303-964-5053

**Email Contact**—kpyatt@regis.edu; **URL**—www.regis.edu

**Contact Person**—Dr. Kevin Pyatt

**Specializations**—Instructional Technology Curriculum, Instruction, and Assessment Ed Leadership for Innovation and Change—Principal Licensure Adult Learning, Training, and Development Reading.

**Features**—The majority of our programs are offered in the online format.

**Admission Requirements**—Essay Letters of Recommendation Minimum GPA of 2.75.

**Number of Full Time Faculty**—15; **Number of Other Faculty**—150

**Degrees awarded in 2012–2013 Academic Year**—Master's—200; PhD—0; Other—0

**Grant Monies awarded in 2012–2013 Academic Year**—0


**Name of Institution**—University of Florida

**Name of Department or Program**—School of Teaching and Learning

**Address:**
2403 Norman Hall
Gainesville, FL
32611-7048
USA

**Phone Number**—352-273-4180; **Fax Number**—352-392-9193

**Email     Contact**—aritzhaupt@coe.ufl.edu;     **URL**—http://education.ufl.edu/educational-technology/

**Contact Person**—Albert Ritzhaupt

**Specializations**—Educational technology students may earn MAE, MEd, EdS, EdD or PhD degrees. The MEd, EdS, and EdD programs are online. The MAE and PhD programs are blended.

**Features**—Students take core courses listed on our Educational Technology website. Opportunities to collaborative research, write and design with faculty members. Strong community of graduate students.

**Admission Requirements**—Please see the Educational Technology website for the most up-to-date information.

**Degree Requirements**—Please see the Educational Technology website for the most up-to-date information. Program and college requirements must be met but there is considerable flexibility for doctoral students to plan an appropriate program with their advisers.

**Number of Full Time Faculty**—5; **Number of Other Faculty**—3

**Degrees awarded in 2012–2013 Academic Year**—Master's—10; **PhD**—2; **Other**—5

**Grant Monies awarded in 2012–2013 Academic Year**—459,871

**Name of Institution**—University of West Florida

**Name of Department or Program**—Instructional and Performance Technology

**Address:**
11000 University Parkway
Pensacola, FL
32514
USA

**Phone Number**—850-474-2300; **Fax Number**—850-474-2804

**Email Contact**—nhastings@uwf.edu; **URL**—http://onlinecampus.uwf.edu

**Contact Person**—Nancy B. Hastings

**Specializations**—MEd, Instructional Technology: Distance Learning Human Performance Technology MSA., H.P.T.: Human Performance Technology EdD, Curriculum and Instruction, Instructional Technology Specialization: Performance Technology Distance Learning Certificate Programs: Instructional Design and Technology Human Performance Technology Virtual Educator.

**Features**—Fully online programs at all levels Small classes Recognized nationally as a "Best Buy" in Online Master's in Administration Like us on Facebook and Follow us on Twitter Military Friendly University Out-of-State Tuition Waivers for admitted students in fully online programs.

**Admission Requirements**—GRE or MAT Score (dependent upon previous GPA) Official Transcripts Letter of Intent See Department Website for additional information for specific programs.

**Degree Requirements**—MEd, 36 credit hours MSA, 36 credit hours EdD, minimum 66 credit hours.

**Number of Full Time Faculty**—4; **Number of Other Faculty**—2

**Degrees awarded in 2012–2013 Academic Year**—Master's—21; PhD—0; Other—8

**Grant Monies awarded in 2012–2013 Academic Year**—260,000

**Name of Institution**—Kennesaw State University

**Name of Department or Program**—Instructional Technology

**Address:**
585 Cobb Avenue
Kennesaw, GA
30144
USA

**Phone Number**—470-578-3262; **Fax Number**—470-578-9100

**Email Contact**—tredish@kennesaw.edu; **URL**—http://bagwell.kennesaw.edu/departments/itec

**Contact Person**—Dr. Traci Redish

**Specializations**—Kennesaw State University offers MEd, EdS (Certification and Advanced Tracks) and EdD degrees in Instructional Technology. MEd and EdS Certification Track degrees prepare students to integrate technology into their teaching and assist other educators in utilizing technology to improve teaching and learning. These degrees are organized around the ISTE Technology Coach Standards. The Advanced Track EdS and EdD degrees prepare students for a variety of instructional technology leadership positions and to conduct research in the field of instructional technology. These degrees are built upon the ISTE Technology Director Standards and the CoSN Framework of Essential Skills. Our programs are B-12 focused.

**Features**—All programs are entirely online.

**Admission Requirements**—MEd Program:—Transcripts from each college attended—Bachelor's degree in Education—2.75 GPA—Clear Renewable Teaching

Certificate—1 Year of Teaching Experience—Professional Resume—One Evaluation Form—Mentor Form EdS Program (Certification Track). (1) An earned master's degree in professional education or a related field; (2) A clear and renewable Georgia Teaching (T), Service (S), Technical Specialist, or Leadership (L or PL) Certificate or departmentally approved equivalent. The Department of Instructional Technology recognizes and appreciates that many independent schools and twenty-first century learning environments do not require educators to hold traditional state teaching certification. In such instances, the Department will make a case-by-case determination as to whether the educators qualifications are sufficiently equivalent to a traditional teaching certificate and/or whether the educator has the background necessary to ensure successful completion of the program. (3) At least 3 years of professional teaching or administrative experience or both in P-12 education (current full-time employment as a professional educator is preferred); EdS Program (Advanced Track): (1) An earned master's degree in professional education or a related field; (2) A clear and renewable Georgia Teaching (T), Service (S), Technical Specialist, or Leadership (L or PL) Certificate or departmentally approved equivalent. The Department of Instructional Technology recognizes and appreciates that many independent schools and twenty-first century learning environments do not require educators to hold traditional state teaching certification. In such instances, the Department will make a case-by-case determination as to whether the educators qualifications are sufficiently equivalent to a traditional teaching certificate and/or whether the educator has the background necessary to ensure successful completion of the program. (3) At least 3 years of professional teaching or administrative experience or both in P-12 education (current full-time employment as a professional educator is preferred); EdD Program. (1) An earned master's degree in education or a closely related field. (2) A clear renewable professional certificate (T, S, L, PL, or Life) OR a departmentally approved equivalent. The Department of Instructional Technology recognizes and appreciates that many charter, independent schools, IE2, and twenty-first century learning environments do not require educators to hold traditional state teaching certification. In such instances, the Department will make a case-by-case determination as to whether the educators qualifications are sufficiently equivalent to a traditional teaching certificate and/or whether the educator has the background necessary to ensure successful completion of the program. (3) At least 3 years of professional teaching or administrative experience (or a combination thereof), or a related role serving B-12 education. (To facilitate candidates' field experiences, current full-time employment as a professional educator is preferred.). (4) A competitive Graduate Record Exam (GRE) score and Graduate GPA. The GPA and GRE will be utilized with other admission criteria to determine program eligibility. Although no minimum scores are required, candidates are encouraged to prepare and score well since admission to the program is competitive. Please note: The Analytical/Writing score one receives as part of the GRE exam is used competitively in the admission review process. It is strongly encouraged for applicants to do well on this portion of the exam.

**Degree Requirements**—MEd—36 h EdS—30 h EdD—66 h.

**Number of Full Time Faculty**—6; **Number of Other Faculty**—40

**Degrees awarded in 2012–2013 Academic Year**—Master's—59; **PhD**—1; **Other**—62

**Grant Monies awarded in 2012–2013 Academic Year**—0


**Name of Institution**—Boise State University

**Name of Department or Program**—Educational Technology

**Address:**
1910 University Drive
Boise, ID
83725
USA

**Phone Number**—208-426-4008; **Fax Number**—208-426-1451

**Email Contact**—kbranson@boisestate.edu; **URL**—edtech.boisestate.edu

**Contact Person**—Kellie Branson

**Specializations**—Boise State's Master of Educational Technology is a hands-on, skills-focused, project-oriented degree program for educators who want to make a difference in student performance. Doctor of Educational Technology Master of Educational Technology Graduate Certificate in Online Teaching MS Educational Technology Graduate Certificate in School Technology Coordination Graduate Certificate in Technology Integration Graduate Certificate in Online Teaching.

**Features**—100 % Online Innovative Curriculum. Recently featured as one of Americas best online graduate programs by U.S. News & World Report. Flexibility to focus on students professional needs. Award-winning faculty. Small classes Excellent Financial Aid options for students.

**Admission Requirements**—3.0 undergraduate GPA, personal essay, no GRE required. No admission deadlines.

**Degree Requirements**—MS and MET—33 credits Doctorate—66 credits.

**Number of Full Time Faculty**—14; **Number of Other Faculty**—12

**Degrees awarded in 2012–2013 Academic Year**—Master's—186; **PhD**—0; **Other**—0

**Grant Monies awarded in 2012–2013 Academic Year**—12,000,000


**Name of Institution**—Ball State University

**Name of Department or Program**—Master's of Arts in Curriculum and Educational Technology

**Address:**
Teachers College
Muncie, IN
47306
USA

**Phone Number**—(765)285-5461; **Fax Number**—(765)285-5489

**Email Contact**—sadaf@bsu.edu; **URL**—http://cms.bsu.edu/Academics/
CollegesandDepartments/Teachers/Departments/EdStudies/AcProgram/GradDegr/
MACurriEdTech.aspx

**Contact Person**—Ayesha Sadaf

**Specializations**—Specialization tracks in curriculum or educational technology.

**Features**—The Master's of Arts in Curriculum and Educational Technology is a
30-h program designed for educators seeking to integrate technology into K12 curriculum and other instructional contexts where teaching and learning occur.
Graduates are prepared to become leaders within their instructional contexts by
coursework and experiences that focus on development of a conceptual framework
in which technology is an embedded aspect of the teaching and learning process.
The program prepares graduates to utilize technology to meet learning needs of
students and to critically examine technology ever-changing presence within
schools and society.

**Admission Requirements**—Prospective students should apply to the Graduate
College and provide official transcripts from all universities/colleges attended. A
student seeking admittance for a Master's degree must meet the following minimum criteria:—Hold an earned bachelor's degree from a college or university that
is accredited by its regional accrediting association—Have one of the following:—
An undergraduate cumulative GPA of at least 2.75 on a scale of 4.0—A cumulative
GPA of at least 3.0 on a 4.0 scale in the latter half of the baccalaureate. Additional
Information regarding application and admission to the graduate college can be
found at the following website. http://www.bsu.edu/gradschool.

**Degree Requirements**—Successful completion of 30 graduate hours.

**Number of Full Time Faculty**—8; **Number of Other Faculty**—4

**Degrees awarded in 2012–2013 Academic Year**—Master's—22; **PhD**—0;
**Other**—0

**Grant Monies awarded in 2012–2013 Academic Year**—0

**Name of Institution**—Indiana University

**Name of Department or Program**—Instructional Systems Technology, School of
Education

**Address:**
W. W. Wright Education Bldg., Rm 2276, 201 N. Rose Ave.
Bloomington, IN
47405-1006
USA

**Phone Number**—(812)856-8450; **Fax Number**—(812)856-8239

**Email Contact**—istdept@indiana.edu; **URL**—http://education.indiana.edu/~ist/

**Contact Person**—Thomas Brush, Chair, Dept. of Instructional Systems Technology

**Specializations**—The MS and EdS degrees are designed for individuals seeking to be practitioners in the field of Instructional Technology. The MS degree is also offered in a web-based format with instructional product and portfolio requirements, with specializations in Workplace Learning and Performance Improvement; Instructional Systems Design Practice; and Learning Technologies. A Studio specialization is available to residential students. Online certificate and licensure programs are also available.

An online EdD is now being offered as well. Our first cohort of students began in the Fall of 2012. Applications are now being accepted for our Fall 2015 cohort. The emphasis of the EdD is the application of theory to practice.

The PhD degree features a heavy research emphasis via faculty-mentored research groups and student dossiers for assessing research, teaching and service competencies.

**Features**—Requires computer skills as a prerequisite and makes technology utilization an integral part of the curriculum; eliminates separation of various media formats; and establishes a series of courses of increasing complexity integrating production and development. The latest in technical capabilities have been incorporated, including teaching, computer, and laptop-ready laboratories, a multimedia laboratory, and video and audio production studios. Residential master's students have a studio facility available for their exclusive use for two semesters.

PhD students participate in faculty-mentored research groups throughout their program. Students construct dossiers with evidence of research, teaching and service that are evaluated by faculty on three occasions during the program. The second and third dossier reviews replace the traditional written and oral examinations.

**Admission Requirements**—MS: Bachelor's degree from an accredited institution, 1350 GRE (three tests required) or combined verbal+math=291, analytical writing=3.5 (new format), 2.75 undergraduate GPA. EdS, EdD and PhD: 1650 GRE (three tests required) or combined verbal+math=302, analytical writing=4.0 (new format), 3.5 graduate GPA.

**Degree Requirements**—MS: 36 credit hours (including 15 credits in required courses); an instructional product; nine credits in outside electives, and portfolio. EdS: 65 h, capstone project with written report and a portfolio. EdD: 60 h post-master's

(MS credits not counted towards 60 h), with written and oral qualifying exams, and dissertation. PhD: 90 h, dossier reviews, and thesis.

**Number of Full Time Faculty**— 12; **Number of Other Faculty**— 10

**Degrees awarded in 2012–2013 Academic Year**—Master's—20; **PhD**—8; **Other**—0

**Grant Monies awarded in 2012–2013 Academic Year**—600,000

**Name of Institution**—Emporia State University

**Name of Department or Program**—Instructional Design and Technology

**Address:**
1 Kellogg Circle—Campus Box 4037
Emporia, KS
66801
USA

**Phone Number**—620-341-5829; **Fax Number**—620-341-5785

**Email Contact**—jcolorad@emporia.edu; **URL**—http://idt.emporia.edu

**Contact Person**—Dr. Zeni Colorado, Chair

**Specializations**—Distance learning, online learning, corporate education, P-12 technology integration

**Features**—All program courses are offered both online and face to face on the ESU campus. The Master of Science in Instructional Design and Technology program prepares individuals for leadership in the systematic design, development, implementation, evaluation, and management of technology-rich learning in a variety of settings. Individuals obtaining the IDT degree serve as instructional designers/trainers in business, industry, health professions, and the military and are charged with training, development, and eLearning programs within their organizations. Other graduates hold leadership positions in P-12 and post-secondary institutions. In addition to positions in the workplace, graduates regularly choose to pursue their PhD degrees in IDT at top-ranked universities. IDT faculty members hold leadership positions on the Association for Educational Communications and Technology (AECT) board of directors, executive committee, and research and theory division. Forms and application materials available at the website, http://idt.emporia.edu. Other social media contacts, Facebook—http://facebook.com/idtesu, Twitter—http://twitter.com/idtesu, Blogspot—http://idtesu.blogspot.com/, YouTube—http://www.youtube.com/idtesu.

**Admission Requirements**—Graduate application, official transcripts, GPA of 2.75 or more based on a four-point scale in the last 60 semester hours of undergraduate study, resume, two current recommendations, writing competency. The program admits on a rolling basis. The departmental admission committee reviews and decides on applications as they are received, until there are no remaining openings.

**Degree Requirements**—36 credit hours: Non-thesis Track: 21 cr. core, 3 cr. research, 3 cr. learning, 9 cr. electives. Thesis Track: 24 cr. core, 3 cr. learning, 6 cr. research, 3 cr. electives.

**Number of Full Time Faculty**—6; **Number of Other Faculty**—7

**Degrees awarded in 2012–2013 Academic Year**—Master's—33; PhD—0; Other—0

**Grant Monies awarded in 2012–2013 Academic Year**—284,112


**Name of Institution**—Morehead State University

**Name of Department or Program**—Educational Technology Program

**Address:**
Ginger Hall
Morehead, KY
40351
USA

**Phone Number**—606-783-2040; **Fax Number**—606-783-5032

**Email Contact**—c.miller@morehead-st.edu; **URL**—www.moreheadstate.edu/education

**Contact Person**—Christopher T. Miller

**Specializations**—Master of Arts in Education degree focuses on technology integration, multimedia, distance education, educational games, and instructional design. Educational Leadership Doctor of Education in Educational Technology Leadership is a practitioner-based doctoral degree program focused on the development of leaders in the field of educational technology.

**Features**—Master's program is fully online. EdD program is fully online with the exception of a 1 week face-to-face seminar course each year.

**Admission Requirements**—Admission requirements for Master's degree: * Standard or provisional teaching certification, a statement of eligibility for teaching, or letter describing your role as educational support. Those students who fit the criteria of educational support will be able to obtain the master's degree, but it cannot be used for initial teacher certification. * A GRE minimum combined score of 750 (verbal and quantitative) and 2.5 on the analytic writing portion or a minimum 31 raw score (381–386 Scaled Score) on the Miller Analogies Test. * For students who have not met testing requirements for admission into the program, but who have successfully completed 12 h of coursework required for the program with a 3.5 or above GPA, the department chair may waive the testing requirement. * The testing requirement is waived for students who have already completed a master's degree. * A minimum of 2.75 undergraduate GPA. * Demonstrated competency of computer fluency (i.e., undergraduate or graduate computer competency course or computer competency assessment). EdD admission requirements: * GRE, Miller Analogies Test (MAT), or GMAT scores including GRE writing score or on-demand writing sample. * Official transcripts of all undergraduate and graduate coursework. * Documentation of a master's degree from an institution accredited by a nationally recognized accreditation body. * Resume or vita documenting years of related professional/leadership or educational technology, instructional design and training experience. * Letter of introduction/interest stating professional goals, leadership style, and educational philosophy. * Recommendation forms: at least three professional references from persons in a position to evaluate the applicants potential for success in a doctoral program. At least one to be completed by immediate or up-line supervisor or (for Ed. Tech track) professional familiarity with candidates use of technology, instructional design, and training. Other recommendation forms to be completed by professional colleagues or university faculty who are familiar with the applicant. * Documentation of previous statistical methodology, research related coursework or evidence of use and application of data-informed decision making to determine possible need for statistical methodology coursework. * International students and ESL students must meet university minimum TOEFL score or its equivalent. * No more than 24 h of previously completed postgraduate work from MSU may be counted in the EdD program.

**Degree Requirements**—Master's program degree requirements * Satisfy general degree requirements. * Must submit a professional portfolio demonstrating work completed within the program during the final semester of graduate work. * Must apply for graduation in the Graduate Office, 701 Ginger Hall, in the beginning of the term that completion is anticipated. * Maintain a 3.0 GPA in all courses taken after completing the bachelor's degree. *Must be unconditionally admitted. EdD Degree Requirements: * Satisfy all degree requirements. * The student must successfully complete and defend a qualifying examination to enroll in EDD 899 capstone courses and continue within the doctoral program. * Students are required to successfully complete and defend a doctoral capstone. * Students must apply for graduation with the Graduate Office at the beginning of the semester in which they intend to complete. * Maintain a cumulative 3.0 GPA in all courses taken. Must be unconditionally admitted. If a student is not unconditionally admitted after completing 12 graduate hours, he/she will not be permitted to register for additional credit hours. * Students are encouraged to complete the program within the cohort time limit. The maximum allowed time for completion is 10 years. * A total of 18 h will be permitted to be transferred from other universities.

**Number of Full Time Faculty**—4; **Number of Other Faculty**—0

**Degrees awarded in 2012–2013 Academic Year**—Master's—12; **PhD**—5; **Other**—0

**Grant Monies awarded in 2012–2013 Academic Year**—0

**Name of Institution**—University of Massachusetts, Amherst

**Name of Department or Program**—Learning, Media and Technology Master's Program/Math Science and Learning Technology Doctoral Program

**Address:**
813 N. Pleasant St.
Amherst, MA
01003
USA

**Phone Number**—413-545-0246; **Fax Number**—413-545-2879

**Email Contact**—fsullivan@educ.umass.edu; **URL**—http://www.umass.edu/education/academics/tecs/ed_tech.shtml

**Contact Person**—Florence R. Sullivan

**Specializations**—The Master of Education concentration in Learning, Media and Technology prepares students to understand, critique and improve technology- and media-based learning and teaching. The program is structured such that students construct solid knowledge of theories of learning and instruction, as well as theories of the design and use of educational technologies and media. Just as importantly, we offer a number of courses and research experiences through which students develop facility with applied aspects of technology-centered educational practices (e.g., developing digital media utilizing a number of authoring tools). By encountering multiple opportunities for the analysis, design and testing of educational technology/media, students develop a principled approach to technology- and media-based instruction and learning. The Math, Science and Learning Technology doctoral program prepares graduate students to improve the learning and instruction of Science, Technology, Engineering, and Mathematics (STEM) disciplines. To achieve that goal, we are deeply committed to research and scholarship, using both basic and applied research. We put a premium on developing principled approaches to affect educational practice and pursuing rigorous theory building about educational phenomena. We apply such knowledge in developing state of the art instructional designs. These efforts grow from an understanding of educational practice and close work with practitioners in both formal and informal learning settings. Importantly we recognized that certain social groups have been historically marginalized from STEM disciplines, education, and work. We seek to understand the processes and structures contributing to the systematic exclusion of these groups and to actively contribute to correcting such inequities. Our work draws from a variety of disciplines including cognitive science, sociology, anthropology, the learning sciences, psychology, and computer science.

**Features**—In the master's program, we consider media and technology both as tools in learning and teaching specific disciplines (e.g., mathematics and science) and as objects of study in and of themselves. With regard to the former, and in line with the affiliated faculty's expertise, students explore the educational uses of a variety of technological forms (e.g., robotics systems for learning engineering, physics, programming, and the arts) and computer-based environments (e.g., software systems for learning scientific image processing). As for the latter, students actively engage in designing and using various learning technologies and media, including Web-based environments, computer-mediated communications systems, computer-based virtual worlds, and new media for new literacies. The features of the doctoral program of study are: * provide an interconnected locus of intellectual activity for graduate students and faculty; * increase equity (in gender, ethnicity, and opportunities) in recruitment, admission, and retention of students and faculty and pursue issues of equity in science education; * teach relevant courses, seminars, and independent studies in mathematics and science education; * conduct pertinent research studies in mathematics and science learning, teaching, curriculum development, and assessment; * build a base of scholarship, disseminate new knowledge, and apply it actively in education; * provide apprenticeship opportunities for graduate students; * understand and support effective practice in mathematics and science education; * coordinate outreach efforts with K-12 schools and related projects; * collaborate with faculty in the Department, School, and University as well as in the wider profession throughout the Commonwealth of Massachusetts, nationally, and internationally.

**Admission Requirements**—For the master's program—GPA of 2.75 or higher, TESOL test score of 80 points or higher, excellent letters of recommendation, clear statement of purpose. For the doctoral program—earned master's degree in math, natural sciences, learning technology or education, GPA of 2.75 or higher, TESOL test score of 80 points or higher, excellent letters of recommendation, clear statement of purpose.

**Degree Requirements**—Master's degree—33 credit hours and thesis. Doctoral degree—36 credit hours beyond the master's degree, 18 dissertation credit hours, successful completion of comprehensive exams, successful completion of doctoral dissertation.

**Number of Full Time Faculty**—6; **Number of Other Faculty**—2

**Degrees awarded in 2012–2013 Academic Year**—Master's—6; PhD—2; Other—0

**Grant Monies awarded in 2012–2013 Academic Year**—5,300,000

**Name of Institution**—Oakland University

**Name of Department or Program**—Master of Training and Development Program

**Address:**
2200 North Squirrel Road
Rochester, MI
48309-4494
USA

**Phone Number**—248 370-4171; **Fax Number**—248 370-4095

**Email Contact**—ouhrdmtd@gmail.com; **URL**—www2.oakland.edu/sehs/hrd/

**Contact Person**—Dr. Chaunda L. Scott—Graduate Coordinator

**Specializations**—The Master of Training and Development Program at Oakland University provides a unique blend of knowledge and skills in all aspects of training and development. Students can choose between two area of emphasis: * Instructional Design and Technology. * Organizational Development and Leadership.

**Features**—The Master of Training and Development Program develops practitioners with the knowledge and skills required to enhance individual performance. Graduates of the program will be able to lead interventions associated with diagnosing performance problems and opportunities. Graduates will also be able to design and implement individual and organizational solutions and evaluate results. All courses are taught by outstanding faculty who have diverse backgrounds and experience in business and academia. The Master of Training and Development Program and be completed in two and one half years. Graduates of the program will be qualified to work as human resource development professionals. including directors of training centers, organizational development consultants, instructional designers and performance technologists.

**Admission Requirements**—Official transcripts for undergraduate and graduate coursework showing a bachelor's degree from a regionally accredited institution and a cumulative GPA of 3.0 or higher. A formal statement, between 100 and 1500 words, highlighting work and life experience—preferably 1 year or longer that have led to desire to pursue the Master of Training and Development Degree. Three letters of recommendations to attest to the quality and scope of the applicants academic and professional ability and a interview will be required.

**Degree Requirements**—The completion of 36 credits approved credits with an overall GPA of 3.0 or better and a grade of 2.8 or above in each additional course. The completion of five core courses is also required; HRD 530 Instructional Design, HRD 506 Theoretical Foundations of Training and Development, HRD 507 Needs Assessment, HRD 605 Program Evaluation and HRD 611 Program Administration along with four elective courses.

**Number of Full Time Faculty**—4; **Number of Other Faculty**—4

**Degrees awarded in 2012–2013 Academic Year**—Master's—15; PhD—0; Other—0

**Grant Monies awarded in 2012–2013 Academic Year**—0

**Name of Institution**—East Carolina University

**Name of Department or Program**—Mathematics, Science, and Instructional Technology Education

**Address:**
MSITE Department, Flanagan Hall
Greenville, NC
27858
USA

**Phone Number**—252-328-9355; **Fax Number**—252-328-9371

**Email Contact**—sugarw@coe.ecu.edu; **URL**—http://www.ecu.edu/educ/msite/it/

**Contact Person**—William Sugar

**Specializations**—MS in Instructional Technology MAEd in Instructional Technology (see corresponding Educational Media and Technology Yearbook entry) Certificates in Computer-based Instruction, Special Endorsement in Computer Education, and Distance Learning and Administration.

**Features**—All required and elective courses are offered online. Courses include innovative approaches to online instruction.

**Admission Requirements**—MAT or GRE exam score.

**Degree Requirements**—Bachelor's degree.

**Number of Full Time Faculty**—7; **Number of Other Faculty**—3

**Degrees awarded in 2012–2013 Academic Year**—Master's—20; PhD—0; Other—0

**Grant Monies awarded in 2012–2013 Academic Year**—0


**Name of Institution**—University of North Carolina, Wilmington

**Name of Department or Program**—Master of Science in Instructional Technology—Dept. of Instructional Technology, Foundations and Secondary Education

**Address:**
601 South College Rd
Wilmington, NC
28403
USA

**Phone Number**—910-962-4183; **Fax Number**—910-962-3609

**Email Contact**—moallemm@uncw.edu; **URL**—http://www.uncw.edu/ed/mit

**Contact Person**—Mahnaz Moallem

**Specializations**—The Master of Science degree in Instructional Technology (MIT) program provides advanced professional training for teachers and school technology coordinators; business and industry personnel such as executives, trainers, and human resource development employees; persons in the health care field; and community college instructors. The program focuses on the theory and practice of design and development, utilization, management, and evaluation of processes and resources for learning. It emphasizes product development and utilization of advanced technology and provides applied training in the total design, development, implementation, and evaluation of educational and training programs. Instructional Technology Specialist (ITS) and 079 Special Endorsement In Educational Computing and Technology Facilitation (TF): An Online Post-Baccalaureate Certificate. The ITS/TF Certificate Program is designed to address the needs of K-12 teachers, as well as instructional technology specialists, community college faculty/staff, and individuals interested in the design and development, implementation and management of educational and training materials. The Certificate program serves individuals who do not wish to earn a Master of Science degree but wish to expand their knowledge and skills in design, development, implementation and management of instructional materials for different delivery systems. It is also designed for students who are already enrolled in other graduate programs and desire the additional concentration in instructional technology to improve their employment candidacy. The certificate is not a license to teach but rather a University endorsement of instructional technology competence. The program uses an online delivery system for the majority of courses. Some courses may require real-time virtual or face-to-face meetings to provide hands-on activities for production purposes or to offer site visitations. The certificate program in Online Teaching and Learning. This graduate certificate program in Online Teaching and Learning (OTandL) is designed to meet the needs of K-12 educators, higher education faculty, instructional design specialists, chief learning officers, and other professionals and individuals who wish to design, develop, implement, manage, and evaluate online learning environments. The certificate program serves individuals who do not wish to earn a Master of Science degree, but wish to expand their knowledge and skills in teaching online courses and managing online learning environments.

**Features**—As an exciting and innovative program, MIT provides students the opportunity to gain skills and knowledge from educational and applied psychology, instructional systems design, computer science, systems theory, and communication theory, allowing for considerable flexibility to tailor individual needs across other academic disciplines. Students from diverse fields can plan programs which are consistent with their long-range academic and professional goals. MIT courses are offered both on campus and online, allowing professionals to earn their degrees and/or certificates by taking MIT on-campus courses, or MIT online courses, or a combination of both types. In addition, the MIT program is directed toward preparing students to function in a variety of roles to be performed in a broad range of settings, including business and industry, human services, health institutions, higher education, government, military, and public and private K-12 education.

**Admission Requirements**—Students desiring admission into the graduate program in instructional technology must present the following: A bachelor's degree from an accredited college or university or its equivalent from a foreign institution of higher education based on a 4-year program. A strong academic record (an average GPA of 3.0 or better is expected) in the basic courses required in the area of the proposed graduate study. Academic potential as indicated by satisfactory performance on standardized test scores (e.g., Miller Analogy Test or Graduate Record Examination). The MAT or GRE must have been taken within the last 5 years. Three recommendations from individuals who are in a position to evaluate the students professional competence as well as potential for graduate study. A statement of career goals and degree objectives. A letter describing educational and professional experiences, their reasons for pursuing graduate study, and the contributions that the student hopes to make after completing the degree. North Carolina essential and advanced technology competencies. Individuals who fall below a specified criterion may be admitted if other factors indicate potential for success. Individuals with identified deficiencies may be accepted provisionally with specified plans and goals for the remediation of those deficiencies. Such remediation may include a requirement of additional hours beyond those normally required for the degree.

**Degree Requirements**—Applicants should submit the following to the UNCW Graduate School:—Official graduate application. (Use the following link https://app.applyyourself.com/?id=uncw-grad to apply electronically.)—Official transcripts of all college work (undergraduate and graduate). The transcripts should be mailed directly to UNCW Graduate School—Official scores on the Miller Analogy Test (MAT) or Graduate Record Examination (GRE). Scores more than 5 years old will not be accepted. The UNCW institution code for the MAT and GRE is 5907—Three recommendations from individuals in professionally relevant fields, addressing the applicants demonstrated academic skills and/or potential for successful graduate study—Evidence of a bachelor's degree at the time of entrance—International students: TOEFL score of 550 or higher or IELTS (International English Language Testing System) score of 217 or better (computerized test), 550 or better (paper test), or a minimum score of 79 on the Internet-based test (TOEFL iBT) or IELTS minimum score of 6.5 or 7.0 to be eligible for a teaching assistantship—Letter of application and a statement of professional goals describing applicant's educational and professional experiences, reasons for pursuing a master's degree in instructional technology, and contributions that applicant hopes to make after degree completion.

**Number of Full Time Faculty**—5; **Number of Other Faculty**—6

**Degrees awarded in 2012–2013 Academic Year**—Master's—20; **PhD**—0; **Other**—0

**Grant Monies awarded in 2012–2013 Academic Year**—1,199,546


**Name of Institution**—University of North Dakota

**Name of Department or Program**—Instructional Design and Technology

**Address:**
231 Centennial Drive, Stop 7189
Grand Forks, ND
58202
USA

**Phone Number**—701-777-3486; **Fax Number**—701-777-3246

**Email  Contact**—Woei.hung@email.und.edu;  **URL**—http://education.und.edu/teaching-and-learning/idt/index.cfm

**Contact Person**—Woei Hung

**Specializations**—Problem-Based Learning, Problem Solving, K-12 Technology Integration eLearning Game-Based Learning Human Performance Technology.

**Features**—Online Hybrid with synchronous and asynchronous learning Master's and Certificates fully available at a distance Three graduate certificates (K-12 Technology Integration; Corporate Training and Performance; eLearning) MS and MEd PhD Interdisciplinary studies Research Opportunities: Northern Plains Center for Behavioral Research Odegard School of Aerospace Sciences (Aviation and Radar simulators; Unmanned Aerial Systems Training).

**Admission  Requirements**—http://education.und.edu/teaching-and-learning/idt/index.cfm.

**Degree Requirements**—Master's: http://education.und.edu/teaching-and-learning/idt/master's.cfm; Doctoral: http://education.und.edu/teaching-and-learning/idt/doctor.cfm.

**Number of Full Time Faculty**—2; **Number of Other Faculty**—4

**Degrees awarded in 2012–2013 Academic Year**—Master's—8; PhD—2; Other—3

**Grant Monies awarded in 2012–2013 Academic Year**—0

**Name of Institution**—Valley City State University

**Name of Department or Program**—School of Education and Graduate Studies

**Address:**
101 College St
Valley City, ND
58072
USA

**Phone Number**—701-845-7304; **Fax Number**—701-845-7190

**Email Contact**—jim.boe@vcsu.edu; **URL**—www.vcsu.edu/graduate

**Contact Person**—James Boe

**Specializations**—The Master of Education Degree has four concentrations that focus on technology and the learner. Teaching and Technology concentration Technology Education concentration Library and Information Technologies concentration Teaching English Language Learners concentration Elementary Education concentration English Education concentration. The program also offers Graduate Certificates in the following areas: Library and Information Technologies certificate Teaching English Language Learners certificate Elementary and Secondary STEM certificates.

**Features**—This is a completely online program which focuses on how technology can be used in a school setting to enhance student learning.

**Admission Requirements**—(1) Baccalaureate degree with a 3.0 undergraduate GPA or a test is required. (2) Three letters of recommendation. (3) Written goals statement. (4) Resume. (5) $35 fee for application.

**Degree Requirements**—Completion of 32–37 credits depending on concentration. Action Research Study. Final portfolio demonstrating program core values.

**Number of Full Time Faculty**—20; **Number of Other Faculty**—11

**Degrees awarded in 2012–2013 Academic Year**—Master's—36; **PhD**—0; **Other**—0

**Grant Monies awarded in 2012–2013 Academic Year**—0


**Name of Institution**—New York Institute of Technology

**Name of Department or Program**—Dept. of Instructional Technology and Educational Leadership

**Address:**
Northern Blvd/26 61st Street
Old Westbury/New York City, NY
11568/10023
USA

**Phone Number**—(516)686-7777/(212)261-1529; **Fax Number**—(516)686-7655

**Email Contact**—smcphers@nyit.edu; **URL**—http://www.nyit.edu/education

**Contact Person**—Dr. Sarah McPherson, Chair, Dept. of Instructional Technology and Educational Leadership

**Specializations**—Master of Science in Instructional Technology for Educators and Professional Trainers; Certificates in Computers in Education, Teaching Twenty-first Century Skills, Science, Technology, Engineering, and Mathematics (STEM), and Virtual Education; Advanced Diploma Educational Leadership and Technology for School Building Leader; MS in Childhood Education and School Counseling.

**Features**—Courses are offered face to face and hybrid in Long Island, New York City, upstate New York in partnership with NYS Teacher Centers, in School District partnerships and internationally (incl. Turkey and Abu Dhabi). Courses are also offered 100 % online statewide, nationally and internationally. The Instructional Technology program features: Integration into content area curriculum and instruction for K-12 teachers; Leadership and instructional technology for school building administrators; Professional trainer program for adult learning in corporate, government, and nonprofit agencies. All courses are hand-on instruction in technology labs; or online and hybrid delivery. Evening, weekend, and summer courses are available in all formats.

**Admission Requirements**—All program require bachelor's degree from accredited college with 3.0 cumulative grade point average; Advanced Diploma require Master's and 3 years teaching for admission.

**Degree Requirements**—Master of Science: completion of 36 credits and 3.0 GPA. Advanced Certificates: completion of 12–18 credits (depending on min. credits for certificate) and 3.0 GPA. Advanced Diploma—completion of 33 credits and 3.0 GPA.

**Number of Full Time Faculty**—6; **Number of Other Faculty**—30

**Degrees awarded in 2012–2013 Academic Year**—Master's—75; **PhD**—0; **Other**—12

**Grant Monies awarded in 2012–2013 Academic Year**—0

**Name of Institution**—Stockton University

**Name of Department or Program**—Master of Arts in Instructional Technology (MAIT)

**Address:**
101 Vera King Farris Drive
Galloway, NJ
08205
USA

**Phone Number**—609-652-4949; **Fax Number**—609-626-5528

**Email Contact**—leej@stockton.edu; **URL**—http://intraweb.stockton.edu/eyos/page.cfm?siteID=73andpageID=276

**Contact Person**—Jung Lee

**Specializations**—The Master of Arts in Instructional Technology offered by Stockton University is designed to bring the best instructional technologies into both public and corporate curricula. With a strong theoretical foundation, the degree enables graduates to use technology as a tool to enhance learning and training.

**Features**—The program serves (1) students who seek or will continue employment in the K-12 schools; (2) students who wish to pursue coordinator or supervisor positions in P-12 schools and districts; and (3) students seeking or holding careers in business, industry, or nonprofit organizations.

**Admission Requirements**—Minimum 3.0 GPA, relevant experience, reference letters and GRE General Exam scores or MAT (Miller Analogies Test scores).

**Degree Requirements**—11 graduate courses (33 credits) including capstone project course.

**Number of Full Time Faculty**—3; **Number of Other Faculty**—5

**Degrees awarded in 2012–2013 Academic Year**—Master's—25; **PhD**—0; **Other**—0

**Grant Monies awarded in 2012–2013 Academic Year**—0


**Name of Institution**—New York University

**Name of Department or Program**—Educational Communication and Technology

**Address:**
MAGNET (Media and Games Network), 2 Metrotech Center Suite 800
New York (Brooklyn), NY
11201
USA
**Phone Number**—(646) 997-0734; **Fax Number**—(212)995-4041

**Email Contact**—ectdmdl@nyu.edu; **URL**—http://steinhardt.nyu.edu/alt/ect

**Contact Person**—Jan L. Plass (Program Director); Ricki Goldman (Doctoral Program Coordinator)

**Specializations**—MA in Digital Media Design for Learning, MS in Games for Learning, and PhD in Educational Communication and Technology:—for the preparation of individuals as educational media designers, developers, media producers, and/or researchers in education, business and industry, health and medicine, community services, government, museums and other cultural institutions; and to teach or become involved in administration in educational communications and educational technology or learning sciences programs in higher education, including instructional video, multimedia, web, serious games, and simulations, and interactive toys. The program also offers a post-Master's 30-credit Certificate of Advanced Study in Education. The degrees emphasize design and learning sciences research in learning in all contexts throughout the life span, including both formal and informal/nonformal environments. Faculty research areas include technology and media in collaborative learning, simulations and games for learning, medical education, language and literacy learning, global development, STEM education, early childhood education, and health education. Emphasizes theoretical foundations, especially a cognitive science and learning sciences perspective of learning and instruction, and their implications for designing media-based learning environments and materials. All efforts focus on video, multimedia, instructional television, Web-based technology and simulations and games; participation in special research and production projects and field internships. Uses an apprenticeship model to provide doctoral students and advanced MA students with research opportunities in collaboration with faculty.

**Features**—Program twitter: @ectdmdl; see http://steinhardt.nyu.edu/alt/ect/social/ for information about mailing lists, our private Facebook group; also see our blog of educational technology events and jobs at http://blogs.nyu.edu/steinhardt/edtech/.

**Admission Requirements**—MA/MS: Bachelor's degree or international equivalent required. Typically 3.0 undergraduate GPA, statement of purpose (no GRE required), optional portfolio. PhD: Master's degree or international equivalent required. 3.0 GPA, GRE, responses to essay questions, interview related to academic or professional preparation and career goals. (TOEFL required for international students.)

**Degree Requirements**—MA/MS: 36 semester credit hours including specialization, elective courses, thesis, English Essay Examination. PhD: 57 semester credit hours beyond Master's, including specialization, foundations, research, content seminar, and elective course work; candidacy papers; dissertation; English Essay Examination. Full-time or part-time study available; *no online option available*.

**Number of Full Time Faculty**—6; **Number of Other Faculty**—4

**Degrees awarded in 2012–2013 Academic Year**—Master's—22; PhD—2; **Other**—0

**Grant Monies awarded in 2012–2013 Academic Year**—1,500,000

**Name of Institution**—Syracuse University

**Name of Department or Program**—Instructional Design, Development, and Evaluation Program, School of Education

**Address:**
330 Huntington Hall
Syracuse, NY
13244-2340
USA

**Phone Number**—(315)443-3703; **Fax Number**—(315)443-1218

**Email Contact**—takoszal@syr.edu; **URL**—http://idde.syr.edu

**Contact Person**—Tiffany A. Koszalka, Professor and Department Chair

**Specializations**—Certificates in Educational Technology and Instructional Design, MS, MS in Instructional Technology, C.A.S., and PhD degree programs in Instructional Design, Educational Evaluation, Human Issues in Instructional Development, Technology Integration, and Educational Research and Theory (learning theory, application of theory, and educational media research). Graduates are prepared to serve as curriculum developers, instructional designers, program and project evaluators, researchers, resource center administrators, technology coordinators, educational technology specialist, distance learning design and delivery specialists, trainers and training managers, and higher education faculty.

**Features**—The courses and programs are typically project-centered. Collaborative project experience, field work and internships are emphasized throughout. There are special issue seminars, as well as student- and faculty-initiated mini-courses, seminars and guest lecturers, faculty-student formulation of department policies, and multiple international perspectives. International collaborations are an ongoing feature of the program. The graduate student population is highly diverse.

**Admission Requirements**—Certificates and MS: undergraduate transcripts, recommendations, personal statement, interview recommended; TOEFL for international applicants; GRE recommended. Certificate of Advanced Study: Relevant Master's degree from accredited institution or equivalent, GRE scores, recommendations, personal statement, TOEFL for international applicants; interview recommended. Doctoral: Relevant Master's degree from accredited institution or equivalent, GRE scores, recommendations, personal statement, TOEFL for international applicants; interview strongly encouraged.

**Degree Requirements**—Certificates: 12, 15, and 24 semester hours. MS: 30 semester hours, portfolio required. MS in Instructional Technology: 30 semester hours, practicum and portfolio required. C.A.S.: 60 semester hours, exam and project required. PhD: 90 semester hours, research apprenticeship, portfolio, qualifying exams and dissertation required.

**Number of Full Time Faculty**—3; **Number of Other Faculty**—6

**Degrees awarded in 2012–2013 Academic Year**—Master's—28; **PhD**—2; **Other**—4

**Grant Monies awarded in 2012–2013 Academic Year**—0


**Name of Institution**—East Stroudsburg University of Pennsylvania

**Name of Department or Program**—Instructional Technology: Department of Digital Media Technologies

**Address:**
200 Prospect Street
East Stroudsburg, PA
18301
USA

**Phone Number**—(570)422-3621; **Fax Number**—(570)422-3876

**Email Contact**—bsockman@.esu.edu; **URL**—www.esu.edu/gradit

**Contact Person**—Beth Rajan Sockman PhD

**Specializations**—Mission: The graduate programs are designed to prepare instructional technologists to utilize critical reflection with research in order to design, produce, and implement technological tools to improve learning in a global society. Instructional Technology Students can obtain a Master's of Education degree in

Instructional Technology and/or a Pennsylvania Instructional Technologist Specialist Certificate. Students interested in PK-12 education may choose to concentrate in Technology Integration. Instructional technologist can be prepared for 5 areas: * PK-12 Educators: technology literacy of educators and specialists to work in K-12 schools, school districts, or instructional technology personnel in education. * Edu-business Entrepreneurs: technology to facilitate learning in customized learning environments. * Instructional Designer: technology and instructional designer in the business, training or cooperate environment. * Higher Education Technology Integrators: learning management systems and work with faculty SMEs for technology integration into their curriculum.

**Features**—The program provides students with an opportunity to take courses from ESU University. Students who successfully complete the program become proficient in using technology in teaching. Students can choose courses that explore that following areas: * Interactive web design (Including Web 2.0 applications). * Convergence of Technology. * Desktop publishing. * Graphics. * Video. * New and emerging technologies. * Instructional design. * Learning theories. * Research in Instructional Technology.

**Admission Requirements**—For MEd degree: * Two letters of recommendation. * Portfolio or interview (Interview is granted after the application is received). * For full admission a minimum overall undergraduate 2.5 QPA For certification: * Contact the graduate coordinator for additional admission information to comply with Pennsylvania Department of Education requirements. * Minimum overall undergraduate QPA 3.0 (Pennsylvania Act 354). * If not 3.0 QPA, then completion of nine credits of Media Communication and Technology Department courses with prior written approval of department faculty adviser. * Two letters of recommendation. * Rolling deadline.

**Degree Requirements**—Total = 33 credits # Take courses and learn—Take 30 credits of courses for the master's and learn based on your needs. You will learn to use and implement technologies outside average persons experience. # Create, Submit and Present your Portfolio—This is the time to display your learning in a professional manner. In the portfolio you articulate your goals and may identify learning goals for your internship. Click here for the Portfolio Guidelines. # Complete an Internship—You complete a 90 h internship that extends your knowledge base—three credits. # Complete Portfolio and Graduate.

**Number of Full Time Faculty**—6; **Number of Other Faculty**—4

**Degrees awarded in 2012–2013 Academic Year**—Master's—7; PhD—0; Other—0

**Grant Monies awarded in 2012–2013 Academic Year**—11,000

**Name of Institution**—University of Memphis

**Name of Department or Program**—Instructional Design and Technology

**Address:**
406 Ball Hall
Memphis, TN
38152
USA

**Phone Number**—901-678-5672; **Fax Number**—901-678-3881

**Email Contact**—treymartindale@gmail.com; **URL**—http://idt.memphis.edu

**Contact Person**—Dr. Trey Martindale

**Specializations**—Instructional Design, Educational Technology, Technology Integration, Web 2.0 and Social Media, Web-Based Instruction, E-Learning, Computer-Based Instruction, Professional Development, Online Teaching, Consulting and Project Management.

**Features**—IDT program: http://idt.memphis.edu. Twitter: https://twitter.com/idt-memphis. IDT Program News: http://idtmemphis.wordpress.com/. Google Plus: https://plus.google.com/+IDTMemphis/posts. All our degrees and certificates are offered completely online. Our master's degree is 30 credit hours, and our doctoral degree is 54 credit hours. Our educational technology certificate is 12 credit hours, and our e-learning design and development certificate is 12 credit hours. All are completely online. The IDT Studio, staffed and run by IDT faculty and students, serves as an RandD space for coursework and research involving technologies such as digital media, WBT/CBT, pedagogical agents, gaming, and simulation. The IDT Studio contracts with local partners to give students real-world consulting and ID experience. The IDT program is an active partner in the Martin Institute for Teaching Excellence (http://martininstitute.org). We have also partnered with the Institute for Intelligent Systems and the Tutoring Research Group (www.autotutor.org) to work on intelligent agent development and research.

**Admission Requirements**—An official transcript showing a bachelor's degree awarded by an accredited college or university with a minimum GPA of 2.0 on a 4.0 scale, two letters of recommendation, graduate school and departmental application. Doctoral students must also be interviewed by at least two members of the program. Full details here: http://www.memphis.edu/idt/apply.php.

**Degree Requirements**—MS: 30 credit hours total. EdD: 54 credit hours total. 45 in major, nine in research; residency project; comprehensive exams; dissertation. IDT Certificate: 12 credit hours total.

**Number of Full Time Faculty**—4; **Number of Other Faculty**—5

**Degrees awarded in 2012–2013 Academic Year**—Master's—5; **PhD**—4; **Other**—8

**Grant Monies awarded in 2012–2013 Academic Year**—300,000

**Name of Institution**—University of Texas at Brownsville

**Name of Department or Program**—Educational Technology

**Address:**
One West University Boulevard
Brownsville, TX
78520
USA

**Phone Number**—(956) 882-7540; **Fax Number**—(956) 882-8929

**Email Contact**—Rene.Corbeil@UTB.edu; **URL**—http://edtech.utb.edu

**Contact Person**—J. Rene Corbeil, EdD

**Specializations**—E-Learning Instructional Design Web-Based Instruction Multimedia Design

**Features**—The Online M. Ed. in Educational Technology is a 36-h program designed to prepare persons in K-12, higher education, corporate, and military settings to develop the skills and knowledge necessary for the classrooms of tomorrow. Graduates of this program will have a much better understanding of the uses of technology and how they can be applied in instructional/training settings. The program focuses on the theory, research and applications related to the field of educational technology and is intended to help individuals: — use instructional technology (computers, telecommunications and related technologies) as resources for the delivery of instruction — serve as facilitators or directors of instructional technology in educational settings and/or be developers of instructional programs and materials for new technologies — design instructional materials in a variety of media. In addition to earning an MEd in Educational Technology, students working in K-12 environments also have the opportunity to complete the Educational Technology Leader Certificate program. This certificate program is provided through the three graduate elective courses offered as an option in the degree program. An E-Learning Certificate is also available for individuals working in higher education or at e-learning industries. This certificate program is provided through the four graduate elective courses offered as an option in the degree program.

**Admission Requirements**—Proof of a baccalaureate degree from a 4-year institution which has regional accreditation. GPA of 2.5 or higher (3.0 GPA for "unconditional" admission. Between 2.5–2.9 for "conditional" admission). Application Essay/Statement of Goals. Please provide a carefully considered statement of: (1) your academic and professional objectives and (2) explain how graduate study will help you to attain your goals. Note: The GRE is not required for students with undergraduate GPAs above 3.0.

**Degree Requirements**—The MEd in Educational Technology consists of 27 h from core courses plus 9 h of electives for a total of 36 h. Students can select the 9 h of electives based upon their professional needs and academic interests (e.g., Master Technology Teacher—MTT Certificate, e-Learning Certificate, or 12 h in a specific content area such as reading, mathematics, science) with advisor approval. Core Courses: (24 h) EDTC 6320—Educational Technology EDTC 6321—Instructional Design EDTC 6323—Multimedia/Hypermedia EDTC 6325—Educational Communications EDTC 6329—Selected Topics in Educational Technology EDTC 6332—Practicum in Educational Technology EDFR 6300—Foundations of Research in Education EPSY 6304—Learning and Cognition EDFR 6388—Socio Cultural Foundations Electives: (9 h) EDCI 6301—Instructional Technology in Teaching EDCI 6336—Problems in Education: International Technology Issues EDTC 6340—Applications of Advanced Technologies in the Pk-12 Classroom EDTC 6341—Student-Centered Learning Using Technology EDTC 6342—Technology Leadership EDTC 6343—Master Teacher of Technology Practicum* EDTC 6351—Web-Based Multimedia in Instruction EDTC 6358—Theory and Practice of e-Learning.

**Number of Full Time Faculty**—4; **Number of Other Faculty**—2

**Degrees awarded in 2012–2013 Academic Year**—Master's—45; **PhD**—0; **Other**—0

**Grant Monies awarded in 2012–2013 Academic Year**—0

**Name of Institution**—Old Dominion University

**Name of Department or Program**—Instructional Design and Technology
**Address:**
Education 228
Norfolk, VA
23529
USA

**Phone Number**—757-683-3246; **Fax Number**—757-683-5862

**Email Contact**—gswatson@odu.edu; **URL**—http://education.odu.edu/eci/idt/

**Contact Person**—Gingers S. Watson

**Specializations**—Our faculty engages students in a rigorous course of study tailored to meet individual educational and career interests. Research opportunities and course work ensures that all students receive a solid foundation in Instructional Design and Technology Instructional Design Theory Human Performance Technology Modeling, Simulation and Gaming Distance Education Evaluation and Assessment Trends and Issues in Instructional Technology Quantitative and Qualitative Research.

**Features**—All of our courses are offered via distance using a hybrid format. Classroom instruction uses a virtual classroom that allows all students to participate in a face-to-face classroom. A reduced tuition rate is available for students living outside of Virginia who are accepted into the program.

**Admission Requirements**—MS degree: GRE scores or MAT scores; transcripts for undergraduate and graduate courses PhD: GRE scores, transcripts for undergraduate and graduate courses, letters of recommendation, and an essay describing professional goals.

**Degree Requirements**—MS program is 30–36 h PhD program is a post-master degree consisting of 60 h.

**Number of Full Time Faculty**—4; **Number of Other Faculty**—1

**Degrees awarded in 2012–2013 Academic Year**—Master's—5; **PhD**—7; **Other**—0

**Grant Monies awarded in 2012–2013 Academic Year**—25,000,000

**Name of Institution**—Concordia University Wisconsin

**Name of Department or Program**—Educational Design and Technology

**Address:**
12800 N Lakeshore Drive
Mequon, WI
53092
USA

**Phone Number**—262-243-4595; **Fax Number**—262-243-3595

**Email Contact**—bernard.bull@cuw.edu; **URL**—http://www.cuw.edu/go/edtech

**Contact Person**—Dr. Bernard Bull

**Specializations**—Designing digital age learning experiences, educational innovation, social and ethical implications of technology.

**Features**—This program is built around competency-based digital badges. Students earn digital badges as they progress through the courses, and these badges can be immediately exported to an open backpack to display in an online portfolio, website, resume, or social network. Courses are available online or face-to-face. Some cohorts may also be offered at off-campus sites in Wisconsin and beyond. In addition, we run occasional thematic cohorts where a group of students work through the program together over an 18–24 month period, all agreeing to focus their thesis or culminating project upon the cohort theme (e.g., new literacies, bridging the digital divide, global education, discipleship in the digital age).

**Admission Requirements**—To be considered for admission, a student must: Have a bachelor's degree from an accredited college or university. Have a minimum GPA of 3.00 in the undergraduate program.

**Degree Requirements**—Required Courses EDT 970—Integrating Technology in the Classroom (3) EDT 889—Applying Technology in the Content Areas (3) EDT 908—Critical Issues in Educational Technology (3) EDT 892—Instructional

Design (3) EDT 893—Theories of Learning and Design (3) EDT 815—Research in Educational Technology (3) EDT 927, 928, 929—Portfolio I, II, and III (0) EDT 895—Capstone Project (3) OR EDT 890—Thesis Completion Seminar (3) Electives EDT 805—Online Teaching and Learning (3) EDT 814—Educational Ministry in the Digital World (3) EDT 894—Digital Literacy (3) EDT 907—Multimedia for the Classroom (3) EDT 939—School Leadership in Technology (3) EDT 851—Support and Troubleshooting for Teaching and Learning with Technology (3) EDT 957—Building Online Learning Communities (Web 2.0/ Learning 2.0) (3) EDT 971—Grants and Funding for Educational Technology Initiatives (3) EDT 804—Strategies for Teaching and Learning with Interactive Whiteboards (1) EDT 945—Readings in Educational Design and Technology EDT 815—Innovation in Education EDT 820—Blended Learning Other electives as approved by the program director.

**Number of Full Time Faculty**—3; **Number of Other Faculty**—8

**Degrees awarded in 2012–2013 Academic Year**—**Master's**—25; **PhD**—0; **Other**—0

**Grant Monies awarded in 2012–2013 Academic Year**—0

# Part V
# Mediagraphy

# Chapter 17
# Introduction

**Sheng-Shiang Tseng**

## Contents

This resource lists journals and other resources of interest to practitioners, researchers, students, and others concerned with educational technology and educational media. The primary goal of this section is to list current publications in the field. The majority of materials cited here were published in 2014 or mid-2015. Media-related journals include those listed in past issues of EMTY, as well as new entries in the field. A thorough list of journals in the educational technology field has been updated for the 2014 edition using Ulrich's Periodical Index Online and journal websites. This chapter is not intended to serve as a specific resource location tool, although it may be used for that purpose in the absence of database access. Rather, readers are encouraged to peruse the categories of interest in this chapter to gain an idea of recent developments within the field. For archival purposes, this chapter serves as a snapshot of the field of instructional technology publications in 2014. Readers must bear in mind that technological developments occur well in advance of publication and should take that fact into consideration when judging the timeliness of resources listed in this chapter.

## Selection

Items were selected for the Mediagraphy in several ways. The EBSCO Host Databases were used to locate most of the journal citations. Others were taken from the journal listings of large publishing companies. Items were chosen for this list

S.-S. Tseng (✉)
The University of Georgia, 116 River's Crossing, Athens, GA 30602-4809, USA
e-mail: pattseng@uga.edu

© Springer International Publishing Switzerland 2017                        331
M. Orey, R.M. Branch (eds.), *Educational Media and Technology Yearbook,*
Educational Media and Technology Yearbook 40,
DOI 10.1007/978-3-319-45001-8_17

when they met one or more of the following criteria: reputable publisher, broad circulation, coverage by indexing services, peer review, and coverage of a gap in the literature. The author chose items on subjects that seem to reflect the instructional technology field as it is today. Because of the increasing tendency for media producers to package their products in more than one format and for single titles to contain mixed media, titles are no longer separated by media type. The author makes no claims as to the comprehensiveness of this list. It is, instead, intended to be representative.

## Obtaining Resources

*Media-related periodicals*: The author has attempted to provide various ways to obtain the resources listed in this Mediagraphy, including telephone and fax numbers, Web and postal addresses, as well as e-mail contacts. Prices are also included for student (stud), individual (indiv), K-12 educator (k12), and institutional (inst) subscriptions. The information presented reflects the most current information available at the time of publication.

*ERIC Documents*: As of December 31, 2003, ERIC was no longer funded. However, ERIC documents can still be read and copied from their microfiche form at any library holding an ERIC microfiche collection. The identification number beginning with ED (for example, ED 332 677) locates the document in the collection. Document delivery services and copies of most ERIC documents can also continue to be available from the ERIC Document Reproduction Service. Prices charged depend on format chosen (microfiche or paper copy), length of the document, and method of shipping. Online orders, fax orders, and expedited delivery are available.

To find the closest library with an ERIC microfiche collection, contact: ACCESS ERIC, 1600 Research Blvd, Rockville, MD 20850-3172, USA; (800) LET-ERIC (538-3742); e-mail: acceric@inet.ed.gov.

To order ERIC documents, contact:

ERIC Document Reproduction Services (EDRS)
7420 Fullerton Rd, Suite 110, Springfield, VA 22153-2852, USA
(800) 433-ERIC (433-3742); (703) 440-1400
Fax: (703) 440-1408
E-mail: service@edrs.com.

*Journal articles*: Photocopies of journal articles can be obtained in one of the following ways: (1) from a library subscribing to the title, (2) through interlibrary loan, (3) through the purchase of a back issue from the journal publisher, or (4) from an article reprint service such as ProQuest Microfilm.

ProQuest Microfilm, 789 E. Eisenhower Parkway, PO Box 1346
Ann Arbor, MI 48106-1346, USA
(734) 761-4700

Fax: (734) 997-4222
E-mail: sandra.piver@proquest.com.

Journal articles can also be obtained through the Institute for Scientific Information (ISI).
ISI Document Solution
PO Box 7649
Philadelphia, PA 19104-3389, USA
(800) 336-4474, option 5
Fax: (215) 222-0840 or (215) 386-4343
E-mail: ids@isinet.com.

## Arrangement

Mediagraphy entries are classified according to major subject emphasis under the following headings:

- Artificial Intelligence, Robotics, and Electronic Performance Support Systems
- Computer-Assisted Instruction
- Distance Education
- Educational Research
- Educational Technology
- Information Science and Technology
- Instructional Design and Development
- Learning Sciences
- Libraries and Media Centers
- Media Technologies
- Professional Development
- Simulation, Gaming, and Virtual Reality
- Special Education and Disabilities
- Telecommunications and Networking

# Chapter 18
# Mediagraphy

Sheng-Shiang Tseng

## Artificial Intelligence, Robotics, and Electronic Performance Support Systems

**Artificial Intelligence Review.** Springer Science+Business Media, PO Box 2485, Secaucus, NJ 07096-2485. http://www.springer.com/journal/10462, tel: 800-777-4643, fax: 201-348-4505, service-ny@springer.com [8/yr; $1225 inst (print/online), $1470 inst (print+online, content through 1997)]. Publishes reports and evaluations, as well as commentary on issues and development in artificial intelligence foundations and current research.

**AI Magazine.** Association for the Advancement of Artificial Intelligence, 2275 East Bayshore Road, Suite 160, Palo Alto, California 94303. http://www.aaai.org/Magazine, tel: 650-328-3123, fax: 650-321-4457, info08@aaai.org [4/yr; $75 stud (print), $145 indiv (print), $285 inst (print), $290 inst (online)]. Proclaimed "journal of record for the AI community," this magazine provides full-length articles on new research and literature, but is written to allow access to those reading outside their area of expertise.

**International Journal of Human-Computer Interaction.** Taylor & Francis Group, Customer Services Department, 325 Chestnut St, Suite 800, Philadelphia, PA 19106. http://www.tandfonline.com/hihc, tel: 800-354-1420, fax: 215-625-2940, subscriptions@tandf.co.uk [12/yr; $265 indiv (print), $277 indiv (print+online), $2090 inst (online), $2389 inst (print+online)]. Addresses the cognitive, creative, social, health, and ergonomic aspects of interactive computing.

S.-S. Tseng (✉)
The University of Georgia, 116 River's Crossing, Athens, GA 30602-4809, USA
e-mail: mikeorey@uga.edu

© Springer International Publishing Switzerland 2017
M. Orey, R.M. Branch (eds.), *Educational Media and Technology Yearbook*,
Educational Media and Technology Yearbook 40,
DOI 10.1007/978-3-319-45001-8_18

**International Journal of Robotics Research.** Sage Publications, 2455 Teller Rd, Thousand Oaks, CA 91320. http://ijr.sagepub.com, tel: 805-499-9774, journals@ sagepub.com [14/yr; $243 indiv (print), $2390 inst (online), $2603 inst (print), $2656 inst (print+online)]. Interdisciplinary approach to the study of robotics for researchers, scientists, and students. The first scholarly publication on robotics research.

**Journal of Intelligent and Robotic Systems.** Springer Science+Business Media, PO Box 2485, Secaucus, NJ 07096-2485. http://www.springer.com/journal/10846, tel: 800-777-4643, fax: 201-348-4505, service-ny@springer.com [16/yr; $2686 inst (print/online), $3223 inst (print+online, content through 1997)] Main objective is to provide a forum for the fruitful interaction of ideas and techniques that combine systems and control science with artificial intelligence and other related computer science concepts. It bridges the gap between theory and practice.

**Journal of Interactive Learning Research.** Association for the Advancement of Computing in Education, PO Box 1545, Chesapeake, VA 23327-1545. http://www. aace.org/pubs/jilr, tel: 757-366-5606, fax: 703-997-8760, info@editlib.org [4/yr; $150 indiv, $2095 inst]. Publishes articles on how intelligent computer technologies can be used in education to enhance learning and teaching. Reports on research and developments, integration, and applications of artificial intelligence in education.

**Knowledge-Based Systems.** Elsevier, Inc., Journals Customer Service, 3251 Riverport Lane, Maryland Heights, MO 63043. http://www.elsevier.com/locate/ knosys, tel: 877-839-7126, fax: 314-447-8077, journalcustomerservice-usa@else-vier.com [12/yr; $247 indiv, $618.93 inst (online), $2022 inst (print)]. Interdisciplinary applications-oriented journal on fifth-generation computing, expert systems, and knowledge-based methods in system design.

**Minds and Machines.** Springer Science+Business Media, PO Box 2485, Secaucus, NJ 07096-2485. http://www.springer.com/journal/11023, tel: 800-777-4643, fax: 201-348-4505, service-ny@springer.com [4/yr; $986 inst (print/online), $1183 inst (print+online, content through 1997)]. Discusses issues concerning machines and mentality, artificial intelligence, epistemology, simulation, and modeling.

# Computer-Assisted Instruction

**AACE Journal.** Association for the Advancement of Computing in Education, PO Box 1545, Chesapeake, VA 23327-1545. http://www.aace.org/pubs/jilr, tel: 757-366-5606, fax: 703-997-8760, info@editlib.org [4/yr; $150 indiv, $2095 inst]. Publishes articles dealing with issues in instructional technology.

**CALICO Journal.** Computer-Assisted Language Instruction Consortium, 214 Centennial Hall, Texas State University, San Marcos, TX 78666. http://calico.org, tel: 512-245-1417, fax: 512-245-9089, info@calico.org [3/yr; $20 stud, $65 indiv, $50 k12, $105 inst]. Provides information on the applications of technology in teaching and learning languages.

**Children's Technology Review.** Active Learning Associates, 120 Main St, Flemington, NJ 08822. http://childrenstech.com, tel: 800-993-9499, fax: 908-284-0405, lisa@childrenstech.com [12/yr; $30 indiv (online), $60 indiv (print + online)]. Provides reviews and other information about software to help parents and educators more effectively use computers with children.

**Computers and Composition.** Elsevier, Inc., Journals Customer Service, 3251 Riverport Lane, Maryland Heights, MO 63043. http://www.elsevier.com/locate/compcom, tel: 877-839-7126, fax: 314-447-8077, journalcustomerservice-usa@elsevier.com [4/yr; $98 indiv, $190.13 inst (online), $618 inst (print)]. International journal for teachers of writing that focuses on the use of computers in writing instruction and related research.

**Computers & Education.** Elsevier, Inc., Journals Customer Service, 3251 Riverport Lane, Maryland Heights, MO 63043. http://www.elsevier.com/locate/compedu, tel: 877-839-7126, fax: 314-447-8077, journalcustomerservice-usa@elsevier.com [12/yr; $476 indiv, $940 inst (online), $3084 inst (print)]. Presents technical papers covering a broad range of subjects for users of analog, digital, and hybrid computers in all aspects of higher education.

**Computer assisted language learning.** Taylor & Francis Group, Customer Services Department, 325 Chestnut St, Suite 800, Philadelphia, PA 19106. http://www.tandfonline.com/ncal, tel: 800-354-1420, fax: 215-625-2940, subscriptions@tandf.co.uk [6/yr; $234 indiv, $719 inst (online), $822 inst (print + online)]. An intercontinental and interdisciplinary journal which leads the field in its dedication to all matters associated with the use of computers in language learning (L1 and L2), teaching, and testing.

**Computers in Human Behavior.** Elsevier, Inc., Journals Customer Service, 3251 Riverport Lane, Maryland Heights, MO 63043. http://www.elsevier.com/locate/comphumbeh, tel: 877-839-7126, fax: 314-447-8077, journalcustomerservice-usa@elsevier.com [12/yr; $377 indiv, $751.47 inst (online), $2475 inst (print)]. Scholarly journal dedicated to examining the use of computers from a psychological perspective.

**Computers in the Schools.** Taylor & Francis Group, Customer Service Department, 325 Chestnut Street, Suite 800, Philadelphia, PA 19106. http://www.tandf.co.uk/journals/titles/07380569, tel: 800-354-1420, fax: 215-625-2940, subscriptions@tandf.co.uk [4/yr; $148 indiv (online), $160 indiv (print + online), $797 inst (online), $911 inst (print + online)]. Features articles that combine theory and practical applications of small computers in schools for educators and school administrators.

**Center for Digital Education.** e.Republic, Inc., 100 Blue Ravine Rd, Folsom, CA 95630. http://www.centerdigitaled.com/, tel: 800-940-6039 ext 1319, fax: 916-932-1470, subscriptions@erepublic.com [4/yr; free]. Explores the revolution of technology in education.

**Dr. Dobb's Journal.** United Business Media LLC, Customer Service, PO Box 1093, Skokie, IL 60076. http://www.ddj.com, tel: 888-664-3332, fax: 847-763-

9606, drdobbsjournal@halldata.com [12/yr; free to qualified applicants]. Articles on the latest in operating systems, programming languages, algorithms, hardware design and architecture, data structures, and telecommunications; including hardware and software reviews.

**Instructor.** Scholastic Inc., PO Box 420235, Palm Coast, FL 32142-0235. http://www.scholastic.com/teachers/instructor, tel: 866-436-2455, fax: 215-625-2940, instructor@emailcustomerservice.com [8/yr; $8)]. Features articles on applications and advances of technology in education for K-12 and college educators and administrators.

**Interactive Learning Environments.** Taylor & Francis Group, Customer Services Department, 325 Chestnut St, Suite 800, Philadelphia, PA 19106. http://www.tandf. co.uk/journals/titles/10494820, tel: 800-354-1420, fax: 215-625-2940, subscriptions@tandf.co.uk [6/yr; $320 indiv, $924 inst (online), $1056 inst (print+online)]. Explores the implications of the Internet and multimedia presentation software in education and training environments that support collaboration amongst groups of learners or co-workers.

**Journal of Computer Assisted Learning.** John Wiley & Sons, Inc., Journal Customer Services, 350 Main St, Malden, MA 02148. http://www.blackwellpublishing.com/journals/JCA, tel: 800-835-6770, fax: 781-388-8232, cs-agency@ wiley.com [6/yr; $253 indiv (print+online), $1660 inst (print/online), $1992 inst (print+online)]. Articles and research on the use of computer-assisted learning.

**Journal of Educational Computing Research.** Baywood Publishing Co., Inc., 26 Austin Ave, PO Box 337, Amityville, NY 11701-0337. http://www.baywood.com/ journals/previewjournals.asp?id=0735-6331, tel: 800-638-7819, fax: 631-691-1770, info@baywood.com [8/yr; $289 indiv (online), $275 indiv (print+online), $717 inst (online), $755 inst (print+online)]. Presents original research papers, critical analyses, reports on research in progress, design and development studies, article reviews, and grant award listings.

**Journal of Educational Multimedia and Hypermedia.** Association for the Advancement of Computing in Education, PO Box 1545, Chesapeake, VA 23327-1545. http://www.aace.org/pubs/jemh, tel: 757-366-5606, fax: 703-997-8760, info@editlib.org [4/yr; $150 indiv, $2095 inst]. A multidisciplinary information source presenting research about and applications for multimedia and hypermedia tools.

**Journal of Research on Technology in Education.** International Society for Technology in Education, 180 West 8th Ave., Suite 300, Eugene, OR 97401-2916. http://www.iste.org/jrte, tel: 800-336-5191, fax: 541-434-8948, iste@iste.org [4/yr; $173 indiv (print+online), $260 inst (online), $297 (print+online)]. Contains articles reporting on the latest research findings related to classroom and administrative uses of technology, including system and project evaluations.

**Language Resources and Evaluation.** Springer Science+Business Media, PO Box 2485, Secaucus, NJ 07096-2485. http://www.springer.com/journal/10579, tel: 800-

777-4643, fax: 201-348-4505, service-ny@springer.com [4/yr; $1045 inst (print/ online), $1254 inst (print+online, content through 1997)]. Contains papers on computer-aided studies, applications, automation, and computer-assisted instruction.

**MacWorld.** Mac Publishing, Macworld Subscription Services, PO Box 37781, Boone, IA 50037. http://www.macworld.com, tel: 800-288-6848, fax: 515-432-6994, subhelp@macworld.com [12/yr; $22]. Describes hardware, software, tutorials, and applications for users of the Macintosh microcomputer.

**PC Magazine.** Ziff Davis Media Inc., 28 E 28th St, New York, NY 10016-7930. http://www.pcmag.com, tel: 212-503-3500, fax: 212-503-4399, pcmag@ziffdavis.com [12/yr; $20]. Comparative reviews of computer hardware and general business software programs.

**System.** Elsevier, Inc., Journals Customer Service, 3251 Riverport Lane, Maryland Heights, MO 63043. http://www.journals.elsevier.com/system, tel: 877-839-7126, fax: 314-447-8077, journalcustomerservice-usa@elsevier.com [8/yr; $167 indiv, $317.87 inst (online), $1043 inst (print)]. International journal covering educational technology and applied linguistics with a focus on foreign language teaching and learning.

**Social Science Computer Review.** Sage Publications, 2455 Teller Rd, Thousand Oaks, CA 91320. http://ssc.sagepub.com, tel: 800-818-7243, fax: 800-583-2665, journals@sagepub.com [4/yr; $146 indiv (print), $908 inst (online), $989 inst (print), $1009 inst (online+online)]. Interdisciplinary peer-reviewed scholarly publication covering social science research and instructional applications in computing and telecommunications; also covers societal impacts of information technology.

**Wireless Networks.** Springer Science+Business Media, PO Box 2485, Secaucus, NJ 07096-2485. http://www.springer.com/journal/11276, tel: 800-777-4643, fax: 201-348-4505, service-ny@springer.com [8/yr; $1017 inst (print/online), $1220 inst (print+online, content through 1997)]. Devoted to the technological innovations that result from the mobility allowed by wireless technology.

## Distance Education

**American Journal of Distance Education.** Taylor & Francis Group, Customer Services Department, 325 Chestnut St, Suite 800, Philadelphia, PA 19106. http://www.tandf.co.uk/journals/titles/08923647, tel: 800-354-1420, fax: 215-625-2940, subscriptions@tandf.co.uk [4/yr; $99 indiv (print+online), $348 inst (online), $398 inst (print+online)]. Created to disseminate information and act as a forum for criticism and debate about research on and practice of systems, management, and administration of distance education.

**Journal of E-learning & Distance Education.** Canadian Network for Innovation in Education, BCIT Learning & Teaching Centre, British Columbia Institute of Technology, 3700 Willingdon Ave., Burnaby, BC, V5G 3H2, Canada. http://www.

jofde.ca, tel: 604-454-2280, fax: 604-431-7267, journalofde@gmail.com [at least 2/ yr; free]. Aims to promote and encourage scholarly work of empirical and theoretical nature relating to distance education in Canada and throughout the world.

**Journal of Library & Information Services in Distance Learning.** Taylor & Francis Group, Customer Service Department, 325 Chestnut Street, Suite 800, Philadelphia, PA 19106. http://www.tandf.co.uk/journals/titles/1533290X, tel: 800-354-1420, fax: 215-625-2940, subscriptions@tandf.co.uk [4/yr; $88 indiv (online), $99 indiv (print+online), $225 inst (online), $257 inst (print+online)]. Contains peer-reviewed articles, essays, narratives, current events, and letters from distance learning and information science experts.

**Journal of Research on Technology in Education.** International Society for Technology in Education, 180 West 8th Ave., Suite 300, Eugene, OR 97401 -2916. http://www.iste.org/jrte, tel: 800-336-5191, fax: 541-434-8948, iste@iste.org [4/yr; $54 member, $200 nonmember]. Contains articles reporting on the latest research findings related to classroom and administrative uses of technology, including system and project evaluations.

**Open Learning.** Taylor & Francis Group, Customer Services Department, 325 Chestnut St, Suite 800, Philadelphia, PA 19106. http://www.tandf.co.uk/journals/titles/02680513, tel: 800-354-1420, fax: 215-625-2940, subscriptions@tandf.co.uk [3/yr; $138 indiv (print), $392 inst (online), $448 inst (print+online)]. Academic, scholarly publication on aspects of open and distance learning anywhere in the world. Includes issues for debate and research notes.

# Educational Research

**American Educational Research Journal.** Sage Publications, 2455 Teller Rd, Thousand Oaks, CA 91320. http://aer.sagepub.com, tel: 800-818-7243, fax: 800-583-2665, journals@sagepub.com [6/yr; $77 indiv (print+online), $933 inst (online), $1016 inst (print), $1037 inst (print+online)]. Reports original research, both empirical and theoretical, and brief synopses of research.

**Asia-Pacific Education Researcher**. Springer Science+Business Media, PO Box 2485, Secaucus, NJ 07096-2485. http://www.springer.com/journal/40299, tel: 800-777-4643, fax: 201-348-4505, service-ny@springer.com [4/yr; $308 inst (print/online), $370 inst (print+online, content through 1997)]. Reports on the successful educational systems in the Asia-Pacific Region and of the national educational systems that underrepresented.

**Educational Research.** Taylor & Francis Group, Customer Services Department, 325 Chestnut St, Suite 800, Philadelphia, PA 19106. http://www.tandf.co.uk/journals/titles/00131881, tel: 800-354-1420, fax: 215-625-2940, subscriptions@tandf.co.uk [4/yr; $231 indiv, $616 inst (online), $704 inst (print+online)]. Reports on current educational research, evaluation, and applications.

**Educational Researcher.** Sage Publications, 2455 Teller Rd, Thousand Oaks, CA 91320. http://edr.sagepub.com, tel: 800-818-7243, fax: 800-583-2665, journals@ sagepub.com [9/yr; $66 indiv (print+online), $499 inst (online), $543 inst (print), $554 inst (print+online)]. Contains news and features of general significance in educational research.

**Innovations in Education and Teaching International.** Taylor & Francis Group, Customer Services Department, 325 Chestnut St, Suite 800, Philadelphia, PA 19106. http://www.tandfonline.com/riie, tel: 800-354-1420, fax: 215-625-2940, subscriptions@tandf.co.uk [6/yr; $229 indiv, $751 inst (online), $858 inst (print+online)]. Essential reading for all practitioners and decision makers who want to stay good practice in higher education through staff and educational development and subject-related practices.

**Journal of Interactive Learning Research.** Association for the Advancement of Computing in Education, PO Box 1545, Chesapeake, VA 23327-1545. http://www. aace.org/pubs/jilr, tel: 757-366-5606, fax: 703-997-8760, info@editlib.org [4/yr; $150 indiv, $2095 inst]. Publishes articles on how intelligent computer technologies can be used in education to enhance learning and teaching. Reports on research and developments, integration, and applications of artificial intelligence in education.

**Learning Technology.** IEEE Computer Society, Technical Committee on Learning Technology, 150 Androutsou Street, Piraeus GR-18352, Greece. http://lttf.ieee.org/ content/ieee-trlt, tel: (+30) 210-4142766, fax: (+30) 210-4142767, sampson@unipi. gr [4/yr; $17 stud member, $64 member, $205 nonmember]. Online publication that reports developments, projects, conferences, and findings of the Learning Technology Task Force.

**Meridian.** North Carolina State University, College of Education, Poe Hall, PO Box 7801, Raleigh, NC 27695-7801. http://www.ncsu.edu/meridian, meridian_ mail@ncsu.edu [2/yr; free] Online journal dedicated to research in middle school educational technology use.

**Research in Science & Technological Education.** Taylor & Francis Group, Customer Services Department, 325 Chestnut St, Suite 800, Philadelphia, PA 19106. http://www.tandf.co.uk/journals/titles/02635143, tel: 800-354-1420, fax: 215-625-2940, subscriptions@tandf.co.uk [3/yr; $440 indiv, $2010 inst (online), $2297 inst (print+online)] Publication of original research in the science and technological fields. Includes articles on psychological, sociological, economic, and organizational aspects of technological education.

# Educational Technology

**Appropriate Technology.** Research Information Ltd., Grenville Court, Britwell Rd, Burnham, Bucks SL1 8DF, UK. http://www.researchinformation.co.uk/apte. php, tel: +44 (0) 1628 600499, fax: +44 (0) 1628 600488, info@

researchinformation.co.uk [4/yr; free]. Articles on less technologically advanced, but more environmentally sustainable solutions to problems in developing countries.

**British Journal of Educational Technology.** John Wiley & Sons, Inc., Journal Customer Services, 350 Main St, Malden, MA 02148. http://www.blackwellpublishing.com/journals/BJET, tel: 800-835-6770, fax: 781-388-8232, cs-agency@wiley.com [6/yr; $234 indiv, $1596 inst (print/online), $1916 inst (print+online)]. Published by the National Council for Educational Technology, this journal includes articles on education and training, especially theory, applications, and development of educational technology and communications.

**Canadian Journal of Learning and Technology.** Canadian Network for Innovation in Education (CNIE), 260 Dalhousie St., Suite 204, Ottawa, ON, K1N 7E4, Canada. http://www.cjlt.ca, tel: 613-241-0018, fax: 613-241-0019, cjlt@ucalgary.ca [3/yr; free]. Concerned with all aspects of educational systems and technology.

**Educational Technology.** Educational Technology Publications, Inc., 700 Palisade Ave, Englewood Cliffs, NJ 07632-0564. http://www.bookstoread.com/etp, tel: 800-952-2665, fax: 201-871-4009, edtecpubs@aol.com [6/yr; $259]. Covers telecommunications, computer-aided instruction, information retrieval, educational television, and electronic media in the classroom.

**Educational Technology Research & Development.** Springer Science+Business Media, PO Box 2485, Secaucus, NJ 07096-2485. http://www.springer.com/journal/11423, tel: 800-777-4643, fax: 201-348-4505, service-ny@springer.com [6/yr; $439 inst (print/online), $527 inst (print+online, content through 1997)]. Focuses on research, instructional development, and applied theory in the field of educational technology.

**International Journal of Technology and Design Education.** Springer Science+Business Media, PO Box 2485, Secaucus, NJ 07096-2485. http://www.springer.com/journal/10798, tel: 800-777-4643, fax: 201-348-4505, service-ny@springer.com [4/yr; $582 inst (print/online), $698 inst (print+online, content through 1997)]. Publishes research reports and scholarly writing about aspects of technology and design education.

**Journal of Computing in Higher Education.** Springer Science+Business Media, PO Box 2485, Secaucus, NJ 07096-2485. http://www.springer.com/journal/12528, tel: 800-777-4643, fax: 201-348-4505, service-ny@springer.com [3/yr; $173 inst (print/online), $208 inst (print+online, content through 1997)]. Publishes scholarly essays, case studies, and research that discuss instructional technologies.

**Journal of Educational Technology Systems.** Baywood Publishing Co., Inc., 26 Austin Ave., Box 337, Amityville, NY 11701-0337. http://www.baywood.com/journals/previewjournals.asp?id=0047-2395, tel: 800-638-7819, fax: 631-691-1770, info@baywood.com [4/yr; $489 inst (online), $515 inst (print+online)]. Deals with systems in which technology and education interface; designed to inform educators who are interested in making optimum use of technology.

**Journal of Interactive Media in Education.** Open University, Knowledge Media Institute, Milton Keynes MK7 6AA UK. http://www-jime.open.ac.uk, tel: +44 (0) 1908 653800, fax: +44 (0) 1908 653169, jime@open.ac.uk [Irregular; free]. A multidisciplinary forum for debate and idea sharing concerning the practical aspects of interactive media and instructional technology.

**Journal of Science Education and Technology.** Springer Science+Business Media, PO Box 2485, Secaucus, NJ 07096-2485. http://www.springer.com/journal/10956, tel: 800-777-4643, fax: 201-348-4505, service-ny@springer.com [6/yr; $1335 inst (print/online), $1602 inst (print+online, content through 1997)]. Publishes studies aimed at improving science education at all levels in the USA.

**MultiMedia & Internet@Schools.** Information Today, Inc., 143 Old Marlton Pike, Medford, NJ 08055-8750. http://www.mmischools.com, tel: 609-654-6266, fax: 609-654-4309, custserv@infotoday.com [5/yr; $50]. Reviews and evaluates hardware and software. Presents information pertaining to basic troubleshooting skills.

**Science Communication.** Sage Publications, 2455 Teller Rd, Thousand Oaks, CA 91320. http://scx.sagepub.com, tel: 800-818-7243, fax: 800-583-2665, journals@sagepub.com [8/yr; $188 indiv (print+online), $1123 inst (online), $1223 inst (print), $1248 inst (print+online)]. An international, interdisciplinary journal examining the nature of expertise and the translation of knowledge into practice and policy.

**Social Science Computer Review.** Sage Publications, 2455 Teller Rd, Thousand Oaks, CA 91320. http://ssc.sagepub.com, tel: 800-818-7243, fax: 800-583-2665, journals@sagepub.com [4/yr; $146 indiv (print), $908 inst (online), $989 inst (print), $1009 inst (print+online)]. Interdisciplinary peer-reviewed scholarly publication covering social science research and instructional applications in computing and telecommunications; also covers societal impacts of information technology.

**TechTrends.** Springer Science+Business Media, PO Box 2485, Secaucus, NJ 07096-2485. http://www.springer.com/journal/11528, tel: 800-777-4643, fax: 201-348-4505, service-ny@springer.com [6/yr; $161 inst (print/online), $193 inst (print+online, content through 1997)]. Targeted at leaders in education and training; features authoritative, practical articles about technology and its integration into the learning environment.

**T.H.E.** Journal. PO Box 2166, Skokie, IL 60076. http://www.thejournal.com, tel: 866-293-3194, fax: 847-763-9564, thejournal@1105service.com [9/yr; free] For educators of all levels; focuses on a specific topic for each issue, as well as technological innovations as they apply to education.

# Information Science and Technology

**Canadian Journal of Information and Library Science.** University of Toronto Press, Journals Division, 5201 Dufferin St, Toronto, ON, M3H 5T8, Canada. http://www.utpjournals.com/cjils, tel: 416-667-7777, fax: 800-221-9985, journals@

utpress.utoronto.ca [4/yr; $55 stud (online), $100 stud (print+online), $90 indiv (online), $140 indiv (print+online), $160 inst (print)]. Published by the Canadian Association for Information Science to contribute to the advancement of library and information science in Canada.

**E-Content.** Information Today, Inc., 143 Old Marlton Pike, Medford, NJ 08055-8750. http://www.econtentmag.com, tel: 800-300-9868, fax: 609-654-4309, custserv@infotoday.com [10/yr; $119, free to qualified applicants]. Features articles on topics of interest to online database users; includes database search aids.

**Information Processing & Management.** Elsevier, Inc., Journals Customer Service, 3251 Riverport Lane, Maryland Heights, MO 63043. http://www.elsevier.com/locate/infoproman, tel: 877-839-7126, fax: 314-447-8077, journalcustomerservice-usa@elsevier.com [6/yr; $337 indiv, $870 inst (online), $2790 inst (print)]. International journal covering data processing, database building, and retrieval.

**Information Services & Use.** IOS Press, Nieuwe Hemweg 6B, 1013 BG Amsterdam, The Netherlands. http://www.iospress.nl/html/01675265.php, tel: +31 20 688 3 indiv (online), $616 inst (print), $560 inst (online)]. An international journal for those in the information management field. Includes online and offline systems, library automation, micrographics, videotex, and telecommunications.

**The Information Society.** Taylor & Francis Group, Customer Services Department, 325 Chestnut St, Suite 800, Philadelphia, PA 19106. http://www.tandf.co.uk/journals/titles/01972243, tel: 800-354-1420, fax: 215-625-2940, subscriptions@tandf.co.uk [5/yr; $219 indiv, $533 inst (online), $609 inst (print+online)]. Provides a forum for discussion of the world of information, including transborder data flow, regulatory issues, and the impact of the information industry.

**Information Technology and Libraries.** American Library Association, Subscriptions, 50 E Huron St, Chicago, IL 60611-2795. http://www.ala.org/lita/ital, tel: 800-545-2433, fax: 312-944-2641, subscription@ala.org [4/yr; free]. Articles on library automation, communication technology, cable systems, computerized information processing, and video technologies.

**Information Today.** Information Today, Inc., 143 Old Marlton Pike, Medford, NJ 08055-8750. http://www.infotoday.com/it, tel: 609-654-6266, fax: 609-654-4309, custserv@infotoday.com [10/yr; $97]. Newspaper for users and producers of electronic information services. Includes articles and news about the industry, calendar of events, and product information.

**Internet Reference Service Quarterly.** Taylor & Francis Group, Customer Services Department, 325 Chestnut St, Suite 800, Philadelphia, PA 19106. http://www.tandf.co.uk/journals/WIRS, tel: 800-354-1420, fax: 215-625-2940, subscriptions@tandf.co.uk [4/yr; $102 indiv (online), $109 indiv (print+online), $248 inst (online), $283 inst (print+online)]. Discusses multidisciplinary aspects of incorporating the Internet as a tool for reference service.

**Journal of Access Services.** Taylor & Francis Group, Customer Services Department, 325 Chestnut St, Suite 800, Philadelphia, PA 19106. http://www.tandf.co.uk/journals/WJAS, tel: 800-354-1420, fax: 215-625-2940, subscriptions@tandf.co.uk [4/yr; $93 indiv (online), $102 indiv (print+online), $248 inst (online), $283 inst (print+online)]. Explores topics and issues surrounding the organization, administration, and development of information technology on access services and resources.

**Journal of the Association for Information Science and Technology.** John Wiley & Sons, Inc., Journal Customer Services, 350 Main St, Malden, MA 02148. http://onlinelibrary.wiley.com/journal/10.1002/(ISSN)1532-2890, tel: 800-835-6770, fax: 781-388-8232, cs-agency@wiley.com [12/yr; $2889 inst (print/online), $3533 inst (print+online)]. Provides an overall forum for new research in information transfer and communication processes, with particular attention paid to the context of recorded knowledge.

**Journal of Database Management.** IGI Global, 701 E Chocolate Ave., Suite 200, Hershey, PA 17033-1240. http://www.igi-global.com/journal/journal-database-management-jdm/1072, tel: 866-342-6657, fax: 717-533-8661, cust@igi-global.com [4/yr; $196 indiv (print+online), $556 inst (print+online)]. Provides state-of-the-art research to those who design, develop, and administer DBMS-based information systems.

**Journal of Documentation.** Emerald Group Publishing Inc., Brickyard Office Park, 84 Sherman Street, Cambridge, MA 02140. http://www.emeraldinsight.com/loi/jd, tel: 617-945-9130, fax: 617-945-9136, america@emeraldinsight.com [6/yr; inst prices vary]. Focuses on theories, concepts, models, frameworks, and philosophies in the information sciences.

**Journal of Interlibrary Loan, Document Delivery & Electronic Reserve.** Taylor & Francis Group, Customer Services Department, 325 Chestnut St, Suite 800, Philadelphia, PA 19106. http://www.tandf.co.uk/journals/titles/1072303X, tel: 800-354-1420, fax: 215-625-2940, subscriptions@tandf.co.uk [5/yr; $125 indiv (online), $132 indiv (print+online), $468 inst (online), $535 inst (print+online)]. A forum for ideas on the basic theoretical and practical problems regarding all aspects of library resource sharing faced by planners, practitioners, and users of network services.

**Journal of Library Metadata.** Taylor & Francis Group, Customer Services Department, 325 Chestnut St, Suite 800, Philadelphia, PA 19106. http://www.tandf.co.uk/journals/titles/19386389, tel: 800-354-1420, fax: 215-625-2940, subscriptions@tandf.co.uk [4/yr; $99 indiv (online), $104 indiv (print+online), $295 inst (online), $337 inst (print+online)]. A forum for the latest research, innovations, news, and expert views about all aspects of metadata applications and information retrieval in libraries.

## Instructional Design and Development

**Human-Computer Interaction.** Taylor & Francis Group, Customer Services Department, 325 Chestnut St, Suite 800, Philadelphia, PA 19106. http://www.tandf. co.uk/journals/titles/07370024, tel: 800-354-1420, fax: 215-625-2940, subscriptions@tandf.co.uk [4/yr; $110 indiv, $917 inst (online), $1048 institution (print+online)]. A journal of theoretical, empirical, and methodological issues of user science and of system design.

**Instructional Science.** Springer Science+Business Media, PO Box 2485, Secaucus, NJ 07096-2485. http://www.springer.com/journal/11251, tel: 800-777-4643, fax: 201-348-4505, service-ny@springer.com [6/yr; $1062 inst (print/online), $1274 inst (print+online, content through 1997)]. Promotes a deeper understanding of the nature, theory, and practice of the instructional process and the learning resulting from this process.

**International Journal of Human-Computer Interaction.** Taylor & Francis Group, Customer Services Department, 325 Chestnut St, Suite 800, Philadelphia, PA 19106. http://www.tandf.co.uk/journals/titles/10447318, tel: 800-354-1420, fax: 215-625-2940, subscriptions@tandf.co.uk [12/yr; $265 indiv (print), $277 indiv (print+online), $2090 inst (online), $2389 inst (print+online)]. Addresses the cognitive, social, health, and ergonomic aspects of work with computers. It also emphasizes both the human and computer science aspects of the effective design and use of computer interactive systems.

**Journal of Educational Technology Systems.** Baywood Publishing Co., Inc., 26 Austin Ave., PO Box 337, Amityville, NY 11701-0337. https://us.sagepub.com/en-us/nam/journal-of-educational-technology-systems/journal202400, tel: 800-638-7819, fax: 631-691-1770, info@baywood.com [4/yr; $143 individ (print+online), $493 inst (online), $537 inst (print), $548 inst (print+online)]. Deals with systems in which technology and education interface; designed to inform educators who are interested in making optimum use of technology.

**Journal of Technical Writing and Communication.** Baywood Publishing Co., Inc., 26 Austin Ave., PO Box 337, Amityville, NY 11701-0337. https://us.sagepub. com/en-us/nam/journal-of-technical-writing-and-communication/journal202406, tel: 800-638-7819, fax: 631-691-1770, info@baywood.com [4/yr; $143 indiv (online), $493 inst (online), $537 inst (print), $548 inst (print+online)]. Essays on oral and written communication, for purposes ranging from pure research to needs of business and industry.

**Journal of Visual Literacy.** International Visual Literacy Association, Dr. David R. Moore, IVLA Executive Treasurer, Ohio University, 250 McCracken Hall, Athens, OH 45701. http://www.ivla.org/drupal2/content/journal-visual-literacy, tel: 740-597-1322, jvleditor@ohio.edu [2/yr; $30 student, $55 indiv, $75 inst]. Explores empirical, theoretical, practical, and applied aspects of visual literacy and communication.

**Performance Improvement.** John Wiley & Sons, Inc., Journal Customer Services, 350 Main St, Malden, MA 02148. http://onlinelibrary.wiley.com/journal/10.1002/

(ISSN)1930-8272, tel: 800-835-6770, fax: 781-388-8232, cs-agency@wiley.com [10/yr; $95 indiv (print/online), $105 indiv (print+online), $481 inst (print/online), $578 inst (print+online)]. Promotes performance science and technology. Contains articles, research, and case studies relating to improving human performance.

**Performance Improvement Quarterly.** John Wiley & Sons, Inc., Journal Customer Services, 350 Main St, Malden, MA 02148. http://www3.interscience. wiley.com/journal/117865970/home, tel: 800-835-6770, fax: 781-388-8232, cs-agency@wiley.com [4/yr; $65 indiv (print), $256 inst (print/online/print+online)]. Presents the cutting edge in research and theory in performance technology.

**Training.** Lakewood Media Group, PO Box 247, Excelsior, MN 55331. http://www.trainingmag.com, tel: 877-865-9361, fax: 847-291-4816, ntrn@omeda.com [6/yr; $79, free to qualified applicants]. Covers all aspects of training, management, and organizational development, motivation, and performance improvement.

# Learning Sciences

**International Journal of Computer-Supported Collaborative Learning.** Springer Science+Business Media, PO Box 2485, Secaucus, NJ 07096-2485. http://www.springer.com/journal/11412, tel: 800-777-4643, fax: 201-348-4505, service-ny@springer.com [4/yr; $591 inst (print/online), $709 inst (print+online, content through 1997)]. Promotes a deeper understanding of the nature, theory, and practice of the uses of computer-supported collaborative learning.

**Journal of the Learning Sciences.** Taylor & Francis Group, Customer Services Department, 325 Chestnut St, Suite 800, Philadelphia, PA 19106. http://www.tandf. co.uk/journals/titles/10508406, tel: 800-354-1420, fax: 215-625-2940, subscriptions@ tandf.co.uk [4/yr; $93 indiv, $860 inst (online), $983 inst (print+online)]. Provides a forum for the discussion of research on education and learning, with emphasis on the idea of changing one's understanding of learning and the practice of education.

**International Journal of Science Education.** Taylor & Francis Group, Customer Services Department, 325 Chestnut St, Suite 800, Philadelphia, PA 19106. http://www.tandfonline.com/tsed, tel: 800-354-1420, fax: 215-625-2940 subscriptions@ tandf.co.uk [18/yr; $1346 indiv, $3973 inst (print), $4541 (print+online)]. Special emphasis is placed on applicable research relevant to educational practice, guided by educational realities in systems, schools, colleges and universities.

# Libraries and Media Centers

**Collection Building.** Emerald Group Publishing Inc., Brickyard Office Park, 84 Sherman Street, Cambridge, MA 02140. http://www.emeraldinsight.com/loi/cb, tel: 617-945-9130, fax: 617-945-9136, america@emeraldinsight.com [4/yr; inst prices vary]. Provides well-researched and authoritative information on collection maintenance and development for librarians in all sectors.

**Computers in Libraries.** Information Today, Inc., 143 Old Marlton Pike, Medford, NJ 08055-8750. http://www.infotoday.com/cilmag/default.shtml, tel: 609-654-6266, fax: 609-654-4309, custserv@infotoday.com [10/yr; $100]. Covers practical applications of microcomputers to library situations and recent news items.

**The Electronic Library.** Emerald Group Publishing Inc., Brickyard Office Park, 84 Sherman Street, Cambridge, MA 02140. http://www.emeraldgrouppublishing.com/el.htm, tel: 617-945-9130, fax: 617-945-9136, america@emeraldinsight.com [6/yr; inst prices vary]. International journal for minicomputer, microcomputer, and software applications in libraries; independently assesses current and forthcoming information technologies.

**Government Information Quarterly.** Elsevier, Inc., Journals Customer Service, 3251 Riverport Lane, Maryland Heights, MO 63043. http://www.elsevier.com/locate/govinf, tel: 877-839-7126, fax: 314-447-8077, journalcustomerservice-usa@elsevier.com [4/yr; $226 indiv, $288 inst (online), $946 inst (print)]. International journal of resources, services, policies, and practices.

**Information Outlook.** Special Libraries Association, Information Outlook Subscriptions, 1700 Eighteenth Street, NW, Washington, DC 20009-2514. http://www.sla.org/access-membership/io, tel: 703-647-4900, fax: 1-202-234-2442, magazine@sla.org [12/yr; $40 stud member, $114 member]. Discusses administration, organization, and operations. Includes reports on research, technology, and professional standards.

**The Journal of Academic Librarianship.** Elsevier, Inc., Journals Customer Service, 3251 Riverport Lane, Maryland Heights, MO 63043. http://www.elsevier.com/locate/jacalib, tel: 877-839-7126, fax: 314-447-8077, journalcustomerservice-usa@elsevier.com [6/yr; $177 indiv, $169 inst (online), $552 inst (print)]. Results of significant research, issues, and problems facing academic libraries, book reviews, and innovations in academic libraries.

**Journal of Librarianship and Information Science.** Sage Publications, 2455 Teller Rd, Thousand Oaks, CA 91320. http://lis.sagepub.com, tel: 800-818-7243, fax: 800-583-2665, journals@sagepub.com [4/yr; $122 indiv (print), $845 inst (online), $920 inst (print), $939 inst (print+online)]. Deals with all aspects of library and information work in the UK and reviews literature from international sources.

**Journal of Library Administration.** Taylor & Francis Group, Customer Services Department, 325 Chestnut St, Suite 800, Philadelphia, PA 19106. http://www.tandf.co.uk/journals/titles/01930826, tel: 800-354-1420, fax: 215-625-2940, subscriptions@tandf.co.uk [8/yr; $248 indiv (online), $275 indiv (print+online), $922 inst (online), $1054 inst (print+online)]. Provides information on all aspects of effective library management, with emphasis on practical applications.

**Library & Information Science Research.** Elsevier, Inc., Journals Customer Service, 3251 Riverport Lane, Maryland Heights, MO 63043. http://www.elsevier.com/locate/lisres, tel: 877-839-7126, fax: 314-447-8077, journalcustomerservice-usa@elsevier.com [4/yr; $188 indiv, $213 inst (online), $716 inst (print)]. Research articles, dissertation reviews, and book reviews on issues concerning information resources management.

**Library Hi Tech.** Emerald Group Publishing Inc., Brickyard Office Park, 84 Sherman Street, Cambridge, MA 02140. http://www.emeraldinsight.com/loi/lht, tel: 617-945-9130, fax: 617-945-9136, america@emeraldinsight.com [4/yr; inst prices vary]. Concentrates on reporting on the selection, installation, maintenance, and integration of systems and hardware.

**Library Hi Tech News.** Emerald Group Publishing Inc., Brickyard Office Park, 84 Sherman Street, Cambridge, MA 02140. http://www.emeraldinsight.com/loi/lhtn, tel: 617-945-9130, fax: 617-945-9136, america@emeraldinsight.com [10/yr; inst prices vary]. Supplements Library Hi Tech and updates many of the issues addressed in-Departmenth in the journal; keeps the reader fully informed of the latest developments in library automation, new products, network news, new software and hardware, and people in technology.

**Library Journal.** Media Source, Inc., 160 Varick Street, 11th Floor, New York, NY 10013. http://www.libraryjournal.com, tel: 800-588-1030, fax: 712-733-8019, LJLcustserv@cds-global.com [20/yr; $102 indiv]. A professional periodical for librarians, with current issues and news, professional reading, a lengthy book review section, and classified advertisements.

**Library Media Connection.** Linworth Publishing, Inc., PO Box 204, Vandalia, Ohio 45377. http://www.librarymediaconnection.com/lmc, tel: 800-607-4410, fax: 937-890-0221, linworth@linworthpublishing.com [6/yr; $69 indiv]. Journal for junior and senior high school librarians; provides articles, tips, and ideas for day-to-day school library management, as well as reviews of audiovisuals and software, all written by school librarians.

**The Library Quarterly: Information, Community, Policy.** University of Chicago Press, Journals Division, PO Box 37005, Chicago, IL 60637. http://www.journals.uchicago.edu/LQ, tel: 877-705-1878, fax: 877-705-1879, subscriptions@press.uchicago.edu [$27 students (online), $49 indiv (print), $48 indiv (online), $54 indiv (print + online), inst prices vary]. Scholarly articles of interest to librarians.

**Library Resources & Technical Services.** American Library Association, Subscriptions, 50 E Huron St, Chicago, IL 60611-2795. http://www.ala.org/ala/mgrps/divs/alcts/resources/lrts/index.cfm, tel: 800-545-2433, fax: 312-944-2641, subscription@ala.org [4/yr; $100 print, $95 online, $105 print + online]. Scholarly papers on bibliographic access and control, preservation, conservation, and reproduction of library materials.

**Library Trends.** Johns Hopkins University Press, PO Box 19966, Baltimore, MD 21211-0966. http://www.press.jhu.edu/journals/library_trends, tel: 800-548-1784, fax: 410-516-3866, jrnlcirc@press.jhu.edu [4/yr; $80 indiv (print), $85 indiv (online), $163 inst (print)]. Each issue is concerned with one aspect of library and information science, analyzing current thought and practice and examining ideas that hold the greatest potential for the field.

**Public Libraries.** American Library Association, Subscriptions, 50 E Huron St, Chicago, IL 60611-2795. http://www.ala.org/pla/publications/publiclibraries, tel: 800-545-2433, fax: 312-944-2641, subscription@ala.org [6/yr; $65 indiv]. News and articles of interest to public librarians.

**Public Library Quarterly.** Taylor & Francis Group, Customer Services Department, 325 Chestnut St, Suite 800, Philadelphia, PA 19106. http://www.tandf. co.uk/journals/WPLQ, tel: 800-354-1420, fax: 215-625-2940, subscriptions@ tandf.co.uk [4/yr; $138 indiv (online), $148 indiv (print + online), $425 inst (online), $486 inst (print + online)]. Addresses the major administrative challenges and opportunities that face the nation's public libraries.

**Reference and User Services Quarterly.** American Library Association, Subscriptions, 50 E Huron St, Chicago, IL 60611-2795. http://rusa.metapress.com/ content/l74261, tel: 800-545-2433, fax: 312-944-2641, subscription@ala.org [4/yr; $25 student, $60 member, $65 nonmember]. Disseminates information of interest to reference librarians, bibliographers, adult services librarians, those in collection development and selection, and others interested in public services.

**The Reference Librarian.** Taylor & Francis Group, Customer Services Department, 325 Chestnut St, Suite 800, Philadelphia, PA 19106. http://www.tandf.co.uk/jour-nals/wref, tel: 800-354-1420, fax: 215-625-2940, subscriptions@tandf.co.uk [4/yr; $297 indiv (online), $324 indiv (print + online), $1202 inst (online), $1374 inst (print + online)]. Each issue focuses on a topic of current concern, interest, or practi-cal value to reference librarians.

**Reference Services Review.** Emerald Group Publishing Inc., Brickyard Office Park, 84 Sherman Street, Cambridge, MA 02140. http://www.emeraldinsight.com/ loi/rsr, tel: 617-945-9130, fax: 617-945-9136, america@emeraldinsight.com [4/yr; inst prices vary]. Dedicated to the enrichment of reference knowledge and the advancement of reference services. It prepares its readers to understand and embrace current and emerging technologies affecting reference functions and information needs of library users.

**School Library Journal.** Media Source, Inc., 160 Varick Street, 11th Floor, New York, NY 10013. http://www.slj.com, tel: 800-595-1066, fax: 712-733-8019, sljcustserv@cds-global.com [12/yr; $89 indiv]. For school and youth service librar-ians. Reviews about 4000 children's books and 1000 educational media titles annually.

**School Library Monthly.** Libraries Unlimited, Inc., PO Box 291846, Kettering OH 45429. http://www.schoollibrarymedia.com, tel: 800-771-5579, fax: 937-890-0221, schoollibrarymonthly@sfsdayton.com [12/yr; $89 indiv]. A vehicle for dis-tributing ideas for teaching library media skills and for the development and implementation of library media skills programs.

**School Library Research.** American Library Association and American Association of School Librarians, Subscriptions, 50 E Huron St, Chicago, IL 60611-2795. http://www.ala.org/aasl/slr, tel: 800-545-2433, fax: 312-944-2641, subscription@ala.org [annual compilation; free online]. For library media specialists, district supervisors, and others concerned with the selection and purchase of print and non-print media and with the development of programs and services for preschool through high school libraries.

**Teacher Librarian.** The Scarecrow Press, Inc., 4501 Forbes Blvd, Suite 200, Lanham, MD 20706. http://www.teacherlibrarian.com, tel: 800-462-6420, fax: 800-338-4550, admin@teacherlibrarian.com [5/yr; $62 indiv] "The journal for school library professionals"; previously known as Emergency Librarian. Articles, review columns, and critical analyses of management and programming issues.

# Media Technologies

**Broadcasting & Cable.** NewBay Media, LLC., 28 E. 28th St, 12th Floor, New York, NY 10016. http://www.broadcastingcable.com, tel: 800-554-5729, fax: 712-733-8019, bcbcustserv@cdsfulfillment.com [47/yr; $169 indiv]. All-inclusive news-weekly for radio, television, cable, and allied business.

**Educational Media International.** Taylor & Francis Group, Customer Services Department, 325 Chestnut St, Suite 800, Philadelphia, PA 19106. http://www.tandf.co.uk/journals/titles/09523987, tel: 800-354-1420, fax: 215-625-2940, subscriptions@tandf.co.uk [4/yr; $170 indiv, $605 inst (online), $691 inst (print+online)]. The official journal of the International Council for Educational Media.

**Historical Journal of Film, Radio and Television.** Taylor & Francis Group, Customer Services Department, 325 Chestnut St, Suite 800, Philadelphia, PA 19106. http://www.tandf.co.uk/journals/titles/01439685, tel: 800-354-1420, fax: 215-625-2940, subscriptions@tandf.co.uk [4/yr; $511 indiv, $1351 inst (online), $1544 inst (print+online)]. Articles by international experts in the field, news and notices, and book reviews concerning the impact of mass communications on political and social history of the twentieth century.

**Journal of Educational Multimedia and Hypermedia.** Association for the Advancement of Computing in Education, PO Box 1545, Chesapeake, VA 23327-1545. http://www.aace.org/pubs/jemh, tel: 757-366-5606, fax: 703-997-8760, info@editlib.org [4/yr; $150 indiv, $2095 inst]. A multidisciplinary information source presenting research about and applications for multimedia and hypermedia tools.

**Journal of Popular Film and Television.** Taylor & Francis Group, Customer Service Department, 325 Chestnut Street, Suite 800, Philadelphia, PA 19106. http://www.tandf.co.uk/journals/titles/01956051, tel: 800-354-1420, fax: 215-625-2940, subscriptions@tandf.co.uk [4/yr; $77 indiv, $203 inst (online), $232 (print+online)]. Articles on film and television, book reviews, and theory. Dedicated to popular film and television in the broadest sense. Concentrates on commercial cinema and television, film and television theory or criticism, filmographies, and bibliographies. Edited at the College of Arts and Sciences of Northern Michigan University and the Department of Popular Culture, Bowling Green State University.

**Learning, Media & Technology.** Taylor & Francis Group, Customer Services Department, 325 Chestnut St, Suite 800, Philadelphia, PA 19106. http://www.tandf.co.uk/journals/titles/17439884, tel: 800-354-1420, fax: 215-625-2940, subscriptions@tandf.co.uk [4/yr; $610 indiv, $2055 inst (online), $2349 inst (print + online)]. This journal of the Educational Television Association serves as an international forum for discussions and reports on developments in the field of television and related media in teaching, learning, and training.

**Media & Methods.** American Society of Educators, 1429 Walnut St, Philadelphia, PA 19102. http://www.media-methods.com, tel: 215-563-6005, fax: 215-587-9706, info@media-methods.com [5/yr; $35 indiv]. The only magazine published for the elementary school library media and technology specialist. A forum for K-12 educators who use technology as an educational resource, this journal includes information on what works and what does not, new product reviews, tips and pointers, and emerging technologies.

**Multichannel News.** NewBay Media, LLC., 28 E. 28th St, 12th Floor, New York, NY 10016. http://www.multichannel.com, tel: 888-343-5563, fax: 712-733-8019, mulcustserv@cdsfulfillment.com [47/yr; $249 indiv]. A newsmagazine for the cable television industry. Covers programming, marketing, advertising, business, and other topics.

**MultiMedia & Internet@Schools.** Information Today, Inc., 143 Old Marlton Pike, Medford, NJ 08055-8750. http://www.mmischools.com, tel: 609-654-6266, fax: 609-654-4309, custserv@infotoday.com [5/yr; $50 indiv]. Reviews and evaluates hardware and software. Presents information pertaining to basic troubleshooting skills.

**Multimedia Systems.** Springer Science+Business Media, PO Box 2485, Secaucus, NJ 07096-2485. http://www.springer.com/journal/00530, tel: 800-777-4643, fax: 201-348-4505, service-ny@springer.com [6/yr; $773 inst (print/online), $928 inst (print + online, content through 1997)]. Publishes original research articles and serves as a forum for stimulating and disseminating innovative research ideas, emerging technologies, state-of-the-art methods, and tools in all aspects of multimedia computing, communication, storage, and applications among researchers, engineers, and practitioners.

**Telematics and Informatics.** Elsevier, Inc., Journals Customer Service, 3251 Riverport Lane, Maryland Heights, MO 63043. http://www.elsevier.com/locate/tele, tel: 877-839-7126, fax: 314-447-8077, journalcustomerservice-usa@elsevier.com [4/yr; $165 indiv, $1771 inst (print), $1771 inst (online)]. Publishes research and review articles in applied telecommunications and information sciences in business, industry, government, and educational establishments. Focuses on important current technologies, including microelectronics, computer graphics, speech synthesis and voice recognition, database management, data encryption, satellite television, artificial intelligence, and the ongoing computer revolution.

## Professional Development

**Journal of Digital Learning in Teacher Education.** International Society for Technology in Education, Special Interest Group for Teacher Educators, 180 West 8th Ave., Suite 300, Eugene, OR 97401. http://www.iste.org/jdlte, tel: 800-336-5191, fax: 541-302-3778, iste@iste.org [4/yr; $151 indiv (print+online), $260 inst (online), $297 inst (print+online)]. Contains refereed articles on preservice and in-service training, research in computer education and certification issues, and reviews of training materials and texts.

**Journal of Technology and Teacher Education.** Association for the Advancement of Computing in Education, PO Box 1545, Chesapeake, VA 23327-1545. http://www.aace.org/pubs/jtate, tel: 757-366-5606, fax: 703-997-8760, info@editlib.org [4/yr; $150 indiv, $2095 inst]. Serves as an international forum to report research and applications of technology in preservice, in-service, and graduate teacher education.

## Simulation, Gaming, and Virtual Reality

**Simulation & Gaming.** Sage Publications, 2455 Teller Rd, Thousand Oaks, CA 91320. http://sag.sagepub.com, tel: 800-818-7243, fax: 800-583-2665, journals@sagepub.com [6/yr; $166 indiv (online), $1302 inst (online)]. An international journal of theory, design, and research focusing on issues in simulation, gaming, modeling, role-playing, and experiential learning.

## Special Education and Disabilities

**Journal of Special Education Technology.** Technology and Media Division, JSET, PO Box 3853, Reston, VA 20195. http://www.tamcec.org/jset, tel: 703-709-0136, fax: 405-325-7661, info@exinn.net [4/yr; $100 indiv, $260 inst]. Provides information, research, and reports of innovative practices regarding the application of educational technology toward the education of exceptional children.

## Telecommunications and Networking

**Canadian Journal of Learning and Technology.** Canadian Network for Innovation in Education (CNIE), 260 Dalhousie St., Suite 204, Ottawa, ON, K1N 7E4, Canada. http://www.cjlt.ca, tel: 613-241-0018, fax: 613-241-0019, cjlt@ucalgary.ca [3/yr; free]. Concerned with all aspects of educational systems and technology.

**Computer Communications.** Elsevier, Inc., Journals Customer Service, 3251 Riverport Lane, Maryland Heights, MO 63043. http://www.elsevier.com/locate/comcom, tel: 877-839-7126, fax: 314-447-8077, journalcustomerservice-usa@elsevier.com [24/yr; $3106 inst(online/print)]. Focuses on networking and distributed computing techniques, communications hardware and software, and standardization.

**EDUCAUSE Review.** EDUCAUSE, 4772 Walnut St, Suite 206, Boulder, CO 80301-2536. http://www.educause.edu/er, tel: 303-449-4430, fax: 303-440-0461, er-subs@educause.edu [6/yr; $39 indiv (print), free online]. Features articles on current issues and applications of computing and communications technology in higher education. Reports on EDUCAUSE consortium activities.

**International Journal on E-Learning.** Association for the Advancement of Computing in Education, PO Box 1545, Chesapeake, VA 23327-1545. http://www.aace.org/pubs/ijel, tel: 757-366-5606, fax: 703-997-8760, info@editlib.org [4/yr; $150 indiv, $2095 inst]. Reports on current theory, research, development, and practice of telecommunications in education at all levels.

**The Internet and Higher Education.** Elsevier, Inc., Journals Customer Service, 3251 Riverport Lane, Maryland Heights, MO 63043. http://www.elsevier.com/locate/iheduc, tel: 877-839-7126, fax: 314-447-8077, journalcustomerservice-usa@elsevier.com [4/yr; $103 indiv, $646 inst (print), $648 inst (online)]. Designed to reach faculty, staff, and administrators responsible for enhancing instructional practices and productivity via the use of information technology and the Internet in their institutions.

**Internet Reference Services Quarterly.** Taylor & Francis Group, Customer Services Department, 325 Chestnut St, Suite 800, Philadelphia, PA 19106. http://www.tandf.co.uk/journals/titles/10875301, tel: 800-354-1420, fax: 215-625-2940, subscriptions@tandf.co.uk [4/yr; $102 indiv (online), $109 indiv (print+online), $248 inst (online), $283 inst (print+online)]. Describes innovative information practice, technologies, and practice. For librarians of all kinds.

**Internet Research.** Emerald Group Publishing Inc., Brickyard Office Park, 84 Sherman Street, Cambridge, MA 02140. http://www.emeraldinsight.com/loi/intr.htm, tel: 617-945-9130, fax: 617-945-9136, america@emeraldinsight.com [5/yr; inst prices vary]. A cross-disciplinary journal presenting research findings related to electronic networks, analyses of policy issues related to networking, and descriptions of current and potential applications of electronic networking for communication, computation, and provision of information services.

**Online Searcher.** Information Today, Inc., 143 Old Marlton Pike, Medford, NJ 08055-8750. http://www.infotoday.com/online, tel: 609-654-6266, fax: 609-654-4309, custserv@infotoday.com [6/yr; $139 indiv] For online information system users. Articles cover a variety of online applications for general and business use.

# Index

© Springer International Publishing Switzerland 2017
M. Orey, R.M. Branch (eds.), *Educational Media and Technology Yearbook*,
Educational Media and Technology Yearbook 40,
DOI 10.1007/978-3-319-45001-8

CPSIA information can be obtained
at www.ICGtesting.com
Printed in the USA
LVOW02*1821181216

517726LV00003BC/24/P